PRAISE FOR

TRUE BELIEVER

—

"[A] serious biography . . . What [*True Believer*] does best is unfurl a Künstlerroman, a story about the growth of an art form and an art-ist, who was also a director and a leading man, unable to admit that the show could go on without him."   —*The New Yorker*

"*True Believer* . . . has the thunderous sweep of a Kirby epic, begin-ning with a Romanian pogrom . . . and ending with the pitiful Götterdämmerung of Lee's last quarter-century. "
                                        —J. Hoberman, *New York Review of Books*

"Absorbing . . . One need not be a comics nerd to find Riesman's portrait of the deeply flawed and relatably human pop-culture icon an absorbing read, and some of its revelations are stunning."
                                                                —*USA Today*

"Striking . . . *True Believer* paints a portrait of a man who was just as flawed as his heroes, and he emerges all the more human for it. . . . [Riesman is] a must-read chronicler of the comic book industry."
                                                —*The Hollywood Reporter*

"A serious look from someone who holds an abiding love for Lee's work, without letting it blind a critical, journalistic eye."
                                                                —*Jewish Exponent*

"Well-researched and thorough."   —*The New Republic*

"A significant contribution to comics history scholarship . . . It's a book that anyone concerned with the hard truths of human nature and the business of popular culture over the last 80 years needs."

—*Forbes*

"This detailed, clear-eyed examination pulls back the curtain on one of America's great storytellers and is sure to reignite debates over Lee's legacy." —*Publishers Weekly,* starred review

"*True Believer* is smart, well-researched, and likely to change Lee's legacy outside of comics." —*ComicBook.com*

"[An] illuminating new biography." —*Fast Company*

"Tantalizing . . . Riesman puts in the hard yards to separate fact from myth." —Dorian Lynskey, *The Spectator*

"An illuminating and reliable account of Lee's improbable odyssey."

—Jacob Heilbrunn, *Washington Monthly*

"For those who know Stan Lee from his sunny, funny cameos in Marvel films, get ready for an unputdownable deep dive. The man lived a life—warts and all—and Riesman captures the shadow and sunshine in equal measure." —Patton Oswalt

"*True Believer* is in every imaginable way the biography that Stan Lee deserves—ambitious, audacious, daring, and unflinchingly clear-eyed about the man's significance, his shortcomings, his transgressions, his accomplishments, and his astonishing legacy."

—Robert Kolker, author of *Hidden Valley Road*

"Stan Lee was a mythmaker, both creatively and autobiographically. To reach the truth of his troubled and troubling life story, Riesman has had to peel away layers of quarrel, exaggeration, credit-grabbing, dispute, and faulty memory. The result is an enthralling, vibrantly written portrait of one of American popular culture's great innovators."

—Mark Harris, author of *Pictures at a Revolution*
and *Five Came Back*

"The story of Stan Lee is a wild ride, sometimes breathtaking, often shocking—but it is also a wholly American one, rooted in the transformation of hardscrabble reality into glorious dreams, of legends into truth, of absence into action, of immigration into assimilation." —Sarah Weinman, author of *The Real Lolita*

"Stan Lee was, all at once, a genius, a schlepper, a hack, a huckster, and a marvel. Riesman painstakingly digs into how much credit each of those overlapping personae deserves, and then he spins all those threads into a book that reads with the supple speed of Mr. Fantastic himself."

—Christopher Bonanos, author of *Flash:
The Making of Weegee the Famous*

"A life rich with unexpected turns and a biography filled with personality. In looking at a man who created heroic stories for a living, Riesman bravely examines the trace lines underneath the legends of his life. The result is a startling, fresh portrait of a truly American career." —Nathan Heller, author of *The Private Order*

"Jam-packed with carefully compiled evidence of just how much delectable bullshit, staggering failure, and vicious backbiting goes into the making of a great American genius. I genuinely could not put it down." —Penny Lane, director of *Hail Satan?*

"Take it from someone who has always found comic books alluring but knew next to nothing about the medium's history before reading *True Believer*: this book will pull you in no matter what level of knowledge or built-in curiosity you bring to it."

—Leon Neyfakh, co-creator of *Slow Burn* and *Fiasco*

"The first great biography to emerge since Lee's death, *True Believer* is an origin story of the modern entertainment industry, a portrait of a man who never felt comfortable with the industry his tastes came to dominate, and—in its dizzying last third—a true crime story that rivals *Bad Blood*."

—Adam Westcott, *Politics & Prose staff pick*

TRUE BELIEVER

TRUE BELIEVER

THE
RISE AND FALL OF
STAN LEE

ABRAHAM
RIESMAN

 CROWN
NEW YORK

2022 Crown Trade Paperback Edition

Copyright © 2021 by Abraham Riesman

This Is Not a Secret Jewish History of Stan Lee by Abraham Riesman
in *Jewish Currents,* copyright © 2021 by Abraham Riesman

Published in the United States by Crown,
an imprint of Random House, a division of
Penguin Random House LLC, New York.

Crown and the Crown colophon are registered trademarks
of Penguin Random House LLC.

Random House Book Club and colophon are trademarks
of Penguin Random House LLC.

Originally published in hardcover in the United States by Crown,
an imprint of Random House, a division of
Penguin Random House LLC, New York, in 2021.

Library of Congress Cataloging-in-Publication Data
Names: Riesman, Abraham, author.
Title: True believer / Abraham Riesman.
Description: First paperback edition. | New York: Crown, [2022] |
Includes index.
Identifiers: LCCN 2020016622 (print) | LCCN 2020016623 (ebook) |
ISBN 9780593135730 (trade paperback) | ISBN 9780593135723 (ebook)
Subjects: LCSH: Lee, Stan, 1922–2018. | Cartoonists—
United States—Biography.
Classification: LCC PN6727.L39 Z89 2020 (print) |
LCC PN6727.L39 (ebook) |
DDC 741.5/973092 [B]—dc23
LC record available at https://lccn.loc.gov/2020016622
LC ebook record available at https://lccn.loc.gov/2020016623

Printed in the United States of America on acid-free paper

crownpublishing.com

randomhousebookclub.com

1st Printing

Book design by Barbara M. Bachman

For Tom Spurgeon,

who took comics just seriously enough

For my father,

the first biographer in the family

"I have no spur
To prick the sides of my intent, but only
Vaulting ambition, which o'erleaps itself
And falls on th' other."

—*Macbeth*, ACT I, SCENE 7

CONTENTS

TRUE BELIEVER

WHAT IT
TAKES

WE CANNOT KNOW FOR CERTAIN WHETHER SOFIE AND ZANFIR Solomon saw the celebrity when he returned, but we may presume they got word of his arrival soon enough. It was the bitter winter of 1899 and the couple were in their mid-thirties, married for sixteen years and raising a growing nest of children. Their home county, Vaslui, was a sparsely populated chunk of land in eastern Romania, containing just over 110,000 people, roughly 6,800 of them Jews like the Solomons, all of them struggling through a devastating recession. But even in the long, bleak nights, there was cause for excitement in the local Jewish community: The prodigal son was on his way.

"For months before, if you had put your ear to the ground, you might have heard the distant rumble of his approach, and Vaslui held not only its ear to the ground, but its breath," wrote Marcus Eli Ravage, a Vasluiander of the Solomons' era. "On the street, in the market, at the synagogue, we kept asking one another the one question, 'When will *he* arrive?'" At last, the long-anticipated *landsman* rode a midnight train into town, and on his finely tailored frock coat lay the scarcely visible dust of a place the Solomons may have heard of but could barely imagine; a place where the laws of the Old World didn't apply (perhaps even the laws of physics—given that it was on the other side of the world, it was said that people walked upside down there); a place where a Jew could be whatever he saw fit to be. "I had heard of people going to Vienna and Germany and Paris, and even to England for business or pleasure, but no one, to my knowledge, had ever gone to America of his own free will," Ravage continued. And yet here was one of their own, back from fourteen years in what they called "Nev-York," decked out in finery such as they'd never seen.

"The streets were lined with craning, round-eyed, tiptoeing Vasluianders, open-mouthed peasants, and gay-attired holiday visitors from neighboring towns who, having heard of the glory that had come to Vaslui, had driven in in their ox-carts and dog-carts to partake of it," Ravage recalled. Perhaps Zanfir and Sofie and their nine-year-old daughter, Celia, were among the rubber-neckers; if so, they would have been astounded by the man's diamonds, his capacity to rattle off words in the alien tongue of English, and his trunkful of presents: "There were railways that were wound up like clocks and ran around in their tracks like real trains, and dancing negroes, and squawking dolls, and jews'-harps, and scores of other delights for the palate as well as the fancy," Ravage reported. The returnee said he was working for the American government in a high post and, though he maintained a humble demeanor, he alluded to a significant fortune. Surely the Solomons heard tell of what happened when the man went to synagogue on Saturday: He received the honor of an *aliyah*—an opportunity to recite a blessing alongside the holy scrolls of the Torah—which came with the obligation to make a donation, and instead of the customary three or four francs, the man calmly offered 125 of them. "From that day on," wrote Ravage, "Vaslui became a changed town." Suddenly, it seemed like everyone had the notion to pack up and leave.

But wait. Was it true that, as one local with information from overseas said, the man was wildly exaggerating his success? Sure. Did Ravage later find out that this revered individual—whom he nicknamed Couza, a Romanian word denoting royalty—was actually a mere foreman in a bedspring factory, his wife a dressmaker, and his palatial New York estate just a fraction of a flat? Of course. Did any of that matter? Not one jot. "There was a country somewhere beyond the seas where a man was a man in spite of his religion and his origin," mused Ravage. "Even if the informer were right, and Couza were a sham, America surely was no sham." Perhaps we are to take the story as allegory; either way, the point stood: In the new Jerusalem they called the United States, you could make it just fine as a bullshitter.

SOFIE AND ZANFIR BEGAT CELIA. Celia and a man named Jack Lieber begat Stanley. Less famously, Celia and Jack also begat Larry, and that was it for their begetting. Stanley, as it turned out, sort of begat himself—he invented a character to play named Stan Lee and never got around to being Stanley again. The character is well known to myriad people in America and around the globe: a jovial, energetic man with a pedigree in comic books, bearing tinted glasses and a white mustache, bounding through the world with a gusto for life and community, spouting catchphrases ("Face front!" "'Nuff said!" "Excelsior!") and winning the affections of both the young and the young at heart. But as the sun set on the year 2018, Stan was dead and Larry was the only living human who remembered what it was like *before*.

Before Spider-Man, before the Avengers, before the X-Men, before the Fantastic Four. Before Marvel Comics, before Atlas Comics, before Timely Comics. Before Stan Lee Media, before POW Entertainment, before the accusations of investor fraud and criminal activity. Before the movie cameos, before the mobile games, before the webisodes, before the straight-to-DVD movies that no one seemed to see. Before *Stripperella,* before the second coming of *Stripperella*. Before the elder-abuse allegations, before the sexual-assault allegations, before the 911 calls, before the comics signed in blood. Before the lawsuits, before the arrests, before the

Supreme Court, before the guilty pleas. Before Jack Kirby, before Steve Ditko, before Peter Paul, before the Clintons (yes, those Clintons), before Gill Champion, before Jerry Olivarez, before Keya Morgan. Before Joan, before Jan, before JC. Before the name "Stan Lee" was trademarked, before it was signed away, before it was signed away again, before people started fighting over it like jackals at a bloodied wildebeest. Before everything was built, before it all fell apart. Before anything, there was Larry.

And after everything, there was still Larry. It had been forty-five days since Stan died just shy of age ninety-six. Larry, eighty-seven, sat on a beige couch in a breadbox-size studio apartment on the Upper East Side of Manhattan, pants hiked up past his belly button and a green button-down covering his withered chest. The scene around Larry's place was chaotic: papers piled atop a disused drawing board, boxes of miscellany lying haphazardly on the floor, a priceless personal sketch from the creators of Captain America yellowing in a cheap frame, a bedroom pillow bungee-corded to a computer chair for ergonomic purposes, pictures of dead women he once loved adorning nondescript shelving units. His goatee scraggled its way across the lower part of his face, and his eyes were mournful behind Coke-bottle lenses. He sighed.

"He had different sides to him," Larry said of his late brother in the near-extinct New York Jewish accent the two of them had shared. "I feel like I'm almost talking about Charles Foster Kane. Who was he? *What* was he? What was he *like*?" Larry paused and pondered his own questions. His answer was simple, though entirely accurate: "It depends on who you talk to at what moment."

By way of example, you could fast-forward a few weeks to a massive Stan Lee tribute show held at the famed Chinese Theatre in Hollywood. There, thousands of admirers waited in line to flash their tickets—the cheapest of them cost $150—and be admitted into the auditorium to see various entertainment professionals who knew or looked up to Stan talk about his impact on their lives. Outside, a fan mused on why he'd come. "I felt it was the best way to honor and celebrate the life of Stan Lee," he said, "who in many ways shaped and formed the person I am today with all the comics and creations he made." Another called Stan "the Mark Twain of Marvel" and said he belonged on a "Mount Rushmore of comic books." Yet another said, "He's an icon. You can't beat Stan the Man. You can't take that legacy away." One well-wisher had driven all the way from Las Vegas, and with understandable cause: "For me, Stan Lee was actually pretty close to a father figure," he said, "just because of growing up with his comics and everything. That's how I learned a lot of my morality and got to connect on a deeper level with other people. I had a single mom, so it was nice to have a male person to look up to that I didn't have in the household." They waxed rhapsodic about his narratives, his interactions with fans, and his plentiful appearances in dozens upon dozens of superhero movies, where he'd pop in to offer wisdom or comic relief, often both at the same time. To these people, Stan had been an inspiration, something close to a god.

Months later, an even higher-profile tribute event was held by Stan's former employer, Marvel, in his honor at New York City's New Amsterdam Theatre on 42nd Street and recorded for subsequent broadcast on ABC. There, the praise was even more effusive. "Stan Lee started a story with no end, and it changed the world," said Marvel movie actor Tom Hiddleston. "For me, Stan Lee was probably the most important writer and artist of my life," said talk-show host Jimmy Kimmel. "Stan was a superhero when it came to creating great characters and telling memorable stories," said Disney CEO Bob Iger. "Stan was a visionary whose passion for art and storytelling left a lasting impact on pop culture and entertainment," said Marvel TV star Clark Gregg. "I was so grateful for him being such a big part of my childhood, and I never outgrew it," said *Star Wars* icon Mark Hamill. "He's one of the founding fathers of American mythology," said Marvel Comics editor Sana Amanat, "and I think that is going to outlast all of us." There were laughs, cheers, and moments of tender remembrance that left wet eyes from the orchestra section to the balconies.

The New Amsterdam event was invite-only, and most members of Stan's inner circle weren't there, which made sense, given that most of them were by then either suing one another, awaiting trial, or trashing Marvel in the press—and, in one case, doing all three at once. So the tribute at the Chinese Theatre was the closest thing to a funeral that Stan had, and Larry wasn't in attendance. He wasn't entirely sure he had been invited, but, if he had, one suspects he wouldn't have attended. There was his fear of flying, for one thing. But there was also a lingering bitterness he felt when it came to Stan. Larry, despite working for Stan on and off for fifty years as both a writer and an artist, was always kept at arm's length emotionally by his brother. His voice breaking and his eyes watery, Larry recalled a story from the 1970s, when he was struggling to get Stan to throw some work his way. Stan kept passing the buck, saying he was the publisher of Marvel Comics now, not an editor, and that the matter was simply out of his hands. Larry knew that was a load of nonsense and eventually turned to one of the editors for help. "Well, Larry," he recalls the editor saying, "it's the consensus of opinion here that the only people Stan thinks about are himself and his family, and that doesn't include you."

No, Stan's family ever really consisted of only two people: his wife and his daughter. The former, Joan Boocock Lee, died a little more than a year before he did, so the only member of the triad left was their sixty-eight-year-old daughter, Joan Celia Lee (named, in a rare bit of ancestor acknowledgment, after Sofie and Zanfir's kid), more commonly known as JC. She had recently become the subject of some very bad press: There had been reports in major news outlets that she was verbally and physically abusive of her parents in their waning days, was a profligate spender of her father's money, and had made a full-court press to break into a trust that had been set up to prevent her from spending all of Stan's cash after her parents' deaths. However, she deserved some sympathy: She was allegedly (and her father privately adopted this assessment) schizophrenic, bipolar, and an addict. I'd spent weeks trying to get her lawyer/ publicist/business partner, Kirk Schenck, to set up an interview. He'd said it would happen, but he never delivered and, strangely enough, instead tried to get me to participate in a movie project he and JC were putting together. A few days after recording Larry's lament, I obtained JC's phone number from a source and decided to try my luck, hoping we could have an initial on-the-record conversation and set up a larger interview later. She picked up.

"This is worse than fake news," JC said of those nasty media items about her, shortly after we began speaking. "It's just evil. My father had a terrible time, my mother had a terrible time, and now *I'm* having a terrible time." She began to cry. "Nobody was hurting anybody!" she said. "It was all about love." (This was, apparently, a favored phrase: She had self-published a strange book of captioned family photos a few years earlier, entitled *Stan Lee's Love Story: "It's All About Love!"*) As she went on about her father, her tears turned to sobs and her words became unintelligible. She collected herself, then, without my prompting, she started to talk about the rumors of her spending habits: "Let's just say I bought a pair of shoes or I bought thirty pairs of shoes. Is it anybody's business? Am I asking anyone else to pay for it? Whose business is anything about this? *Whose?*" Her words became paranoid. "I'm just curious: Who sent in the creeps? They're the lowlifes. And who are the people who sent them in? Who are the higher-uppers? The people flying around in Learjets they got because of my father. I really consider everything that's happened a conspiracy. You wanna call Stan Lee's daughter crazy? Go right ahead and do it. I'll sit with any doctors and lawyers any week."

At last she said she'd be willing to speak to me for my article. I told her there must have been a misunderstanding—I was writing a biography, not an article. Immediately she changed her mind. "Tell Random House that JC Lee is coming to New York—I have a two-thousand-page book," she said, defiance rising in her voice. "They know me by name and have since the eighties." Abruptly, she was screaming at me. "I'm not interested in your book, and I'm interested in *one* book: *mine!*" she bellowed. "It's called *My Father Bought Me a House*. It just has to start there!" She hung up; our conversation had lasted for only about three minutes. A few moments later, a source from Stan's inner circle (these people, despite hating one another, are in constant and instant communication) texted me to say JC was telling everyone I had stolen her book manuscript and was trying to publish it under my own name. I texted Schenck to apologize for going behind his back and to ask what we should do next. He called me. "Now," he said wearily, "you see what I have to deal with."

The only thing predictable about Stan's only surviving progeny was that she was unpredictable, and that was never more evident than when I got a text a few months later from a man I'd been in touch with named Peter Paul. "JC is sending me a locket containing Stan's ashes," it read. This was more than a little shocking, as Stan had gone to his grave loathing Paul, and the feeling was mutual. When I expressed my surprise, Paul texted me a picture of a locket that, presumably, contained a bit of the late maven's remains. "Wow," I texted. Paul's reply: "Abe—I don't bullshit."

That particular claim was a questionable one, as Paul is full of stories that at least *feel* too amazing to be true. Back in the 1990s, he and Stan had been the closest of friends, wining and dining together while Stan languished in uselessness at Marvel. Paul, a longtime hidden hand pushing along the careers of various C-listers—Fabio and Buzz Aldrin being two of the most notable—had decided to help Stan out in breaking free from his contract with the company that had made him famous. Subsequently, the two got into business together, forming an online-entertainment company called Stan Lee Media around the turn of the millennium. It was a cash cow in the early going, working up a froth on Wall Street and briefly eclipsing Marvel's own market cap. However, by the end of 2000, it had very publicly and spectacularly collapsed due to the end of the dot-com bubble, malfeasance, and, more important, a DOJ and SEC crack-down on major financial crimes that had been committed at the top of the company. Stan was cleared of wrongdoing, but Paul was hit with a heap of charges, pleaded guilty to one of them, and was sent to prison. It was his fourth felony conviction, believe it or not: Back in the 1970s and '80s, he'd done time for possession of large amounts of cocaine, using a dead man's identity to cross the Canadian border, and defrauding the Cuban government (that one's a long story). Stan believed that Paul was responsible for the destruction of Stan Lee Media and openly denounced him on multiple occasions. As Stan put it in his second memoir while describing the whole debacle: "I'll never be so stupidly trusting again."

If only that were true. Stan was an astoundingly poor judge of character and was very susceptible to being conned, or at least woe-fully manipulated. He lived to regret it. His final year and a half, after his departed wife could no longer act as a bulwark against mountebanks, had been a hellish maelstrom of abuse and theft. But who was at fault? It was like a game of Clue. Was the biggest villain Keya Morgan, a memorabilia collector and Hollywood hanger-on who was arrested multiple times for various alleged crimes involv-ing Stan? Was it Jerry Olivarez, who had set up a fake for-profit charity and roped Stan into it, then made off with a massive, alleg-edly forged check from Stan's bank account? Was it Max Anderson, Stan's road manager, who was accused of stealing countless expen-sive artifacts from Stan's career? Was it JC? Was it an alliance of some or all of them? All of the aforementioned people will tell you that they were the only one who had Stan's best interests at heart and that all the rest were sticky-fingered criminals who are not to be trusted.

For what it's worth, Morgan was and is the most flamboyant of these suspects, making sure to appear in red-carpet photos with Stan at every turn during their years of acquaintance and attending con-fabs between Stan and various celebrities, from Leonardo DiCaprio and Robert De Niro to David Copperfield and Buzz Aldrin (there Aldrin is again, bizarrely enough), typically wearing a dark suit and a black bowler hat he says he received as a gift from Michael Jackson. Nearly a year after Stan's death, a suited and shades-wearing Morgan strode into a restaurant in the Los Angeles suburbs and sat down at a booth along with me and his armed bodyguard. He demanded a seat where he could face the exit, because "I never put my back to the door." Given the fact that he was about to go to trial over alleged elder abuse toward Stan, it was supremely odd that he brought no lawyer. Over the course of nearly five hours, Morgan spoke about how the whole world was arrayed against him and depicted himself as a paragon of virtue. He made a self-aggrandizing point of showing me books, newspapers, and magazines that cited his role as a collector of celebrity artifacts, then opened his laptop. He'd come to play me audio and video of Stan in his twilight months, media that forever changed the way I thought about Stan. I couldn't help but wonder whether any of what I saw and heard then was legitimate and believable, which is sadly appropriate: After all, Stan Lee's story is where objective truth goes to die.

WE CAN BE CERTAIN of one thing: Stan Lee was far less than truthful about his life and accomplishments. He lied about little things, he lied about big things, he lied about strange things, and there's one massive, very consequential thing he may very well have lied about. If he did lie about that last thing—and there's substantial reason to believe he did—it completely changes his legacy.

Stan became a name and face recognizable to literally billions of people because he said he created the Marvel Universe. And, to be sure, he played a key role in doing that. In 1961, after more than two decades of toiling away in obscurity as a writer/editor at an unremarkable comic-book publishing house, he and a writer/artist named Jack Kirby put together a superhero comic book called *The Fantastic Four* #1. It was action-packed, with dynamic illustrations and propulsive dialogue, and—most important—unlike the superhero comics that preceded it, it depicted protagonists who hated each other almost as much as they hated their superpowers. It is no exaggeration to say that this comic was an inflection point in global popular culture, as its success led to a bevy of revolutionarily humanistic superhero comics from the publisher, which had been known by various names but renamed itself Marvel Comics. Spider-Man, Iron Man, the Incredible Hulk, Black Panther—these pieces of intellectual property and many more, all of them eventually lucrative beyond anyone's wildest dreams, emerged in an axial period, a handful of years of fevered creativity.

But whose creativity? Stan always said it was mainly his, that he dreamed up all these characters, then handed them to Kirby to merely draw. Ever since then, a credulous public has believed him. Countless articles and interviews have taken him at his word and he has thus been canonized as one of the greatest cultural sources in American history—"the Homer of the twentieth century," as an oft-repeated line goes. Yet none of these tributes acknowledge a bizarre and shocking fact: It's very possible, maybe even probable, that the characters and plots Stan was famous for all sprang from the brain and pen of Kirby, who spent much of his life despising Stan for, as he saw it, stealing credit. It's already provable that Stan lied blatantly and often about Kirby's contributions to their comics together. How far did this deception go? There are those who claim, more than a little convincingly, that Stan pulled off one of the most daring acts of artistic theft in modern history.

Stan Lee was, by most accounts, a remarkably pleasant man to deal with. He was charming, self-effacing, kind, warm, and gracious. He passionately loved his wife, he unceasingly supported his daughter, he uplifted many of the creators who worked for him, and he was always nice to his legions of fans. Certainly there were scores of people far more cruel than he in the comics industry and the creative arts in general. And there is no doubt that he contributed greatly to the Marvel Universe: He wrote snappy dialogue and ruminative narration, and his wizardry at management and editing created a never-rivaled roster of comics creators and an ever-expanding sequence of interconnected stories that continues to this day. What's more, his remarkable gift for promotion is what sold Marvel to the world and made it the multibillion-dollar brand it is today.

But at his core, Stan was a man whose success came more from ambition than talent. He lived a quintessentially American life, one in which he came from virtually nothing, struggled in middle-class purgatory, then reached the heights of fame and fortune. And yet, like the prodigal son of Vaslui, he was unsatisfied with what he actually achieved and always boasted of more. His is a tale of triumph, but it is also one of overreach and agony.

The often-false story Stan Lee told about himself and his work was that of the American dream: success earned through hard work, optimism, and staying true to oneself. But the true story of his life is that of the American reality: success won in no small part through nepotism, corner-cutting, dissembling, and stealing. Perhaps this approach to life gave him a blind spot, as he was ultimately beset by caricatures of his own ambitious self, people who had far fewer personal limits in their quests for cash and recognition. Taken as a whole and with sober eyes, the man's journey adds up to one of the more fascinating stories of the past century of American arts and letters, and it is a journey that has heretofore gone unexamined in public. The time has come to tell that story.

One of Stan's trademark phrases was "True Believer." He used it to address his followers—"Face front, True Believer!" and the like— but perhaps, when it came to his own legend, his truest believer was he himself. That kind of commitment to his own hype would prove to be his undoing. Another slogan of his was "Excelsior!"—Latin for "ever upward." And up he rose. But so, too, did he fall.

PART 1

AMBITION AND ITS DISCONTENTS

*"Of what import
are brief,
nameless lives . . .
to Galactus??"*

—*The Fantastic Four* #49

ESCAPE AT ANY COST

——

(TO 1939)

THE POGROM THAT STAN LEE'S FATHER SURVIVED AS A CHILD could hardly have come at a more sacred time. It was the evening of Tuesday, September 11, 1890, and the Jews of the eastern Romanian city of Botoșani—likely numbering just below sixteen thousand, putting them roughly at parity with the Gentile population—were beginning their observance of the holiest twenty-five hours of the year, the supremely important fast day known as Yom Kippur, or the Day of Atonement. As they beat their chests and wailed to God in a collective plea for mercy, a congress of more than two hundred Romanian students were screaming at one another beneath a newly unveiled statue of national poet Mihai Eminescu, incensed over the great dilemma of the day: what to do with the Jews. All Jewish people had recently been expelled from the student congress, and the matter of the members' concern that day was a resolution, raised by a group of socialists, that would have allowed Jews to return to their number. Opponents of that proposal were furious and, after about two hours of arguments, people were starting to throw punches, so the matter was dropped and the students went to a banquet.

At around 9:30 P.M., the group, now likely inebriated, stumbled out into the streets, and some of the students from the anti-Semitic faction wandered into a Jewish neighborhood. They smashed stones through the windows of a school, then made their way to a synagogue, where they saw, through a window, people lost in prayer. Suddenly the Gentiles broke into the house of worship and hurled insults at the frightened and somber congregants, demanding that they dance and shout cheerful phrases. The Jews did so, but it wasn't enough—soon, the Romanians were screaming, "Down with the kikes!" and setting holy books aflame.

Having done all this, the students returned to the streets and continued their rampage, attacking and desecrating more synagogues full of worshippers, as well as looting dozens of Jewish-owned homes and businesses. At one synagogue, the rioters found a Jewish doorman and a Christian who helped the Jews out on holidays and the Sabbath; some held the former down and set his beard on fire, while others physically attacked the latter for debasing himself through servitude to Jews. At the Sticlarilor School, they beat a Jewish guard named Nachman. In the home of Ştrul Herş Schwarz, a teacher of calligraphy, the students destroyed the furniture and forced the man's wife and daughters to run into the night clad only in their sleeping clothes. The Săvener synagogue, the Reb Eizig synagogue, the Simchi synagogue—all were targeted, all were defiled. Exhausted, the Jew-hating youths eventually abandoned their task and went to bed, leaving the traumatized Jewish community of Botoşani to pick up the pieces in the cold light of dawn. It was just a few days before Iancu Urn Liber's fourth birthday, and already he knew the cruelty of our unredeemed world.

Gray-eyed, brown-haired Iancu was born into a community that was fast crumbling under the weight of the world's oldest prejudice. Most or all of his family were so-called Ashkenazim, Jews whose proximate origins lay in Mitteleuropa ("Ashkenaz" is an antiquated Hebrew term for Germany) and who, after various expulsions and massacres, had traversed Eastern Europe in more-recent centuries. That said, we must here take a pause, as Iancu's paternal grandmother, Pesseh, was born with the surname Pesica, which perhaps placed her origins in the far-western Romanian town of Pecica. There had been Jews in that part of the world as long ago as the days of Roman antiquity: Could it be that one of Iancu's bloodlines stretched through to the age of the empire, thus making his birthright even firmer than that of many of those Gentiles who would tar him as an alien? Either way, the monikers of Iancu's other forebears suggest they themselves were of more-recent vintage. We can surmise this based on the fact that their names all emerge from Yiddish, the German dialect that was the proprietary lingua franca of the Ashkenazim.

On Iancu's father's side, his grandfather—Pesseh's groom—was Bercu Liber; on the boy's mother's side, his grandparents were Haia Sura (her birth surname is unknown) and Sloim Leibovici. Leibovici and Liber are Romanian domestications of the Yiddish names Leibowitz and Lieber, respectively. We can hazard a guess that most of Iancu's forebears were drawn from the mass of Ashkenazi migrants who fled the poverty and persecution of Galicia and Poland beginning in the fifteenth century and found themselves in the principality of Moldavia, which is where Botoșani can be found. Pesseh and Bercu had a son, Simon Liber, around 1843, but his birth location is unknown. His bride was Estera Malca Leibovici, child of Haia Sura and Sloim, born circa 1856, though she went by the nicknames Manta and Minnie; the place of her birth, like that of the groom, is a mystery. However, we do know they were wed in Botoșani, and it is entirely possible that that was the only city they'd ever known. After all, there had been Jews in Botoșani since at least the 1600s, and by the time the Romanian-illiterate, intermittently employed, and profoundly religious Simon and Manta welcomed Iancu to the world on the afternoon of September 21, 1886, it was a bustling Jewish center.

It's hard to pinpoint the inception of the towering wave of anti-Semitism that engulfed Romania in the last decade of the nineteenth century and the first of the twentieth, driving Stan Lee's parents to flee the continent. But if we are to understand the forces that shaped Stan's parents and, in turn, Stan himself—as well as the origins of the cold distance between Stan and his father—we must attempt to sort the historical narrative out. On the one hand, Jew hatred in the Romanian territories had been present for centuries. Vlad Tepes, the infamous impaler of men and alleged inspiration for Dracula, had been a sworn foe of the Jews of his principality during the mid-1400s. Romanian church literature of the 1600s punished with excommunication any Christians who made contact with Jews. Greek-born overlords of the region made accusations of Jewish ritual murder during the 1700s. Russian invaders of the early 1800s propagated czarist anti-Jewish literature, sentiment, and legal codes. But the particular brand of anti-Semitism that permanently changed the lot of Romania's Jews came in the late 1800s, with the rise of romantic nationalism in the region. As is so often the case with downturns in the fortunes of a minority, the hatred came after a period of hope. A continent-wide series of revolutions in 1848 led to promises from liberal Romanian nationalists that the Jews would be granted full citizenship, civil and political rights, and the freedom to cease wearing the Polish-style caftans and *shtreimels* (large, furry hats) they were obligated to don. The revolution turned out to be a failure, and there was a subsequent political tug-of-war between promises and disappointments that lasted decades.

The 1878 Treaty of Berlin, authored by a convention of the great powers of the day, mandated equal rights and emancipation for the Jews of Romania. Yet it was there that the horrors truly began. In an age when nationalism meant uniformity, the Jews were seen as a fly in the ointment; in a populace drunk on the ecstasy of national independence, the Jews were targeted as a foreign element. The Treaty of Berlin was overruled time and time again by the Romanian leadership, and more than fifty specifically anti-Semitic laws were put into place. Jewish activists were deported; Jews were blocked from being doctors, lawyers, or pharmacists; Jewish businesses were barred from selling certain products; Jewish children were booted from schools; and so on. Life for the Jews became increasingly impoverished and intolerable. We do not know what Stan's grandparents did for a living in Romania, but it is entirely possible they lost skilled jobs and were forced to choose menial professions instead. Racist orators roamed the streets. Reactionary pamphlets papered the reading rooms of the country. A gathering with the straightforward official title "the Romanian–European Anti-Semitic Convention" was held in Bucharest with government endorsement, and speech after speech in the legislature excoriated the Jewish population.

"It is immaterial in which country they live, the Jews do not become assimilated," one senator bellowed in a legislative session. "They form a nation within the nation and remain immobile in a state of barbarism." It was against this backdrop that Stan's father saw the Jews of his city assaulted and learned he would never be at home in his homeland. The impact of such trauma on a human being and its reverberations in that person's children should never be underestimated. Stan would walk away from Judaism and the institutions of Jewish life—even, it can be argued, from Jewishness as a concept—but his parents' and grandparents' experience must have been an influence. Iancu, forged in tragedy, grew up to be a harsh and bitter man, as well as one who was passionate about being Jewish. The contrast between him and his firstborn is striking and intriguing.

And what of Stan's mother? Celia was a half decade younger than Iancu and came from a family whose names similarly imply an Ashkenazi background—indeed, they don't appear to have Romanianized their names the way the Libers and Leibovicis had, which might mean they were more-recent arrivals to the region, perhaps coming during a massive influx of Jews that occurred in the 1830s. Isaac Solomon and Sarah Bernstein gave birth to Zanfir in 1863; Moses Hoffman and Rachel Seigel brought about a child named Sofie in roughly the same year. The pair wed around 1883 and resided in Vaslui county, possibly in the small town of Perieni. They brought Celia into the world on January 3, 1890, and within a few years they were either newly or still in a slightly larger municipality known as Huşi. Huşi was smaller than Botoşani, containing some 16,000 people as of 1899, but about 4,000 of them were Jewish, making for another significantly Jewish area. These high concentrations of Jews in urban locales should come as no surprise, given that Romanians had, through stigma, violence, and legislation, long seen to it that Jewish people couldn't live in the countryside among the Romanian peasantry. Nevertheless, Jewish life grew in these quasi-ghettos, and Huşi was no exception: In Celia's time, multiple Jewish cemeteries and houses of worship were there. Life carried on, even under horrible conditions.

It was not to last. An 1899 crop failure brought a devastating economic recession to Romania, and that, combined with continuing anti-Semitic persecution, pushed Jewish life in the country to a breaking point. A mass exodus began. Starting in that year, Romanian Jews sailed to the United States in astounding numbers: more than 1,300 in 1899, more than 6,000 in 1900, and well over 54,000 in total by the end of the century's first decade. Great masses of them exited the country on foot, marching long miles to ports that would allow them to commence a journey to the Americas. They became known as the *fusgeyers*—Yiddish for "foot-wanderers"—and their exodus was the single most important story in the Jewish world of their day. Although their numbers were not as great as those of the Russian Jews who had arrived in North America in droves in the 1880s, the Romanian cousins bore a tragic distinction: While the Russian Jews had been only one stream among many Russian migrants who were departing to escape turmoil and poverty, there were hardly any non-Jewish Romanian departures in the run that began in 1900. The only reason to leave Romania was a Jewish heritage. These were, first and foremost, refugees escaping political persecution that had befallen them by virtue of their birth.

As was true for countless millions of immigrants of the day, the Romanian Jews fled largely to New York City, and Celia and

Iancu—who, at this point, still had not met—were among the horde. The Solomons arrived first, on the day after Christmas in 1901, when Zanfir, Sofie, and their children disembarked from a ship known as the *Majestic*. Zanfir was listed at Ellis Island as a "laborer," a catchall for someone whom the authorities deemed to have no particular profession—perhaps they didn't understand him when he spoke, perhaps he declined to share the nature of his work, or perhaps he simply wanted to start with a fresh slate. Whatever the case, he took his clan to 4th Street—now known as part of the East Village, but then considered part of the Lower East Side—not too far from the heart of the sub-neighborhood known as "Little Rumania." Although the Jewish Lower East Side is today remembered with a certain degree of romance and wistfulness, it was often hellish for the new arrivals, widely known as "greenhorns." Perhaps the Solomons knew the aforementioned Marcus Eli Ravage, the fellow Jewish Vasluiander who had arrived in 1900 and later wrote vividly of the awful conditions in this boiling pot of humanity, which was one of the most densely populated areas civilization had ever seen.

"So far is the immigrant from being accustomed to such living conditions," wrote Ravage, "that the first thing that repels him on his arrival in New York is the realization of the dreadful level of life to which his fellows have sunk. And when by sheer use he comes to accept these conditions himself, it is with something of a fatalistic resignation to the idea that such is America." People were shoved into dark tenements where a dozen might share an apartment that was divided from their neighbors only by a dangling sheet. Men who had been doctors and lawyers in the Old Country were reduced to roving as street peddlers. "This was the boasted American freedom and opportunity," said Ravage, "the freedom for respectable citizens to sell cabbages from hideous carts, the opportunity to live in those monstrous, dirty caves that shut out the sunshine."

Despite such challenges, the Solomons planted a stake in the ground. The family entered the hat-making business, and Celia, once she was old enough, got a job as a salesgirl at the Woolworth's department store, then ascended to being an accountant there. Having come to the United States at an early age, she quickly discarded any trace of an accent—so much so that her own sons were never quite sure whether she had actually been born in Romania. The groundwork was being laid for a child like Stan to have a foothold in the American experiment.

Iancu got out relatively late in the Romanian Jewish exodus, showing up at Ellis Island only on August 6, 1906. When he sailed from Rotterdam to New York on the *Nieuw Amsterdam,* he came with the clothes on his back, four dollars in his pocket, and a brother, Litman, about whom we know little. Short, lean Iancu Urn, just shy of the age of twenty, spoke to the immigration agents and was given the Anglicization of his name, which he carried for the rest of his life: Jacob Aaron. He soon started going by an even more American name, which he'd utter in a Romanian-Yiddish accent that he never quite shook: Jack. He had been trained in Romania as a saddlemaker, an important artisanal trade for an era in which horses had yet to be replaced by motorcars. At some point during his new life in New York, he abandoned that profession to become a dress-cutter in Manhattan's Garment District.

A huge portion of New York's new Jewish immigrants worked in the garment industry, so Jack was no exception to the general rule, but his status as a cutter meant he rose to the top of the crop. Cutters were relatively well paid and had to demonstrate incredible skill, as they were the ones who carefully sliced through stacks of fabric to create the outlines of a given piece of clothing. While a slipup in sewing would ruin only one dress, a mistake in cutting could destroy far more, all in one go. In other words, Jack was good with his hands. Though there are no extant records of his initial dwelling place, it's likely that Jack, like virtually every other new Jewish arrival, dwelled on the Lower East Side, where, by then, Romanian Jews had made a significant impact. They were known as the bons vivants of the Jewish population, as spicy as the pastrami—a Romanian dish influenced by years of Turkish occupation—that they introduced to American cuisine. Romanian Jews were heavily involved in the culinary trades and were pioneers of the Yiddish theater, bringing raucous and impassioned performances (not unlike Stan's eventual self-presentation) in the tongue of the Eastern European Jews.

There are no known records or stories, even from Larry, about how Jack and Celia met, but it may well have happened far from the Lower East Side. As the years of the twentieth century wore on and New York's subway system was born, Jews started leaving that sardine-packed pit and spreading out to enclaves across the city. By 1918, Jack was living at 40 West 116th Street in Manhattan, near Columbia University. We know this from his World War I draft-registration card, which also reveals a sad aspect of his existence at the time: When asked for his closest relative, he listed his father and said the man was still living in Romania. This was a curious choice, given that Jack already had family in the United States: There was Litman but also a sister, Rebecca (or Beckie), and another brother, Welwel (or Willie), who ended up in Titusville, Pennsylvania. Larry says Jack hardly ever spoke about his family of origin, but Willie's daughter, Martha Leiber Dermer (that branch of the family went with an alternate spelling of their surname), recalls her dad visiting Jack in New York regularly and that "Jack was always happy to see my father; he and my father were close"—although she hastens to point out that Jack never returned the favor by visiting them, as far as she knew. As for Jack's father, Simon, Martha says he ended up in what was then Palestine and later became Israel. It stands to reason that Stan Lee may have cousins wandering the Holy Land.

Whatever the case, the year 1920 found Jack living as a bachelor boarder in East Harlem, on East 114th Street, deprived of the family presence that the Solomons enjoyed. However, he soon entered their embrace: At some point, Jack and Celia found each other, and they wed in the spring of 1920 in the home of a rabbi from Botoşani. The newlyweds moved to a building at 777 West End Avenue, at the corner of 98th Street, on Manhattan's Upper West Side, where they were childless for more than two years. But on December 28, 1922, they had their first son and gave him a pair of distinctly non-Jewish names followed by a very Jewish one that he would come to discard: Stanley Martin Lieber. Perhaps those first two English monikers were Jack and Celia's way of declaring that this lad, whatever his troubles, would be distinctly of the New World to which they had fled at such great cost.

THE BIOGRAPHER'S CHALLENGE IS similar to the psychoanalyst's but far more futile. Both professions seek to understand a human being by analyzing recurring themes and motifs in that human's external and internal worlds. Both will tell you there is no more formative period than one's childhood—as the saying often attributed to Saint Ignatius goes, "Give me the child for the first seven years and I will give you the man." Both are held back by the unreliability of a subject's memory about those early years of shaping and growth. However, the psychoanalyst is far more likely to get honest answers about the young life of a patient than is the biographer, who must largely rely on the stories the subject wants spoken about publicly. There is no more unreliable narrator of a person's life than that person. This is a particularly thorny problem when it comes to Stan, given his tendency toward deceit and exaggeration.

Case in point: the tale of the essay-writing contest. At age fifteen, Stan entered a competition for young scribes held by the *New York Herald Tribune,* a publication that would come to be significant in Stan's later life on multiple occasions. The challenge was to write a nonfiction piece about the news of the week. "I won it three weeks running," he said in 1977, "and finally the editor called me down to the *Herald Tribune*. He said, 'Will you stop entering the contest and give someone else a chance?'" Per the story, this editor asked Stan what he wanted to be when he grew up, and the lad said he dreamed of being an actor. "He said, 'Well, why don't you think of being a writer? I don't know how good you act, but you seem pretty good with words.'"

Surely Stan never expected that anyone would bother fact-checking something as trivial as that little anecdote. And a dive into the paper's archives reveals that young Stanley Martin Lieber had, indeed, competed and won seventh place on May 7, 1938, then netted an honorable mention (as did ninety-nine other kids) on two subsequent weeks. But that was it. No first-place finish at any time, much less a jealousy-inducing streak at the top, which makes the idea of his having an inspirational audience with an editor quite unlikely. That incident should give us pause about believing that anything Stan said about his youth was strictly—or even remotely—factual. But that doesn't mean his stories lack significance. They tell us much about how Stan perceived himself and, more important, how he wanted to be perceived by others.

The overarching theme of all the stories Stan Lee told about his childhood is that of escape: from his economic class, from obscurity, even from his own family. All three of those escapes were readily visible in the opening portions of 2002's *Excelsior!: The Amazing Life of Stan Lee,* a curious quasi-autobiography co-written by a celebrity biographer named George Mair, in which first-person recollections are interspersed with third-person narration. Stan begins his account of his own life on a somewhat Oedipal note:

> I always felt sorry for my father. He was a good man, honest and caring. He wanted the best for his family, as most parents do. But the times were against him. At the height of the Depression there were just no jobs to be had.
>
> Seeing the demoralizing effect that his unemployment had on his spirit, making him feel that he just wasn't needed, gave me a feeling I've never been able to shake. It's a feeling that the most important thing for a man is to have work to do, to be busy, to be needed. Today, I never feel more fulfilled than when I'm working on a number of projects at once, which is

really nuts because I'm always wishing I had more free time. Still, when I'm busy I feel needed, and that makes me feel good.

There you have it, instant psychiatry, and it didn't cost either of us a cent.

This is, perhaps, the lens through which we should look at Stan's entire life. Stan was not a publicly self-reflective man and showed virtually no interest in talking about his parents—their deaths go nearly unmentioned in *Excelsior,* despite the fact that both were tragic and surely impactful in their own ways—so it must be deeply significant that, on a rare occasion when he mentioned his dad, he spoke of him this way. By his own admission, Stan wanted to be wealthier, more needed, and generally better than the man who had sired him.

If we want to consume more information about the kind of people Jack and Celia were and how Stan saw them, we must subsist on breadcrumbs. According to Stan, Jack "was a brilliant man, I think. He was very well read, mainly on current events. He read every newspaper you could find." It appears that his marriage was turbulent: "I always wished my mother and father would lavish as much love on each other as they did on my younger brother, Larry, and me," Stan said in *Excelsior*. He continued:

They were both good, loving parents, and I think the only thing that gave them any pleasure was their children. My brother and I always regretted that fate had not been kinder to them and that they couldn't have had happier lives. They must have loved each other when they married, but my earliest recollections were of the two of them arguing, quarreling incessantly. Almost always it was over money, or the lack of it. I realized at an early age how the specter of poverty, the never-ending worry about not having enough money to buy groceries or to pay the rent, can cast a cloud over a marriage. I'll always regret the fact that, by the time I was earning enough money to make things easier for them, it was too late.

There, again, is that Depression-kid avarice (as well as, perhaps, an echo of his own fights over money with his wife and daughter, which we shall get into later). But there, too, is a dubious claim: that of a loving relationship between father and son. It seems that Stan was stretching the truth in that regard. "Often he was, I'd say, a difficult man," Larry recalls when asked about Jack. "I don't know what made him tick." Jean Davis Goodman, the boys' cousin (and wife of the publisher of what became Marvel Comics, Martin Goodman), called Jack "demanding" and assessed the situation this way before she died: "He was exacting with his boys—brush your teeth a certain way, wash your tongue, and so on." That squares with Larry's estimation: "He was worried about doing what's right all the time, and he did it in a way that made me worry about things other kids didn't have to worry about. Let's say we were in front of a store. He'd say, 'Come here, don't stand in front of the man's window. He has to sell his goods and you're blocking it.'" Larry says Jack was never abusive, but he was cold, cryptic, and "always worried about disturbing somebody else." He had particular views about how people should act and was unafraid of enforcing them, even with strangers, in Larry's recollection: "I used to go to the movies with him, and he sometimes argued with the woman sitting in front who— women wore big hats then—refused to take off her hat," he says. "So I got embarrassed and stopped going." When Stan let his guard down late in life, he contradicted his memoir's warm account of his father. "Even when I made a good living, my dad didn't think of me as a success," Stan told an interviewer in 2014. "He was pretty wrapped up in himself most of the time. Some of that rubbed off on me."

The slender and quiet Celia, on the other hand, appears to have been a more welcoming presence, albeit one in chronic distress. "She was very honest, and if she believed in something, she'd speak up,"

Larry says. "Otherwise, she didn't." She left her job to raise her children and, as Stan put it, she "spent almost all her time cleaning our small apartment or cooking in the kitchen." Larry says his mother "was a worrier. If I went anyplace, I had to be back on time, not because she'd be angry but because she'd be worried. She worried a lot." Jean Goodman said Celia was a "persecuted mother" and that her relationship with her husband "made the atmosphere difficult." Larry confirms this: "I think my father didn't—I don't want to go into it—didn't get along with my mother," he says. Nevertheless, Celia seems to have adored Stan. "My mother was my biggest fan," Stan would eventually write in an early outline for his memoir. "Always led me to think a talent scout would grab me the next time I walked down the street."

By the time Larry was born, on October 26, 1931, there was a nearly nine-year gap between him and his older brother, and thanks to their mother, the eldest perpetually cast a long shadow over the youngest—a fact of life that never stopped being true. "My mother used to say to me, 'Be like your brother,'" Larry says. "That's what I remember. 'Why aren't you more like your brother?' That was my childhood." He recalls a specific incident that stuck with him all his life: His mother "told me the story that one day, when she went to school for Stan, the teacher said, 'He is so wonderful. He reminds me of our president Roosevelt.'" That kind of praise for her older son never ceased, as Larry tells it. "I lived with that and I had an enormous respect for this image," he says. "It was almost like the movie *Rebecca,* where she kept hearing about Rebecca but never met her, you know?"

The location of all of this family drama was constantly shifting. The Upper West Side was an expensive place for a struggling immigrant family to live, and perhaps the price drove them away, as they decamped much farther north, to 619 West 163rd Street in Washington Heights, by the end of 1924. At some point, the family packed up again and moved to 1720 University Avenue in the Bronx. Both areas were solidly lower-middle class and heavily—though by no means exclusively—populated by Jews, including a number of members of Celia's family. The Solomons were a large brood and the boys interacted with them regularly, a fact that would prove to be highly significant in Stan's career. That said, young Stan seems to have loathed his relatives. "Hated to visit my family," he would eventually write in that memoir outline, "but every so often, on a Sunday, I had to."

The dramatis personae for these dreaded meetups was colorful. There was glamorous Aunt Mitzi and her British husband, Arthur, who worked as a fixer in the movie industry. There was Aunt Freda and her overly generous groom, Sam, who gave away their money and left her with virtually nothing. There were cousins Mort and Midge, the former of whom was a salesman and the latter of whom died young of hepatitis. There was "Little" Ed, who sold hats and had a son, Stuart Solomon, who would go on to don the name Mel Stuart and become a filmmaker, directing *Willy Wonka & the Chocolate Factory* and *If It's Tuesday, This Must Be Belgium*. (Despite the fact that they both worked in the entertainment industry, Mel and Stan don't appear to have had much contact over the course of their adult lives; in fact, in some notes Stan wrote down for the co-author of *Excelsior,* he cryptically comments, "My one celeb relative—MEL STUART—disliked at sight.") Most important, there was the aforementioned cousin Jean and an uncle from a different branch of the Solomon tree, Robbie. Robbie had been an athlete in his youth and grew up to be, as Larry puts it, "a nice guy," working for and marrying the sister of publisher Martin Goodman. Jean further solidified the familial connection to Martin by marrying the man. Those two marriages would prove to be crucial in changing the history of the arts.

The groundwork for those momentous changes was also being laid in the homes and schools of young Stan. The boy was, by all accounts, a voracious consumer of whatever media he could take in. Newspaper comic strips were an early love—he would later cite *The Katzenjammer Kids, Skippy, Dick Tracy, Smitty,* and *The Gumps* as some of his favorites. Like millions of other Americans, he and his family got into the nascent technology of radio: "Sunday night, we listened to the comedians," he'd later recall. "There was Fred Allen and Jack Benny, Edgar Bergen and Charlie McCarthy, and there was W. C. Fields." Although Stan rarely cited radio as an influence, the evocative and percussive verbiage of golden-age radio would later be echoed in his dialogue and narration at Marvel. Movies were another obsession; he recalled there being five movie houses near his home in Washington Heights, giving him plenty of options. Young Stan reveled in the films of Charlie Chaplin, Roy Rogers, and his screen idol, the swashbuckling Errol Flynn—a proto-superhero if there ever was one. "Errol Flynn was my god," he would say many decades later. "I was about ten years old, I don't know. I'd walk out of the theater after an Errol Flynn movie; I'd have a crooked little smile on my face, the way I thought he smiled, and an imaginary sword at my side, and I'd be hoping that I could find some bully picking on a little girl so I could come to her rescue, you know?"

But, above all, Stan was a nut for reading. "At every meal at home—breakfast, lunch, or dinner—I'd have a book or magazine to read while I ate," he wrote. "One of the first presents my mother bought me was a little stand to keep on the kitchen table to rest a book against while eating. . . . My mother used to say that if there was nothing to read, I'd read the labels on ketchup bottles, which I did." In his memoir and interviews, he'd list examples of his early favorites throughout the canons of both high and low art. "Some of the books I most enjoyed were H. G. Wells, Arthur Conan Doyle, Mark Twain, and Edgar Rice Burroughs," he wrote. "Then there were the seemingly limitless tales of the Hardy Boys, Don Sturdy, Tom Swift, the Boy Allies . . . After a while, my tastes in reading became more eclectic. I discovered Edgar Allan Poe, Charles Dickens, Edmond Rostand, Omar Khayyam, Émile Zola, and, of course, Shakespeare." Early Modern English became a passion of his, both in Shakespeare ("While I'm sure most of the Bard's work was way over my then-juvenile head, I was fascinated by the rhythm of his words, by the flowery language, the 'What ho, Horatio' type of outpourings") and the King James Bible ("I love that style of writing, the almost poetical phrasing and the 'thees' and 'thous' and 'begats,' which can make the simplest thought seem fraught with drama").

And yet, although all of these famed works no doubt moved Stan, one can argue that the most influential texts for his eventual impact on the world were the now-forgotten children's book cycles *Jerry Todd* and *Poppy Ott,* both penned by the pseudonymous scribe Leo Edwards. Oddly enough, Edwards's influence on Stan's life and career had less to do with his stories than his backmatter, specifically a section Edwards dubbed "Chatterbox." "At the end of each book, there were letters pages where the writer, Leo Edwards, would write a little message to the readers and print some of their letters with answers," Stan would say later in life. "I loved the fact that they had letters and commentary by the author. Leo Edwards was the only guy that did that. Maybe I remembered the warm, friendly feeling of those letters." Stan would go on to ape Edwards's innovation to great effect during the heyday of Marvel, answering readers' missives with a peppy, conversational tone in the so-called Bullpen Bulletins section of each comic he put out. This connection is no mere surmise—Stan eventually made it explicit, saying of "Chatterbox": "In fact, that's what gave me the idea to do the 'Bullpen Bulletins' pages in the comics years later."

Unsurprisingly, this fixation on words made Stan a successful student in elementary school—perhaps to his emotional detriment. Like many working-class parents of that era, Celia, it seems, wanted her son to be able to help support the family through wage labor, and that meant getting done with his school career ahead of schedule. "Was always the youngest kid in my class and in my social group," he wrote in his memoir outline. "It happened because my mother wanted me to finish school as soon as possible, so I'd work hard in order to get into the 'A' classes, the 'skipping' grades—and I was usually in classes with kids older." There were occasional bright spots in these classes, such as his experiences with an instructor named Leon B. Ginsberg, Jr., who made a lasting impression on young Stan: "He would entertain the class with humorous and exciting stories to illustrate teaching points," Stan later wrote. "It was Mr. Ginsberg who first made me realize that learning could be fun, that it was easier to reach people, to hold their attention, to get points across, with humor than any other way. It was a lesson I never forgot, a lesson I've tried to apply to everything I do." But, on the whole, Stan's status as the runt of his class overshadowed his early education: "It made my early years hell," he would later write, "'cause I was the one they always picked on."

In Stan's framing, that bullying was just one of many factors that drove him to feel as though he had to leave his life behind. His recounting of his childhood never portrayed it as idyllic. Even the view outside his window depressed him. "Though it may seem like a trivial thing, I was saddened by the fact that my family always lived in a rear apartment—never one facing the street," he wrote in his memoir. "Looking out the window, all we could see was the brick wall of the building across the alley. I could never look and see if the other kids were out in the street playing stickball or doing anything that I might join in." (He then boasted that, as of the memoir's writing, "my home is on a hilltop in Los Angeles, where we have a view stretching from the Pacific Ocean to downtown.")

He hated that poverty kept him from certain social situations, as well. "A real depressing time for me was summer, when most of the kids went away to camps with unpronounceable Indian names," he wrote. "What made this depressing for me—aside from not being able to send postcards home from places like Camp UgaUgaTa and Camp Monga-Wonga-Donga, or whatever—was that I was usually alone in the city. Most of my friends would be at camp and I'd be hanging around the school yard, hoping someone would come by for a game of handball." He certainly felt no kinship with the Jewish community and was allergic to the very idea of religion. "I never believed in religion. I don't mean the Jewish religion—I mean in religion," he would later say. "To me, faith is the opposite of intelligence, because faith means believing something blindly. I don't know why God—if there is a God—gave us these brains if we're going to believe things blindly."

This was a stark contrast with his parents. Jack had been raised in a deeply observant Jewish family and, although he became more moderate in his observance than his brother Willie, Jack still went to synagogue somewhat regularly and was passionate about his Jewish identity. Celia lit Sabbath candles and said the prayer for the dead every Friday night and, at Jack and Celia's behest, Stan and Larry both had the coming-of-age ceremony known as a bar mitzvah. None of that moved Stan. "My father insisted I be bar mitzvahed, and I took a crash course in learning to read Hebrew, all of which I'm sorry to say I've forgotten now," he said in old age. "My parents didn't have much money at that time, and I remember during the ceremony at the temple, there was my father and me, and maybe two other people had wandered in. That was the whole thing." In 2015, I was allowed to send Stan a few interview questions via email, and when I asked him, "How important was New York Jewish culture in forming the way you talk, write, and think?" he completely dodged the Jewish part and simply replied, "The city of New York itself informed the way I talked, wrote and thought. There was something about New York culture that seemed to be, and still seems to be, different than any other place in the world."

In order to explore the city he loved so well, he used one object that brought him great joy: a bicycle. "When I rode it, in my imagination I was a mighty knight atop a noble steed," he wrote. "That bike was my best friend because it gave me a feeling of freedom. So what if our family didn't have a car. I finally had wheels. I could ride all over the city, go wherever I pleased. No kid ever loved a bike more than I loved mine." Larry says he doesn't remember his brother riding a bicycle especially often, but even if this story is an exaggeration, it's one that evokes that recurring motif of Stan's urge to leave behind everything he'd been born into. "Stan never spoke about his past, about Mother and Father, with any great warmth, because I think he was trying to escape from it," says Larry. "That's why he mentioned it, I think, in his book, getting on the bicycle to ride. He wanted to get away from it all. And he got away from it, all right."

WHATEVER WAS IN THE WATER at the Bronx's DeWitt Clinton High School in the twentieth century, it should have been bottled and studied. The all-male public school—named after the early U.S. senator, New York City mayor, and New York State governor DeWitt Clinton—was first established in Lower Manhattan in 1897 and subsequently moved to the north-central Bronx in 1929, where it has remained ever since. By the time Stan studied there in the mid-1930s, the institution had already served as the alma mater of future luminaries such as author Richard Condon, journalist Daniel Schorr, and composer/lyricist Frank Loesser. Later, it would produce even bigger names: Neil Simon, Ralph Lauren, Judd Hirsch, and many more. And while Stan studied there, the school bustled with a mish-mash of geniuses. He may well have shared classes with James Baldwin, Paddy Chayefsky, Richard Avedon, or Sugar Ray Robinson, just to name a few contemporaries.

But perhaps the oddest fact of all was the way the school, in Stan's day, influenced the development of the American comic book. In addition to Stan, DeWitt Clinton gave diplomas to both of Batman's creators, Bob Kane and Bill Finger, as well as to the first master of the full-length graphic novel, Will Eisner, who is often regarded as the greatest American cartoonist of all time. However, Stan never spoke of having any relationships with these men. Indeed, the only fellow student he ever spoke of at any length was a boy named John J. McKenna, Jr. McKenna never went on to fame or fortune, but he made an impression on Stan, thanks to his part-time job: selling subscriptions to *The New York Times* to fellow students. Stan waxed rhapsodic about this boy in *Excelsior,* devoting about as much space, if not more, to him as he did to his own family members. Here's just a portion of the remembrance:

> I was one of the first to subscribe, but the main thing on my mind was, *Man, if only I could address an audience as confidently as that and speak off the cuff as glibly as he.* He spoke for about ten full minutes, looking his audience straight in the eye, never once fumbling or losing the attention of the class. I was terribly impressed by the smooth, easygoing way he made his pitch and the way he managed to hold the interest of the students while talking about a subject that normally would bore the pants off them.
>
> I decided that I wanted to be able to speak that way, to be able to hold the attention of an audience the way he did.

There does appear to have been a New Yorker named John J. McKenna, Jr., whose birth date would make him roughly Stan's age, but the rest of the story may well be apocryphal. What matters is that Stan devoted so much energy to conveying it to his fans. "He never knew it," Stan wrote, "but McKenna, with his great gift of gab, who could make a tough teenage audience listen attentively to every word he had to say, was one of my first role models (after the aforementioned Leon B. Ginsberg, Jr., of course)." In this tale, Stan laid out a trio of traits that he valued enormously throughout his professional life: confidence, charisma, and salesmanship. McKenna knew how to generate demand and move product, and Stan wanted in on that action. In a very concrete way, he achieved that goal insofar as he said he subsequently got his own job selling newspaper subscriptions, albeit for the publication that had so lukewarmly reviewed him in that essay contest, the *Herald Tribune*.

That was only one of Stan's micro-professions in that era. Dress-cutting was a gig-based trade, without much in the way of stability, and Jack's chronic unemployment during the years following the Great Crash of 1929 took a toll on the familial wallet. According to

Stan, Jack once owned a diner—something relatively common among Romanian Jews—but it swiftly went bankrupt. Even while Stan was a student at DeWitt Clinton, he was regularly employed in one odd job or another, according to his recollections. The anecdotes about these jobs would roll out of him whenever he recounted his youth, their order getting mixed up, and it was always unclear which ones he did in high school and which came after graduation. There was the time he wrote advance obituaries about celebrities who had yet to die. There was the time the Goodman family apparently linked him up with a Jewish employment network that netted him a remote job writing publicity copy for a tuberculosis hospital in Denver called the National Jewish Health ("I could never understand what I was trying to do—get people to get tuberculosis so they go to the hospital?"), although the hospital tells me they have no record of his doing so. He said he did paid acting work in a theater program run by the Works Progress Administration, in no small part because a girl he liked was doing the same—but no record of his being employed there has survived, if there ever was one. He said he delivered sandwiches from the Jack May drugstore to the offices of Rockefeller Center and that he was faster than all of his fellow delivery boys. He spoke of working as an office boy for a trousers manufacturer and, feeling exploited and disrespected by the higher-ups, throwing a pile of informational papers into disarray after being fired. He said he worked as an usher at Midtown Manhattan's Rivoli Theatre and once walked Eleanor Roosevelt to her seat, tripping over someone's foot in the process.

In contrast to all these jobs, school held little interest for Stan. "I didn't hate being in school," he would later tell an interviewer, "but I just kept wishing it was over and I could get into the real world." That said, he did find himself involved in school life, albeit in an extracurricular manner. The yearbook for his DeWitt Clinton graduating class of 1939 reveals an array of clubs in which he was a member, from the Future Lawyers Club to the school literary magazine, *The Magpie*, for which he served as—appropriately enough—the publicist. He was fond of telling a story about that job, one that, in true Stan Lee style, deviated from the truth: He would tell of climbing a painter's ladder in the room where *The Magpie* operated and painting the words "Stan Lee Is God" on the ceiling, but very late in life, when questioned about his use of that nom de plume at such an early age, he said he probably wrote "Stan Lieber Is God." Or maybe none of that story happened at all. Whatever the case, his yearbook entry summed up a philosophy that would stay with him for the rest of his life: When asked for his life's goal, he wrote, "Reach the Top—and STAY There."

In Stan's retelling, around the time he graduated, he rented an apartment in Manhattan's West Village to have some space to himself and, no doubt, to romance a few young ladies along the way—he was growing into something of a hound for them. Along those lines, he said he briefly attended night school at the City College of New York solely to spend time with a young woman he was seeing. "I don't remember what I studied or what course I took, but I enrolled just so I could be with her," he later said; within six months, the pair had split and Stan, who would eventually become a sought-after speaker on college campuses around the country, abandoned his own attempts at higher education forever. He bounced from job to job, searching for permanent employment, without any sense of where his future lay. There is a kind of irony in what happened next. When he told stories about those early years, Stan always portrayed his family as ancillary to his own career ambitions and autodidactic sense of purpose. He wanted you to believe he'd gotten where he was through sheer hard work and talent. But an unexpected bit of nepotism allowed him to set foot on the path toward—to use his words—reaching the top and staying there: A pair of family members offered young Stanley Martin Lieber an insider deal that would, in its way, alter the shape of global public consciousness.

2.

MEANS OF
ASCENT

(1 9 3 9 – 1 9 4 5)

ABOUT FIVE DECADES AFTER A TEENAGE STAN STARTED WORK-
ing for Martin Goodman at the publishing imprint initially known
as Timely Comics, an interviewer asked him how he had landed the
job. "Well, I answered this ad," he said. "There was an assistant
wanted at a publishing company and I figured, *Hey, great!* I was just
out of high school. I wanted to be a writer. I didn't know it was a
comic-book company. Particularly when you say 'publishing company,' I figured books or regular magazines. And I got up there and
when I found out that the opening was for an assistant in the comic-
book department, I was really surprised." The interviewer was
friendly, but he'd done his homework and confessed to Stan that he
was a little confused: Wasn't Goodman Stan's relative? Was their
professional link really the result of happenstance? "Martin was
my . . . I had a cousin, and he was my cousin's husband," Stan said,
waving his finger in the air near his chest, as though drawing the
family tree. "And I'm not sure . . ." Stan trailed off and started again.
"The whole thing was quite a coincidence, because he saw me in the
hall one day and said, 'What are you doing here?' and I said, 'I'm
working here!'"

That could have been a slightly plausible account of events, and Stan often spoke of boldly answering an ad in the paper (sometimes he said the ad acknowledged it was for a comics job, sometimes not) and then finding himself working for Timely. That is, except for the fact that he quietly threw the story out the window in his later years, perhaps after being caught wrong-footed in the lie one too many times. By the time he and Mair put together *Excelsior,* he'd updated his official line. "My uncle, Robbie Solomon, told me they might be able to use someone at a publishing company where he worked," he wrote. "So I contacted the man Robbie said did the hiring, Joe Simon, and applied for a job. He took me on and I began working as a gofer for eight dollars a week at this small company located in the McGraw-Hill Building on Forty-second Street at Ninth Avenue, on the west side of Manhattan. I didn't realize it at the time, but I had embarked on my life's career."

That last bit about not knowing that comic books would be his destiny rings true, if only because virtually no one working on the things back then had any sense that they were going to be toiling in that medium for the long haul. Comic books hadn't even existed ten years prior and, despite an initial streak of success, few took them seriously as art; there was no reason to believe they were anything more than a children's fad that would die out within a matter of years, if not months.

Before the comic book, there was the nudie and the smoosh. In the late 1920s, New York City publishing was in no small part built on disreputable publications, crammed with slapdash material and slammed onto cheap paper before being thrown to a populace with an insatiable appetite for content of low moral fiber in an increasingly libertine age. Smooshes were text-based magazines about illicit liaisons, while nudies were pictographic celebrations of the female form that just barely eluded decency laws. And even if they *were* indecent, a publisher could always grease a palm in Tammany Hall to get a pass. The average Gentile publisher would never stoop to print such content, so certain Jewish businessmen, far removed from the strict codes of their parents' Old World life, were happy to satisfy the demands of the debased consumer.

Though these publishers were undoubtedly the ones who would come to popularize the comic book, it's a matter of debate who actually invented the art form. People had been putting newspaper comic strips into compiled editions since at least the 1840s, and an 1897 set of reprints of New York newspaper staple *The Yellow Kid* coined the term "comic book" on its back cover. However, the size and shape of these publications looked nothing like what we'd today identify as a standard-issue comic book. That only came in early 1929, when New York-based publisher George T. Delacorte, Jr., put out *The Funnies,* an insert for tabloid newspapers that was filled with strips that had been rejected by the syndicates. It was arguably the first real comic book—and it was a consistent sales failure, eventually getting the ax in the autumn of 1930.

Enter New Yorker Maxwell Charles Gaines, a Jewish former teacher and necktie salesman with a serious limp who was desperate for a big break during the nadir of the Great Depression. After making contact with Connecticut-based Eastern Color Printing, he arranged to republish some of the most popular newspaper strips of the time in a comic book called *Funnies on Parade* in 1933. It was distributed as a coupon giveaway through Procter & Gamble, was a smash hit, and was followed by sophomore effort *Famous Funnies.* The latter, also released in 1933, was the first publication we can undoubtedly refer to as a comic book, insofar as it featured a wraparound cover and was sold individually on stands, not through a coupon mail order. Another ambitious publisher and former cavalry officer, Malcolm Wheeler-Nicholson, one-upped Gaines in late 1934 by forming National Allied Publications and subsequently putting out *New Fun,* the first comic book to feature new material, but it lasted only a handful of issues.

It wasn't until pornography maven Harry Donenfeld got into the action that the comic book really took off. A Romanian-born Jew who was raised on the Lower East Side and whose publishing business was astoundingly mobbed up (he allegedly helped gangster Frank Costello move Prohibition-era liquor from Canada in boxes for shipping paper), Donenfeld faced a crisis in the mid-thirties. New mayor Fiorello H. La Guardia was cracking down on vice and indecency, and that meant a slump for the smooshes and the nudies. Donenfeld and his uptight business manager, fellow Lower East Side Jew Jack Liebowitz, somehow ran into the desperate Wheeler-Nicholson and were inspired to get into the nascent comics business. It had a special pecuniary appeal: Retailers were nervous about selling girlie mags, but Donenfeld and Liebowitz could persuade them by throwing in some clean comic-book fun for the kids.

Donenfeld and Liebowitz were in the right place at the right time. Other publishers at the margins of good taste got in on the action and the comic-book fad started to rise nationwide, built on versions of the sci-fi, crime, and adventure tales of the day's youth magazines. However, the medium didn't explode until Donenfeld and Liebowitz ousted Wheeler-Nicholson from National and one of their employees discovered a slush-pile submission. It was the creation of two Jewish kids from Cleveland, Jerry Siegel and Joe Shuster, and the lead character was called Superman. His 1938 debut in National's *Action Comics* #1 made comic books the single hottest item in the entertainment market of the time, and an industry was finally born.

Although Stan was a reader of newspaper strips, there is no evidence that he was in any way a regular consumer of comic books prior to obtaining a job at a company that put them out. Nevertheless, he swiftly became a key player in the budding ecosystem of the American comic book. Indeed, the story of Stan's early years in comics is one of a stunningly quick rise to prominence and material success, spurred by both his undeniable talent and the family-first attitude that dominated so many immigrant-owned workplaces in

New York City at the time. Well, that and a bitter act of betrayal, which, although it may or may not have been perpetrated by Stan himself, certainly gave him a huge leg up.

NONE OF WHAT HAPPENED in Stan's life past the age of sixteen would have been possible without the efforts of the controversial and under-sung founder of the company that became Marvel Comics. He was another ambitious second-generation American Jew who wasn't afraid to cut corners and do a little backstabbing here and there in order to get ahead. If you were to invent him as a fictional character, you might be accused of mild anti-Semitism. In fact, he was just one of the first in a long succession of domineering and ambitious—and, as it happened, Jewish—men who loomed large in Stan's life until its end.

Moses Goodman was born to Lithuanian Jewish émigrés Isaac Goodman and Anna Gleichenhaus on January 18, 1908, in Brooklyn, though the child would eventually come to be known as Martin. Theirs was a large family, even by the standards of the time: thirteen children in twenty-two years. Martin was the eighth child but, improbably, the first male, and before he could reach the sixth grade, he dropped out of school to supplement the peddler's wages of his father with scattered jobs. Members of the Goodman family speak of how young Martin developed a precocious interest in publishing as a kid, cutting out articles from magazines and rearranging them with paste into his own mock compilations. He was an iconic American type, not just in his entrepreneurial desires but in his lust to understand the inner workings of the country his parents had adopted: People who knew him would often tell—perhaps inaccurately—of the days of wanderlust Goodman spent hitching rides on trains across the United States in the middle of the 1920s. "Before his publishing days, there were many tramp trips, freight cars, cooking beans over a fire," one of his lawyers, Jerry Perles, would later say. "I don't think you could mention a town to him that he didn't know about. He is knowledgeable about this country. It helped him a great deal later on in magazine circulation."

The circumstances under which Goodman came to that trade are murky. He most likely worked for the so-called Father of Magazine Science Fiction, publisher Hugo Gernsback (birth name Hugo Gernsbacher—another Jewish immigrant, albeit one from Luxembourg), but evidence of such employment is limited to hearsay. Somehow or other, Goodman came into contact with Gernsback's onetime circulation manager, a Jewish law school graduate named Louis Silberkleit. As of late 1929, Silberkleit was working as circulation manager for Eastern Distributing Corporation, a national distributor of dozens of magazines, and he took Goodman on to work in the circulation department. There Goodman got a firsthand view of the world of the so-called pulps. So named for the cheap paper, often made from low-grade wood pulp, on which they were printed, pulp magazines were deliciously trashy items, chock-full of punchy text about everything high culture wouldn't touch, from lurid tales of sex and death to the still-forming genre of sci-fi. The pulps were a sensation with youths around the country, particularly a certain kind of obsessive young man, the likes of which would go on to become Stan's bread and butter: Gernsback and his ilk were cultivating the first generation of what would one day be referred to as geeks.

Though Gernsback was worshipped by adolescent nerds, he was hardly beloved by the people who knew him best in the industry. He was infamous for, as one of his contemporaries put it, his "venality and corruption, his sleaziness, and his utter disregard for the financial rights of authors." Goodman was assigned to Gernsback's account with Eastern and doesn't seem to have been repulsed by any of the older man's traits; as it turned out, he went on to adopt many of them as his own. When Eastern went under in 1932, Silberkleit started two companies, Newsstand Publications, Inc. and Mutual Magazine Distributors, and took Goodman along with him, only for the two to part ways in 1934 after their distributor went under.

Goodman was left in control of Newsstand and managed to bring it back from the brink of insolvency with a killer's instinct that would come to serve him well throughout the years—except, that is, for the handful of times when it disastrously failed him.

As publishing historians Michael J. Vassallo and Blake Bell put it, "For [Goodman], success meant jumping and pumping—jumping on a successful trend and pumping multiple similar titles (with the least possible investment) through the pipeline as fast as possible in order to rake in as much profit as possible." They point out that Goodman set up more than eighty quasi-fictitious companies over the years, shady publishing entities that could buy and sell their intellectual property from one another when one or a few went bankrupt or got into legal trouble—as Vassallo and Bell say, Goodman "put more effort into building his corporate web of shell publishers than he did into building a strong brand (which, right there, reveals the priorities of the quick buck, low-brow publishing mindset of the 1930s)." Oddly enough, the slender, prematurely white-haired, generally quiet Goodman would be the first to cop to this not-so-generous assessment. "If you get a title that catches on, then add a few more, you're in for a nice profit," he once told *The Literary Digest*. "Fans are not interested in quality," he said on another occasion. By way of justification for this mindset, we have yet another cutthroat line from Goodman: "This field is full of pirates."

This was the business-psychology milieu that Stan entered while he was still in his impressionable teenage years. When the lad went to work for Goodman, the latter had only just started to publish comic books, having launched *Marvel Comics* #1 through shell publisher Timely in August 1939. Timely became the name most closely associated with Goodman's early comics publishing, although the books were actually published under a variety of headings prior to the line's renaming in the early 1960s: Timely, Atlas, Manvis—even, on a few occasions, Marvel. Whatever you wanted to call it, the comics operation was a near-instant smash for Goodman. *Marvel Comics* #1 had introduced the company's first superheroes, the

Human Torch and the Sub-Mariner. Superhero comics, first introduced in the form of National's Superman the previous year, had abruptly become one of the most popular items in the cultural marketplace, and Goodman wanted to secure his foothold.

Marvel Comics (renamed *Marvel Mystery Comics* in the second issue for no extant reason) had been produced through a partnership with Funnies, Inc., a third-party "packaging" vendor that produced comic books, and, seeing the success that the series brought him, Goodman opted to bring the action into his own tent. He enticed one of the packager's star writer/artists, Joe Simon, to come aboard and work for him directly. The young man, lanky and in his mid-twenties, had been born Hymie Simon to an English and an American Jew in western New York. He was confident and charismatic, in addition to being remarkably good at juggling assignments: While cranking out work for Funnies, Inc., he simultaneously acted as an editor at comics packager Fox Feature Syndicate. It was there that Simon met another twentysomething writer/artist with a prodigious work ethic. The squat, serious man's name was Jacob Kurtzberg—yet another Jewish name that would eventually be discarded in favor of something a little more Establishment-ish. In his case, the nom de guerre became "Jack Kirby."

Kirby was born to Jews of Austro-Hungarian extraction on August 28, 1917, on Essex Street in the Lower East Side. Kirby was, in many ways, Stan's dispositional polar opposite. Where Stan had been enamored of silver-tongued rhetoricians in his youth, Kirby looked up to the brawlers—and, indeed, became one. "Each street had its own gang of kids, and we'd fight all the time," Kirby would remember later in life. "We'd cross over the roofs and bombard the Norfolk Street Gang with bottles and rocks and mix it up with them." He learned to temper his more violent impulses, but he never lost his pugilistic sense of right and wrong and never—often to his own detriment—became a schmoozer or a glad-hander. Like Stan, he started working while he was still a youngster and ultimately did most of his learning outside class, by scarfing down the popular entertainments of the day. "The pulps were my writing school," Kirby said. "Movies and newspaper strips were my drawing school. I learned from everything. My heroes were the men who wrote the pulps and the men who made the movies. Every hero I've written or drawn since then has been an amalgam of what I believed them to be."

Though he was never formally trained in artwork, Kirby had a precocious and natural talent for drawing, and before he could even enter twelfth grade, he dropped out of school to make a living as a working artist in order to support his family. He did a number of low-level gigs—drawing fill-in art for *Popeye* animations, doing knockoffs of popular comic strips for a syndicate, penning single-panel cartoons about politics and personal health—before he stumbled into the still-new medium of comic books by working for a packager run by Will Eisner and partner Jerry Iger. There, he experimented with a bizarre array of pseudonyms: "Fred Sande," "Ted Grey," "Teddy," "Curt Davis," "Jack Curtiss," and, ultimately, the one he permanently settled on. Having so dubbed himself, the newly minted Jack Kirby moved to the glorified sweatshop that was Fox Feature Syndicate to earn a wage. It wasn't a ton of money and the boss was a jerk, so Kirby didn't have to think too hard when his new pal and collaborator, Simon, offered the chance for the two of them to jump ship and sign on for salaried work with Goodman in 1940.

It would be another two decades before Stan would have any appreciable impact on pop culture, but Simon and Kirby didn't have to wait nearly that long. They changed the course of American folk art before the country even entered World War II. Indeed, it was that looming overseas conflict that fueled the success of Kirby's longest-lasting co-creation: the star-spangled avenger known as Captain America.

After Simon and Kirby had produced the lackluster superhero Red Raven and the moderately successful Vision and Marvel Boy (not to be confused with two better-known Marvel characters of the same names who came much later), Simon allegedly brainstormed an all-American Aryan übermensch wrapped in Betsy Ross's finest and initially named him Super-American. "No, it didn't work," Simon recalled in his memoir. "There were too many 'Supers' around. 'Captain America' had a good sound to it. There weren't a lot of captains in comics. It was as easy as that." He and Kirby filled out the visual and thematic details, and a new piece of intellectual property was born. This two-fisted paragon had been a mild-mannered everyman before a strange serum granted him massive strength, and his debut adventure in December 1940's *Captain America Comics* #1 (for arcane reasons, the cover date was a few months later than the date of the actual release, an industry-wide policy that would remain in practice for decades to come) resonated with all the force of the punch its title character landed on Hitler in the cover image.

However, a cynic might point out that rival publisher MLJ Comics—co-run, as it happened, by Goodman's erstwhile partner and mentor Silberkleit—had already put out a flag-draped and chemically altered superhero named the Shield in 1939 and that the good captain was just another entrant in Goodman's endless parade of rip-offs. MLJ chief John Goldwater was one such cynic and threatened legal action after Simon and Kirby's strapping adventurer first appeared—adding insult to injury, Cap bore an arm-held shield that looked exactly like the Shield's angular insignia. No matter; the boys changed the shape of Cap's shield to an enduringly iconic circle for the second issue, and Goldwater conceded defeat. It was an early message from the company that would become Marvel: Our legal agility will always trump your creative integrity.

Around the time that Simon was helping to cook up Cap's first foray into print and settling in as Timely's first editor (a stickler for detail, he always went out of his way to point out that "editor," not "editor-in-chief," was his title), he was, according to Simon, pulled aside by Robbie Solomon, whose role at Goodman's company was as ambiguous as his familial relation to the boss was clear. Simon and Solomon never got along. "I don't really know why he was there except to take messages," Simon recalled late in life. "As far as I could tell, his only other job was to make certain those cushions were on all of the chairs, fluffed up and ready for Martin's behind. . . . He was a big mouth with a lot of opinions on subjects about which he knew nothing." Although Larry Lieber recalled enjoying Solomon's company as a relative, that sentiment was not shared by the growing staff of creatives that Goodman had hired for the new comic-book bullpen.

" 'Uncle Robbie,' as he was known by the staff of the bullpen, they looked at him as a spy for Martin Goodman, and nobody trusted him," recalls another bullpen member, artist Allen Bellman. "He was a former ladies'-hat salesman and was always trying to tell the artists how to draw." But Goodman wanted Solomon there and Goodman wrote the checks, so everyone kept their mouths shut. And when Solomon came to Simon with some nepotistic marching orders, he went right along with them. "Robbie had a sister named Celia Lieber, and one day he brought in this sixteen-year-old kid who was her son, Stanley," Simon wrote (Stan was likely seventeen, but leave that be). " 'Martin wants you to just keep him out of the way,' he said. 'Put him to work.' So young Stanley Lieber became my assistant and gopher."

That latter title was a workplace neologism derived from the sort of orders one would give a person like Stan: Go for this thing I need, go for that thing I want delivered, and so on. "Mostly we had Stan erasing the pencils off of the inked artwork, and going out for coffee," Simon wrote. "He followed us around, we took him to lunch, and he tried to be friends with us. When he didn't have anything to do, he would sit in a corner of the art department and play his little flute or piccolo, whatever it was, driving Kirby nuts. Jack would yell at him to shut up." Stan's chronic abuse of that musical instrument, variously remembered as an ocarina or whistle or some such, left an early negative impression of Stan on Kirby. "I remember him sitting on my desk and playing the flute, interfering with my work," Kirby later said. "I remember being serious about what

I was working on, and Stan was never serious about anything." Simon recalled Kirby periodically growling, "Someday, I'm gonna kill that kid." Strike one.

Stan at least concurred with Kirby on one count: Despite the titanic changes the two of them would unleash on the world later in their lives, they were not close in the beginning. "We never became very friendly at the time because they never thought of me as a peer, and there's no reason why they should have," Stan conceded while describing Simon and Kirby in *Excelsior*. "I had started as an inexperienced apprentice, and it's hard to live that first impression down. Anyway, I didn't work with them long enough for our relationship to change significantly—or for them to learn the sheer wonderfulness of me." That said, in the handful of months that Stan spent working for the dynamic duo, Simon, in an offhand gesture, made what would turn out to be a momentous decision: He gave Stan his first professional written work. "One day I made his life," Simon wrote. "I gave him a text page to do in *Captain America*." The bottom-line-conscious Goodman was always looking for a way to cut costs, and one common trick was to put at least two pages of non-comics text in a comic book, to get it to qualify for the postage rate of a magazine. The cheat took the form of two interior pages with blocks of narrative prose, adorned by an illustration or two in the margins, like one would see in a children's book. Simon, overworked and probably looking for something to keep Goodman's irritating little relative busy, assigned one of those toss-offs to Stan for March 1941's *Captain America Comics #3*.

The result was a short prose story called "Captain America Foils the Traitor's Revenge." It began *in medias res,* with a colonel dressing down a grunt in terms that, ironically, Stan's harshest critics would later apply to him: "I'm sorry, Haines, but there is no place in this army for the likes of you. You have lied, cheated, spied and stolen." As a whole, the story was a perfectly serviceable piece of writing, especially given the age and inexperience of its author—and one that, in its brief length, presented a few notable attributes. For one thing, Stan appears to have been the first person to dream up the eventually ubiquitous idea of Cap using his lawsuit-proof shield as a kind of boomerang, tossing it in such a way that it hits a target and then bounces back to its owner. Second, and more subtly, the story was a precursor of Stan's eventual obsession with giving his heroes quirkily non-heroic action to play out, in this case taking the form of a goofy pillow fight between Cap and his underage sidekick, Bucky. What's more, the two pages featured header and footer illustrations drawn by Kirby, technically making the story the first published collaboration between the two legendary frenemies.

Finally, the story bore not the byline "Stanley Lieber" but rather "Stan Lee," a name that had never before appeared in print. "Being only seventeen at the time and not yet having become the incredibly sophisticated and knowledgeable superperson that I am today, I somehow felt it would not be seemly to take my name, which was certain to one day win a Pulitzer, and sign it to mere, humble comic strips," Stan would later write. "Thus, I was caught up in the fantasy of using a pen name, something suitable for strips, while saving my real name for the saga that would make me immortal. And that's how Stan Lee was born. I simply cut my first name in half and slyly changed the 'y' to a second 'e.'" Simon recalled seeing the byline and being confused. "Who's Stan Lee?" he asked the boy. "I'm changing my name," came the reply. "For journalistic reasons." Simon was puzzled by the last name, which sounded vaguely Chinese, and remarked, "It would be better for a laundry." "I hadn't considered that," Stan said, then added presciently, "I wonder what the comic book prospects are in China."

The new name, so casually created, would later come to be its bearer's platform, but also a feint—perhaps intentional, perhaps not—that obscured his Ashkenazi heritage. "Alas, I never did write that novel and ended up eventually changing my name legally to Stan Lee"—that wouldn't come until thirty years later, after Marvel had struck it big—"because that was the name by which I had come to be known just about everywhere," he wrote in the foreword to a

2007 book about Jews in the comics industry. "But I have a confession to make. To this day I regret that name change." He didn't elaborate on why in the foreword, but the context perhaps suggests some late-in-life regret about hiding his ancestry. One struggles to imagine anyone in 1941 bothering to read that two-page story, but it nonetheless made history.

Stan, now demonstrably competent at writing and eager to show his mettle, was given more work at the typewriter. The very next issue of *Captain America Comics* featured another Stan-penned and Kirby-illustrated text piece, "Captain America and the Bomb Sight Thieves," followed by one starring the Human Torch in *Marvel Mystery Comics* #21. But all of that was a lead-up to Stan's debut as a writer of full-on comics stories, word balloons and all. Simon and Stan may have had their disagreements later, but at the time, Simon seemed to think somewhat highly of Stan, given that he tossed not one, not two, but three comics stories to the novice in quick succession, all of them appearing on newsstands in May of 1941.

The first-ever published Stan Lee comics story appeared on May 15 in *U.S.A. Comics* #1. The six-page piece was illustrated by Charles Nicholas (another Anglicized pseudonym, actually used by multiple people, but in this case referring to the Polish American Charles Wojtkoski) and called "Jack Frost." It was a bizarre one. In it, an anthropomorphized spirit of freezing weather named Jack Frost meets a gold prospector on a frozen plain in Alaska; unfazed by meeting a muscular being made of ice, the prospector tells Frost in his dying breaths of a rogue in New York who shot him while stealing his riches and now threatens the man's daughter. "I have heard that crime flourishes throughout the world, but it has now reached my land," Frost declares to no one in particular. "I will avenge this deed and prevent more like it!"

He freezes the man in a block of ice for some reason and "speeds away" to New York City, where he tries to alert the police commissioner and the chief of detectives, who mock the ice-blue gent and are punished with dripping icicles and abruptly cold temperatures, establishing Frost as a kind of super-anti-hero. He tracks down the baddies and leaves them to die in a fire, further establishing his misanthropic bona fides. When he's chastised by cops on the scene, he declares that the poor reception he's received has brought him to a grim conclusion: "If I can't work with you, I'll work against you—the next time we meet—*beware!*" Frost "vanishes from the eyes of mortal men, leaving only two icicles as a reminder that he has promised to return!" The whole thing was slightly derivative of the Sub-Mariner, who was also a crank with an ambivalent attitude toward humankind, but it was far stranger. This comics debut for Stan presaged a running motif in the vast majority of the super-characters he created *after* his Marvel heyday: a figure based on a weird gimmick that doesn't quite work and leaves no trace on the cultural psyche.

Afterward came comics stories about existing superhero the Black Marvel, newly minted and eminently human foreign correspondent "Headline" Hunter, Simon and Kirby's clock-themed superhero Father Time, and a Stan superhero creation named the Destroyer ("A man who has sworn never to rest until he has destroyed the Nazi hordes"). Suddenly, a byline crediting Stan as the writer was common, which was unusual for the comic books of the time, when writers' names were typically hidden; it appears that Stan saw them as more of a vehicle to fame than his peers did. A few months later, Stan branched out beyond Goodman's comics lineup and into the boss's humor mags, writing some gag pages for a publication called *Joker*. One was a brief "modern fairy tale" in which a "l'il sailor" tries to entice a "l'il girl" to "sit on the grass" with him and she refuses, leading to a situation in which the sailor for some reason went to "the l'il girl's house instead and sat all night and talked with her family!" The end. A comedic list of things to do at an army camp was aimed at the small group of young men who had been enlisted since the September 1940 institution of the draft (preemptive, what with the United States not yet at war), and a prose piece called "Laugh It Off!!" was about a man who follows fitness and nutrition advice of the day but ends up "a thin, sickly, unpopular young goon who lives in a city called Goonville, where the people believe all the advertisements."

Though none of these pieces induce a giggle eight decades later, Stan would go on to spend a significant amount of his career, right into the twenty-first century, trying to make it as a writer of prose humor. When that humor came in the form of the Marvel ephemera that he wrote in the first person—letters pages, columns, introductions—it was titanically successful. When, as here, it was done in a more detached mode, it never stuck. One more notable bit of career foreshadowing came in September 1941's *Marvel Mystery Comics* #25, in which Stan penned a text story about various superheroes who were series regulars coming together for a confab. Although it wasn't superhero fiction's first crossover—that honor belonged to a Namor and Human Torch epic in issue #8, written by someone else—it was the first to suggest that *everyone* in Timely's stable could occupy the same space. Twenty years later, when Stan established the endlessly interconnected Marvel Universe, he likely didn't remember those two pages of prose, but perhaps they were the seed that grew into a framework that fundamentally changed popular fiction on both page and screen.

While Stan was executing all these obscure and un-ballyhooed—but nonetheless noteworthy—firsts, an era was abruptly coming to an end. Simon and Kirby, in Simon's account, had negotiated a handshake deal with Goodman when they created Captain America, whereby they would get a 25 percent share of the profits on the character's books. Goodman, however, allegedly paid virtually nothing out to the men, despite the character's runaway success on the newsstands, lying to them that it wasn't actually earning much. When Simon and Kirby learned that they were being screwed, they took up moonlighting for rival National (later, and often retrospectively, known as DC Comics) on the sly, working out of a nearby hotel room in their off hours. This is where Stan comes in, and not necessarily favorably. "We were spending a lot of time in our hotel studio, and one time Stan Lee followed us—like he always did—

refusing to be sent back," Simon recalled. "When he saw what we were working on, we swore him to secrecy."

A couple of days later, in Simon's account, a pack of Goodman relatives who worked for the boss (Stan and Solomon were hardly the only ones to get a nepotistic spot on the payroll) surrounded Simon and Kirby in the bullpen. "You guys are working for DC," Abe Goodman allegedly said. "You haven't been true to us. You haven't been loyal to us. You should be ashamed of yourselves," then, "You have to finish the issue of *Captain America*. After that, you're fired!"

The timing is suspicious. Could it be that gabby Stan ratted the pair of them? Simon, for his part, was doubtful. "My theory was that in comics, everybody knew everything," he wrote. "The guys at DC knew that we were coming up and negotiating, working on contracts, and they talked to other guys. Some of them might even have been jealous of us, since we were getting a different page rate than they were. There were no secrets there. So I'm not so sure it was Stan, after all." Stan, in *Excelsior,* said, "They quit Timely a few months after I started working there. And no, it wasn't because of me!" But—and this is crucial—there was one person who seems to not have shared their estimation of the events. "Jack always thought Stan had told his uncle that we were working for DC," Simon recalled. "He never gave up on that idea, and hated him for the rest of his life—to the day he died." Strike two.

With Simon gone, Goodman needed a new editor for his comics line as of late 1941. In a wild act of familial favor, he first chose his brother Abe, then, for reasons unknown, gave the title to Stan, a kid with barely any experience in any kind of profession, much less the increasingly high-stakes world of comic books. Nevertheless, on January 5, 1942, the contents page of *Captain America Comics* #12 bore the text "Stan Lee, Editor," not mentioning that this high-powered individual had just turned nineteen. "I assume [Goodman] wanted to find someone who wasn't still in his teens to wear the mantle of editor," Stan later recalled. "But apparently he had a short

interest span and eventually stopped looking." Stan now had to contend with the mercurial Goodman more directly and with greater
responsibility, and he was never quite clear about what that relationship was like, though it seems to have been turbulent. In his 1978
autobiography outline, Stan wrote, "MG was father figure to me—
most successful man I'd ever known." But later, in *Excelsior,* he was
lightly damning and described distance rather than familial bonhomie. The paragraph in which he describes Goodman is worth repeating in full, given how verbose it is, as well as how crucial were the
lessons that Stan learned from that unsteady bond:

> As bosses go, Martin was pretty much okay. He was some-
> what aloof in the beginning, but why not—we weren't ex-
> actly drinking buddies. Timely was a fairly small company
> and most of the staff called him by his first name. One thing
> about him was obvious—he enjoyed being a boss. He took
> lots of time off to play golf, would nap on his office couch
> almost every afternoon, and, in later years, enjoyed playing
> Scrabble with anyone in the company who had the time. Alas,
> that was never me. But he still managed to keep an eye on
> things and he knew the publishing business inside and out. A
> self-educated man, he was sharp as a tack and nobody knew
> the intricacies of magazine circulation better than he. If he
> had been more ambitious, I think his company could have be-
> come one of the giants in publishing, but Martin seemed quite
> satisfied just to make a good living and not have to work too
> hard. It frustrated me, because I always wished we could have
> done more and gone farther. But I kept those thoughts to my-
> self. In those days I considered myself lucky to have a job, and
> an interesting job at that.

What becomes clear is that if Goodman was a father figure, he
was one like Stan's biological father: somewhat pathetic, in Stan's
eyes, and a person to learn from largely by opposite example. On

top of managing a staff and a relationship with his cousin-in-law, Stan had to deal with the stress of continuing to write. Here, too, we see Stan, later in life, ragging on Goodman and convincing his audience that he had eventually bested his Oedipal oft-nemesis by becoming a trendsetter, an inventive creator, and a generally fun guy. "Martin's mandate was to keep the stories simple enough to be understood by young children," Stan wrote. "We're not talking *War and Peace* here." The struggle to escape Goodman's perceived philosophy of grim underachievement would come to define Stan's worldview.

Despite his resentment and hectic editing schedule, the new editorial chief became beloved by the bullpen. "Everybody felt Stan was wonderful. He kept things pretty loose," recalled artist Vince Fago. "He used to play a recorder all day long. It was like a clarinet. It made it very nice for everybody; it made things relaxing. He'd make us wait while he finished whatever tune he was playing. He'd even go into Martin Goodman's office and blow it at him." Stan would go on long walks with employees and offer them pay increases of a dollar a page, which was quite a lot of money in those days and very much appreciated. He also had a natural ability to balance micromanaging and granting creators free rein. On the one hand, "He was good-natured but strict with his editing," Allen Bellman recalled. "He wanted perfection. If you drew a cup on a table in one panel, do not leave that cup out in the next panel." On the other, as Fago put it, when Stan was mapping out stories for artists, he trusted them to do good work without too much guidance: "He wrote the story and dialogue, but he didn't break the story down into panels. That was left up to me."

This latter idea, that he could come up with a bit of an outline and write the text but leave the artists to do the bulk of the actual plotting and storytelling, would eventually evolve into what was known as the Marvel Method. It would be enormously controversial due to the fact that it obscured the artist's dual role as penciler and writer. But even in its prototype stage, it was useful for triage in a hectic environment and gave the artist the freedom to run wild. Not even in his third decade of life, Stan was already playing with fire.

A year after Captain America had entered the fray of World War II, the country that shared his name took his lead. Here, we must once again cast doubt on Stan's account of events. For years, he spoke of feeling a nationalistic duty to jump right in, and reporters and historians have regurgitated that version. "And shortly after the war started, I said to myself, 'What am I doing here, writing comic books?'" he told an interviewer in 1977. "'Gotta get in the army, be a hero like Errol Flynn or John Wayne,' so I enlisted." In 2017, he waxed even more patriotic: "I think I could have gotten a deferment, but . . . it was the kind of war you were a son of a bitch if you didn't get into it. It was too important not to fight." But Pearl Harbor was bombed on December 7, 1941, and Stan only enlisted on November 9, 1942—more than eleven months later. In that gap, the only way in which he served his country was by producing stories about Timely heroes roughing up the Axis, cranking out humorous text bits (uninformed by any lived experience) about life in the army, distracting adults with some decent short stories in Goodman's grown-up magazines, and placating nervous kids with silly bits about a goofy creature named the Imp. Could it be that Goodman pressured Stan to stick around? Stan mentioned in *Excelsior* that "my parents were worried about me" getting into the war—maybe he stalled in order to placate them until he could stall no more? Or perhaps, understandably, this scrawny, bookish young man didn't want to face the horrors of combat? Whatever the case, Stan did end up enlisting and was prepared to be shipped off on the Atlantic or Pacific. As it turned out, he never left his country of birth. He barely even left his typewriter.

THE KEY THING TO remember about Stan Lee's war years is that he was a propagandist. He never portrayed himself that way, and his

work then (or at least the work we know about) was eminently ano-
dyne. But the fact remains that it was all aimed at accomplishing
official military goals through simple, direct messaging designed to
instill emotional reactions of loyalty and excitement. Up until this
point, with the slight exception of doing publicity copy for that
tuberculosis hospital, Stan's writing was meant to entertain, not gal-
vanize. By the time he became famous—indeed, it's arguably the
reason he *did* become famous—he was a wizard at stirring his readers
up with direct addresses, often using the martial phrase "face front"
and referring to himself as "Generalissimo." Such verbiage sought
to make the masses feel as though they were members of a legion of
devoted followers who would do whatever their commander asked
of them. There is cause to think about the influence of his wartime
environment.

There's no way Stan could have known his service would have
any direct impact on his writing, given that he assumed, as did every
enlisted man, that he'd be sent off to fight. "I used to go to penny
arcades in New York and shoot those little guns and win prizes all
the time—I figured I was a shoo-in to handle real guns," he recalled.
"What little we know when we're young."

"Martin wasn't happy about my leaving," Stan continued, but
the soldier-to-be arranged to have Fago (who was, funny enough,
yet another DeWitt Clinton grad) take over as editor of Timely, and
Goodman accepted the new status quo. The selection of Fago may
have been something of a power play. "I think Stan was protecting
himself," Timely artist Dave Gantz would later recall. "He didn't
want anyone to upstage him. Vince had the type of nature that
would never allow him to do a thing like that." Whatever the case,
there would be a hand on the tiller.

According to Stan, his father—though, oddly, not his brother or
mother—accompanied him to New York's Penn Station as he departed on a train for basic training at New Jersey's Fort Monmouth.
There, he was put on sentinel duty overlooking the Atlantic, freezing his *tuchus* off in what he assumed was a kind of official hazing

ritual. He chafed at army hierarchy: "Hated non-coms far more than I could ever hate the enemy," he wrote in his outline, referring to non-commissioned officers. While still at Monmouth, Stan was assigned to the Signal Corps, the division of the army largely tasked with establishing and maintaining communications lines on the battlefield. Stan recalled being excited about the prospect but was disappointed to learn that he had a much more mundane duty, one that would leave him stateside: educating soldiers.

"I couldn't believe it," Stan recalled with an implicit sigh. "The army felt it had found something even more important for me to do than guarding New Jersey from an impending enemy invasion. They wanted me to write training films." He was, improbably, one of only nine men assigned to the so-called playwright division, along with such luminaries as director Frank Capra, writer William Saroyan, cartoonist Charles Addams, and even Dr. Seuss. It doesn't seem that Stan worked too closely with any of these individuals, though some of them shared his new digs at a repurposed movie studio in Queens, New York, but he was proud to identify himself as one of their number. The official military manual on the classification of enlisted personnel described the playwright position thusly: "Writes scenarios and scripts for theatrical, radio, or motion picture productions for entertainment or instruction of military personnel, or for publicity purposes . . . Civilian experience in writing or adapting scripts or scenarios for radio, stage, or motion pictures required." Stan was an odd fit, by that standard. Comic books were not included in the list of required experiences; it's unclear how often Stan had even been writing full scripts for his comics, as opposed to outlines with dialogue; and it appears that he felt out of place, given that he later wrote (though this may have been his trademark false modesty), "There could be only one explanation for my inclusion in that august group. They must have felt they needed one token nonentity in the crowd. I guess political correctness mattered even then."

Adding further intrigue is the fact that documentation of Stan's time in the military is notably spotty. There are no extant records of most of his claimed accomplishments in the playwright division, though his accounts seem plausible enough. He served at Duke University and at Indiana's Fort Benjamin Harrison, all the while cranking out increasingly bouncy products. He said he began by writing troop-training films with such thrilling titles as *The Nomenclature and Operation of an M-10 Rifle Under Battle Conditions* and *The G.I. Method of Organizing a Footlocker*. In an echo of the fib about the childhood writing contest for the *Herald Tribune,* Stan would often tell a possibly apocryphal story about being too good at his job: "Officer-in-charge asked me to write slower—I was making it look bad for the others," he pithily recounted in his autobiography outline. He soon moved on to comparatively more-joyful material. He said he wrote a marching song for the army finance department, which he remembered as going like this:

> Off we go, into our office yonder
> At our desks, morning till night
> Far away from any battle's thunder
> We pay off the fellas who fight
> Clerks alert, guarding our books from blunder
> Payroll forms clutter the floor
> We write, compute, sit tight, don't shoot
> Nothing can stop the Fiscal D'rector!

So successful was this effort, in Stan's telling, that he was tasked with making the finance department's payroll manuals easier to read and thus filled them with little cartoons and puzzles starring a character named Fiscal Freddy. But nothing pleased him more than a poster he designed to prevent overseas soldiers from contracting venereal disease during R&R sessions. He claimed to have drawn the image: a cartoonish serviceman marching along with a smile and pointing at himself while he boasted, "VD? Not me!" As Stan would tell it, he was so eager to serve his country—and escape the tedium—

that he asked to be made an officer and sent into battle. His commanding officer, so the story goes, replied, "Stan, if you become an officer, we'll lose you. They'll send you overseas. And we don't have enough writers to do all our instructional manuals and films." Perhaps it's true, perhaps not—either way, his mentioning of the story was part and parcel of the Stan Lee method of self-aggrandizement.

None of this was particularly arduous work, nor was Stan ever very far removed from civilization, so he still embraced many aspects of civilian life. He bought his first car, a used 1936 Plymouth, followed by a four-door Buick Phaeton. It was the beginning of a lifelong love affair—friends often remarked on Stan's adoration of automobiles. Speaking of love affairs: He also established a reputation as something of a ladies' man. He spoke of dating a wealthy woman in Indianapolis, but it "didn't turn out to be a love affair." An army employee in the laundry department was another crush, but "she had one horrible habit I couldn't stand. Anytime anything displeased her, which was quite often, she'd go, 'Oh, rats! Oh, rats!' I just couldn't see myself spending my life with a girl who kept saying, 'Oh, rats!'"

But most important—and most mysterious—was Stan's almost-bride, a woman we only know by the unusual name Kiye. She gets a brief mention in the autobiography outline ("Met Kiye—almost got married"), and in an interview he spoke of her as a "girl I was really serious with, and I thought I could marry her when I got out of the army." However, there was a complication for the twenty-something Stan: "I found out she was only sixteen. I felt that wouldn't be fair to her, so I walked away from it." Though Kiye may have been the most relevant romantic prospect Stan had during the war, the most intriguing was none other than the eventual author of *The Price of Salt* and *The Talented Mr. Ripley,* Patricia Highsmith, who was at the time writing comic books for Timely. Fago had set up the potentially romantic meeting for Stan. Highsmith was a notoriously flinty person, as well as one who is best known as a woman who loved other women, and unfortunately for posterity, Stan didn't remember—or at least reveal—any details of their confab. Fago reported that the meetup didn't blossom into a formal date because "Stan Lee was only interested in Stan Lee."

And all the while, in his off-hours, Stan managed to somehow keep writing comics for Timely, with the name "Pvt. Stan Lee, Consulting Editor" sometimes appearing in the credits. They were frivolous outings about cartoonish creatures and patriotic heroes (in keeping with his propaganda work, he even wrote at least one story designed to get readers to buy war bonds), with the occasional humor piece for one of the standard magazines. He often told a story about nearly getting court-martialed for breaking into a mailroom in order to get a time-sensitive comics assignment from Fago. Again, who knows if it happened, but the story fits with Stan's presentation of himself as a workaholic with a mischievous streak.

By the time Stan was honorably discharged on September 29, 1945, he'd accomplished a remarkable amount of creative work for a grunt. He explicitly said, later in life, that he thought the war had no effect on him. "I was just three years older," he told an interviewer. "I served, I did what I had to do, I came home, and I looked for a girl to marry." This is too simplistic. He often said he admired advertising men and wanted to emulate them in his ability to sell the brands he worked for and his own personal brand (and the two were often one and the same). But he never worked in advertising for a Madison Avenue agency. He worked in advertising for the U.S. government— and while he did, he put another set of tools for rhetoric in his mental toolbox. When he returned to his native New York City, Stan Lee had everything he needed to ascend to a new level of success in arts and letters. But, like so many men of the Greatest Generation, who demobilized and got back to the ordinariness of postwar life, his next phase was one of dashed hopes and thwarted ambition.

3.

QUIET
DESPERATION

———

———

AS SOON AS STAN HAD THE OPPORTUNITY TO GO BACK TO HIS full-time job in comic books, he started trying to get out of it. In his autobiography outline, the first item he typed under the heading BACK TO CIVILIAN LIFE was "Wanted to start educational textbook biz. Bennett Cerf. Should have tried other publisher. Oh well." Cerf was the venerable co-founder and head of Random House, as well as a famed humorist—an established literary celebrity as of the end of the war. Elsewhere in the Lee archives, one can find the text of a speech Stan delivered much later in life, in which he claims he "spent six months working on" an effort to establish a "subsidiary to publish textbooks" with Cerf before giving up when he realized how "convoluted" the government approvals process for such volumes was. "Unfortunately, being so young and stupid and inexperienced, it didn't occur to me to just go to somebody else in the textbook field," he went on. "I figured, 'Well, it didn't work,' and I went back to comic books again." He provided no clue as to why he wanted in on the textbook industry, though his recent experience as a composer of educational materials for the U.S. Army may have led him to believe that he had special didactic talent. He had a habit of getting worked up about whatever the most recent thing he'd accomplished was. Plus, he'd never really shown any special love of comics as a medium or an industry and was no doubt unenthused about having to interact with the difficult, often-dour Goodman on a daily basis again. Textbooks must have seemed like as good an exit as any, and if the years between Stan's military discharge and the advent of *The Fantastic Four* teach us anything, it's that he wanted out.

His schemes for departure from the comic-book trade in the 1940s and '50s were varied, but they all hit dead ends for one reason or another: tragic luck, infertile business climate, deficit of inspiration, what have you. As a result, he never quit his day job. Timely Comics, or whatever it was called on a given week, continued to churn out four-color narratives, and Stan was back to being in charge of the whole line, despite his still-young age. Fago was relieved of his duties as head editor and would later note that Goodman, whatever his flaws, seemed to trust Stan. "Goodman never interfered with what Stan was doing," Fago said. "He had faith in Stan. He knew Stan was in control and that his work was good." Stan had associate editors, but was firmly in charge and trusted his gut instincts while navigating the waters of the adolescent comics industry—waters that would soon become dangerously choppy.

Reviews of his leadership in this period were mixed. "Stan's management style was probably considered brusque by some people," recalls cartoonist Al Jaffee, who worked for him as a creative and, briefly, as an associate editor—and would later go on to become a humor legend at EC Comics' *Mad* magazine. "He was friendly but somewhat aloof. He protected his editor position by not becoming palsy-walsy." Allen Bellman, the artist, says, "He was good to his employees." Writer Daniel Keyes, who went on to pen the novel *Flowers for Algernon,* wrote for Stan in the fifties and wasn't impressed, saying he was "the shyest person I had ever met up until that time. He would not talk to anyone. He'd hole up in his back office. My memory of him is that he's got a glass on the floor, and a putter, and he's putting golf balls." Adele Kurtzman, one of Stan's secretaries in this period and the wife of Timely artist and future

Mad creator Harvey Kurtzman, says of the latter's time working with Stan, "Working for Stan was not a happy episode. I think he felt that the criticism wasn't warranted. The comics were printed in black and white and Stan would say, 'More blacks! More whites!' It wasn't going anywhere. It was . . . humiliating is the only word I can think of." But she herself had few complaints and says Stan created a lighthearted work environment: "He never fired me or was angry, none of that stuff. He impressed me. . . . [Once,] he climbed to the top of a filing cabinet in the room next to ours and said, 'I am God and I want all of you to bow to me!' It was silly kid stuff." Artist Gene Colan started working for Stan in mid-1947 and always got a kick out of him. "Stan was a very jolly guy, always like a kid," he later said. "And if he wanted to express himself fully, he would actually stand on his desk and get into a pose so that we had an idea of what he was looking for. The very first time I ever met him, even then he had on his head a beanie cap with a propeller on the top, and the window was open. That thing would just spin around. I couldn't believe it. I always got along well with him."

Whatever people thought of him, they certainly thought far worse of any number of bloviators and hard-asses who edited at other companies. Stan was about as good as it got. He knew how to find and keep talent, as well as how to pair writers and artists, with a matchmaker's eye. The work at Timely in this era may not have been revolutionary, but it was solid. Indeed, it's entirely possible that his greatest talent was editing; the only other skill that competed with it was his flair for promotion. Of course, he never sold himself as comics' greatest editor but rather as its greatest ideas man. One can argue that that was a core tragedy of Stan's existence and legacy: He was never able to put his most inarguable achievements front and center and instead opted for the ones that were most debatable.

As it turned out, editing was basically Stan's *only* job in comic books for the first two years after he got out of the service. Vassallo, the publishing historian, who owns what he claims is the largest collection of Goodman publications in the world, put it this way: "In this immediate postwar period of late 1945 through mid-1947, Stan Lee was supervising all the comic books but doing no real actual writing at all." Goodman's company had only grown in size and complexity during Stan's interregnum, even moving to a physically larger space in the Empire State Building in his absence. The bullpen now held dozens of artists on staff, and there was a growing legion of freelance writers to whom Stan would, in a further anticipation of the controversial Marvel Method, toss a few lines of story idea, then let them run wild with their scripts and the subsequent work of the artists.

The product they would deliver was vastly different from that which had dominated in Stan's initial days as a professional scribe. At the end of World War II and its perceived epic clash between the forces of light and darkness, the sun set on the first age of the super-heroes. Who were they to fight now that the Nazis were gone? Per-haps simple street hoods just didn't feel big enough, or maybe American youths were weary of Manichaean battle. Though DC continued to publish Superman, Batman, and Wonder Woman, it phased out most of its tales of spandex-clad derring-do. Timely did the same, publishing a dribble of stories about Namor, the Human Torch, and Captain America for a little while, then dropping them.

In their place came an ever-changing bandwagon of genre trends, all of which Goodman and Stan dutifully jumped on and off of as the market dictated. There were funny-animal tales, *Archie*-esque teen goofs, Westerns, hard-boiled crime sagas, horror stories, comics about young female professionals making their way in the world, licensed movie and TV tie-ins, even retellings of the Bible. Another genre Stan occasionally dipped his toe into was romance comics. These usually fake stories, often expressed as "true confessions" from young women about their love lives, were, ironically enough, the invention of a pair of men: Simon and Kirby, who were work-ing outside Timely and DC. Romance comics became a dominant force in the comic books of the 1950s, often ascending to the top of the charts and leaving a legacy of melodrama to comics storytelling that lasts to this day. Stan had yet to produce any major innovations in the medium of sequential art, but his future partner was already on to changing the industry a second time.

Meanwhile, Stan was trying to transcend that industry by positioning himself as an expert on it. In 1947, he made two daring attempts to break into mainstream nonfiction prose about comics. The first took the form of a cover story for *Writer's Digest* that fall, bearing the borderline-cynical headline THERE'S MONEY IN COMICS! Stan himself was the cover model, looking perfectly paternal with a slicked-back haircut (his hairline was retreating at an alarming rate for a man his age) and a pipe in his mouth (although he didn't smoke). "Well, what are you waiting for?" asked the first sentence, and the rest read like any number of chipper self-help guides for postwar working men. It laid out how to write and sell a comic, as well as the "5 Elements of a Good Comic Script."

The most interesting of these was number three, "Good Dialogue," which presaged Stan's eventual revolution in superhero dialoguing and denigrated his company's own past work: "The era of Captain America hitting Red Skull and shouting, 'So you want to play, eh?' is over!" he declared, adding that you should "have your characters speak like real people, not the inhabitants of a strange and baffling new world!" The conclusion was brimming with Truman-esque can-do spirit: "So, those of you writers who are itching to crack new markets have a market waiting for you that's just made to order. . . . I'm sure you won't regret spending the time—I didn't!" This long, first-person piece was the first published appearance of the character of Stan Lee, comics maven. He hadn't even come close to finding the full voice that character would later assume, but the it's-just-you-and-me-having-a-chat tone was present and, in retrospect, an obvious building block of his later success.

The second and more revealing stab at mainstream success was a self-published ninety-nine-page monograph called *Secrets Behind the Comics,* published on October 28. It wasn't quite a comic book, though it featured extensive illustrations by Stan's friend and employee Ken Bald. It, like the *Writer's Digest* essay, aimed to position Stan as a kind of spokesman for the comics industry and a translator of insider lore for lay readers—a native guide, if you will. He would later embrace that role and ride it to great success, aided by his talent for hyperbolic verbiage, which was also on display in *Secrets Behind the Comics*. "Never before have you read a book like this!" declared the introduction. "It will amuse you and astound you! Take good care of this book, for you will want to read it and re-read it and show it to your friends many times in the years to come! And now settle back comfortably and get set to enjoy a new reading thrill!" The rest claimed to elucidate every key step in the process of creating a comic book, from the germ of an idea to the printed object in a reader's hands, all presented as a numbered series of "Secrets." The content was bland, but the presentation had a cheerful bounce that one doesn't necessarily expect from a nuts-and-bolts look at what was essentially an assembly line for low-grade entertainment products.

However, *Secrets Behind the Comics* contained Stan's first provable commission of a cardinal sin for the arts, one that he would commit countless times, to a degree that would eventually be catastrophic for his reputation: obscuring credit. Secret #12 was all about the creation of Captain America, who was still probably Timely's most famous creation. It presented, in comics-panel form over the course of a few pages, a dubious narrative never uttered by anyone else. In it, Martin Goodman gains initial success with *Marvel Comics* #1 in a noble quest born of his belief that the "young American reading public must be made aware of the dangers of Nazis and fascism!" Seeing his early victories, he then notes, "I must do still more! I must create a comic character who will represent freedom's battle against fascism!" The narration then claims, "During the next few weeks, Martin Goodman had the nation's top writers and artists submitting ideas for a new patriotic type of character, until finally, one character was chosen! Captain America, sentinel of liberty!" A portrait of Cap and Bucky stood astride the following page. But the book didn't mention Simon or Kirby even once in all of its ninety-nine pages. Of course, the average human knew nothing about Cap's real provenance, and, if Stan is to be believed, a credulous reading public somehow found out about the tome and it sold out its initial print run. A precedent had been set.

There was a significant personal victory that year, as well, making 1947 something of an *annus mirabilis* for Stan. He'd furthered his career as a ladies' man from his extended-stay room at Manhattan's Alamac Hotel—he was particularly proud of one odd conquest, in which he dated a woman who turned out to be an escort and who was eager to tell him of her sex work. "I became one of the best-informed people about the world of erotic experiences, even though those torrid tidbits of information were, on my part, mostly gained secondhand," he would later write. "And, as attractive as she was, I'm sure it's clear to the observant reader that we remained together for many months mainly because of my unquenchable thirst for knowledge." (Ironically, or perhaps hypocritically, Stan would later write an essay for one of Goodman's magazines entitled "Don't Legalize Prostitution.") That was all prelude, as it turned out.

One winter night, he was scheduled to meet a professional model named Betty at a holiday party thrown by his cousin Morton Feldman at the latter's hat company. As the story goes, Stan knocked on the door and it was answered by a different model, an English brunette named Joan Clayton Boocock. "And I remember it very clearly," Joan would recall decades later, in her impeccably posh intonations. "He came to the door and he had his raincoat thrown over his shoulder . . . and a scarf or something, like a cravat." The two locked eyes, and Stan always said he was struck by her uncanny resemblance to an archetype from his childhood: "I used to draw cartoons when I was very young, little drawings," he said. "Almost everybody who draws—every guy, I guess—you like to draw girls and you usually draw your idealized girl's face. And it has been the same face that I had been drawing all the time: big, beautiful eyes and a turned-up nose and nice lips." In that moment of winter's chill, the world clicked into place for Stan. "I took one look at her and it was the face I had been drawing all my life." Joan said Stan's first line was dynamite: "He said, 'Hello, I think I'm going to fall in love with you.' And I thought, *This is one I can't let get away.*"

There was a slight snag, in the form of her still-fresh marriage to an American soldier who'd been stationed in her native England—her status as a war bride was what had brought her to the States in the first place. But no matter: Joan's mind was set on Stan, and she trekked to Reno, Nevada, where one could obtain a divorce after a short period of residency. Stan stayed in New York initially; the two said they corresponded, but when Joan allegedly sent Stan a letter addressed to someone named Jack, he panicked at the prospect of becoming a cuckold and flew to Reno to ensure that everything went according to plan. There was nothing to worry about: Joan got her divorce and, as the story goes, moments later, the same judge who'd granted it then married the blushing couple. It was December 5, 1947, almost exactly a year after they'd met, and the pair immediately flew back to New York for a second wedding ceremony, this one with friends and family, officiated by a rabbi, and held in the Liebers' current apartment, on 170th Street in Washington Heights. Intermarriage between Jews and non-Jews was extremely uncommon back then. Jack was fiercely tribal in his Judaism, and Celia was, as Stan put it, a "rather old-fashioned Jewish lady," so it's believable when Larry says it was "a big concern" to Jack that Stan was "marrying outside of the religion." However, the scion of the Lieber clan always insisted that his parents had been welcoming of his Christian bride. If they had objections, Stan certainly wasn't going to let that stop him and his love.

But even in the midst of this joy, there was a strong whiff of imminent tragedy. Celia was near death at the ceremony. "She first had allergies and arthritis and finally stomach cancer," recalls Larry. On December 16, just eleven days after Stan was cleaved to the woman of his dreams, he lost the woman of his birth. Celia Solomon Lieber was buried at the Jewish cemetery of Mount Lebanon in Queens.

She was not even fifty-eight. For whatever reason, Stan made little mention of this sad turn of events, referencing it only in one sentence in his memoir: "When my mother died, our life changed dramatically." The change was not born of grief but rather of logistics. Sixteen-year-old Larry—who had been very close to his mother and changed radically from a carefree youth to a neurotic one due to her death—had to live with someone. Jack, who moved to a smaller apartment on 70th Street, refused to be a single parent. Larry speculated that his father "did not ask me to live with him because I think he knew we wouldn't get along so easily. . . . He did not ask me to live with him, and nobody else in the family even suggested that I should."

So Stan and Joan allowed Larry to reside with them in their newly purchased house on Long Island, which Stan said they moved to in order to accommodate the boy. The new arrangement seems not to have gone well. Stan wrote that Joan took her new quasi-maternal duties "like a trouper and couldn't have been nicer or more considerate of Larry." However, the sensitive Larry, who compares his disposition then and now to that of Blanche DuBois, tells of an unwelcoming atmosphere. "I felt very strongly that he had ambivalent feelings about me being out there," the younger brother says. When I ask him why there was ambivalence, he demurs, saying only, "You'd have to get into him and Joan—and mostly Joan—and it becomes a different story. And that's the part I don't want to go into." However, he speaks generally about Joan's being a poor influence on Stan. "I think whatever he was that was admirable, Joan may have changed somewhat," Larry says. "If he had faults, she made the faults worse." When I ask what faults he's talking about, he replies, "Well, about being unsympathetic to things, about just making money. He could snap at people." The living arrangement lasted only a few months before Larry opted to live with his cousins Martin and Jean Goodman.

What's more, the *Writer's Digest* cover story and *Secrets Behind the Comics* added up to nothing in terms of Stan's prospects, spawning no sequels or great acclaim. (That said, in 1951, famed media theorist Marshall McLuhan briefly mentioned the cover story in a meditation on media in his book *The Mechanical Bride,* though he didn't seem interested in the story's author.) Stan couldn't bring himself to care about the art form in which he toiled: "The funny thing is, I never was a comic-book reader," he would later say. "I only wrote 'em, but I didn't like to read 'em, particularly." He got back into the grind of writing comics around the time of his nuptials, but Larry recalls Stan being primarily interested in quantitative measures of his writing rather than in qualitative ones: "I remember him saying, 'Joan'—he enjoyed the speed of it—'Joan, I did a Western in twenty minutes!'" Later, when Larry asked Stan if he'd ever thought about writing a novel, the younger brother recalls the elder replying, "I don't enjoy writing that much. I write because I can do it and I do it easily and to earn a living." Stan himself would later say he barely thought about his pre–*Fantastic Four* work if he didn't have to. "Being the ultimate hack, I would start doing my thinking when I sat down in front of the typewriter, and not a minute before," he wrote in *Excelsior.* "While I got a kick out of doing comics, it was just a job to me."

That job continued apace, for better or worse. As the forties wound down, Stan primarily penned humor stories, which included the adventures of easygoing female figures like Patsy Walker and Millie the Model as well as a number of blatant rip-offs of more-popular comics on the racks: Awful Oscar aped Dennis the Menace, Archie Comics' titular teen was transmogrified into a lad named Georgie, and so on. Then professional calamity struck, and it may well have been Stan's fault. The oft-told story goes that he had become overly kind to freelancers, accumulating semi-secret piles of "inventory" comics—evergreen pages that he could hold on to and publish if filler or replacement content was needed—and paying them for their work. In this narrative, Goodman found out about the closets filled with finished work and decided to fire the staffers of the bullpen in favor of relying on his voluminous existing stock and the exploitation of freelance labor. There's also speculation that Goodman replaced the bullpen with freelancers for tax reasons, but either way, the bullpen was, indeed, shut down.

In late 1949 and early 1950, Stan was tasked with firing them all, sometimes on his own and sometimes through associate editors or his secretary. There was an intercom system in the building, and, thanks to the layoffs, the speakers gained a not-so-affectionate nickname: " 'Bitch boxes,' we called 'em," recalls Allen Bellman. "Every day, one person or two people were called in. I was holding my breath—I was a newly married guy. And finally, they called my name." Bellman at least gives his former boss credit for not delegating the dirty work in his case: "Stan himself fired me."

THE ARRIVAL OF A CHILD is typically rather consequential in one's life, but Stan couldn't have anticipated just what kind of an impact his first offspring would have. April 18, 1950, saw the birth by cesarean of Joan Celia Lee, who would, much later, be dubbed "JC," in an interaction with Eric Clapton when she was a young adult—or at least that's what she said. By the time of Stan's death, JC became someone that writer/director Kevin Smith, a friend of Stan's, would call "the worst fucking human being in the world," a person Stan himself would refer to as "the most dangerous person in the world," a figure who occupied the majority of Stan's thoughts in the last years of his life, an ongoing concern who tormented him but from whom he could never bring himself to detach. Her life was controversial from the start: At Joan's behest, she and Stan had their child baptized into Christianity. According to Larry, Joan was the one charged with informing Jack, and the latter didn't take it well. "The cruelty, to tell him that the daughter was baptized," Larry bemoans. "Then the letters probably came even more."

The letters he speaks of were missives that the increasingly disgruntled Jack would send to Stan, excoriating him for being unfaithful to Judaism and the Jewish people. "He'd send him letters all the time, drive him nuts," Larry recalls. "'Be more Jewish,' 'Observe the holidays,' that kind of thing." The still-new Jewish state of Israel was a passionate concern of Jack's, and Larry suspects the letters told Stan that "he should be doing something for it," which isn't surprising, if, in fact, Jack's father—and Stan's grandfather—Simon Lieber, was possibly living over there. Such pleas apparently fell on deaf ears. Larry says Jack's relations with Stan and Joan remained cordial in person, and Stan would send money to Jack, but it was clear the father had no love for the sharp turn into Gentile life that his elder son had taken. As it turned out, JC would spend her life singing Christian devotional music with her mother, putting crosses up in her houses, and even going so far as to attempt to record a single about the infant Jesus when she was in middle age. If Jack had been worried about millennia of Jewish heritage in his familial line coming to an end, his fears were well founded.

Though the family expanded, it didn't expand as much as Stan and Joan would have liked. Three years later, Joan was pregnant again and she gave birth to another girl: "We called her Jan, which Joan felt was the closest thing to Stan," Stan would later recall. "Joan had her room all prepared, it was so beautifully decorated." However, the infant was born with serious health problems. "I just insisted that I see her," Joan said. "And she was small, smaller than JC, pretty little baby. And I'll never forget, because they were so thrilled—they kept telling me, 'Oh, she took a little water today, she took a little of this today.'" Joan recalled being at the incubator, watching intently for days, but eventually, "the nurse that was there just came and said, 'Baby done died.'" It was a trauma that neither parent quite recovered from. "It was the first, and most heartbreaking, tragedy of our lives," Stan wrote. When he and Joan were filmed for a documentary fifty-three years later, their voices shuddered and Stan, in a supremely uncharacteristic moment, cried on camera. That said, in the documentary, Joan said she and Stan "never really discussed it. It's interesting. We never really went in a great discussion about Jan."

To make matters worse, there was no hope of a replacement. They'd had trouble conceiving in the past and, for reasons unexplained, Joan's doctors tied her tubes. "And not only did my doctor tie them off—because tubes can be changed—but he cut them so they could not be ever undone," she recalled. "I tried to adopt, and I couldn't adopt. I couldn't adopt a Jewish baby, because I'm not Jewish. I couldn't adopt from a Catholic family, because I'm Episcopalian . . . and you couldn't adopt into any mixed marriage at that time." And so it was that JC became Stan and Joan's only child, a status that gave her pride of place in their hearts no matter how difficult she made their lives. As Joan put it, "Perhaps that is why Stan, our daughter, and I have always been such a close-knit family."

There's old footage in the official Stan Lee archives at the University of Wyoming (Stan donated papers and recordings to the institution's American Heritage Center), much of it seemingly shot by Stan, of that close-knit family frolicking in their Eisenhower-era idyll. Wintertime shots of Joan in a red dress and her grade-school-aged daughter in a white coat, waving and dancing in their backyard. JC, slightly older, cavorting with her mother and a big black dog. JC on a hobbyhorse. JC rolling around in a toy truck. Joan and JC at the pool, the former in a black one-piece and swim cap, the latter in an orange life preserver. The family at the zoo, gazing at ostriches, gazelles, alligators, and elephants. JC performing choreographed dance routines, loving the gaze of the camera. Occasionally, Stan will pop in to mug, perhaps striking a pose as though he's belting an aria to a grateful audience. It almost looks like a parody of suburban domestic harmony. For many, a life such as Stan's in that era would have been perfectly satisfactory: a steady job he was good at, a doting and astoundingly beautiful wife, a growing and energetic daughter, a few dogs, and a home a mere train ride away from the greatest city in the world.

But venture elsewhere in the archives and you'll find declarations from Stan that he was miserable. Perhaps it's all retrospective assessment, but in his autobiographical outline from 1978, he dubs his time in the fifties THE LIMBO YEARS. The halting sentences Stan typed in that section, describing the quotidian agony of suburban life, are among the most riveting and depressing lines he ever wrote in any medium, like something from an Updike novel. "Vicious cycle—we spent money because we felt we ought to be getting something out of all the writing—and I kept writing to be able to pay for the lifestyle we had due to the writing," the outline reads. "My biggest hobby was looking at used cars. And going to the service station and kibitzing—it was our social center. Also, going to dinner with Joan. That was my schedule. Go to the office—come home and write—weekends and evenings."

He was getting paid a salary for his editorial work, but the writing was technically done on a freelance basis, which meant added income, but it wasn't enough for the lifestyle his family was getting used to. "Saved no $," he wrote. "Too dumb to realize my $ went to taxes—kept getting increases in pay and [freelance] rate but it didn't mean anything—just higher bracket. Couldn't save, unless we changed our way of life—but then, what's the sense of working and earning good dough if you don't live like you're earning it?" On top of all that, his hairline was receding ever more drastically. The section on the Limbo Years concludes on a grim note: "Anyway, I did do one positive thing. I finally decided I hated being bald, and I bought a toupee. But I still felt I was going nowhere—and how could I keep getting older and older and still be writing comic books? Where and when would it stop?"

It seems Stan was utterly humiliated by his profession. He and Joan would throw and attend lavish soirees, and Stan later told of doing everything he could to avoid discussing work when he was out partying. "Occasionally, some people who we weren't too familiar with would come over to me and say, 'Well, what do you do?'" he recalled. "Oh, man, I didn't wanna admit what I did. So I'd say something like, 'Oh, I'm a writer' and start to walk away, but he'd follow me. 'Whaddaya write?' I'd say, 'Umm, stories for children.' I'd walk away again; he'd follow me. 'What kind of stories?'

At some point, I had to say, 'Comic books.' At that point, *he* would turn around and walk away." The parties at their home would occasionally make the local society pages, but—at least among the excerpts that are extant today—they fail to mention that the paterfamilias was a writer of comics.

There was an element of sheer professional embarrassment to these omissions, of course. But there was also one of self-preservation. As the fifties progressed, comic books became the object of a nationwide moral panic, and no sensible, self-respecting member of a wholesome community would want to be associated with them. There had been rumblings of criticism toward the comics industry since the late forties, when crime and horror comics were proliferating at a rapid rate. Some complaints in those days came from aestheticians like critic John Mason Brown, who called comic books "the marijuana of the nursery," but the more devastating attacks came from the corridors of psychology.

On March 19, 1948, the Association for the Advancement of Psychotherapy held a symposium in New York City entitled "The Psychopathology of Comic Books," at which experts on ailments of the mind declared—not entirely without merit—that comics were rotting away America's children with their quasi-fascist worship of the powerful. "Children's fantasies, stimulated by comic book pictures, make them imagine violence as the only way out," said one expert at the conference. "For even as the 'good' conquers the 'evil,' it does so by violence only. No one ever lives happily ever after. Alex turns the page and knows there will be a new story with the same people solving the same problems by slightly varied methods of direct and bloody violence." Said another: "Instead of teaching obedience to law, Superman glorifies the 'right' of the individual to take that law into his own hands. Instead of being brave and fearless, Superman lives in continuous guilty terror, projecting outward in every direction his readers' inward aggression." There was a larger terror in the air of the United States about so-called juvenile delinquency, and comics were being labeled as one of its causes.

Just eight days later, *Collier's* magazine ran an article about the comics hullabaloo that centered on the symposium's organizer, a man who would almost single-handedly change the comics industry for generations: Dr. Fredric Wertham. Born in Germany, he'd been an avid student of the works of Freud and had an enviable educational pedigree, having received his medical degree from the elite University of Würzburg before emigrating to the United States to teach at Johns Hopkins. Although Wertham is regularly identified as a conservative by comics fandom due to his pro-censorship stance, he was, in general, a die-hard liberal progressive. He was profoundly committed to the advancement of black people in America, having treated them extensively at a time when white doctors typically eschewed such responsibilities, and his writings on the psychological damage of racism were cited in the landmark anti-segregation Supreme Court case *Brown v. Board of Education*.

However, it was his fixation on comic books—which also came from a progressive belief in improving the lot of all mankind—that has placed him in the history books. The *Collier's* article was headlined HORROR IN THE NURSERY and presented a mass audience with Wertham's combative views on the funny books. "The comic books, in intent and effect, are demoralizing the morals of youth," he was quoted as saying. "They are sexually aggressive in an abnormal way. They make violence alluring and cruelty heroic. They are not educational but stultifying. If those responsible refuse to clean up the comic-book market—and to all appearances most of them do—the time has come to legislate these books off the newsstands and out of the candy stores." Ideas such as these found a serious foothold in the American psyche, and at least fifty cities banned or censored comic books by the end of 1948.

Stan was not immune to the effects of this sentiment. Oddly enough, it was a bit of a boon to him in one small way: It led to one of his first pieces of media coverage. A May 9, 1948, article in the *New York Herald Tribune* (there it is in his life again) quoted "Stanley Lieber" as saying, "We're not selling books on the basis of bosoms and blood. We're businessmen who can't be expected to protect mal-adjusted children who might be affected by cops-and-robbers stories. We feel we use stringent self-censorship." That last sentence was at least partially true. An editorial published in Timely's comics in the autumn of 1948 claimed a psychiatrist named Dr. Jean Thompson was inspecting all of their comics output to "insure the fact that our comics contain nothing that might meet with objections from your parents, teachers, or friends." Increasingly strident editorials about the matter, possibly penned by Stan, followed in subsequent comics: "Let these critics of today look to their history. Let them decide if they want to be remembered as the 20th century counterpart of the people who called *Robinson Crusoe* 'slop.'" "Just as there are good and bad people, good and bad radio programs, good and bad movies, so there is good and bad literature," and so on. For a time, this was enough: Timely was far less offensive with its content than its increasingly popular rival EC, and Goodman's bottom line was largely unaffected by the crusade in the beginning. Indeed, by 1952, Timely was, by some estimates, the most successful publisher in comics, with sales outpacing those of DC roughly two times over.

Nevertheless, Wertham battled on and Stan battled against him—although probably not in quite the way he would later claim he did. "To me, Wertham was a fanatic, pure and simple," Stan wrote in his memoir. "I used to debate with him, which was fun because I usually won—but *that* was rarely publicized. He once claimed he did a survey that demonstrated that most of the kids in reform schools were comic-book readers. So I said to him, 'If you do another survey, you'll find that most of the kids who drink milk are comic-book readers. Should we ban milk?'" There's just one problem with these "Lee/Wertham debates," as Stan called them: They don't appear to have ever happened. Historians have pored over archives to find out about these supposed verbal tussles and have turned up nothing.

The closest thing to a contemporary broadside against Wertham that we can attribute to Stan with reasonable assurance was a story he penned for the twenty-ninth issue of the Goodman series *Suspense,* entitled "The Raving Maniac," in which a crazed man bursts into the office of a comic-book editor who looks just like Stan, ranting about the "miserable magazines" the editor publishes. He points to comics panels depicting vampires, werewolves, and the like, asking, "How can you print stories like these?" Faux-Stan replies with characteristic glibness: "It's easy! We just send 'em to the printer and presto . . . it's all done!" However, Faux-Stan eventually grants the titular maniac a real counterargument: "I'll show you *why* people enjoy reading our magazines! Look at this newspaper!" He points to articles about famine, murder, and nuclear war, then screams, "At least our readers *know* that our stories aren't true!! They can put our magazines down and forget about it! But you can scare yourself to death by reading a newspaper nowadays!!" The maniac says he doesn't like the comics the editor makes; the editor replies, "Okay! So don't read 'em! Nobody's shoving 'em down your throat!! That's one of the wonderful things about this great nation of ours . . . everybody is free to do what he wants to do . . . as long as it doesn't injure anybody else!"

That dogged belief in the supremacy of free speech was not, as it turned out, shared by the rest of the comics industry. April 1954 brought two titanic developments in the war against comics. Wertham released a book summing up his case against the industry with the indelible title *Seduction of the Innocent,* and U.S. senator Estes Kefauver led a series of hearings about juvenile delinquency and comic books in the halls of Congress. Timely was put in the hot seat, along with most of the rest of the big publishers; the committee's investigator, Richard Clendenen, highlighted an issue of Goodman's *Strange Tales* that "has five stories in which 13 people die violently," including one in which a doctor "commits suicide by plunging a scalpel into his own chest." Goodman dispatched his business manager, Monroe Froehlich, Jr., to testify, and the latter claimed the moral high ground with statements like, "Would not this nation have suffered had Harriett Beecher Stowe not written *Uncle Tom's*

Cabin? It, too, was replete with action, torture scenes, violence, and death."

This was not enough. The one-two punch of the runaway success of *Seduction of the Innocent* and the industry's poor performance at the hearings led to a general public-relations catastrophe for those who made comic books for a living. Publishers united to form a group called the Comics Magazine Association of America (CMAA) and immediately set about establishing the Comics Code, an industry-wide censorship schema akin to the Hays Code of Hollywood. The bullet points were puritanical in the extreme: "No drawing should show a female indecently or unduly exposed, and in no event more nude than in a bathing suit commonly worn in the United States of America." "Crime should not be presented in such a way as to throw sympathy against law and justice or to inspire others with the desire for imitation." "Vulgar and obscene language should never be used." "Divorce should not be treated humorously or represented as glamorous or alluring," et cetera, et cetera. More than a dozen companies went under, and a far greater number of professionals never worked in the medium again. The number of comics series on the stands was cut in half across the industry. Stan later recalled that, a few months after the hearings, he spoke of editing comic books to a man he'd met on vacation and the man responded, "You do comic books? That is absolutely criminal—totally reprehensible. You should go to jail for the crime you're committing."

Nevertheless, in spite of this public ridicule, Stan continued to come to work, albeit with a provision from Goodman whereby he was able to write from home on Wednesdays. The comics he produced were, by and large, nothing special: tales of cowboys, knights, fantastical beings, chaste romances, and the like. Goodman, like everyone else in the business, wanted to match the success of the nascent *Mad* magazine, and thus Stan also launched a humor mag called *Snafu,* writing comedic copy for the credits ("Founded by Irving Forbush . . . Losted by Marvin Forbush") and silly captions for photographs (including ones of Joan, posing for cheesecake shots like the model she'd aspired to be before becoming a homemaker). Even this inertia was disrupted by an ill-advised business decision on the part of Goodman. After the mass firings of 1949–50, Goodman had begun distributing his comics himself through a company called Atlas News and slowly reestablished a limited bullpen of staff creators. But in 1956, for reasons that remain unclear but may have had to do with a desire to cut costs to get out of the sales slump that followed the Kefauver hearings, Goodman chose to close Atlas and start distributing through a company called American News Company. Then, in early 1957, American abruptly closed shop. A panicked Goodman signed on with a distributor called Independent News. The only trouble was, it was owned by his competitor DC. Independent forced Goodman to cut his output to merely eight comics a month—a whopping reduction of about 80 percent of his output. The bloodletting began.

"I remember the dark day when Martin told me, 'Stan, we have to let the whole staff go. I want you to fire everybody,'" Stan wrote in *Excelsior*. "I said, 'I can't do that!' He replied, 'You have to. I'm going to Florida on vacation and someone's got to do it.' And that was that." One by one, just as he'd done seven years prior, Stan called staffers into his office and told them they were no longer needed. "It was the toughest thing I ever did in my life," he later said. "I had to tell them, and I was friends with these people. So many of them, I had dinner with them at their homes—I knew their wives, their kids, and I had to tell them this." One possibly apocryphal story had Stan repeatedly excusing himself to the bathroom to throw up between firings. Virtually no one was left by the time it was all over. Though Stan would often write of the "merry Marvel bullpen" later, after the Marvel revolution kicked off, the fact is that any such thing was long dead by the time of its supposed heyday. "I was like a human pilot light," he would later write, "left burning in the hope that we would reactivate our production at a future date." If comics had seemed like a drag before, they now seemed like a radioactive disaster site. Something had to change.

STAN HAD BEEN MAKING attempts at reaching escape velocity for years. "I was constantly free-lancing other things," he wrote in his autobiography outline. It appears that some of this work was in broadcasting, surprisingly enough. In that outline, Stan also said he ghostwrote radio scripts, and Joan would later tell an interviewer that Stan "would go and be involved with very early TV." A list of his accomplishments written in the late 1950s claimed Stan was a member of the Academy of Television Arts and Sciences—the Academy says they have no record of his membership but also that their documentation from that era is spotty. There don't appear to be any records of what radio or television shows Stan worked on, but it's certainly possible that he dabbled in those mediums. He would occasionally mention writing copy for advertising agencies and newspapers on a freelance basis. Additionally, he had periodically tried his hand at longer prose pieces for Goodman's magazines, such as that reported essay on prostitution and short stories with titles like "The Madman of Peakskill Point" and "Where Is Thy Sting?" None of this material led to substantial or sustained non-comics work.

The one area in which Stan *did* have success was the sister medium of the comic book: the newspaper comic strip. It may seem strange now, but given newspaper strips' longer history and their pride of place in high-circulation periodicals, they were seen as a far more respectable gig as of the 1950s. It's no wonder, then, that Stan would attempt an upwardly diagonal jump into them. He'd done a little bit of fill-in scripting in the early fifties for the comedic strips *My Friend Irma* and *Howdy Doody,* but that hadn't led to full-time gigs. In the middle of the decade, Stan persuaded Goodman to allow him to exploit an obscure division of Goodman's company, called

Timely Illustrated Features, which would in part be dedicated to putting together and selling samples of newspaper-strip work. (Oddly, Goodman seems to have allowed Stan to do this as a personal project that didn't benefit the company, given that his eventual comic-strip contracts don't appear to include Goodman's publishing empire.) His subsequent journey through the strip world has typically been ignored, but it's hard to understand the man without digging into the desperate, tireless, and partially successful efforts he made to break into it.

Much of what we know about this journey comes from the letters and documents in the archives of comic-strip agent Toni Mendez, housed at Ohio State's Billy Ireland Cartoon Library, which were helpfully pored over by comics historian Ger Apeldoorn in recent years. In his research, Apeldoorn uncovered an extensive correspondence between Stan and Mendez, whom Stan first hired circa 1956, after the Wertham crusade had devastated the comic-book ecosystem and just before the Timely collapse. Mendez was a fascinating character in her own right: a native New Yorker who briefly studied at Columbia University before becoming, of all things, a dancer in the Rockettes. She went on to be a choreographer and member of the American Theatre Wing, which led to a deeper involvement in the arts; that in turn brought her into contact with various comic-strip creators and ultimately drove her to become an agent for them. She soon had an array of clients, including the enormously successful artist of *Steve Canyon,* Milton Caniff. It was only natural that Stan would turn to such a well-connected woman.

There's no record in the archives of Mendez's first communication with Stan, which may have been by phone, but it appears that his first effort with her was to pitch a strip called *Clay Murdock, V.P.*, with eventual Marvel staple Vince Colletta as his artist collaborator. It was to be a soap opera set in an advertising agency—a kind of "*Mad Men* without the retro sarcasm," as Apeldoorn put it. Mendez sent it to the Chicago Sun-Times Syndicate, the Publishers Syndicate, King Features, and the Chicago Tribune–New York News

Syndicate, enthusiastically billing the proposal as "the best continuity strip I have seen in a while." Everyone turned them down. That was it for *Clay Murdock*. No matter—Stan had another idea in the hopper.

This next effort was built on Stan's belief in a key, but oft-forgotten, figure of the pre-Marvel era. His name was Joe Maneely, he was a crackerjack comics artist, and Stan loved him dearly. Over the course of the 1950s, Stan and Maneely collaborated on an array of projects in the comic-book world. The Philadelphia-born Maneely's elegant figures and dynamic action enchanted Stan, and the two grew close. When Stan wanted to launch a new series and make a splash with readers, he regularly turned to Maneely to draw it. He could do Westerns (*Rawhide Kid*), sword-and-sorcery yarns (*Black Knight*), spy tales (*Yellow Claw*)—nothing was beyond his abilities. He even created that pitch-perfect pastiche of the *Dennis the Menace* strip for one of Stan's *Mad* rip-offs, demonstrating that humor strips were within his range, as well.

So it only made sense that Stan would turn to Maneely for a real strip idea, in this case a pitch to Mendez called *Mr. Lyons' Den*. It was to be a family sitcom but with a slight gimmick: It would sometimes feature a bunch of kids in the all-American boys' club known as the Cub Scouts. Of course, Stan had only a daughter and therefore had no direct experience with the Cub Scouts or their parent organization, the Boy Scouts of America (BSA), but that didn't deter him. He and Maneely concocted some sample strips, and he and Mendez reached out to the BSA with their proposal and samples to see if they'd be interested in backing the strip.

The message they received in reply was disheartening, at best. BSA executive George C. Frickel ripped into the samples for getting a bevy of details wrong (e.g., "In No. 3 the implication is that Cub Scouts go camping, which is definitively not the policy") and suggested that the focus shift from the titular Mr. Lyons to his wife, Mrs. Lyons, with a name change to *Mrs. Lyons' Cubs*. Alterations—including the title switch—were made, and a connection with the public-relations office of the BSA led to a letter from the organization endorsing the strip, which in turn led to a renewed pitch and, to its creators' delight, a pickup from the Chicago Sun-Times Syndicate in the fall of 1957. The syndicate had a devil of a time selling the strip to newspapers: As one of its representatives reported in a letter, "I think we have a good thing here, but are missing the beat. All we have is little boys dressed in cub uniforms doing things any kids—cubs or not—might." It was a fair point.

A publicity push to drum up interest led to a feature about Stan and Maneely and their fledgling strip in a newspaper-industry trade magazine called *Editor & Publisher.* It was one of Stan's first pieces of news coverage and, like nearly all of the subsequent ones he would receive over the decades, it remarked on how charismatic he was. "Stan is tall, Madison-Avenue-ish in appearance, with a smile that reaches across the room," the writer gushed, also noting the clear friendship between writer and artist: "It was difficult pinning these two witty fellows down. They laughed hard in their excitement, and words rippled like water in a fast-moving brook." Nevertheless, despite a few major papers picking up *Mrs. Lyons' Cubs,* it still wasn't catching on with the public. According to Stan, Joan had the idea of calling up various local BSA leaders to see if they liked the strip and, if so, whether they might write to their papers to tell them to grab it. Stan reported that these calls had mixed results: Some leaders had seen it and liked it; others had no idea what it was. Simultaneous to all this, Stan attempted to sell another soap-opera strip alongside Colletta, this one called *For the Love of Linda.* As Stan's pitch put it, the strip was to follow "Gorgeous Linda Hale, orphan," who "is graduating from college when a momentous telegram arrives": Her "grand-uncle has died" and left her a newspaper in a "small, unglamorous town." She arrives there, encounters a varied cast of characters, and "faces the future as a tried and proven newspaper gal." Two syndicates turned Stan and Mendez down in mid-1958, and they gave up on poor Linda.

Nevertheless, *Mrs. Lyons' Cubs* was still coming out on a daily basis, albeit in fewer papers than its creators would've liked. Stan, always looking for legitimacy, immediately leapt to join the National Cartoonists Society and the Newspaper Comics Council. The content in the strip was of questionable comedic value: To wit, one installment featured three panels of a lad getting uniformed and coiffured, only to have his off-panel parent say, "Time for bed, young man," which was followed by a final panel of the boy looking distraught and commenting, "What! And let all this go to waste!" It's possible that the strip would have become stronger if it had a chance to mature, but that was not to be. Tragedy doomed the project in the early morning of June 7, 1958, when Maneely fell between two cars of a commuter train and was killed. It was a devastating personal and professional blow to Stan, leading him (as well as comics historians) to often wonder what the beloved artist would have contributed to the Marvel revolution, had he survived. (The death also resonated for Jack Kirby, who, according to his eventual assistant Steve Sherman, would periodically state his belief that Maneely fell because he was exhausted from being overworked by Stan and that Kirby himself would never allow Stan to exert that kind of control over him.) Stan got Timely artist Al Hartley to take over for Maneely, and the strip limped along for a few months, then was canceled in December. It was a sad and humiliating end.

Nevertheless, hope sprang eternal. Stan and Mendez tried to sell a variety of ideas around the time of Maneely's fatal accident. There was a proposal for a book called *Art Script,* which would have paired famous works of fine art with humorous captions. There was a pitch for something called *Stag Line,* whose details remain mysterious but appears to have been an illustrated advice column from a male perspective. There was an idea for a strip about the adventures of a physically appealing young woman called *Li'l Repute.* There was a proposed team-up with artist Dan DeCarlo—who would later be best known for his style-defining work on the comic-book escapades of America's favorite teenager, Archie—called *Main Street.* Stan and Mendez even pitched a coloring book. None of it went anywhere. At long last, Stan, DeCarlo, and Mendez sold a strip idea that had begun as the daily experiences of a New York City cop, called *Barney's Beat,* but had mutated into a goofy strip about a small-town mailman, called *Willie Lumpkin.* In a stunning reversal of fortune, it debuted in print in December 1959 and got picked up by more than fifty papers, many of them with huge circulations. However, the strip quickly lost momentum and was canceled by the end of 1960.

In light of all these failures, Stan got truly desperate and turned to self-publishing, something he hadn't done since *Secrets Behind the Comics* almost a decade and a half prior. He set up a one-man company called Madison Publishing and put out two books in 1961: *Golfers Anonymous: The Perfect Book for the Imperfect Golfer (and Aren't We All?)* and *Blushing Blurbs: A Ribald Reader for the Bon Vivant.* Each mixed photos—in the former, ones of golfers (sometimes with Stan's own face superimposed upon them), and the latter, ones of pretty girls (including, of course, Joan)—with comedic captions from Stan. (He would continue trying this captioning game throughout his career, well into the new millennium, despite the fact that it never caught on.) The pair were to be followed by a third publication, *My Own Executive ABC Doodle Book,* a gag piece in which jokes about being stuck in wage slavery were combined with simple illustrations by Stan, as well as space for the reader to do his own doodling. The first two books landed with a thud, and the third, though fully mocked up, was never published. Stan, despite his relentless efforts, was stuck in comic books for the time being. But, although he couldn't have known it at the time, it was in the soil of that medium that the seeds of his future fame were being laid.

THE DAWN OF THE MARVEL empire in 1961 would likely have been impossible if not for three arrivals at Goodman's door in the 1950s. Each brought a different set of talents that would come into sync with Stan's own. Each, to varying degrees, contributed ideas that would eventually revolutionize comics (though not in this period). And each would end up with an intense ambivalence, if not downright dislike, toward Stan.

The first to show up was a quiet, mysterious eccentric named Steve Ditko. Little is known about his early life—or his middle and later life, for that matter. Ditko was an intensely private man who, in stark contrast to Stan, vehemently disavowed the spotlight and avoided all the trappings of fame. Ditko was almost five years younger than Stan, having been born on November 2, 1927, into a Pennsylvania family headed by an Eastern European immigrant carpenter father and a homemaker mother. The father—also named Stephen Ditko—was apparently an avid reader of newspaper comic strips and passed his love of them along to his children, who would read them in hand-bound volumes stitched together by their mother, Anna. Young Ditko went on to become a huge fan of the nascent comic-book medium and started drawing fervently, first as an amateur and then for an army newspaper while stationed in Germany in the final days of World War II. What's remarkable here is that, unlike his elders and contemporaries, who generally started working in comic books accidentally or as a stepping-stone to other things, Ditko had dreamed of becoming a comic-book artist—indeed, he was possibly the first comic-book fan to end up as a top talent in the industry.

Ditko idolized *Batman* artist Jerry Robinson and, thanks to the G.I. Bill of Rights, was able to study with him at the Cartoonists and Illustrators School in New York City shortly after the end of the war. Robinson would later recall that Ditko was "quiet and retiring, a very hard worker," and that he possessed a talent that allowed him to rise above the rest of the crop of students. Robinson would often bring comics professionals to his classes and once, in the early 1950s, invited Stan, who dutifully attended, hardly knowing that one of the lads to whom he was speaking would go on to be one of his most important collaborators. After graduation, Ditko worked for various comics publishers and at Simon and Kirby's studio, both as a primary artist and as an inker (a crucial, underappreciated job that entails embellishing the pencils of the primary artist, also known as the penciler, so as to make a completed work that can be printed). His budding career was interrupted by a near-fatal bout of tuberculosis that took him back to Pennsylvania in 1954, and when he returned to comics the next year, he sought work at one of his previous employers, Charlton Comics, only to learn that it had been devastated by a flood. Eager to keep working, he thought he'd try his hand in the house that Martin Goodman built.

Stan was apparently impressed by Ditko's portfolio and signed him up right away. Ditko produced seventeen stories for Stan over the course of six months, most of them horror, mystery, and suspense yarns. Goodman's 1957 distribution fiasco and the ensuing mass firing spelled the end of Ditko's initial run as a collaborator with Stan, but the latter lured the former back in mid-1958 for freelance projects. The pair started to produce work that was remarkable primarily for Ditko's evolving and unique draftsmanship. Eventually, Stan's plots for Ditko started to fit into the O. Henry mold, with narratives that relied heavily on twist endings to present a harsh moral or at least a shock. Ditko took this raw material and presented it in a distinctively eerie way, filled with uncanny motion (levitating buildings, men walking through walls, and the like) and, most important, deeply unsettling human beings. Their bodies were slender and angular, with joints twisting in ways that just seemed ever so slightly *off,* and their faces were wrought with menace, shock, or a spooky ugliness—sometimes all three at once. These elements would, bizarrely and fruitfully, still be present when Ditko did his later superhero work.

The second recruit was a man Stan knew better than he knew Ditko, although not by as much as one might think: his brother. Since his brief stint living with Stan and Joan, Larry had taken his lifelong love of art and started to translate it into concrete work. Despite the difficulties between him and Stan, he'd done a bit of menial printing work for his older brother at Timely around 1950. It hadn't gone well. "We had a relationship where he was always the boss, even when I was at work," Larry recalls. "He was established. He was married. He had a child. I was who? I was Larry Lieber, and I had no friends at that point. I had no friends. So I didn't like where things were going." Dejected, Larry left Goodman's shop and worked odd jobs—for example, at one point he got a gig as a delivery boy at *The New York Times,* transporting items and memos throughout their building. "Stan was always very clever," Larry recalls, "and he said, 'Don't tell people you're in delivery. Tell them you're working in transportation and communications.' That was Stan." Larry enlisted for the Korean War in 1951 and served as a draftsman in Okinawa—although he hastens to say he wasn't terribly good at such technical drawing—and after his discharge, he honed his skills in classes at the Art Students League of New York.

But his attempt to develop his career on his own came to an end after Goodman's 1957 distribution crash, when a desperate Stan asked his younger brother to come work for him again on the cheap. Larry said yes and was tasked with drawing romance comics—and, to his surprise, writing them. "Stan said he wanted somebody to help him write, and he had nobody then; he was doing it all himself," Larry recalled. "I said, 'Stan, I'm not a writer.' He said, 'Oh, you can write. I read your letters from the Air Force. I'll teach you to write comics.'" It was a rare compliment and Larry went along with the suggestion, writing and drawing romance comics, then—according to him and Stan—writing scripts in other genres for the third and most consequential late-fifties arrival at Goodman's shop: Jack Kirby.

The years since Kirby's 1941 departure from Timely had been a roller coaster. He and Simon had decamped for DC and were given relatively free rein to craft groundbreaking stories of their own design. They revamped the company's character the Sandman, invented a new one called Manhunter, and created stories about groups of hard-nosed youths (partially inspired by Kirby's childhood, of course) like the Boy Commandos and the Newsboy Legion. Kirby was drafted into the army in 1943 and served in a significantly more dangerous capacity than did Stan or Ditko, acting as a reconnaissance scout in the European theater and even landing on Omaha Beach, albeit two and a half months after D-Day (he'd later say it was only ten days afterward, from either poor memory or exaggeration). When the war concluded, Kirby and Simon reunited and worked in Westerns and crime comics before making their biggest impact since Captain America by, as we've mentioned, inventing the romance comic in 1947. The romance work was their bread and butter for years, with copies of a given issue regularly selling upward of a million copies a month. They ventured into other genres, too, from horror to sci-fi and beyond. During a brief period in 1954 when Goodman's company revived Captain America as an anti-communist crusader, a ticked-off Simon and Kirby even created a deliberate knockoff called Fighting American and put him into stories that lampooned red-baiters.

Around that time, Simon and Kirby went into business for themselves, creating a company called Mainline Publications, but it became a victim of the Wertham-era collapse and went out of business in 1956, after which he and Simon parted ways. A desperate Kirby had to beg for freelance work from editors, including the guy who he was still sure had ratted him out all those years prior. He worked on fewer than two dozen stories for Stan, but even that was not to last—the 1957 distribution debacle meant Stan couldn't afford a guy like Kirby anymore. Initially, that wasn't the end of the world, because Kirby could still work for DC and happened to be drawing a newspaper strip called *Sky Masters of the Space Force*. However, both of those gigs imploded when DC editor Jack Schiff, who had helped get Kirby the *Sky Masters* job, sued Kirby for allegedly stiffing him on profits he was due from the strip. Kirby was up the creek. That's when he heard that Stan had freed up money to commission freelance work. And so it was that, in early June of 1958, Jack Kirby began working again for a man who had only ever been trouble for him. It is here that everything started to change. It is here, too, that everything gets well and truly complicated.

HERE IS HOW KIRBY, in a 1989 interview, recalled his return to Goodman's shop and Stan's employ:

> It came about very simply. I came in and they were moving out the furniture, they were taking desks out—and I needed the work! I had a family and a house and all of a sudden Marvel is coming apart. Stan Lee is sitting on a chair crying. He didn't know what to do, he's sitting in a chair crying—he was just still out of his adolescence. I told him to stop crying. I says, "Go in to Martin and tell him to stop moving the furniture out, and I'll see that the books make money." And I came up with a raft of new books and all these books began to make money. Somehow they had faith in me. I knew I could do it, but I had to come up with fresh characters that nobody had seen before. I came up with the Fantastic Four. I came up with Thor. Whatever it took to sell a book, I came up with.

Stan, as one might expect, disputed this emasculating account of events. In a 1998 interview, his response was as follows:

> I never remember being there when people were moving out the furniture. If they ever moved the furniture, they did it during the weekend when everybody was home. Jack tended toward hyperbole, just like the time he was quoted as saying that he came in and I was crying and I said, "Please save the company!" I'm not a crier and I would never have said that. I was very happy that Jack was there and I loved working with him, but I never cried to him.

Thus begins the duel of narratives—Kirby's versus Stan's—that will forever muddy the waters about what happened between the two men from 1958 to 1970. The general public is typically aware of only one narrative of the Marvel revolution, and that is Stan's. His can be summarized pretty simply: "Stan came up with all the characters, plots, and dialogue; Jack just came up with the visuals." This notion of Stan as the writer and Kirby as the artist is the conventional wisdom that has been regurgitated in countless retellings and references. Its rival is Kirby's narrative, which can be summarized just as simply: "Jack came up with all the characters, plots, and visuals; Stan just came up with the dialogue." Only in some corners of hardcore comics geekdom is this conception of Kirby as the writer/artist and Stan as the copy boy accepted. In their lifetimes, neither man would publicly admit to any uncertainty about his narrative, nor to any wiggle room that might allow for the ambiguity of collaboration. Each was very firm in saying that he, not the other, was the man primarily responsible for inventing these impossibly valuable stories. To paraphrase Kipling: Stan's is Stan's and Jack's is Jack's, and never the twain shall meet. To make matters worse, both of them would include details in their accounts that made what they said dubious, thus bedeviling historians looking for the one honest man.

For example, let's return to the story about Kirby coming to Goodman's offices in 1958. There is reason to doubt Kirby's retelling. For one thing, Stan was not "just still out of his adolescence" as of June 1958—the man was thirty-five years old. If we write this error off as the misremembering of a septuagenarian, we call into question everything else he said in the interview. If we label it rhetorical hyperbole, we have to wonder where such hyperbole ends and the truth begins: Were the desks really being moved out around a tearful Stan, or are we to take that as metaphor? More important, how do we account for the fact that Kirby appeared to be saying he created the Fantastic Four, Thor, and the rest in 1958, when they didn't see print until the early sixties?

And yet we should not take Stan's rebuttal as gospel, either. As it turns out, it's very plausible that the overall gist of Kirby's story was true. The situation at Goodman's comics-publishing arm was dire as of Kirby's return; of that much we may be reasonably certain. "At one time in the late fifites it was just an alcove, with one window, and Stan was doing all the corrections himself; he had no assistants," Larry would recall. Writer Bruce Jay Friedman, who was doing work for Goodman's magazine arm, recounted that Goodman was trying to phase out his already paltry comics-publishing slate in this period. Artist Dick Ayers, who was doing work for Stan in that lean period, recalled a tense relationship between Stan and Goodman: "Things had started getting really bad, I guess, in 1958," Ayers said. "And still Stan kept me working. And one day, when I went in, he looked at me and he said, 'Gee whiz, my uncle goes by and he doesn't even say hello to me.' He meant Martin Goodman. And he proceeds to tell me, 'You know, it's like a ship sinking and we're the rats. And we've got to get off.'" Adding to this grim atmosphere was the death of Maneely. In fact, when one does the math, it appears that Kirby likely picked up his first new assignment on Monday, June 9, less than 72 hours after Maneely's death. Given how close Stan and Maneely were and how crucial Maneely was to the operations of Goodman's comics publishing, is it not plausible that a devastated Stan may have been shedding tears in the paltry office of a business that was on its last legs?

Whatever the specifics of that particular day, it was followed by three years' worth of stories that are notable mainly for the framework they established rather than for their actual content. Until 1961, Kirby's main job in the comics industry was working on science-fiction stories for Goodman and Stan. They were repetitive affairs, inspired by the popular movies of the time, about titanic monsters and beings from beyond the stars terrorizing hapless mortals. "I was given monsters, so I did them," Kirby would say in 1975. "I would much rather have been drawing *Rawhide Kid*. But I did the monsters. We had 'Grottu' and 'Kurrgo' and 'It.' It was a challenge to try to do something—anything—with such ridiculous characters." Kirby may have thought the characters were ridiculous, but his artwork was coalescing into something truly special: He was a master of thunderous action, conjuring up blocky figures of gargantuan proportions, wondrous machinery that seemed like it was plucked from a thirty-third-century engineering textbook, and explosive foreshortening that made you feel as though every punch were landing right in your face. These talents would be honed as the years went on, but they were already noticeable.

Questions linger about the sci-fi/monster period. For decades, the only thing that was certain about these stories was that Kirby drew them, as his style is unmistakable to an observer. But who was writing them? No one could prove anything, as there were no credits in the printed stories and no one had claimed credit for them. It was only in May 1998, in a friendly interview with Stan's protégé, Roy Thomas, that Stan first claimed credit for writing them. He mentioned no other scribes. Then, the next year, Thomas interviewed Larry, who said the process for the sci-fi stories was as follows: Stan would give Larry a brief plot outline, then Larry would write a detailed script with direction for visuals and copy for dialogue and narration, then Kirby would use that script to do the visuals, to which the scripted dialogue would be added afterward. There's little reason to doubt Larry's account, as he is explicit about how little he cares about his comics career and is never eager to claim credit for anything. I ask Larry whether Kirby came up with the initial stories without any input from Stan; he replies, "Maybe he did. See, I was never there when the two of them were there." We simply don't know conclusively how involved Kirby was, as a writer, in the sci-fi comics of 1958 to 1961.

What does appear to be the case is that, in that period, Stan crystallized, with some set of artists—chiefly Kirby and Ditko—what would come to be known as the Marvel Method. Without understanding the method, you cannot understand the controversy that has ensued for decades about creator credit for the comics Stan worked on. Prior to its advent, comics were usually constructed in the way one might intuitively suspect: A writer would put together a script that specifically identified what images and words should go in each page and panel, give that script to an artist, who would draw the images as directed, then hand it off for editing, inking, and the addition of the pre-written words by the letterer. But the Marvel Method turned all that on its ear. It would begin with some kind of discussion between writer and artist about what should happen in the comic—but, crucially, no script was written. The artist would then go ahead and actually create the plot by taking the vague ideas and making them concrete in panels of storytelling, complete with occasional notes in the margins about what dialogue should be used in a given panel. The writer would then take the pages of plotted art and decide what words should be used for dialogue and narration. By any reasonable standard, this meant the artist was really a writer/artist. Indeed, one can argue that, by mapping out what was happening, the writer/artist was the *primary* writer of the story, with the "writer" just embellishing based on what had come before.

The trouble lies in deciphering what happened in the initial plot conversations for comics created by the Marvel Method. To be blunt, no one really knows what happened in those discussions. If there were recordings of them, none seem to have survived. There were no secretaries taking minutes of the meetings. Comic books were still a fly-by-night industry that few imagined would survive, much less require specific documentation for posterity. It was just two men in a room. Kirby relentlessly claimed until his dying day that his discussions were merely a matter of his telling Stan what was going to happen in a given plot, then going home and creating what he'd said he would create, with some mild editing from Stan at some point in the process. For example, here was a summation Kirby made in a 1990 interview:

I wrote the complete story. I drew the complete story. And after I came in with the pencils, the story was given to an inker and the inker would ink the story and a letterer would letter it and I would give the story to Stan Lee or whoever had the editor's chair and I would leave it there. I would tell them the kind of story I would do to follow up and then I went home and I would do that story, and I wouldn't come into the office until I had that story finished. And nobody else had to work on a story with me.

Once Marvel had become a success, Stan would always say the process consisted of him conceiving the germ of the plot on his own, then hammering it out with Kirby, emphasizing that that germ was his and his alone. For example, here Stan is in 1987, talking about doing the Marvel Method with Kirby and Ditko:

> I wrote the stories and these fellas would draw a lot of them. They both were so good at story that I would just have to give them a few key words and they would do practically the whole thing and then I would just polish it up after they had done it, and it was a wonderful way to work.

However, there is at least one instance of Stan's admitting that Kirby would usually dictate the plot himself. It is a damning one, the closest to a smoking gun that you'll find. He did an interview around 1965, back when few cared about credit, and said the following:

> Some artists, of course, need a more detailed plot than others. Some artists, such as Jack Kirby, need no plot at all. I mean, I'll just say to Jack, "Let's let the next villain be Doctor Doom" . . . or I may not even say that. *He* may tell *me*. And then he goes home and does it. He's so good at plots, I'm sure he's a thousand times better than I. He just about makes up the plots for these stories. All I do is a little editing. . . . I may tell him that he's gone too far in one direction or another. Of

course, occasionally I'll give him a plot, but we're practically both the writers on the things.

It is against this backdrop that we can finally get to the comic that turned the tide for Stan Lee, Jack Kirby, Martin Goodman, and world culture: *The Fantastic Four* #1. When it was conceived in 1961, there was no reason to believe it would be anything special. And yet, here we are.

Stan described his work between 1945 and 1961 as, for the most part, garbage. "In fact, I was probably the ultimate, quintessential hack," he wrote in his memoir. So the question is: How did that hack become world famous as one of the most influential writers in modern history? Nearly everything that Stan had dreamed of during the forties and fifties finally started happening to him in the sixties. And that brings us to a second, perhaps more pertinent question: Would what came next be enough to satisfy his hunger?

MISTER MARVEL

———

*"I knew for a fact
that if I, myself,
possessed a superpower,
I'd never keep it secret."*

—STAN LEE

4.

WHAT PRICE VICTORY?

———

(1961–1966)

———

"**F**ANTASTIC FOUR #1 CRYSTALLIZED AN ART FORM THAT HAS had an impact on our culture rivaling jazz, rock and roll, and hiphop," wrote the author Walter Mosley in 2005. "It not only spoke to the young people of my day and later, but it also helped to form them, to release pressures and tensions that the older generations had no idea existed." This is high praise, and a modern reader may be forgiven for not agreeing upon reading the issue for the first time. Like so many pieces of art that define genres and set trends, *The Fantastic Four* #1 seems archaic and clichéd now to the untrained eye. But for an uncountable number of readers who picked the comic up after it hit stands on August 8, 1961, it was a mind-blower.

However, a question haunts the comic, asked only by the curious few who read between the lines: Who came up with it and, in doing so, began the Marvel revolution? Traditionally, that honor has been reserved for Stan Lee. But outside Stan's own oft-repeated words, there is currently no known evidence that he created the premise, plot, or characters that appeared in *The Fantastic Four* #1. No presentation boards, no contemporary legal documents, no correspondence, no diary entries. Nothing. There is, of course, a chance that something exists and is simply not publicly available at present, but given all the painstaking legal, historical, and journalistic searching to determine the issue's creative origins, that seems highly unlikely. The closest thing to evidence that a pro-Stan argument can offer up is a curious document with a questionable backstory.

It's a summary of that particular and consequential comic book, written on a typewriter, with a heading that reads (complete with a misspelling of "synopsis") "SYNOPSES: THE FANTASTIC FOUR JULY '61 SCHEDULE." Stan's protégé, Roy Thomas, claimed that Stan showed him this document in the late 1960s, years after it was supposedly written. It has since been reprinted by Thomas on multiple occasions as his way of identifying Stan as the prime mover. But the key question is whether the synopsis was composed before or after a discussion of the ideas between Stan and Kirby. If it was written before, that would make Stan the creator of the Fantastic Four. If it was written after, Jack may have been the creator. It's near impossible to know for certain, but there is significant reason to suspect the synopsis was written *after* Stan and Kirby spoke.

Even Stan suggested this was the sequence of events in a 1974 essay about the comic: "After kicking it around with Martin [Goodman] and Jack for a while, I decided to call our quaint quartet the Fantastic Four. I wrote a detailed first synopsis for Jack to follow, and the rest is history." In 1997, Thomas told an interviewer that he "saw Stan's plot for *Fantastic Four* #1, but even Stan would never claim for sure that he and Jack hadn't talked the idea over before he wrote this." Stan would go on to change his story by telling Thomas, in personal correspondence about the synopsis from the late 1990s, "Incidentally, I didn't discuss it with Jack first. I wrote it first, after telling Jack it was for him because I knew he was the best guy to draw it." There is a rumor that the entire document was created after the comic hit stands: In 2009, Kirby's assistant, Steve Sherman, recalled, "I asked Jack about that synopsis. He told me that it was written way after *FF* #1 was published. I believe him." And what of Kirby's direct words on the matter? In 1989, an interviewer said to Kirby, "Stan says he conceptualized virtually everything in *The*

Fantastic Four—that he came up with all the characters. And then he said that he 'wrote a detailed synopsis for Jack to follow.'" Kirby's response was brief and to the point: "I've never seen it, and of course I would say that's an outright lie."

Welcome to the eternal debate over whether it was Stan or Kirby who created the superheroes that emerged in the heady days of the Marvel explosion. For historians of popular culture, it is a debate that is equal parts aggravating and essential. Billions of dollars have hinged on it. Disney's livelihood depends on Stan's interpretation of it. A legal case centered on it came one step away from the Supreme Court and was settled for an unspeakable sum. And, for the purposes of our present narrative, there is simply nothing more important, for one's entire conception of Stan rests on whether or not you think he truly was the originator of this world-changing pantheon. There is almost certainly no definitive item in existence that will settle the matter. The comics industry was simply too haphazard in the axial years of the early 1960s for anyone to have made and saved firm documentation about who did what. Back then, the order of the day was frantically throwing stuff at the wall and moving on to the next thing, which continued to be the case even as Stan started finding renown. It was a period of fevered experimentation and promotion, all of it leading to enormous consequences, none of it being all that closely observed for posterity.

The FF were not actually the first attempt at restarting superhero fiction in Goodman's shop. They were already behind the times to a certain extent. DC had unwittingly inaugurated what is now known as the Silver Age of Comics—the Golden Age having been the first decade and a half or so of the medium's existence—in 1956, with the release of *Showcase* #4, a comic that introduced a retooled version of the Golden Age speed demon known as the Flash. Other super-people had followed at DC and elsewhere, but Goodman's company had lagged at the back of the pack. Then came Doctor Droom—note well the second "r" in that name, as it's what distinguishes the character from a later Marvel staple named Doctor Doom.

Droom was introduced in spring 1961 in the new series *Amazing Adventures,* in a story that was both bizarre and remarkably racist, even by the standards of the time. In it, a white American doctor with the last name Droom overhears some of his colleagues discussing a Tibetan lama who has a serious medical condition. Droom dares himself to cure the man, flying to the Himalayas and passing a series of tests of strength and wits to see him. The dying lama asks Droom to become "the man to continue the never-ending fight against the diabolical forces that exist in the world," bearing magical powers, and the doctor accepts. He abruptly feels his face changing and screams, "My eyes! They're becoming slanted! And I've a— a moustache!" Droom, now looking stereotypically East Asian, is told by the lama, "I have given you an appearance suitable to your new role!" and the newly minted hero ponders his next steps.

For the following few issues of *Amazing Adventures,* drawn and possibly also written by Kirby (though Stan or another writer may also have contributed to the writing), Droom did battle with the forces of darkness but soon vanished into obscurity. Droom is worth mentioning primarily to demonstrate how scattershot the beginning of this new superhero era was, stumbling into existence rather than exploding with fanfare. Though the Marvel Universe has since become an intricate tapestry of stories planned out far in advance in order to connect with one another, there was little in the way of a coherent strategy when the metahumans returned to Goodman's company.

That incoherence is part of the reason why there's no conclusive account of how and why the Fantastic Four were created. Stan told an array of versions that conflict with one another pronouncedly. First came what we might call the Boredom Version. In the late 1960s, when Stan was asked about the inception of the Fantastic Four, he gave no particular narrative, merely random thoughts about ambition on the part of himself and his company. For example, around 1965, a journalist asked Stan about the invention of the quartet of consequential characters. "Well, I guess we were looking for something to hook some new readers," he replied. "Also, I think boredom had a little to do with it. We had been turning out books for about 20 years. Same old type all the time . . . So I figured, let's try something a little more offbeat. . . . I think the big policy was to avoid the clichés." In 1966, he told a young Roger Ebert, "For years we had been producing comics for kids, because they were supposed to be the market. . . . One day, out of sheer boredom, we said—let's do something we would like. So we tried to get rid of the old clichés. Comics were too predictable. Why not accept the premise that the superhero has his superpower, and then keep everything else as realistic as possible?"

But a few years later, Stan started to present a different account, one we might call the Joan Version. In this one, it was his wife who prompted him to get the gumption to shake up his process and create the FF. The earliest use of the Joan Version that I can find was published in 1969, when Stan told an interviewer about how he'd been frustrated by his comics work and had been longing to produce things outside the medium. "Finally, about seven years ago, my wife said to me, 'You know you're a nut, Stan—you're obviously going to be in comics most of your life—why don't you stop thinking of these other things and tearing yourself in two—just concentrate on making a mark in comics,'" he recounted. "And that's when I decided to really give it the old school try, and I forgot everything else for a while. We came out with a new line of Marvel Comics and I tried to make them as well-written and as sophisticated as I could, and I'm happy to say they really caught on." In 1972, he spoke to a group of students at the University of Delaware about how his pre-FF comics were "all the same" until "one day my wife turned to me—she was always looking the other way—and said, 'Why don't you try something new?'"

Then Stan sort of merged these two previous versions into an account that we might call the Martin-and-Joan Version. In 1974,

Stan wrote at length about the FF's real-life beginnings, in a book called *Origins of Marvel Comics,* and he said the process began during a conversation between him and Joan about comics and his various gigs in other media. "She wondered why I didn't put as much effort and creativity into the comics as I seemed to be putting into my other free-lance endeavors," he said. Enter Goodman: "No sooner had the lovely Mrs. Lee filled me with rabid resolution than I had another talk, this time with Martin Goodman," he said. "Martin mentioned that he had noticed one of the titles published by National Comics seemed to be selling better than most. It was a book called *The Justice League of America* and it was composed of a team of superheroes. Well, we didn't need a house to fall on us. 'If *The Justice League* is selling,' spake he, 'why don't we put out a comic book that features a team of superheroes?'" Thus, the Four.

This iteration, too, was tossed by the wayside with time and replaced by a slightly but revealingly altered one, the most commonly repeated one today, which we might call the Quitting Version. It centered on Stan's declaring to Joan that he was going to leave comics altogether—a noted change from all previous versions, which never mentioned anything of the sort and in fact sometimes had included Joan and Stan's assuming he was stuck in the industry for good. The Quitting Version also occasionally included a golf game. As he put it while recounting the Quitting Version in the mid-aughts:

> As far as I remember, it all began when Martin Goodman, who was the publisher and owner of Timely, came to me one day. He told me he had been playing golf with one of the heads of DC Comics, which was called National Comics in those days. The guy told Martin that DC had published a new comic book called *The Justice League of America* and that it was selling very well. If DC had a team of superheroes that was selling well, Martin thought we should also publish one. So he came to me and said, "Stan, I want you to make a team of superheroes for me."

In this same retelling, Stan said a second event soon followed:

> So I told my wife Joanie that I was going to quit comics
> and try something else. So she said, "Well, since Martin asked
> you to do a new book and you've been complaining for years
> that you don't like doing them his way, why don't you do this
> new title the way *you* want to do it? The worst that can hap-
> pen is that he'll fire you. Big deal! You say you want to quit,
> anyway." I thought about it and realized she was right.

And yet, even in this final version, the story would change.
Sometimes Stan said Joan told him to do comics the way he wanted
to do them first and then the pitch from Goodman came next; sometimes, vice versa. Sometimes he didn't even mention the Goodman
part, only the Joan part. Sometimes there was a golf game; sometimes it was just information that Goodman had gathered in an un-
defined way. In short: It's hard to synthesize what, exactly, Stan
wanted his fans to believe about the FF's creation—though by the
end of the line, one message was clear: Other than drawing the characters, Kirby had nothing to do with coming up with them.

For what it's worth, Kirby didn't give much of a streamlined
story about how he allegedly came up with the characters, either.
Kirby was an elliptical thinker and roundabout speaker, rarely telling tales of his own life or process in a linear fashion, and when he
was asked about the FF, he would get facts wrong and speak in vagaries. Even in the space of one interview, he could seem to contra-
dict himself. At one point in 1989, Kirby said he came up with the FF
as soon as he returned to Goodman's company. But elsewhere in the
same conversation, he placed their creation after he'd been working
on the sci-fi comics for a while:

> I had to do something different. The monster stories have
> their limitations—you can just do so many of them. And then
> it becomes a monster book month after month, so there had

to be a switch because the times weren't exactly conducive to good sales. So I felt the idea was to come up with new stuff all the time—in other words there had to be a blitz. And I came up with this blitz. I came up with the Fantastic Four, I came up with Thor—I knew the Thor legends very well—and the Hulk, the X-Men, and the Avengers. I revived what I could and came up with what I could. I tried to blitz the stands with new stuff.

Even beyond that, Kirby's recollections were confusing. In 1993, he told an interviewer, "The Fantastic Four were, well, they were the teens. They were the young people. I love young people. I love teenagers. And you'll find that the Fantastic Four represent that group in many, many ways. They're very vital and they're very active and the teams certainly are in that category. So the Fantastic Four was my admiration for young people." But, as is obvious to anyone who has read the comic, only one of the members of the group—Johnny Storm, the Human Torch—is a teenager; the rest are adults. He once said he had been inspired by mid-century atomic hysteria: "When people began talking about the bomb and its possible effect on human beings, they began talking about mutations because that's a distinct possibility. And I said, *That's a great idea.* That's how the Fantastic Four began, with an atomic explosion and its effect on the characters." But the FF gain their powers from cosmic rays during a failed space flight, not an atomic explosion. Kirby's defenders often say he must have been riffing on a previous comic he'd worked on at DC, *Challengers of the Unknown,* which also featured a quartet of heroes who vow to fight evil after being involved in an accident together. But Kirby would mention the Challengers only glancingly as an influence on the FF. Similar to Stan's various versions, the only thing consistent in Kirby's recollections about the FF was that, as he put it as early as 1970, "It was my idea. It was my idea to do it the way it was; my idea to develop it the way it was."

The temptation, of course, is to conclude that the truth lies somewhere in the middle, that each man was partially responsible for coming up with the team. But this is a dangerous line of thought for a historian, a Solomonic splitting of the baby that mistakes mathematical averages for historical probability. It is absolutely possible that the initial idea emerged in the back-and-forth between the duo. But we should not ignore the possibility, given that both Stan and Kirby were adamant about being the sole progenitor, that one of them was lying and the other telling the truth. We'll probably never know for certain. In the absence of conclusive data, history has been written by the victor.

THE FANTASTIC FOUR #1 begins with the protagonists being summoned by their leader while they're engaged in day-to-day tasks, and when the summons causes them to use their superpowers, the innocent bystanders freak the hell out. Soon we get a flashback to the group's origin story, and it's unlike anything seen before in the medium's twenty-eight-year history.

Superhero stories were supposed to be about genial people who happily stumble upon superhuman abilities, then go on their merry way toward justice. That mold was forever broken in the sequence where powers are forced onto the titular quartet—forced upon them quite painfully, it must be said. Scientist Reed Richards takes his pilot friend Ben Grimm, his girlfriend Susan Storm, and Susan's little brother, Johnny, on an experimental rocket trip, but they're bombarded by cosmic rays. There are six panels of claustrophobic, crimson-shaded agony: "My—my arms are heavy—too heavy—can't move—too heavy—got to lie down—can't move" is Ben's panicked staccato. They slam back down to Earth and immediately find that their situation has gotten even worse. Susan starts to turn invisible and screams as she looks at her disappearing flesh. Ben's skin melts and expands until he resembles a misshapen pile of orange stones; he immediately blames Reed and tries to beat the tar out of him. Johnny calls his friends "monsters" before levitating and bursting into flame. Reed's limbs stretch away from him like distended rubber, and he howls, "What am I *doing*? What *happened* to me? To *all* of us?" The characters seem trapped in a horror fable. Eventually, they calm down and decide to use their powers to help mankind: Reed will become Mr. Fantastic, Sue is dubbed the Invisible Girl, Johnny will be the Human Torch (no relation to the original Timely character of that name), and Ben assumes the identity of the Thing. But even in the scene where they decide to become crimefighters, Lee's dialogue has them trading passive-aggressive barbs and Kirby's pencils show them bearing miserable expressions. The whole thing doesn't feel like a traditional superhero comic; it's more like a David Cronenberg movie or a booze-soaked fight at a Thanksgiving dinner. We cut back to the present, where they do battle with the hideous Mole Man, a villain who brings subterranean creatures to the Earth's surface in a quest for power. That last bit was unremarkable, but the intro and origin sequences were groundbreaking.

It appears that *Fantastic Four* #1 was an immediate hit: In a letter about the issue written on August 29, Stan said, "Judging by early sales reports, I think we have a winner on our hands!" In the same letter, he already seemed to be aiming higher than he had before with his comics work, adding, "We are trying (perhaps vainly?) to reach a slightly older, more sophisticated group." The series initially came out only every other month—Goodman was still laboring under the constraints of the limited production output allowed by his DC-owned distributor—but as it chugged along, it kept accumulating readers. One such reader was a young Alan Moore, who would grow up to write such comics landmarks as *Watchmen, V for Vendetta, From Hell, The League of Extraordinary Gentlemen,* and *Batman: The Killing Joke*. In 1983, Moore recalled reading *Fantastic Four* #3 as a child and how much it changed him. "This comic was utterly stark-raving foaming-at-the-mouth stupendous," he wrote. "The most immediately noticeable thing was the sheer strangeness of Jack Kirby's art. It had a craggy, textured quality that looked almost unpleasant to eyes that had become used to the graceful figures of Carmine Infantino or the smooth inking of Murphy Anderson"—two artists at DC. "That said, it was a taste which quickly grew upon me."

Moore reserved special praise for the Stan-written dialogue: "What was special was the characterization, the way the characters talked, thought, and behaved," he wrote. You had Reed, "who was given to making long-winded and pretentious proclamations on everything from Epsilon radiation to Universal Love"; Sue, "who always looked as if she'd be much happier curled up in an armchair with a bottle of Valium and the latest issue of *Vogue* rather than being captured by the Mole Man or someone of that ilk"; Johnny, "who was brash, loudmouthed and not a little obnoxious, the sort of person who looked like he'd have less trouble picking up an articulated lorry than he would have picking up a steady girlfriend"; and, most important, Ben, about whom "you had the impression that he was always on the verge of turning into a fully fledged villain and quitting the Fantastic Four for good." These are, of course, exaggerations—but only mild ones, and the fact that the material was rich enough for young Moore to extrapolate in those directions was remarkable. The leads were flawed, vivid, and unique, their adventures idiosyncratic and imaginative. Thanks to the Marvel Method, Kirby was probably the primary writer on these FF stories, but the combination of his plotting with Stan's verbiage made for something wholly unique in a marketplace still dominated by the generic pronouncements of bland good guys.

There was a delay between *Fantastic Four* #1 and the arrival of the next batch of superheroes, perhaps because Goodman and Stan hadn't quite expected that the genre would catch on. Whatever the case, the fall of 1961, coming in the wake of the FF's surprise success, appears to have been a period of fevered creativity at Goodman's shop, particularly for Kirby and—to one extent or another—Stan. The next metahuman to pop up was the bulky title character of *The Incredible Hulk* #1. In Stan's 1974 telling, the response to the FF led him to want to top himself. "There I was at my desk, a brand-new sheet of paper in my typewriter, ready to begin anew the agony of creation," he wrote. "What kind of hero was the comic-book reading world waiting for? What could we come up with that would take fandom by storm? How about an Errol Flynn type? Or a Gary Cooper? But then that little voice kept whispering inside my head, 'Be innovative. Be original. They expect you to come up with something that's different.' " He said he realized that the monstrous Thing "was the most popular character in the Fantastic Four, and quite possibly in the entire comic-book field" and noodled on that fact before remembering his love of Victor Hugo's Quasimodo, the Universal Pictures version of Frankenstein's monster, and Robert Louis Stevenson's Dr. Jekyll and Mr. Hyde. "Think of the challenge it would be to make a hero out of a monster," he wrote. "I knew I needed a perfect name for a monstrous, potentially murderous hulking brute who—and then I stopped. It was the word 'hulking' that did it. It conjured up the perfect mental image. I knew I had found his name. He had to be: the Hulk." (Never mind that he, Kirby, and Larry had already released a comic about a non-superhero monster named "the Hulk" just a few months prior.)

Kirby, on the other hand, said the Hulk was entirely his idea, one he based partially on himself: "I created the Hulk, too, and saw him as a kind of handsome Frankenstein," he told an interviewer in 1969. "I never felt the Hulk was a monster, because I felt the Hulk was me. I feel all the characters were me. Being a monster is just the surface thing." In 1982, he cited Stevenson: "What comics were doing all the time was updating the classics. So I borrowed from 'Dr. Jekyll and Mr. Hyde.' I felt there was a Mr. Hyde in all of us and that was a character I wanted and I called him the Hulk." And in 1989, Kirby gave a somewhat implausible, though not impossible, account of the Hulk's creation:

> The Hulk I created when I saw a woman lift a car. Her baby was caught under the running board of this car. The little child was playing in the gutter and he was crawling from the gutter onto the sidewalk under the running board of this

car—he was playing in the gutter. His mother was horrified. She looked from the rear window of the car, and this woman in desperation lifted the rear end of the car. It suddenly came to me that in desperation we can all do that—we can knock down walls, we can go berserk, which we do. You know what happens when we're in a rage—you can tear a house down. I created a character who did all that and called him the Hulk.

Perhaps Kirby really did witness this feat of maternal strength, perhaps he misremembered something he heard about in the news as happening in front of him, or perhaps he made it all up. As of late 1961 and early 1962, all that mattered was producing the eponymous comic in which the character debuted. It was an eerie and unsettling tale in which an experimental test of a bomb laden with "gamma radiation" goes awry, cursing mild-mannered scientist Bruce Banner with the uncontrollable ability to transform into a towering beast. The comic was actually seen as a sales failure upon its debut around March of 1962, making for an early speed bump in Stan and Kirby's road to the future, but the character eventually found a foothold and would go on to become one of their best-known figures.

Even if the Hulk underperformed, it hardly slowed down the overall creative fervor. Stan and Kirby—and, to a lesser extent, Larry, as occasional scriptwriter—were employing the timeworn Goodman process of tossing dart after dart to see if anything could hit the bull's-eye. The middle of 1962 brought the premieres of three consequential super-people. Months prior, Stan, Kirby, and Larry had done a sci-fi story that introduced a scientist named Dr. Henry Pym (the name was Larry's idea), who developed technology to shrink himself to the size of an insect. "That sold so well that I thought making him into a superhero might be fun," Stan would later recall, and, sure enough, in summer 1962's *Tales to Astonish* #35, Pym returned—this time in costume as Ant-Man, commanding an army of ants in a fight against wrongdoing. Kirby never spoke at any length about creating the character, but the notion of people being shrunk down to microscopic size was old hat for him, having been employed in stories he'd done alone or with Joe Simon going back as early as 1940.

Mid-1962 also brought the first appearance of Marvel's take on the Norse god Thor. Stan said the character's origin point was, once again, frustration about one-upping himself. "I kept coming back to the same ludicrous idea: the only way to top the others would be with Super-God," he wrote in 1974. "A thought suddenly struck me. During a recent radio interview the talk-show host and I had been discussing our Marvel stories and he had referred to them as a twentieth-century mythology. . . . One of the points he had made was that Marvel's heroes had some of the charisma, some of the flavor of ancient fairy tales, of ancient Greek and Norse mythology. And that was what grabbed me. That was the answer." In this telling, he turned to the latter of those two legendaria. "As far as I can remember, Norse mythology always turned me on," he wrote. "If ever there was a rich lode of material into which Marvel might dip, it was there—and we would mine it."

The problems with this narrative are twofold. For one thing, it's extremely unlikely that anyone was inviting Stan onto the radio to talk about Marvel during the time when Thor was conceived. Given the many months required to produce a comic in those days, this supposed interview would have had to occur in late 1961, mere weeks after the debut of the Fantastic Four and before even the Hulk had first appeared. Although *The Fantastic Four* #1 had been a hit among the young readers of the comic-book industry, it had in no way broken through to the mainstream adult consciousness, making a radio appearance implausible, and even if it had happened, the company hadn't spawned enough characters to reasonably merit labeling them as a mythology. What's more, Stan had previously displayed no interest in Norse myths, not even in his own accounts of his youth. In stark contrast, Kirby had a long-standing and public fascination with such legends—indeed, he had already done not one but two comics stories starring different versions of Thor in the fifties, one at DC and one for Goodman. "I tried to update Thor and put him in a superhero costume," Kirby said in 1983. "He looked great in it and everybody loved him, but he was still Thor." Larry was recruited to write a script based on a summary typed up by Stan (though that summary could easily have emerged from an initial idea by Kirby, of course), and *Journey into Mystery* #83 introduced what would become the most famous version of Thor to occupy the human imagination in centuries.

However, none of these characters, not even the FF, would swing to the heights that were enjoyed by the final member of the trio of mid-1962 arrivals: Peter Parker, the spectacular Spider-Man. Unfortunately for the historian, his creation story features not one, not two, but three men's conflicting narratives—and one of the narratives involves three additional men on top of that. Stan was fond of beginning his recitation of the origin of Spider-Man with a winking statement about its veracity—as he put it in a 2008 interview, "I've told this story so often that, for all I know, it might even be true." In that interview, he offered up an account that traced Spidey's origin to his own observation of a bug. "I think I was watching a fly walking on a wall, and I said: *Gee, wouldn't it be cool if I had a hero who could stick to walls like an insect?*" he said. "I thought, *I'll get a guy who's like an insect*. So I figured, *Okay, what kind? What'll I call him? Insect-Man?* That didn't sound dramatic. *Mosquito-Man?* No. I went down the list. When I got to Spider-Man—*Spider-Man*—oh, that sounded dramatic. So I figured I'd call him that, and then we had him shoot webs."

This oft-told story, however, comes in direct contradiction to a completely different one Stan used to tell, in which he'd cite the origin point as a riff on author Harry Steeger's 1930s pulp-magazine vigilante, the Spider. "Why the name?" Stan wrote in 1974. "Why Spider-Man? Simple. In the long-dead, practically Paleolithic era when I had been on the verge of approaching teenagerhood, one of my favorite pulp magazine heroes was a stalwart named the Spider. . . . It was his name that grabbed me. But that was enough."

Sometimes he said the idea originated with his wanting to create a teenage superhero and working from there; sometimes not. Sometimes he said it began with wanting to create a hero with realistic problems; sometimes not. Again, the only through line was this notion that he had no assistance from anyone in coming up with the original spark of an idea.

Kirby, as you by now expect, had an entirely different account of Spider-Man's creation. This fact is a bit surprising for a layperson, given that Kirby didn't draw the comic and is thus not commonly associated with the character. Nevertheless, he swore up and down that the process began with him. According to Joe Simon, in 1953, when he and Kirby had their own publishing company, a once-popular artist named C. C. Beck came to them and asked for some work. The publishing duo paired him with writer Jack Oleck (Simon's brother-in-law, demonstrating again how nepotistic comics were back then) and the two concocted a pitch for a character called the Silver Spider. However, things get complicated at this stage, as it's unclear whether Simon and/or Kirby came up with the character and handed it to Oleck and Beck or if it originated with the latter pair. Whatever the case, the Silver Spider bore no resemblance to the eventual Spider-Man in any way, shape, or form save being a superhero with "Spider" in his nom de guerre. What's more, he never made it to a finished comic book, and the only evidence of his existence is oral testimony and a few incomplete documents. Flash-forward a few years: Simon and Kirby, freelancing for Archie Comics, debuted an unsuccessful superhero named the Fly, who had insectoid powers including the ability to spin webs and stick to walls. Once again, there were no thematic or character parallels to Spider-Man, but there were clear echoes in his name and abilities.

Flash-forward again to Kirby's time with Goodman's company after his 1958 return. In Kirby's retelling, at some point during that period he suggested reviving certain aspects of the Silver Spider, which he claimed was created by him and Simon, and developing a character called Spiderman (note the lack of a hyphen). "It was the last thing Joe and I had discussed. We had a strip called the . . . or a script called *The Silver Spider*," Kirby said in 1982. "I had a lot of faith in the superhero characters, that they could be brought back very, very vigorously. They weren't being done at the time. I felt they could regenerate, and I said 'Spiderman' would be a fine character to start with. But Joe had already moved on. So the idea was already there when I talked to Stan." The story goes that Kirby then created some kind of presentation for Stan, which has not survived in readily available form, but one page of it was allegedly seen by eventual Marvel Comics editor-in-chief Jim Shooter. "I've seen it! I've held it in my hands," he told me, and when I asked if the character looked like the finished Spider-Man, he replied:

> No, it looked like Captain America. It was a lot more like some kind of cross between Captain America and the Fly. Because he had the Captain America boots, and he had the belt and he had a web pistol, a gun, and the notes said he was the son of the police commissioner, which is how he found out about all the crimes, but he was drawn like a full-grown man. Big, bulky, Captain America type. No webs on the costume or anything like that.

Enter Steve Ditko. Whether Stan or Kirby was the progenitor, Kirby didn't ultimately end up doing the interiors of the finished comic (though he did draw the cover). In Stan's narrative, he commissioned some sample pages from Kirby and thought the take on the character was too much of "a powerful-looking, handsome, self-confident typical hero type" and took Kirby off the project. In Kirby's telling in 1989, he was just too busy: "I created all those books, but I couldn't do them all. We decided to give the book to Steve Ditko, who was the right man for the job." The demure Ditko, by this point, had become a trusted collaborator of Stan's, working on a series variously titled *Amazing Adventures, Amazing Fantasy,* or *Amazing Adult Fantasy*. Ditko wrote in an essay later in life that Stan discussed a proto-Spidey with him when it was still something Stan and Kirby were working on and that the character "would be a teen-ager with a magic ring that could transform him into an adult hero." He said he later saw five pages of sample story, penciled by Kirby, though he said he didn't know whether Stan had the original ideas. The first of these pages allegedly featured a "typical Kirby hero/action shot" of a hero with "a web gun, never seen in use." The sub-sequent four pages depicted "a teenager living with his aunt and uncle. The aunt was a kindly old woman, the uncle was a retired police captain, hard, gruff." The kid was then shown making his way toward the house of "a whiskered scientist-type involved in some kind of experiment or project," and that was the end of what had been produced.

In Ditko's account, Kirby didn't do the comic for reasons unbe-knownst to Ditko, and he was handed "two synopses" that outlined what came to be the actual, finished plot and character. (Ditko, who refused interviews and broadcast his words solely via paper pam-phlets available only by snail mail even as of his death in 2018, frus-tratingly never clarified who wrote the synopses.) He said he then completely revamped the design into the world-famous image of a spindly lad in a mask with big eyes and a webbed costume of blue, red, and black.

Spider-Man's genesis may be in dispute, but the impact of his big debut is not. The character first appeared in a short story in *Amazing Fantasy* #15. The plot is so well known that it's hardly worth rehash-ing: Dorky teenager Peter Parker is bitten by a radioactive spider and gains the wall-crawling abilities and proportional strength of an arachnid; he builds a machine that allows him to shoot webs from his wrists; he uses his newfound abilities to enrich himself; he cal-lously declines to thwart a robber; his uncle is killed and he chases after the murderer; he discovers that the crook is none other than the man he'd failed to stop earlier; he guiltily devotes himself to fighting crime. The moralistic twist ending, now so familiar, was a clear echo of the sorts of conclusions Stan and Ditko had been creating in their work together for years. It was punctuated with the following narration: "And a lean, silent figure slowly fades into the gathering darkness, aware at last that in this world, with great power there must also come—great responsibility!" Although Stan remains lauded as a writer, even his most loyal fans rarely remember or point to more than one actual quotation from his work. But that one *did* enter the canon. Typically misquoted as "with great power comes great responsibility," it rings in the ears of everyone who enjoys superhero fiction, and many who don't. Fifty-two years later, Brian Michael Bendis, the acclaimed writer of a long-running comic called *Ultimate Spider-Man,* would sum up the ending's impact this way:

> It's a story with a very strong theme: "With great power comes great responsibility." And that theme is so perfect in its simplicity that you could build a religion around it. As a fan, I carried it around with me, but when you start writing it, you realize, *Oh, this is the most important lesson in the world.* It's not a superpower lesson. It's a lesson about power itself. If you have the power to sing, or to grab people's attention, or anything, then with that comes responsibility that you need to identify and raise yourself up to. I had no children when I started [*Ultimate Spider-Man*], and now I have four, and it's what I teach them.

However, the phrase's origins, like everything else from this period of Stan's creative life, are murky. The phrase has a bevy of similar antecedents. A 1793 decree from the French National Convention stated, "They must consider that great responsibility follows inseparably from great power." In 1906, a young Winston Churchill was quoted as saying, "Where there is great power there is great responsibility, where there is less power there is less responsibility, and where there is no power there can, I think, be no responsibility." Franklin Delano Roosevelt, in an unspoken speech that was published posthumously in 1945, wrote, "Today we have learned in the agony of war that great power involves great responsibility." There are more examples, too, but Stan never admitted to being inspired by any of them and, in a 2008 interview, simply referred to the phrase as "the expression that I made up." Perhaps it was a matter of Stan's drawing from the same primordial well of ideas as all those other writers and speakers. Or maybe he ripped somebody off.

WITHIN A FEW MONTHS of *Amazing Fantasy* #15's publication, Stan and Goodman permanently changed the label of their comics line to Marvel Comics, thus retroactively giving a brand name to this burgeoning new era in the medium's history. It's tempting to assume Stan sensed that something was in the air and knew that his ship had come in. Indeed, he often said that was the case. But this assumption is revisionist history. The evidence points to Stan's remaining cautious at best and depressed at worst when it came to his comics career.

In December 1962, Stan, Joan, and twelve-year-old JC traveled to Joan's hometown of Newcastle, in England, and the local paper there—presumably based on information given to them by Stan or Joan—identified Stan as an "American publisher and newspaperman"; comics went unmentioned. In July of 1963, nearly two years into the revolution, one of Stan and Joan's pool parties was listed in Long Island's *South Shore Record,* and the entry didn't mention once that Stan worked in comics. Instead, it promoted his "book of hilarious captions." That book was part of a series entitled *You Don't Say!,* and it was a further demonstration of Stan's trepidation. The first volume, released earlier that year, was made up of more than one hundred news photographs with satirical dialogue bubbles appended to them. It was one of Stan's oldest artistic obsessions, this practice of adding goofy text to photos, and he was constitutionally incapable of admitting that it didn't really land. *You Don't Say!* featured stuff like a picture of Fidel Castro giving a press conference, with text coming out of his mouth reading "And then, after I graduated charm school . . ." or a giddy woman standing next to the amply bosomed Marilyn Monroe while yelling, "They're real!"

He thought well enough of the ninety-six-page pamphlet that he made a similarly sized sequel, *More You Don't Say!,* whose cover image of John F. Kennedy delivering a speech featured a bubble reading, "Allow me to introduce myself." (It also had a cover blurb that purported to be from columnist Walter Winchell, complete with a confusing ellipsis: "Big-Time . . . with hilarious captions.") Kennedy may have proven to be the impetus for the end of the series, as it turned out. Upon the publication of yet another such book, 2008's *Election Daze: What Are They Really Saying?,* Stan gave an interview where he recalled that he and Goodman had made an aborted third volume. "We had Jack Kennedy on the cover with a gag, and while it was at the printer, he was assassinated," he said. "Well, we were so heartsick we couldn't put that book out, so we killed it right at the printers and we just didn't put any more out."

In that same 2008 interview, Stan dropped an intriguing tidbit about his and Goodman's approach to the *You Don't Say* series: "In fact, we were even thinking maybe we'll just drop the comics and do these, 'cause they're easier to do and they make more money because they're more expensive." This is a remarkable revelation, one that squares with a passage in his unpublished autobiography outline referring to this period: "I couldn't forget MG telling me he could make more money raising the price of one of his magazines than I could by working all year—and I knew he was right. Also, I always knew he was basically more interested in, more proud of, and more familiar and comfortable with his slick-paper magazines than with the comics. So I was still nowhere." This could have been a time of triumph for Stan, but he couldn't feel the sunny optimism he was projecting to the outside world. "Things were getting more exciting," he wrote in the outline, "but I still felt I personally was at a dead end."

Readers had no idea that any of this hand-wringing was going on behind the scenes. They were just starting to get to know the man who claimed to be the driving force behind all of these comics they loved so well. The letters-page section of *Fantastic Four* #10, released in late 1962, announced an executive decision from Stan: "Look— enough of that 'Dear Editor' jazz from now on!" he wrote. "Jack Kirby and Stan Lee (that's us!) read every letter personally, and we like to feel that we know you and that you know us! So we changed the salutations in the following letters to show you how much friendlier they sound our way!" Later, he would claim that the readers had started calling them "Stan and Jack" on their own, out of their unprecedented affection, but perhaps they would have done so even without his direction; after all, Stan was doing his level best to suck them in with witty, engaging copy in his printed publications. "I realized we could build our company into a big thing—perhaps another Disney type of operation, if we played our cards right, if we promoted it, and marketed it, and treated it like a huge ad campaign," he wrote in his autobiography outline. Sure enough, Stan started to fill the letters pages and narration boxes with the carnival-barker words of the only character he could truly claim sole credit for: Stan Lee.

Take, for example, *The Amazing Spider-Man* #4, released in mid-1963. It opened with a massive Ditko panel of Spidey attempting to punch a criminal, whose body has turned into sand around the hero's fist, followed by explosive narration that broke the fourth wall and spoke directly to the reader:

> In the space of only the first three issues, you readers have made *Spider-Man* one of the greatest, most phenomenal successes in the history of super characters! And now, with this record-breaking fourth issue, *Spider-Man* soars to still greater heights as he battles the most fantastic foe of all! So, settle back for the thrill of your life—the fateful moment when *Spider-Man* meets—the *Sandman*!

This sort of language was nearly unheard of. EC Comics had done a fair amount of fan outreach in the fifties, and that kind of breathless introduction was common in old radio serials, but direct, postmodern engagement was basically nonexistent in the dour, noble world of superheroes. Stan's narration in the actual story from that same issue was just as thrilling: At one point, Sandman attacks Peter's school, and the panel in which he leaps into costumed action had a header reading "But, outside the classroom door, the returning *Peter Parker* has overheard the commotion, and, making a rapid change, he suddenly bursts into the room like a tornado, as the amazing *Spider-Man!!*" Your average narration panel at DC would likely have just said "Suddenly!" and left it at that. And if we digress from the meta-textual copy for a moment, we can highlight Ditko's acrobatic action and economical plotting, as well as the sparkling banter Stan granted to the protagonist: Where rival companies' heroes would spout various "Have at you!"s and the like, Spidey was sarcastically shouting at Sandman in the heat of battle, "I'll bet you'd be *great* at a party! You're just a barrel of fun, aren't you?!!"

What's more, while those competitors' stories would typically end with everything returned to its right place and no hint of continuity for the issue to come, here, as in so many Marvel stories, we conclude on an unresolved minor chord. The bespectacled Peter stands bereft, a frown upon his face, and contemplates the fact that the public still hates him, no matter how much good he does. "Finally, alone in his room, the amazing individual called *Spider-Man* searches his soul, bewildered, confused, and bitter!" reads the narration. "*One* thing is certain! The world won't have long to wait for *Spider-Man*'s next great thriller! Due to your ever-increasing demand, it will be on sale *soon*! Reserve your copy *now*!"

The pair of letters pages that followed were even more of a delight for a budding geek, what with Stan's snappy personalized responses to his readers' missives. When a Canadian with the improbable name of Bill Schmuck told "Stan and Steve" that he wanted Spidey to have "his own headquarters and maybe a Spider-jet with his insignia on it," Stan replied, "We're all for it, Bill, but where is a superhero without any dough gonna get his own Spider-jet?? Last we heard, he was trying to raise the down-payment on a bike!" No one else in comics was making these kinds of connections with fans. It was all the more remarkable, given his age, that this nearly forty-year-old man had such a rapport with kids and teens. As if all that weren't enough, the letters section ended with a cropped image of the title page of an upcoming Marvel comic. "Like Spider-Man? Then you're sure to flip over . . ." read the text above it, and the image showed a logo for *The X-Men,* combined with the tagline "The Strangest Super-Heroes of All!" The floppy, cheaply printed comic you had just finished and now held in your sweaty palms was a cultural object unlike any that had existed—except, that is, for the rest of the Marvel superhero lineup, all of which credited Stan as the dogged writer/editor.

Speaking of the X-Men, they debuted in the summer of 1963 as a quintet of teenage mutants, born with latent superpowers, who operated out of a school run by a bald-pated gent named Professor X. They would become yet another bone of contention between Stan ("I wanted to do a new team of heroes and I said to myself, *I've run out of radioactivity and gamma rays and cosmic rays—what excuse can I find for these guys getting superpowers?* I took the cowardly way out and said, *Wait a minute—what if they were just mutants? What if they were just born that way?*") and Kirby ("The X-Men, I did the natural thing there. What would you do with mutants who were just plain boys and girls and certainly not dangerous? You school them. You develop their skills. So I gave them a teacher, Professor X"). The X-Men weren't initially much of a hit and certainly a lesser one than another super-team that first assembled in the very same month. This latter squadron, the Avengers, was a confab of various existing Marvel characters: Ant-Man (he leveled up and started going by Giant-Man in the next issue); his girlfriend, the Wasp (a shrinking sprite with a fashion addiction, not exactly a triumph for feminism); the Hulk (too surly to stay on the team for more than the first installment); Thor (his evil brother, Loki, was the impetus for the team's union); and Iron Man (a repentant weapons dealer who had debuted earlier that year and for whom Stan and Kirby both claimed credit). The fourth issue of their eponymous series featured the return of none other than Simon and Kirby's Captain America, unseen for years.

What *The Avengers* demonstrated above all else was the degree to which Stan and Kirby were constructing a massive latticework of stories in which anything that happened in a given individual series—even ones from as far back as the forties—could affect events in any other series. Marvel was a living, breathing, evolving universe, through and through, which couldn't be said for the haphazard worlds of DC, Charlton, or any of the rest of the superhero publishers. It was a brilliant strategy for next-level storytelling, yes, but an even more brilliant marketing ploy. If you wanted to know what the hell was going on in one book, you had to buy all the others, just to be sure you didn't get lost. Kirby never took credit for that idea—indeed, his assistant and biographer, Mark Evanier, says Kirby found it cumbersome and irritating, because it forced him to incorporate other people's ideas into his own comics. But Stan was enormously proud of the notion of the Marvel Universe and maintained it in all the superhero books.

Roger Ebert used to say movies are like a machine designed to create empathy. Stan's line of comics was a machine designed to create addiction. In the new century, Hollywood would finally catch on to this notion and bring it to the multiplex, with massive, lucrative, and controversial consequences. But we're getting ahead of ourselves.

Stan was on fire, working on an extraordinary number of ongoing comics series at once, and his enthusiasm could be infectious. "He worked so hard, but he never got stressed; he was always pleasant to everybody and always appreciated the work everybody did," recalled Flo Steinberg, the cheerful, Bahhhston-accented secretary he hired in 1963, who sat at a desk outside Stan's office. "And people would go in, like Steve Ditko, or Jack Kirby, or Don Heck, or Dick Ayers, and Wally Wood"—all writer/artists—"and so on. They would talk, and voices would get raised in excitement, and Stan would be acting out what he wanted the characters to be doing or saying, their actions, motivations." Stan had been embodying imagery he wanted in his comics in front of artists for decades, but as the superheroic action got wilder, so, too, did his little theatrical scenes. "And there would be jumping around," Steinberg said. "Stan was hopping up on the desk, on the chair. He was very physical, acting out the stuff, and he would run back and forth, and then—*boom-boom-boom*—the sound effects he wanted would come crashing through the walls." In some ways, Stan was making the most artist-friendly environment comics had ever seen. He would crow about his collaborators' visual talents in his published copy, and he started doing something unprecedented when he included itemized credits in the beginnings of the issues. Previously, if you worked on a comic, you were lucky if you even got to sign your name to it, much less identify what you did for it, and God help you if you were lower on the food chain than the penciler or writer. But Stan had the idea to regularly cite the writer, penciler, inker, and letterer, often using effusive poeticism. For example, spring 1964's *The X-Men* #6 was credited as follows:

> *Written: with the flair of Stan Lee*
> *Drawn: with the air of Jack Kirby*
> *Inked: with the care of Chic Stone*
> *Lettered: on a dare by S. Rosen*

Of course, such credits contained two potent lies: First, Stan wasn't the only, or often even the primary, writer on any of these comics, thanks to the Marvel Method; second, the pencilers were not being credited for the writing they were doing. As Ditko would later put it, "Lee started out early with his self-serving, self-claiming, self-gratifying style, of giving credit and then undercutting the giving by taking away or claiming most or all of the credit." Perhaps more important, the writer/artists weren't being *paid* for the massive amounts of writing they were doing. Stan was getting freelance cash for his writing duties, given that his staff job was still as the editor, but guys like Kirby and Ditko, who were laboring without the benefits of staff positions, were also being denied writer's fees that were by all rights theirs. There was no union for comics, and these writer/artists were desperate for the work, so no great commotion was raised about the matter. But it was unfair exploitation of labor, plain and simple. On the rare occasions when writer/artists *did* speak up, Stan was known to shoot them down. Comics historian Barry Pearl once spoke to artist Dick Ayers about the latter's putting-together of an issue of the comic *Sgt. Fury and His Howling Commandos* and was shocked by what he heard:

> Dick told us how Stan called him one day and said, "I can't think of a story for *Sgt. Fury* #23. We won't have an issue unless you think of something!" A worried Dick could not sleep that night and kept [his wife] Lindy awake too. They talked about story after story until, in the middle of the night, Lindy came up with the idea of the Howlers saving a nun and her young charges. Dick said, "Stan will never go for that, he wants nothing about religion . . . But I'll ask him." When Dick did, Stan said, "What a great idea, I'll use it." So they put together a terrific story. When Dick's finished pages were shown to him, he saw the credits where he was only listed as artist. He went to Stan's office and asked if he could also be listed as co-plotter. Stan yelled, "Since when did you develop an ego? Get out of here!"

In his autobiography outline, Stan wrote, "Credits for everyone. Of course, the credits became a Frankenstein monster. Artists and writers began to believe their publicity and became difficult to deal with." The irony is that it was Stan who was beginning to believe his own publicity and becoming difficult to deal with, at least on occasion. Kirby was turning in a truly wild number of pages on a regular basis—1,158 of them in one particular year alone. It's no wonder that, allegedly, when Stan demanded that Kirby redo a set of them for an issue of *The Incredible Hulk,* the two got into a shouting match that resulted in Kirby angrily tearing up the pages and tossing them in the garbage. Stan began talking trash about his writer/artists, too. In a letter to fanzine editor Jerry Bails, Stan blithely insulted an idea Ditko had proposed. "Well, we have a new character in the works for *Strange Tales* (just a 5-page filler named DR. STRANGE—)," he wrote. "Steve Ditko is gonna draw him. Sort of a black magic theme. The first story is nothing great, but perhaps we can make something of him—'twas Steve's idea, and I figgered we'd give it a chance, although again, we had to rush the first one too much." (Doctor Strange would go on to become a key member of the Marvel pantheon, and Stan later claimed it was all *his* idea: "In July of 1963 I gifted the world with another favorite of mine, *Dr. Strange,*" he wrote in *Excelsior.*)

Some of these disses were made out in the open, albeit in the guise of half jest. In the letters pages of *Fantastic Four,* someone congratulated Stan and Kirby on an issue of *Sgt. Fury,* and Stan responded with mock dialogue between him and Kirby: "JACK: SGT. FURY? Is that one of OURS? STAN: You lunkhead, you just drew it a WEEK ago! JACK: Gosh, who can remember that far back?!" In response to a letter about crossing the superheroes over with Marvel's Western comics, Stan pulled a similar trick: " 'Hey, Jack—do we still publish Westerns?' 'You're askin' ME, Stan?? I can't even remember how many fingers to give the Thing!' " Around this time, Ditko went to one of the only comics conventions he ever attended, and an admirer named Ethan Roberts told the writer/artist that he was thinking about becoming a comics professional. Ditko revealed that it wasn't all it was cracked up to be. "He proceeded to tell me how hard the job was and that it paid too little and had few lasting rewards," Roberts later recalled. "It was a real downer."

IN MID-1964, A LETTER from one John Butterworth of Colgate University appeared in *The Amazing Spider-Man* #15 and particularly tickled Stan. "I thought you might be interested in seeing the impact that Spider-Man has had on higher education," it read. "My friends and I have decided that Spider-Man is far ahead of any other super-hero in the field. In an article published in the school newspaper, I tried to sum up the reasons why. Everyone who has read Spider-Man identifies with him, and if Peter Parker ever wants to go to college we'll try to get him a scholarship here—and a fraternity bid, too." Stan's response noted that Butterworth had enclosed the aforementioned article, which was apparently headlined SPIDER-MAN STRIVES FOR STATUS IN COMPETITIVE COMIC BOOK WORLD OF INSECURE SUPER-HEROES. "It's clever as all get-out," Stan said. Around this time, Stan received an invitation from students at New York's Bard College to speak on their campus and he wholeheartedly accepted, beginning a string of college appearances that would continue for decades.

In fall 1964, Stan founded a Marvel fan club called the Merry Marvel Marching Society (MMMS), for which one would pay a dollar and receive membership and assorted goodies. Marvel reading clubs sprouted up all over the United States and even at England's Oxford and Cambridge universities. Playwright Michael McClure unveiled a theatrical production called *The Beard,* which featured an excerpted Doctor Strange monologue from *Strange Tales* #130. Famed visual artist Roy Lichtenstein adapted a Kirby *X-Men* panel for his painting *Image Duplicator*—Kirby was peeved that the Pop Art painter didn't credit him, but Stan seems to have been content to ride the wave, as he started placing the phrase "A Marvel Pop Art Production" on the comics. By 1965, Marvel was getting coverage on major radio stations and in national papers, and Stan was always presented as the voice and creative engine of the company. Stan even pursued a leap back to the medium he'd ghostwritten for a decade earlier: television.

He and Goodman worked out a deal with a company called Grantray-Lawrence Animation to produce a sizzle reel of semi-animated versions of Kirby drawings to shop around to networks, with a live-action introduction from Stan himself. In what is possibly his first appearance on film outside home movies, he looks and sounds nothing like the toupee-wearing, bespectacled, hey-how-ya-doin' character he would later become. Nearly bald and free of glasses, he looks at the camera and calmly boasts that "the Marvel Comics Group is the acknowledged leader in monthly sales of all comic magazines published today" and that "our superheroes are the kind of people that you or I would be if we had a superpower, which sets them apart from all other superheroes published today and seems to be the reason they're far more popular than any others" (never mind that DC, with its much-more-famous Superman and Batman, was actually still number one in sales).

Another reason the Marvel superheroes were so popular, of course, was the writer/artists putting in long hours to craft them. To Stan's credit, he was continuing to put his collaborators out front more than artists typically had been in the industry. Snazzy nicknames started to appear in the credits: "Jolly Jack Kirby," "Sturdy Steve Ditko," "Adorable Artie Simek," "Dazzling Don Heck," and the like. (Stan dubbed himself "Stan the Man," forever placing him in competition with St. Louis Cardinals outfielder Stan Musial for ownership of that nickname.) Despite the fact that there hadn't been a bullpen at Goodman's company for the better part of a decade, Stan regularly wrote about the "Marvel bullpen" and even recorded a short audio play featuring some of the staff and freelancers; one would receive it on a vinyl record upon joining the MMMS. "I realized that most of our readers felt they knew the members of the bullpen because I was always writing about them," Stan would later recall. "So, in a moment of inspiration, I marched the whole gang out of the office one day to a recording studio about five blocks away." In Stan's retelling, the delighted group was "ad-libbing the whole thing." Kirby had a very different recollection of the process:

We rehearsed in the office. Stan treated it like he was producing the Academy Awards. He had this script he'd written. He'd written it and rewritten it and rewritten it and as we were recording it, he kept rewriting it. We all went into the office, more people than there was room for. When you weren't rehearsing your part, you had to go out in the hall and wait. No work was done that day on comics. It was all about the record. We rehearsed all morning. We were supposed to go to lunch and then over to the recording studio, which was over on 55th Street or 56th. I forget where it was. But when lunchtime came, Stan said, "No, no, we're not ready," so most of us skipped lunch and stayed there to rehearse more. Then we took cabs over to the recording studio and we were supposed to be in and out in an hour or two but we were there well into the evening. I don't know how many takes we did.

Entitled "The Voices of Marvel," the record began with Stan, sounding somewhat reserved by the standards of his later persona, addressing the listener with his oft-used, quasi-militaristic catchphrase, "Face front!" (He was getting into the habit of using such catchphrases—the letter that accompanied the record concluded with his second-favorite sign-off, "'Nuff said," although it would still be about three more years until he started using what would become his first-favorite, "Excelsior!") The record continued with a few minutes of goofy doggerel dialogue between Stan, Kirby, Steinberg, and others. To wit:

> **STAN:** Well, well—Jolly Jack Kirby! Say a few words
> to the fans, Jackson!
> **KIRBY:** Okay! A few words!
> **STAN:** Look, pal—I'll take care of the humor around
> here.
> **KIRBY:** You? You've been using the same gags over
> and over for years!

STAN: Well, you can't accuse me of being fickle, can you? By the way, Jack—the readers have been complaining about [Fantastic Four member] Sue [Storm]'s hairdo again.

KIRBY: What am I supposed to do, be a hairdresser? Next time, I'll draw her baldheaded!

STAN: Boy, I'm glad we caught you when you were in a *good* mood!

And so on. The scene was followed by a theme song, "The Merry Marvel Marching Song," performed by a marching band and choir. Notably absent from the record was Ditko, who declined to participate—as Kirby put it in his recounting of the incident, "Steve was much smarter than we were about those things."

Perhaps Ditko was too smart for his own good. There had been artistic tension between him and Stan since the very beginning of *The Amazing Spider-Man*'s run. Though the conventional wisdom has long been that Ditko was the man behind Spidey's action-packed adventures and Stan was the one who infused the enterprise with his humanistic characterization, Ditko vehemently argued that it was the other way around. "I preferred that we have PP/S-m ideas grounded more in a teenager's credible world," he would later write, using the abbreviations for "Peter Parker" and "Spider-Man" that he always used in his mail-order essays. For example, in one issue Spidey rescued an astronaut from a rogue space capsule, and "the story idea undercut the teenage context," in Ditko's estimation: "It's like having a high school football player playing in the Super Bowl." To make matters more awkward, over the years Ditko had become devoted to the ideas of egoist author and ideologue Ayn Rand, developing an unshakable sense of right and wrong and a disgust with those who leeched off others and lacked integrity or conviction. He was repulsed by what he saw as Stan's eagerness to please letter-writing fans, whom Ditko called the "others, outsiders," or "OOs." Stan called Marvel "the House of Ideas" and its rivals "Brand Echh," but Ditko wondered if the roles weren't, in fact, inverted. "Stan bragged that he was doing something unique in 'The House of Ideas,'" Ditko mused. "Was that 'House' to start rejecting its own unique 'ideas' and start appeasing, conforming to, blending down to the common bland level to become another 'Brand Echh'?"

Eventually, the frustrated Ditko requested that Stan allow him to plot *The Amazing Spider-Man* on his own, merely discussing things with Stan and getting edits rather than allowing Stan to pitch ideas. Stan acquiesced, and issue #18 was entirely plotted by Ditko and merely given dialogue and narration by Stan, even though it somewhat brazenly still contained credits that read "Written by: Stan Lee" and "Illustrated by: Steve Ditko." Stan, in a profoundly confrontational move, advertised the comic in Marvel's letters pages by saying, "A lot of readers are sure to hate it, so if you want to know what all the criticism is about, be sure to buy a copy!" Two issues later, the hidden conflict between the two men again seeped above the surface. "Many readers have asked why Stan's name is always first on the credits!" read narration on the first page of late 1964's *The Amazing Spider-Man* #20. "And so, Big-Hearted Lee agreed to put Stevey's name first this time! How about that?!!" Next to those words was a credits box that, yes, put Ditko's name first, but it listed Stan's twice as large and in bold red ink.

Later in life, Stan never publicly acknowledged his digs at his collaborator and always claimed ignorance as to what the problem was. "Little by little I noticed that Steve was beginning to give off hostile vibes," Stan wrote in *Excelsior*. "Steve wasn't the most communicative guy in the world, and to this day I'm not quite sure what the problem was." Then came a decisive rupture: "At some point before issue #25, Stan chose to break off communicating with me," Ditko said. From then on, Ditko would merely bring his completed pages to the Marvel offices and give them to production manager Sol Brodsky, who would then give them to Stan, who, seeing the plot for the first time, would attempt to write narration and dialogue, a task he likened to filling in a crossword puzzle. Perhaps due to Stan's reluctance to take full credit for comics he didn't have much control over and may not have even liked, spring 1965's issue #26 brought something remarkable: the first time a Marvel writer/artist was given anything resembling a writing credit. "Painstakingly Plotted and Drawn by Steve Ditko," read the title page, though "Stealthily Scripted by Stan Lee" still came first in the credits.

Ditko wasn't the only Marvel writer/artist who entered into direct revolt against Stan. A respected industry veteran named Wallace "Wally" Wood had been put on a low-selling series called *Daredevil,* which followed the adventures of a blind crimefighter whose other four senses were heightened. It had been launched by Stan and another old-timer, Bill Everett, but the latter couldn't make his deadlines and was dropped after the first issue. Yet another classic creator, Joe Orlando, was recruited after him and chafed under what he identified as Stan's desire to have art that looked like Kirby's, so he quit. Wood was brought aboard for issue #5 and soon learned that he wasn't in any way happy with the ethics of the Marvel Method. Here's what he told an interviewer many years later:

> I enjoyed working with Stan on *Daredevil* but for one thing. I had to make up the whole story. He was being paid for writing, and I was being paid for drawing, but he didn't have any ideas. I'd go in for a plotting session, and we'd just stare at each other until I came up with a storyline. I felt like I was writing the book but not being paid for writing.

Wood complained about the situation and raised enough of a fuss that Stan allowed him to act as sole credited writer, including dialogue and narration, on *Daredevil* #10, albeit still with just an artist's pay. "I wrote it, handed it in, and he said it was hopeless," Wood recalled. "He said he'd have to rewrite it all and write the next issue himself." Wood complained that he wouldn't do any further work on it unless he got paid as a writer, and, in Wood's telling, Stan said he'd "look into it" but never made the payout. Insult was then added to injury three times over. First, Stan opened the issue with passive-aggressive narration that crowed, "Wally Wood has always wanted to try his hand at writing a story as well as drawing it, and Big-Hearted Stan (who wanted a rest anyway) said okay! So, what follows next is anybody's guess! You may like it or not, but you can be sure of this . . . it's gonna be different!" (Stan was credited only as an editor on that page, but his name still came first in the box.) Second, according to Wood, when it came to the actual story and script, "Stan had changed five words—less than an editor usually changes," thus making his lack of writer's pay all the more frustrating. And finally, there was a kick in the pants in the letters page: "Wonderful Wally decided he doesn't have time to write the conclusion next ish, and he's forgotten most of the answers we'll be needing!" Stan declared there. "So, Sorrowful Stan has inherited the job of tying the whole yarn together and finding a way to make it all come out in the wash! And you think you've got troubles!"

Wood gave up, left, and never forgave Stan as long as he lived. "He despised Stan," recalls Wood's former assistant Ralph Reese. "He was always *on,* he was always being *Stan Lee.* He was just a relentless self-promoter. He was kind of a phony, in Wood's opinion." Years later, according to Reese, Wood and Ditko would spend time together and kvetch about Stan. "They said that Stan's a blowhard and took credit for a lot of stuff he didn't really create," Reese recalls. "Even more than that, they resented the fact that Stan was making millions of dollars and they were still struggling, living in rented apartments."

THE NICHE WORLD OF the comics press had been touting the Marvel revolution since its inception point in 1961, but it took the mainstream media nearly four years to catch up. Marvel's big break came on April 1, 1965, when the hippest newspaper in America, *The Village Voice,* published a long column headlined "Super-Anti-Hero In Forest Hills" (Forest Hills being the Queens neighborhood where Peter

Parker resided), penned by a young reporter named Sally Kempton. After a throat-clearing about the universe of pop-culture "cults" and the comics medium's historical place in it, Kempton introduced her primary subject: "The Marvel Comics Cult is, under the existing Rules of Pop-Cult Spotting, ripe for exposure," she declared. The article claimed to have heard the rumblings of obsession:

> College students interpret Marvel Comics. A Cornell physics professor has pointed them out to his classes. Beatniks read them. Schoolgirls and housewives dream about the Marvel heroes. I myself was deeply in love with a Marvel hero-villain for two whole weeks. The fact is that Marvel Comics are the first comic books in history in which a post-adolescent escapist can get personally involved. For Marvel Comics are the first comic books to evoke, even metaphorically, the Real World.

Amid ads for anti-war meetups and Balkan folk-dancing lessons, Kempton dove into the various Marvel characters and extolled their virtues, albeit with the mild hesitation of an intellectual. It was unlike anything ever written about comic books for the mass market and a significant landmark after the anti-comics panic of a decade before. Kempton concluded with breathless praise for Spider-Man:

> Spiderman, unlike other superheroes, has never yet saved the human race from annihilation. His battles are unfailingly personal, hand-to-hand combats between a young man of precarious courage and the powerful social forces which threaten to destroy his hard-won security. He has no reassuring sense of fighting for a noble purpose, nor has he any outside support. Even the public which cries up his victories invariably deserts him in the clinches. Spiderman is, God save us, an absurd hero, fighting with purely defensive weapons against foes he cannot understand. . . . How can a character as

hopelessly healthy as Superman compete with this living symbol of the modern dilemma, this neurotic's neurotic, Spiderman, the super-anti-hero of our time.

Around this time, Marvel finally found itself flush enough to hire two young men to help Stan out as assistants, Roy Thomas and Denny O'Neil. Both were former residents of small-town Missouri, the former trained as a schoolteacher and the latter as a journalist, and they were the first Marvel fanboys to work at the company they so adored. Thomas had briefly worked for DC under a notoriously confrontational editor named Mort Weisinger and felt that Stan, by contrast, was a breath of fresh air. "He wasn't too much unlike what I could have had in mind, from reading [his comics]," Thomas recalls. "The personality he had, kind of outgoing and informal—you automatically thought that you would call him 'Stan' and not 'Mr. Lee' and that kind of thing. It was all kind of there. He hadn't practiced this personality. . . . It was very friendly, relaxed." O'Neil has a slightly more cynical eye when it comes to his memories of starting out with Stan. "He was the first man I ever knew who really wanted to be rich and famous," O'Neil recalls. "One of the first jobs he gave me the first week I worked for him was to look into the possibility of him getting an honorary degree. I guess I qualified because I was a college graduate. But I said, 'I don't know anything about this, and my impression is, they have to invite you, it's not something you can apply for.'"

Thomas swiftly got into Stan's good graces, but O'Neil wasn't so lucky. "I came in one morning and was called into Stan's office and he fired me, then and there, for no reason I am able to articulate," he recalls. "So I was with a non-working wife and a two-month-old baby and no money and without a job." O'Neil eventually got gigs at DC, and over the decades he and Stan reconciled enough that, in 2001, Stan penned an introduction to a how-to book that O'Neil wrote about writing comics. In it, Stan described the end of O'Neil's Marvel tenure by saying, "I guess because he figured DC Comics needed him more than we did, he left our bullpen," and "Our loss was most definitely DC's gain." O'Neil remains astonished by those words: "He said, 'We should never have let Denny get away,' and I'm thinking, *Get away?* Ten o'clock in the morning, I have no money and I have a baby? I would've taken a job sweeping floors!"

O'Neil was around long enough to experience a watershed moment for Stan and Marvel in November 1965, albeit one that, again, Stan gave conflicting and disputed accounts of. No one argues about the core fact: Federico Fellini, Italian New Wave director of such masterworks as *8 1/2* and *La Dolce Vita,* came to visit the Marvel offices—by then located on Madison Avenue—and told Stan how much he adored Marvel's comics. Soon afterward, in an interview with a journalist about the incident, Stan said Fellini had abruptly called him at his office and said, "Hello, this is Federico Fellini. I like very much your comics. In one hour I come see you, yes," then came over. A few years later, he told another journalist that Fellini had stormed the office without an advance call, flanked by an entourage, and that Marvel's receptionist told Stan, "Federico Fellini is here to see you," to which he said he replied, "Yeah, and tell him Santa Claus is in here." Other times he said the receptionist couldn't pronounce Fellini's name out of ignorance. The one consistent part of Stan's retellings was his professed awe at the love of such a luminary.

But O'Neil has a very different recollection of how Stan reacted. "All the guys who were working on the action stories and crossword puzzles and the romances, up the corridor, there were heads sticking out of office doors because Federico Fellini was on the premises," O'Neil says. "He was there about an hour and he left. And Stan came out to us and said, 'Was that guy somebody important? I thought he was just another fan of mine.' Stan was not terribly hip."

That may have been true, but he was certainly good at projecting an air of hipness. Nowhere was that more apparent than in his dealings with a reporter named Nat Freedland (né Friedland; he changed it for his byline because he "thought 'Friedland' was a

stupid-looking name"), who was working on assignment for—
where else?—the *New York Herald Tribune*. Freedland had been
working for a small paper called the *Long Island Press* and was trying
to do some freelance magazine writing on the side. "I wanted to be
the next Tom Wolfe, I wanted fame, I wanted to be a first-call for
big stories," Freedland recalls. "I was waiting for little niches that
Tom Wolfe hadn't covered yet." He landed on a topic idea: "Spider-
Man, Marvel, and Stan Lee were the really big thing in New York at
the time," he says, citing the *Village Voice* column as something that
had sparked interest among "pop-culture snobs." He pitched a feature on Marvel to the editor of the *Herald Tribune*'s magazine section, James Bellows, and got it approved. "I called Marvel, I got Stan
Lee on the phone, I said what assignment I had, and he was excited,"
he says. The journalist came to the Marvel offices for only one afternoon in late 1965. One component of the visit was an interview
with Stan, who turned on the charm. "There are little touches I can
see now, in retrospect—little touches of being an egomaniac and
taking all the credit," Freedland says. "But he told me about all the
stuff and I thought it was cute and tremendous. I saw artists coming
around, but I didn't talk to them much."

The one quasi-interaction he did have with an artist came when
Stan contrived to have a story conference between him and Kirby to
discuss an upcoming issue of *The Fantastic Four*. "And Lee is talking
to Kirby in very general terms and Kirby's going, 'Uh-huh'—he's
not very verbal," Freedland recalls. Stan started doing his storytelling acrobatics, leaping around and throwing mock punches. "Great,
great," was all Kirby said when Stan was done. Kirby maintained
that the whole thing was a staged stunt. "Jack said that there was not
a plotting session for a real issue," recalls Mark Evanier. "They had
already plotted that issue beforehand, and they were basically recre-
ating it for the reporter. And one of the reasons Jack didn't say more
in the meeting was he wasn't thinking about a story. He wasn't
gonna take anything home and draw that story. The story was done
for him." Indeed, according to Kirby, he was by that point primarily

just dictating to Stan what he was going to do in a given story, and those meager plot conversations weren't even happening in person; they were all over the phone. Freedland knew none of this and didn't bother to find it out. "I was so enchanted by the whole thing," he says.

While chatting with Freedland that day, Stan tore into Ditko with his signature passive-aggression. "I don't plot Spider-Man anymore," he told the reporter. "Steve Ditko, the artist, has been doing the stories. I guess I'll leave him alone until sales start to slip. Since Spidey got so popular, Ditko thinks he's the genius of the world. We were arguing so much over plotlines I told him to start making up his own stories."

One such story came out almost exactly when Freedland was doing his reporting, in *The Amazing Spider-Man* #33, and it has been hailed throughout comicdom as a masterwork. In it, Spidey finds himself trapped under the weight of a massive pile of metal equipment while water rushes down around him, threatening him with death by either crushing or drowning. Near him is a vial of a serum that can save the life of his aunt May, who is on her deathbed elsewhere. He almost gives up, then thinks of her and his late uncle: "If she—doesn't make it—it'll be my fault! Just the way I'll always blame myself for what happened to Uncle Ben!" he says to himself, his face cast down in shame. "The two people in all the world who've been kindest to me! I can't fail again! It can't happen a second time! I won't *let* it—I *won't*!" He strains and struggles, newly powered by his feelings of regret and aspiration. "I must prove *equal* to the task—I must be *worthy* of that strength—or else, I don't *deserve* it!" He gains some purchase, then fights to lift the heavy machinery the final few feet. "*Anyone* can win a fight—when the odds—are easy! It's when the going's tough—when there seems to be no chance— *that's* when—it counts!" At last, he tosses it all off, his muscles rippling and speed lines flying up and away.

It's a scene often cited as one of the greatest in superhero comics, due to Ditko's command of pacing and anatomy, oft-imitated and even adapted more or less verbatim in 2017's hit film *Spider-Man: Homecoming*. In 2005, Stan recalled the process of creating the scene to an interviewer: "So, in the story, in the plot, I believe Steve and I worked out that, eventually, Spider-Man does manage to lift that huge weight off him and get to Aunt May in time," he said. "But I never realized that Steve would draw it so magnificently. . . . [I]t was such a thrill. Even to me, and I was the writer of the story! When I saw that, I almost shouted in triumph. Steve did a wonderful job on that." Only one problem: Stan had nothing to do with the idea for the scene and added the dialogue only after the fact. By then, even by Stan's own admission many times over, Ditko was coming up with the plots and the two weren't speaking, much less having plot conferences. In the letters section of the issue, a fan missive declared, "This truly is the Marvel Age of Comics! 'Nuff said!" Stan replied, "The Marvel Age of Comics! Now *there's* a catchy phrase!" But one of the men who brought that age into being wanted nothing more to do with it.

According to Ditko, his breaking point came when Sol Brodsky, the production manager, called him to convey Stan's message that one of Marvel's yearly extra-large issues, known as an "annual," was due soon. "One day I got a call from Sol," Ditko wrote in an essay. "The next S-M annual is coming up. Okay. Later, thinking about what I could do for the annual, I asked myself, 'Why should I do it?' Why should I continue to do all these monthly issues, original story ideas, material, for a man who is too scared, too angry over something, to even see, talk to me?" The choice, to him, became obvious: "My next visit to Marvel, I told Sol I was quitting Marvel. Sol told Stan. The only person who had the right to know why I was quitting refused to come out of his office or to call me in. Stan refused to know why."

Ditko handed in his pages for his final issues of *The Amazing Spider-Man* and *Strange Tales* and left the building. It was right around Thanksgiving 1965. Roy Thomas was there that day. "Steve walks in and turns his work to Sol Brodsky and walks out," he recalls. "Sol gets up and trots into Stan's office and comes back a minute later and tells me that Ditko has quit. He said Ditko just came in and said he'll finish up the Spider-Man and Doctor Strange [comics] he was working on now, and then that was it. And he didn't give Sol or Stan any kind of a reason." Stan and Ditko agreed on at least one thing: The former didn't ever figure out why the latter left, nor did he want to. "I just remember that I was angry over the way he quit," Stan told an interviewer decades later. "He left in such a way that I wasn't tempted to call him and ask him why." Word of this epochal event leaked within a few days, and the fanzine *The Comic Reader* reported it in December. It was a kick in the gut to fans who had become enamored of the writer/artist's idiosyncratic genius, but there was no information about how or why it had all gone down.

As if that weren't enough, the *Herald Tribune* article hit stands a few weeks later, on January 9, 1966. It was classic New Journalism, its language simultaneously flip and hip, and it fawned over Stan. Freedland wrote that Stan was "an ultra–Madison Avenue, rangy lookalike of Rex Harrison" with "humorous eyes, thinning but tasteful gray hair, the brightest-colored Ivy wardrobe in captivity and a deep suntan" who "dreamed up the 'Marvel Age of Comics' in 1961.'" It recounted Fellini's visit, the Bard College appearance, the bombastic magic of the FF, the neurotic charm of Spidey, and claimed that "practically every costumed hero in Lee's new Marvel Comics mythology displaces enough symbolic weight to become grist for an English Lit. Ph.D. thesis." Freedland even parroted Stan's claim about winning that *Herald Tribune* essay contest as a kid. By contrast, Kirby was un-interviewed, passive, and described in the following terms: "If you stood next to him on the subway you would peg him for the assistant foreman in a girdle factory." Mark Evanier recalled, "Jack's wife, Roz, read the article early the Sunday morning it came out, woke Jack up to read it," then "Jack phoned Stan at home to wake him up and complain. Both men later recalled that the collaboration was never the same after that day, and it was more than just an injured ego at work." Strike three.

Freedland has lived to regret what he wrote. "I feel sad that I was one of the things that made Kirby feel he was being shortchanged, which, in retrospect, decades later, I can see, yeah, he was," he tells me. " 'Girdle factory.' Oh, God. Oh, poor Kirby. What the hell was I thinking?" Freedland says that when the article came out, he promoted it by appearing on Jean Shepherd's popular radio show and repeating his pro-Stan account of Marvel's popularity. As the weeks went on, Freedland was surprised to find that Stan didn't mention all this publicity in the backmatter of any of the comics. He was perplexed—after all, Stan was usually eager to boast about any and all mentions the company received. "I called Marvel and talked to Stan Lee and said, 'How come you didn't put me in your column, now that the thing is out?' " Freedland recalls. "And he told me about Kirby being upset—I think he put it as, 'upset about having his feelings hurt'—and I thought, *Gee, I can see why he would.*"

Nevertheless, Freedland remained enchanted and landed on a new idea: "I wanted to be a Marvel writer," he says. "There was a writing test, and I took it and turned it in, and I got the word back from someone, saying I didn't have the style or quality—by which I mean characteristics—of writing stuff that would work with Marvel Comics." Freedland was one of countless admirers who were now dreaming of working for the House of Ideas. To all appearances, the tide was high for Marvel, and Stan was the glorious captain of the ship. But with Ditko's departure and Kirby's grim resignation to the fact that he would never be fully appreciated, the Marvel Age of Comics was, in a way, already over.

5.

LONELY AT
THE TOP

————

(1966–1972)

————

JACK KIRBY ONCE TOLD A STORY TO HIS ASSISTANT AND FRIEND
Steve Sherman. It took place in the mid-1960s, a few years before he
and Sherman met. The story goes like this: Kirby came to Marvel's
premises one day and found Stan alone, doing something strange.
"The guy was sitting in the dark in his office, all the lights were out,
he had a tape recorder, and he was talking into the tape recorder,"
Sherman says. "Jack sat down and Stan said, 'Now listen to this, this
is great!'" Stan hit PLAY on the device. "And it was just Stan talking:
phrases and speeches and 'Excelsior!' and this and that," Sherman
recalls. Jack asked what this was all about. Stan smiled his Cheshire-
cat smile and said, "I'm going to run for governor." All Kirby could
think to say was "Good for you."

Stan never ended up running for governor, or for any elected office. But the anecdote is revealing nonetheless. If we take it as truth,
it fits perfectly with the feeling of invulnerability and limitless possibility that Stan exhibited as the sixties barreled along. And even if
the event never really happened, the fact that Kirby told the story
was emblematic of the bitterness and alienation that he increasingly
felt toward his boss and collaborator in the back half of the decade.
This was a partnership that shook the world, but like so many such

partnerships, it was torn asunder by a clash of personalities and worldviews. Stan was feeling the wind at his back and running as fast as he could toward greater renown, and he was lucky enough to find it. But the period between Ditko's departure and Stan's eventual assumption of the publisher's chair was one in which he lost Kirby, then his writing duties, and ultimately saw his glory days come to a close. This era was as good as life ever got for Stan, but he remained unsatisfied, and, due to events both within and beyond his control, he would never again feel the mix of achievement and respect that the era brought.

The period's creative height arguably came at its outset. In a bitterly ironic turn of events, at almost the exact time that the *Herald Tribune* article forever soured the already tense relationship between Stan and Kirby in early 1966, Marvel began publishing what is widely regarded as the pair's greatest story, the so-called Galactus Trilogy. Presented over the course of issues #48 through 50 of *The Fantastic Four,* it was a tale of white-knuckle suspense and apocalyptic scope. The series had already been on something of a roll in the previous few issues, having taken the FF to the hidden world of a race of superpowered individuals known as the Inhumans; the story included bombastic combat, clever humor, and unforgettably weird characters (a king whose whispers can cause massive destruction and so never speaks, a warrior monk who can find the weakest point in any object, and a giant dog who can teleport, just to name a few). The first few pages of issue #48 wrap up the Inhumans saga, then move to a stunning Kirby starscape, where "in the deep vastness of outer space, an incredible figure hurtles through the cosmos—a being whom we shall call the *Silver Surfer* for want of a better name!" Sure enough, the reader sees a nude, genital-free man on a silver surfboard careening through the universe.

The rest of the story was somehow more mind-blowing than anything the Kirby/Stan pairing had produced so far. The sky above Earth appears to catch fire. Then it appears to be filled with massive stone objects. Reed communes with a peaceful alien being known as the Watcher, who admits that it was he who created these illusions in order to conceal the planet from detection by the Surfer. "He is the advance scout for *Galactus!*" the Watcher declares, his eyes wide and crazed. "Galactus, who drains entire planets of their elements, and then leaves them dry, unable to support life!" But it's no use. In a fascinating collage of photo images—Kirby was getting fond of that technique—machinery descends from a giant sphere above New York City. Then a massive humanoid being adorned in bizarre straps and a horned crown appears and announces that Earth "shall *sustain* me until it has been drained of all elemental life!"

Both Kirby and Stan claimed credit for inventing Galactus on their own, of course, and both alluded to the idea that they wanted to have the FF fight God. And so the quartet did, first in vain and finally in triumph, but only after the mutiny of the Surfer, who has been convinced that humanity is worth saving after an encounter with the Thing's blind girlfriend. And yet even that wasn't what finished the job: The only thing that brings Galactus to surrender is the threatened use of a tiny device, retrieved in a mad dash to space by Johnny, known as the Ultimate Nullifier. The ravenous titan departs, and, in a slightly incongruous coda, Johnny goes off to start his career at college. The whole endeavor was as tense as it was ambitious, and it has loomed large in the minds of superhero enthusiasts to this day.

The partnership that birthed the story was one Stan was desperately trying to maintain. Throughout 1966, he made efforts to soothe his writer/artist in the wake of the *Herald Tribune* article. On March 10, Stan spoke at Princeton University and made sure to say that Kirby was "every bit as imaginative as I am—I love to say this for public consumption—probably a lot more." Just a few weeks later, the magazine section of the Berkeley-based newspaper *The Daily Californian* ran an article entitled "A Fantastic Five Years of Marvel Age of Comics," which quoted Stan as saying, "Jack Kirby is one of the greatest artists in the world today. The best artists are storytellers and dramatists. You can't be a good artist without having a feeling for the story as well. Jack frequently has as many ideas for a story as I do. If I'm really short on time he even writes the stories sometimes." Kirby claimed he was also promised a substantial raise and a bonus for non-comics uses of his artwork. Perhaps most important, Stan changed the credits for his collaborations with Kirby. No longer did he put himself down as the writer and Kirby as the artist; instead, there were ambiguous declarations like "Another Spellbinding Spectacular by Stan (the Man) Lee and Jack (King) Kirby."

These spellbinding spectaculars displayed even more good work, especially in *The Fantastic Four*. The Galactus Trilogy was immediately followed by a still-lauded single-issue story called "This Man . . . This Monster!" in which an impostor Thing attempts to infiltrate the FF and soon sees the error of his ways amid some of Kirby's most psychedelic sci-fi artwork yet. Right after that came a true landmark in the history of comics: the two-part story that introduced King T'Challa of Wakanda, aka the Black Panther. The character was the ruler of a fictional African nation that, rather than being filled with backward stereotypes, was instead the most technologically advanced country in the entire world, albeit one that lived in secret. What's more, the Panther was able to defeat the FF in a test of combat, further proving his mettle. By the end of the story, the character was firmly ensconced as the first-ever mainstream black superhero.

To this day, Marvel goes out of its way to praise Stan for his progressive foresight in dreaming up Black Panther, and Stan, in his lifetime, was only too happy to support that viewpoint. "I wanted to create the first black superhero, but I wanted to avoid stereotyping," he said in 2005. "See, in doing a superhero, the first thing you have to think of is, what is a good name for him, and what is a good superpower?" He said he had recalled that "some character" in a story from his childhood "had a black panther, and I thought that was so dramatic when I read those stories, and I liked the name, 'the Black Panther.'" In this telling, he then fleshed out the idea—headquarters in Africa, powers of a jungle cat, et cetera—and went to Kirby for the design. Kirby claimed the character was entirely his idea, inspired by his own desire for diversity: "I came up with the Black Panther because I realized I had no blacks in my strip," he said in 1989. "I suddenly discovered that I had a lot of black readers. My first friend was a black! And here I was ignoring them because I was associating with everybody else. It suddenly dawned on me— believe me, it was for human reasons—I suddenly discovered nobody was doing blacks. And here I am a leading cartoonist and I wasn't doing a black." Thus, the Panther. (For what it's worth, neither man claimed to have been inspired by the American radical group of the same name, which emerged at almost that exact time.)

That dispute over credit lay in the future, but Kirby was being disrespected and underpaid in the present as of 1966, as well, despite Stan's efforts at ameliorating the situation. The promised raise turned out to be minimal and the bonuses never arrived, despite the explosion of Marvel in other media. That year brought the debut of a whole line of Marvel merchandise—T-shirts, posters, and the like— which was fed to a hungry and growing consumer base. The items almost exclusively featured artwork by Kirby. He received no extra payment for this use of his work. Shortly thereafter, that Grantray-Lawrence cartoon show that Stan had pitched the previous year made it to air on ABC and would go on to produce more than 190 animated stories. A huge portion of these tales merely consisted of Kirby's comics artwork, lightly manipulated by animators to add motion. Again, Kirby received no extra payment for this mass-media exploitation of his creative work. There were paperback reprints of Kirby comics, too. There were Marvel trading cards with Kirby drawings on them. None of it brought Kirby, or the other artists whose work appeared in these non-comics venues, a single cent in royalties.

A professional from almost any other creative medium would be astonished that Kirby allowed this to happen and didn't file a massive lawsuit for lack of payment. How could this be? The answer is twofold. First, Kirby, like Lee, was a child of the Great Depression, who constantly worried about losing a line of steady income, however meager. He had a growing family and was, according to all who knew him, deeply committed to supporting them by holding on to the only job he had—and, due to that lingering legal dispute with a DC editor over money from an old newspaper strip, he wasn't welcome at the only other big game in town. But the second reason requires some understanding of the general injustices of the superhero-comics industry. Put simply, all of the work that anybody did for Marvel or DC was considered "work for hire," owned totally and exclusively by the publishers, not the creators. This standard had been established in the early days of comics and had been used to screw over a wide array of writers and artists, who didn't have any stake in the intellectual property that was raking in untold dollars for the executives who tossed off exploitative page-rate wages as the only remuneration for the blood and sweat of Kirby and his ilk.

For what it's worth, this applied to Stan, as well—remember, his writing work was being done on a freelance basis; his staff jobs were as editor and art director. He didn't have any expectation of ownership for any of the characters he claimed to have created. The legality of this work-for-hire arrangement was questionable as of the mid-sixties, largely consisting of a message on the back of paychecks that said the persons receiving them waived all copyright claims. Decades later, this slapdash method of retaining rights would come under legal scrutiny and the Kirby estate would assert in a lawsuit that he, in fact, had owned Marvel's core intellectual property. But that was a long way off and, in their sixties heyday, both men simply took the unjust status quo as it was.

Kirby allegedly made an attempt at breaking out of this arrangement around 1966–67, when he went to Stan with the idea that he'd wrap up the story of Thor with a climax in which all the Norse gods would perish and be replaced with new deities that would star in a new series. Most important, he wanted to fully own and be exclusively credited for these figures. Stan would later say Kirby never told him about the idea, but Evanier tells me Kirby presented his concepts to Stan, "who said, in effect, 'Yes, we want them,' but he wanted to just fold them into existing comics; Jack would be expected to just give them away for the same deal he always had. No additional pay, no special credit." That didn't sit well with Kirby. "He thought at that point, *That's too good of an idea to give them, the way they're treating me,*" recalls Evanier. Kirby stuck around and kept his nose to the grindstone, but his unhappiness was steadily rising.

Kirby's former partner, Joe Simon, was just as ticked off with Stan and Martin Goodman, if not more so, but he was more vocal about it. Goodman got word that Simon was going to attempt to assert a copyright on Captain America and, in July 1966, Goodman told Kirby he could get some extra cash if he signed a deposition describing the creation of the character in terms that allowed Marvel to retain ownership. The monetary amount was promised to be equal to whatever Simon would get in a settlement. Simon, on the warpath, wrote a comics story for the forty-eighth issue of a *Mad* magazine knockoff called *Sick,* published in fall 1966 and entitled "The New Age of Comics." It was perhaps the first instance of a comics professional giving fans a behind-the-curtain look at the injustices of the industry they loved so much. And it was, to say the least, vicious.

The strip began with introductory text that talked about the goofiness of superhero characters and declared, "You won't find a human being anywhere in these books. And if you ever meet the guys who turn it out, you'd run into the same trouble." The reader is transported to a comics publisher on Madison Avenue—the location of Marvel's offices—where a grinning editor named Sam Me orders around a sad-looking artist named Dripko: "All right, do the whole book over and have it on my desk in an hour—we've got twenty other books to get out today!" Sam says before adding, "And don't forget to sign my name to it!" Another artist, Plotsky, tells Sam, "Say, I got an idea!" Sam's immediate reply is, "*Great!* Sign my name to it and do six pages!" Sam takes Plotsky to see his secret weapon, a star-spangled hero named Captain American (note the "n"), who leaps into battle through a window and falls to his death. Plotsky has an idea for a replacement: "How about a character called *Sam Me?*" Sam replies, "Plotsky, you're a *genius*! Remind me to put your name in the credits sometime!" In the final panel, Plotsky grazes the fourth wall as he muses, "A character named *Sam Me*— you think anybody would believe one could exist?" Sam, now clad in a superhero uniform with a giant dollar sign on his chest, offers a closing benediction: "Whatever you're mumbling about, Plotsky— write it down and sign my name to it!"

Stan's name was, as it turned out, everywhere. The man was becoming an out-and-out celebrity. In 1966 alone, more than one hundred publications ran articles about Marvel—many of them reprints of one feature written for syndication, but in an age when local papers still dominated the media environment, that redundancy hardly mattered. Stan was nearly always the star of such articles, of course. Mimeographed fanzines praised his perceived writing prowess and hailed him as a genius. He was appearing regularly on broadcast media, as well, featuring in a segment on CBS and appearing in an untold number of radio interviews. He'd chat with anyone, from pioneering talk-radio host Barry Gray to undergrads on Columbia University's in-house station. He hadn't quite created the chipper Stan Lee character that he would embody for the latter five decades of his life; these interviews were subdued affairs in which Stan sounded like a reserved intellectual—albeit one who was unafraid to offer a little self-praise—and always sounded like he was smiling gratefully. On one show, he boasted about the Merry Marvel Marching Society's broad appeal: "We have members who belong to the John Birch Society, and we are tremendously big with Berkeley College in California," he said, referring to two outposts of the extreme right and left, respectively. "I am telling you, I think we are a phenomenon in publishing circles because we absolutely encompass every range and every taste and every age group."

One age group he was particularly proud of capturing, in case it isn't already obvious, was college students. He was hopping from campus to campus with his speaking gigs and received ostentatious praise at each one he went to; posters for an appearance at the University of Chicago billed it as STAN LEE—THE LEGEND IN HIS OWN TIME. In these speaking engagements, he'd generally eschew prepared remarks and instead just take questions from the audience, then offer up impromptu musings as answers. He was a quick and keen mind in those situations, alternately musing on or wittily rejecting whatever was thrown his way. The boy who had longed to be an actor had grown into a different kind of onstage raconteur. Sensing that fans were hungry for more of this still-developing Stan Lee character, he established a feature in Marvel's letters pages in spring 1967 called "Stan's Soapbox," in which he'd pontificate and rile up his base with slogans and jittery word-jazz. "Our rollickin' readers, no matter what their ages, have proven to be bright, imaginative, informal, and sophisticated!" he wrote in one early "Soapbox." "So we don't mind when some of our roguish rivals claim to outsell us. . . . After all, everyone knows there's less of our type of people than theirs! So let them continue catering to the bubblegum brigade—and more power to 'em. The public needs SOME sort of pabulum till it's grown up to Marvel! 'Nuff said?"

In all of these venues, Stan went out of his way to praise Kirby and even brought him along when he was invited to do a live interview on New York City's WBAI radio in March 1967. "I always say that Jack is the greatest mythological creator in the world," Stan said in that appearance, Kirby at his side in the studio. "In fact, I should let Jack say this, but just on the chance that he won't, somebody was asking him how he gets his authenticity in the costumes and everything, and I think he gave a priceless answer. Jack said that 'they're not authentic. If they were authentic, they wouldn't be authentic *enough*.' But he draws them the way they should be, not the way they were." It's important to note that Stan hadn't quite yet developed the party line that the stories were always his initial idea—in that WBAI interview, Stan said Kirby was sometimes the progenitor of their stories. "If we're sitting around dreaming up a plot," he said, "Jack might say to me, 'Gee, you know, we haven't used the Silver Surfer for a while. How would it be if he was doing this, that, or the other?'" Kirby was as polite and charming as Stan in the conversation. A listener would think the pair were wholly in sync.

How far from the truth that was. The year 1967 brought another slew of slights. *The Fantastic Four* #66 and 67 presented a two-part story about the FF encountering a being created by a group of scientists. According to Evanier, Kirby had wanted the story to be a commentary on Ayn Rand–style Objectivist rationalism, with the scientists attempting to create someone who saw the world in black-and-white moral terms and operated only on reason, never emotion. In Kirby's plan, this would have meant the creature would attack his creators for their flaws, given that they are governed by emotion and imperfect logic, as all humans are. It was to be a story about how pure reason, removed from forgiveness and accommodation for imperfection, can be destructive. In Evanier's telling, Kirby brought the story to Stan, who rejected the whole premise. Per his instructions, the story was redone to be a simple plot about mad scientists creating a monster who turns out to be pure of heart and combats his sinister parents. Kirby groaned at the revision and its implicit suggestion that he was getting too intellectually big for his britches.

Kirby watched as the *Herald Tribune* pattern was repeated over and over again: Journalists kept depicting Stan as Marvel's godhead—the "creator of the Marvel Comics Group," as he was billed on a television roundtable—and rarely even mentioned Kirby, who may well have been the creator of the whole kit and caboodle. Building on the success of the initial Grantray-Lawrence animated shorts, Marvel signed a deal to do two new cartoons about the Fantastic Four and Spider-Man, respectively. They wouldn't gank Kirby's artwork the way the previous show had, but he was nevertheless shafted again: Advance ads for the FF show said the characters were "the brainchildren of Stan Lee." Perhaps due to a complaint from Kirby, when the cartoon eventually debuted, the credits said it was "based upon an idea by Stan Lee and Jack Kirby," but it was a paltry bandage on a festering wound.

Around this time, Stan and Kirby were separately interviewed for a fanzine, and a close read reveals that all was not as copacetic as it seemed in the mainstream imagination. When Stan was asked who came up with the FF, he replied, "Both—'twas mainly my idea, but Jack created characters visually." When Kirby was asked who created the Inhumans—who, mind you, had been introduced in a story where Stan was the publicly credited writer—he replied, "I did." Most ominous, when Kirby was asked whether the workflow consisted of his plotting stories that Stan just dialogued, he gave a deeply passive-aggressive response: "This is Stanley's editorial policy. As a Marvel artist, I carry it out." Kirby couldn't bring himself to even use the name "Stan Lee," much less kowtow to the man who had adopted that moniker. He would use only the same name he'd used when Stan first started irritating him decades earlier. When one looks back at the sweep of Stan and Kirby's careers, something becomes clear: By the end of 1967, they weren't coming up with any new major characters. Even the characters they'd already collaborated on were dividing them. After a disagreement about the way the Silver Surfer's origin and character traits should be portrayed, Stan took Kirby's chrome-domed creation entirely out of his hands and selected artist John Buscema to handle plots and pencils for the Surfer's first solo series. The dual-core engine of creativity that had powered so much of the Marvel machine had a spanner in the works and was slowing down.

Lucky for Stan and Goodman, new sources of energy were arriving to keep up the pace. The air was humming in the label's Manhattan headquarters, where minds and hands who would go on to be legends of the comics industry were arriving in droves. By and large, they loved working with Stan. A talented young DC artist named Neal Adams had heard from a colleague about the creative leeway that came with the Marvel Method and made an appointment to meet with Stan and ask for work. "He was exuberant, enthusiastic;

he offered me any book in the house," Adams recalls. "Stan would never dismiss me, in any conversation or anything that we were doing. He had respect. And he had respect for people who had a head on their shoulders and would speak up, because he did have that kind of appreciation for other people's opinions and feelings about things." In other words, it appears that Kirby's downtrodden status was the exception. Further reinforcing that notion are the words of the writer/artist selected to replace Steve Ditko on *The Amazing Spider-Man*, John Romita, Sr., who would go down in the record books as one of the most significant second-wave Stan collaborators of the Marvel Age. Unlike the first wave—Kirby and Ditko—this group was generally enthusiastic about the Marvel Method. "I realized that [drawing] comics from a script was absolutely paralyzing and limiting," Romita says. "When you had the option of deciding how many panels you'd use, where to show everything, how you pace each page out, it's the best thing in the world. Comics becomes a visual medium!"

Writers, too, came aboard and became enamored of Stan. Roy Thomas was given writing duties in addition to his assistant editing and developed a close mentor–mentee relationship with his boss. A college student named Chris Claremont, who would go on to revolutionize comics in the 1970s and '80s, reached out to Stan in 1968 about working for Marvel. He got an unpaid editorial internship for school credit and, despite the breakneck pace of the work and the occasional micromanaging, he couldn't get enough of Stan. "He was equally good as an editor, equally good as a manager, equally good as an inspiration," Claremont recalls. "He was the anchor that held all these disparate planets. He was the sun around which we all orbited with enthusiasm, because he was somebody you could trust even if you wanted to blow his brains out. And that's a level of inspiration that I think no one's ever equaled." Even his secretaries loved him—Flo Steinberg was an enthusiastic comrade-in-arms, and when she left the company, her replacement, Robin Green, developed an admiration for Stan. As she put it in a later remembrance:

He was my boss and sometimes I liked him and sometimes I hated him, but I always did what he told me to, sometimes grudgingly, like when he'd have me run the errands his wife didn't feel like doing, but I always did them. Because he worked so hard, tried so hard, was so enthusiastic, you'd want to make it easier for him. He's got a one-man show going, he won't delegate, which is why he works so hard. In the world of the Marvel Comics Group, God doesn't look like Charlton Heston. He looks like Stan Lee.

If that's true, then Kirby was Marvel's lone atheist.

THE CIRCUMSTANCES OF JACK LIEBER'S last days are shrouded in mystery, but the existing evidence points to them being deeply unpleasant. Stan and Larry's father had lived alone since the death of his wife, never remarrying and becoming a bitter, solitary old man. He never showed a shred of appreciation for Stan's success in the comic-book trade. To him, Stan was just an apostate ex-Jew who had been nothing but a disappointment, and Larry—still toiling as a writer/artist on low-tier Marvel books—was scarcely better. In 1968, the octogenarian Jack suffered a heart attack, but that wasn't what killed him. "He died from a medical mistake," Larry recalls. It seems Jack's heart attack sent him to New York City's famed Belle-vue Hospital, where a doctor "treated his heart perfectly," as Larry puts it, "but he gave him so many depressants." I ask Larry if he means antidepressants and he responds, "The opposite. Things that would make you depressed." He pauses. "Let's just say he died of depression." I ask him if he means his father committed suicide. An even longer pause, then, "That, I don't want to go into anymore."

Our understanding of what happened is further clouded by the fact that Martha Leiber Dermer, the boys' cousin, tells me she had heard only that Jack died due to health problems and that she would've been told if it had been suicide. On the other hand, Martha's niece, Jennifer Bonvouloir, recalls her own mother—also Stan's cousin—telling her that Jack had hung himself: "I know our mother had told us that and that the reason Stan divorced himself from the rest of the family is because of what happened to his dad," she says. Whatever the circumstances, Jack was pronounced dead on February 26, 1968, an ocean and a continent away from the place of his birth, and was buried next to his wife in the Mount Lebanon cemetery in Queens. "I don't remember anything about my father's funeral," Larry says, then corrects himself, saying, "Well, I do, but I don't want to get into it."

Stan was even less descriptive than Larry in talking about their father's passing—the full extent of his public comments about his father's death consists of a brief paragraph in his memoir: "An unexpected phone call from my brother Larry told us, in a voice trembling with sorrow, that my father, who never remarried and had been living in Manhattan all these years, had died unexpectedly," he wrote. "We felt a sudden emptiness as we realized we could look forward to no more visits from him." Maybe such visits had been happening; maybe Stan was manufacturing them for the memoir to present an illusion of familial harmony. Either way, Stan was racked by guilt in the wake of the death, according to Larry. "Stan blamed himself for it, somewhat," the brother says. "My father wanted Stan to buy him a house." Stan never did. "And so Stan often thought, *Maybe I should have given . . .*" Larry trails off, then picks up again: "And I told Stan, 'No. It had nothing to do with a house. Dad had to go with a doctor who was stupid. Not you.' And he said to me, 'I'm so relieved to hear that.' So I was glad I could give him that."

That sort of kindness was not often repaid, says the younger sibling. "He was a stranger to me, really," Larry muses. "His feelings about me might have been ambivalent." He recalls Stan and Joan being cold and withholding toward him in venues both personal and professional. Larry was watching his brother's star rise while he himself "could hardly pay the rent," as he puts it. One day, Stan and Larry had a rare lunch together and Stan told him that he'd just made an investment that had yielded him $250,000. "And I thought to my-self, *What are you telling it to me for?*" Larry recalls with a slight sneer. "To me, that's like walking out in the street if you just had a good meal in a fine restaurant and telling a beggar in the street, 'Hey, you know what a good meal I just had?' . . . I wondered if he didn't do it just to be cruel."

Stan could be very generous toward Larry, paying for a few months of his brother's rent in 1968, when Larry moved into the studio apartment on the Upper East Side where he still resides. But that generosity was often followed by potshots. Larry bought a car around the time he moved into the studio, and the purchase meant obeying New York City's byzantine parking laws and moving his car multiple times a week, something that Stan heard about and decided to exploit. Larry recounts what followed this way:

> One day, he says to me, "Larry, as long as you're moving your car anyway, how about moving mine? I'll give you five dollars a week if you move my car." Five dollars a *week?* I was so insulted. I said, "If we had a close relationship, I'd do it for nothing! I wouldn't even take a dollar. But if you're going to offer money, that's it?" I thought to myself, *Would you offer Jack Kirby five dollars a week? Or anybody?* So I said, "No, I won't do it." Well, the next thing I hear, one of the days that I went over to visit the Goodmans, Jean Goodman tells me, "The strangest thing happened." I says, "What?" . . . They'd been out to dinner when Stan suddenly comes over to Jean and says, "What do you think of that schmuck brother of mine? I offer him fifteen dollars a week to move my car and he turns me down." So I said to Jean, "In the first place, it wasn't fifteen dollars. It was five dollars. In the second place, fifteen dollars a week is sixty dollars a month, and he could put his car in a lot for that much. . . ." So there you have your two opposites of the same man: a man who could be incredibly generous and who could be incredibly cheap.

Stan's generosity may have only intermittently extended to his brother, but it was abundant for his wife and daughter. Joan aspired to a high-society lifestyle and, in Larry's estimation, saw Larry as too déclassé to associate with them. He remembers her coming to the Marvel offices one day when Larry was there and saying to him, "Larry! How are you? You must come and visit us, but don't come for a while, because the weather is getting so nice now and the last time you came, you brought the rain. Ta-ta!" She turned on her heel and walked away. "One sentence and I was invited and disinvited, wasn't I?" Larry says. "That was Joan."

Joan was uninterested in Stan's line of work, as was their daughter. "I don't think my daughter has ever read a comic book in her life, and I doubt that my wife has," he told an interviewer around this time. "They get very bored if I even discuss the subject. All they want is the paycheck every week." Throughout their marriage, Joan was a profligate spender. By the reports of others and Stan's own admissions, she had something of a shopping addiction and accumulated piles of jewelry and strange tchotchkes: statues of animals, excavated minerals, and the like. Stan loved his wife deeply and, as such, rarely turned her down. JC followed in her mother's footsteps and developed a lifelong reputation for spending that was just as wild, if not more so. Stan desperately needed liquidity and a steady flow of income to keep the familial ship afloat. JC, now in her late teenage years, wanted to be an actor, and in 1968 Stan got her her own apartment in Manhattan so she could attend the American Academy of Dramatic Arts. Stan and Joan indulged in their own real estate decision: In addition to their Long Island home, they started renting an apartment in Manhattan where they could stay on weekdays. After a little while, they opted to sell the Long Island place outright and move into a large apartment on 60th Street.

JC dropped out of the academy after a year and began an itinerant existence, living it up in New York's nightclub scene and residing in a studio apartment across the hall from her parents. Around this period, she briefly worked as a receptionist at Marvel Comics, but "there was a pretty tremendously negative attitude toward her," recalls Neal Adams, and Larry Lieber says Stan was "very embarrassed" by her there. That said, she could be capable of great kindness. At one function, she encountered Isaac Tigrett, the man who would one day co-found the international restaurant chains the Hard Rock Cafe and the House of Blues but who was then just another hippie, giving away free LSD at parties. "I had gotten into my own stash of it too much—I was a really young man—and the next thing I knew, I was really in odd shape," Tigrett recalls. "And this beautiful, long-legged, blond, miniskirted lady came and rescued me and took me home with her in New York." There, he met Stan and Joan. "The Lees really nursed me back to health," he recalls, and he and JC "fell madly in love," even going so far as to get engaged for a time. But JC was protean, prone to changing her mood on a dime and often railing against her parents. As Larry recalls, "Stan used to say to me that she reminded him of *The Three Faces of Eve*," the infamous psychological horror film about a woman with dissociative identity disorder.

All family matters were kept extremely close to the vest while Stan set his professional aims higher and higher. In spring 1968, Marvel started advertising autographed photos of Stan—an honor not bestowed upon anyone else in the Marvel stable—and he went on to promote their sale throughout the summer. In a remarkable coup, he booked a spot on one of the most respected televised talk shows in America, *The Dick Cavett Show*, and appeared on May 30 of that year. On the show, he traded zingers with the titular host, who said Stan's comics were "very well written." In response, Stan claimed, as he often did, that he wanted to elevate comic books to the realm of high art. "We've been trying to give them a little more respect," he told Cavett. "After all, they are part of the media today, like radio and television. They are a method of communication, and there's really no reason why a comic book couldn't be well written and well drawn, just like anything else." This was a somewhat disingenuous bit of praise, given that Stan maintained private doubts about whether comics as a medium were worth his attention. But as public relations, it was brilliant: If you were a budding intellectual who enjoyed Marvel, getting a stamp of approval from the witty Cavett was no small endorsement, and it must have been thrilling to see your fearless leader taking to the upper echelons of the airwaves to declare that your obsessions were valid.

Stan even dreamed of starting a talk show of his own and took significant steps toward making that dream a reality. He assembled a roundtable of three young journalists—Louis "Skip" Weiss of *The Daltonian,* Chuck Skoro of the *Columbia Daily Spectator,* and Jeff Shero of underground paper *Rat*—and invited them to a studio, where he filmed about an hour's worth of discussion. The footage, stored in the Stan Lee archives in Wyoming, is disorienting to watch if your only point of reference for Stan is his wall-bouncing final form. Here, he sits in a muted blazer and striped tie, dark toupee atop his head and full beard across his chin, no shades to be found, and speaks with supreme measurement and subdued volume. Perhaps most astonishing, the show has virtually nothing to do with Marvel or comics. Instead, it's all about political issues facing American youth in 1968, that fevered year of rage and revolution. "I've been writing stories for the young generation for the past thirty years, and in the course of that time, well, I would imagine I receive about two to three hundred fan letters every day; probably as much as the Beatles," Stan says at the outset. "During this time, I think I've learned a lot about what young people think. More importantly, I think I've learned a lot about what young people *are.*"

The show's aim, he says, is to provide teens and twentysomethings with a platform to have their voices heard. However, whenever he's confronted with radical ideas, he is swift to denounce them from his point of view as a liberal member of what he calls "the Establishment." The war in Vietnam? He finds it "indefensible," but "there are too many other things involved" for it to just end right away. What of the agony of the African American population in an era of racist candidates calling for "law and order"? "I just don't think the solution is to throw bricks in windows or to say 'If the law doesn't satisfy us and it doesn't make everything perfect, then let's abandon the law or let's make up our own laws' " is Stan's conclusion. By the end, he's more or less throwing his guests entirely under the bus: "I don't think you fellas really have the answer because, while I think your objectives are right, I don't think you have the objectivity which is required, which I think will come later," he says. Perhaps most interesting, when Shero points out how Stan's anti-war leanings don't make sense because Marvel's comics "build up war and the excitement of battle and that sort of thing," Stan will hear none of it: "We *present* war in some stories; we don't try to make it a *fun* thing," he says. The show never made it to air.

All of this self-promotion may have been born from anxiety as much as excitement, given that Stan suddenly had to demonstrate his value to a new set of overlords. In June of 1968, Goodman was approached by thirty-six-year-old Martin Ackerman, the head of a conglomerate known as Perfect Film & Chemical. Perfect was already in the publishing business through its distribution arm, Curtis Circulation, and they wanted to flesh themselves out by snatching up Goodman's empire, comic books and all. Under the terms of the deal, Goodman would remain as publisher, his son, Chip, would become editorial director and eventually replace his father as publisher, and Stan would remain in charge of the comics. The sale moved at a breakneck pace, its terms finalized in July and executed as soon as the early fall.

The deal was a mixed bag for Stan. On the one hand, Ackerman had made it clear to Goodman that he very much wanted the ever-more-famous Stan to stick around as the public face of Marvel Comics. But at the same time, other than reportedly getting a five-year contract (probably the first formal employment contract he'd ever had) with provisions for a raise, Stan would not share in the windfall profit that Goodman had coming to him, despite all his labor over the decades. Goodman is said to have assured Stan it would all turn out right in the end, telling him the night after the deal was signed,

"I'll see to it that you and Joanie will never have to want for anything as long as you live." It was to be a true prediction, although the way in which it played out would ultimately be catastrophic for the relationship between the two old frenemies.

Stan may have still been the voice of Marvel after the sale to Perfect—soon to be renamed Cadence Industries—but it was unclear what exactly that voice was saying when it came to the apocalyptic politics of the time. He received criticism from the underground paper *The East Village Other* for not having enough black characters in his comics, and he indignantly replied with a letter listing the ones they did have. However, that critique may have been the impetus for his co-creation of a high-flying African American hero named the Falcon, who buddied up with Captain America and was allegedly modeled on winsome sports superstar O. J. Simpson. "Stan's Soapbox" columns occasionally denounced bigotry but never got into its root causes or the tough business of rectifying it. Spider-Man and Captain America delved into the campus conflicts of the day and expressed attitudes not dissimilar from Stan's own on his failed talk show.

In *The Amazing Spider-Man* #68, co-plotted by Stan and Romita, supervillain the Kingpin attempts to steal a precious artifact from the fictional Empire State University during a student protest for low-cost dorms led by a black acquaintance of Peter Parker's. Stan's dialogue played with fire, putting words like "whitey," "Uncle Tom," and "soul-brother" into black characters' mouths and depicting Peter as telling them to see the administration's side of the story and yelling, "*Anyone* can paint a *sign,* mister! *That* doesn't make you *right!*" There's no real resolution to the political questions posed by the comic, merely a bizarre deus ex machina in which the protest leaders are arrested on the false belief that they were linked with the Kingpin, something the reader is supposed to see as a positive event because the courts will surely exonerate them. Even jail is a bonus, muses Peter: "And they'll *all* have a chance to *cool off!*"

Captain America was the next to enter the miasma, jumping into the midst of a campus protest in *Captain America* #120, only to find that it's secretly being led by the villainous Advanced Idea Mechanics, whom he defeats. In the conclusion, a member of the radical movement genially shakes hands with a leader of the administration, and the two find a nice, liberal middle ground of cordial compromise. On the final page, Cap muses to a friend that he could never be part of a university because "the job's too *tough* for an old codger like *me!*" It certainly seemed like that had become Stan's general approach to the left/right and old/young divides that were ripping America apart: paternalistic sympathy with both sides but a reluctance to get too involved.

Stan was tentative about using his platform for provocative stances, but he was also contemplating giving up that platform entirely and trying to ascend to another one. Put simply, though he enjoyed the fame comic books had given him, he felt they had outlived their usefulness in his life. In a cinematic coup akin to the Fellini visit, Stan was approached by French filmmaker Alain Resnais, director of such masterworks as *Hiroshima Mon Amour* and *Last Year at Marienbad,* while he was in New York City working on a film about the Marquis de Sade. As it turned out, Resnais was a rabid Stan fan and claimed to have "read everything [Stan] had written" since the dawn of the Marvel revolution. Stan and Resnais became personal friends and, on May 14, 1969, Stan and Joan had the director over for dinner and drinks. For some reason, they chose to record audio of part of the evening's conversation and place the tape in the Wyoming archives. It's revealing, to say the least. For one thing, we learn that if Stan was socially centrist, he was economically somewhat conservative—he goes on and on about how "the taxes are very high in this country."

More important is what the tape uncovers about Stan's private views of the comic-book medium that was bringing him so much success. At one point, Resnais comments that it's "unbearable" to deal with people who read only comic books, and Stan pipes up to concur. "I can't understand people who read comics!" he cries. "I wouldn't read them if I had the time and wasn't in the business. I might look through them and read something good in comics, but I've got so many other interests!" Stan notes that his new contract has a clause stipulating that if he leaves the job, he can't work in publishing for a year afterward, and he points out that he doesn't really fear that. "I figure, for the first time, at my age—and I'm about your age—I feel it's time I started thinking of other things, you know?" he says. "So the contract really doesn't mean much." No, he has his eyes on bigger game, as he points out in a rant:

And I've been thinking myself of trying to write a play, trying to . . . I know some producers in this country who are trying to do a movie scenario. I was even thinking of writing some poems, like Rod McKuen and people like that, with some philosophy and some satire in them. The type of thing I put in the comics, like *The Silver Surfer* and *Spider-Man*. And I think I'm . . . My name may be well known enough that maybe these poems would sell. So the only problem is, as long as I'm here, I don't have the time to write them! And if I leave, I don't get the income, which I need to keep living! So I need to figure out how to do this.

Elsewhere in the conversation, Stan expresses admiration for his writer/artists and posits that "if I do movie work, I could take them with me." However, this seems overly optimistic in retrospect when it comes to the man whose labor had built the foundations of the Stan Lee edifice. Kirby wanted nothing less than to indefinitely continue his association with Stan. In January of 1969, Kirby moved to a suburb of Los Angeles for reasons having to do with the health of his daughter, and the new distance gave him a chance to think things through. Shortly thereafter, interviewer Mark Hebert spoke to Kirby about his life and work and, for perhaps the first time, Kirby openly claimed that he was the progenitor of the Marvel Universe. "You created and drew all of Marvel's standard heroes," Hebert said;

Kirby simply replied, "That's right." Stan didn't have a chance to be ticked off by those two words just yet, because the interview languished and wasn't published until 1976. But another provocation came a few months later, when interviewers Shel Dorf and Rich Rubenfeld spoke with Kirby and asked about Stan Lee; Kirby responded, "Stan Lee is my editor," before grimly adding that "whatever Stan Lee's policies are, they're my policies" because "I feel that's the artist's job, to cooperate with the policy of the publishing house."

That publishing house allegedly screwed Kirby yet again when Goodman paid him less than he paid Simon after the Captain America suit was settled in November 1969, thus violating the devil's bargain Kirby had made by siding with the company years prior. What's more, Kirby ran into trouble while negotiating a contract with the new bosses and turned to Stan for help, which Stan declined to extend. On the creative side, Stan told Kirby he could finally have an Inhumans series all to himself, with no shared creative credits for writing, but the book kept getting pushed further and further back in the schedule and never materialized. It was all too much.

DC chief editor Carmine Infantino had come to a Passover dinner at the Kirby household in California earlier in 1969 and told Kirby that he was welcome to defect to the other side. Kirby had shown him presentation boards for those post-Thor gods he'd been thinking about. Infantino loved them and said Kirby could do stories about them with total creative control. Jack Schiff, the DC editor who held a legal grudge against Kirby over the *Sky Masters* newspaper strip, was gone, opening a path to employment. The offer seemed more and more enticing as all the aforementioned nonsense with Marvel got worse, and finally Kirby came to a conclusion he perhaps should have come to far earlier. In February 1970, Kirby took his newly hired assistants, Sherman and Evanier, out to lunch at Los Angeles's famous Jewish deli, Canter's, and shocked them. "I've made a deal," Evanier recalls Kirby saying. "I'm gonna leave Marvel for DC."

On March 6, Kirby called Stan from California and told him he was leaving Marvel. Six days later, the news broke in the comics fanzine press. It was a development of titanic proportions among those who cared about comics. "When he left Marvel and came to DC," says comics professional, historian, and former fanzine writer Paul Levitz, "it felt like Nixon going to China." Stan always said he was stunned by the turn of events. In 2001, he was asked whether Kirby's departure had been a surprise and he replied, "Yeah. In fact, when he was in California, I remember we were still very friendly. I came to visit him a few times at his house," then reiterated, "We were very friendly until the end." In all the decades afterward, Stan never admitted to getting what the problem was. Evanier would later go on to work with Stan in a number of capacities, and he tells me Stan would often ask him about Kirby's reasons for leaving. "I'd explain them to Stan," Evanier says. "He would nod. And then three months later, he'd say, 'Can you explain to me what Jack is upset about?'"

AS THE LEE–KIRBY MACHINE was grinding to a halt, the problems of labor relations in comics were manifesting elsewhere in Stan's life. In 1969, he and DC's Infantino decided to form a new organization for comic-book professionals—it's unclear who had the initial germ of an idea, though Stan would claim it was all his. "I wanted it to be like the Motion Picture Academy of Arts and Sciences," Stan recalled. They dubbed it the Academy of Comic Book Arts (ACBA). The group was going to elect its leadership, and one day the aforementioned young artist Neal Adams found himself talking to Stan about the upcoming elections. "He insisted on running for the board of the academy," Adams recalls. Adams found this odd, as he thought the group would celebrate labor, not bosses, and Stan was one of the biggest bosses the industry had. "I'm as much a freelancer as anybody," Stan told Adams, referencing the fact that his writing was still technically paid for on a freelance basis. "I know I get a check each week for being editor, but I get freelance checks just like you guys!" "Stan, you're part of management," Adams responded. Stan countered, "No, that's my day job! I'm still a freelancer!" Although Adams remained skeptical, he conceded, and he and Stan ran for vice president and president, respectively.

They won. "I knew I was going to do all the work; it was clearly not in Stan's mind to do all the work of the academy," Adams says. "Stan could be the figurehead. You don't need to know Stan for long to know that's one of the things he likes to do." Stan saw the whole thing as a chance at repute for him and the industry he had come to dominate: "I felt that if we had an awards ceremony every year, we could probably get it on the radio and eventually, after we got a little more prestige, even have it televised," he later said. "I knew there were a lot of celebrities who were into comics, and that's all you need to get something on television—to get this actor or actress to serve as master of ceremonies." However, Adams, a real freelancer who knew the struggles of his fellow toilers, saw the formation of the ACBA as a chance to do something radical.

At a meeting of the group, Adams got up and spoke about how the assembled professionals should unite to demand benefits, higher wages, and ownership of their creations. Stan was aghast. "I remember saying to him and to the gathering in general that he might well be right in everything he said, but this was the wrong forum for that sort of discussion," Stan recalled. "They don't discuss those matters in the television academy; that's the kind of stuff you discuss in a union meeting. If Neal wanted to form a union, he should go ahead and do it, but the purpose of ACBA was to give our industry prestige, not to discuss the fact that artists don't have ownership or things like that." Stan's sympathies for the freelancers he had so wanted to identify with extended only so far, it seemed. "I wasn't interested in starting a union," he said, "so I walked away from it."

But perhaps the words Stan heard from Adams at the ACBA did have some kind of impact on him. On January 20, 1971, he spoke in a roundtable at a meeting of another group, the National Cartoonists Society. To the audience's surprise, Stan used some of his time to denounce comics in bitter terms. "I would say that the comic-book market is the worst market that there is on the face of the Earth for creative talent, and the reasons are numberless and legion," he said, then continued:

> I have had many talented people ask me how to get into the comic-book business. If they were talented enough, the first answer I would give them is, "Why would you want to get into the comic-book business?" Because even if you succeed, even if you reach what might be considered the pinnacle of success in comics, you will be less successful, less secure, and less effective than if you are just an average practitioner of your art in television, radio, movies, or what have you. It is a business in which the creator, as was mentioned before, owns nothing of his creation. . . . Isn't it pathetic to be in a business where the most you can say for the creative person in the business is that he's serving an apprenticeship to enter a better field? Why not go to the other field directly?

Stan may have seen fit to take a rhetorical shot at an unjust system, but overall the system was working just fine for him in 1971. That year saw the highest-profile media coverage of Marvel to date. First came a May 2 article in *The New York Times* about comics, in general, that heavily focused on the House of Ideas. In it, Stan took full credit for the ten-year-old Marvel revolution: "Because sales were down and out of sheer boredom, I changed the whole line around," he reminisced to the reporter. "New ways of talking, hang-ups, introspection, and brooding. I brought out a new magazine called *The Fantastic Four*." The article revealed that, at this point, Stan was actually coming to the office only two days a week—Tuesdays and Thursdays—and was spending the other five days at home, writing. The piece also claimed Stan was now "in the 50 to 60 percent income tax bracket," that "he has a very high-paying, five-year contract with Cadence Industries," and "when the contract expires, he says, he's not sure what he'll do."

In September, Stan's former secretary, Robin Green, wrote a long cover story for that bastion of hipness, *Rolling Stone,* solely about Marvel. It, too, gave full credit to Stan for the changes of the past decade, saying, "Stan had revolutionized the comic industry by giving his characters dimension, character, and personality." Stan told Green that he was primarily interested in entertaining readers but did have a smidge of ideology he wanted to convey. "I think the only message I have ever tried to get across is, For Christ's sake, don't be bigoted, don't be intolerant," he said. But he wasn't referring to bigotry against marginalized groups; he was talking about the virtues of being a centrist: "If you're a radical, don't think that all of the conservatives have horns. Just like if you're a John Bircher, don't think that every radical wants to blow up the nation and rape your daughter."

This kind of highfalutin, muddled liberalism was reaching new levels in his writing, too. In a "Soapbox" column, he responded to a letter (though it's entirely possible no such letter really existed) from a reader that accused Marvel of "trying to brainwash the public" with its tackling of the issues of the day. Stan took the middle path in response. "The radicals claim we're too archaic! The conservatives claim we're too liberal!" he wrote, before saying he and his cohort "represent virtually every shade of opinion" and that he was just happy a conversation had started: "If we can make you think—if we can anger you, arouse you, stimulate and provoke you, then we've served our purpose." Those provocations usually took the form of just depicting a controversial issue rather than digging into its roots and taking a stand. For instance, in partnership with the U.S. government, Stan helmed a story in *The Amazing Spider-Man* that warned kids against doing drugs, but the message was very surface-level: Peter Parker solved his friend Harry's pill addiction simply by beating the crap out of his dealer. Nevertheless, the story garnered significant press attention, bringing further renown to the Stan Lee name. It was a name Stan finally chose to enshrine in 1971 by legally adopting it, with Joan and JC following suit on their own surnames.

Right around that time, Stan was given another name, very much against his will. Kirby had launched three series at DC, acting as writer, artist, and editor on all of them. One was called *Mister Miracle,* and in its sixth issue Kirby introduced readers to a vain, toupee-wearing jerk with the memorable moniker of Funky Flashman, as well as his doting servant, Houseroy. As any hardcore comics devotee could instantly tell you, these were less-than-loving pastiches of Stan and Thomas. Funky loves himself even more than he hates doing real work, and he tries to get the title character on his side by showering him with insincere, alliterative compliments, while repeatedly showing cowardice in the face of battle. Kirby lent the supremely narcissistic figure an endless stream of loathsome dialogue: "*Image* is the thing, Houseroy!"; "I *know* my words drive people into a *frenzy* of adoration!!"; "Why—I look almost—*holy!*"; and the like. The end of the story finds Funky and Houseroy at a former slave plantation, where Funky blithely sacrifices Houseroy to a group of supervillains in order to save himself.

As Funky runs away, the plantation explodes behind him. He marvels at the burning estate and waxes poetic about unpaid labor: "*There it goes*—everything—up in flames! The mockingbird estate— and its *happy* memories! Mint *juleps! Cotillions! Happy* slaves singing for the *family!!!!*" He then launches into linguistic acrobatics ("Looks kinda *pretty,* though—*passion-red* flame against *undulating cyclopean black* smoke! A *marvel of contrast!*") before walking away from the disaster and thinking to himself, "On to *new* conquests, Funky Flashman!! You *winner,* you!!!" It was a brutal narrative assault. Roy Thomas later had lunch with Kirby and told the writer/artist that Stan "was kind of hurt by that Funky Flashman thing you did." In Thomas's recollection, "Jack just gave this nervous laugh. 'Well, you know, it was all in good fun.' And I just kind of shook my head and said, 'Yeah, okay.' Because, I mean, if there's one thing that I knew, it's that it was not in good fun. Stan knew it was not in good fun."

Stan was taking gutshots in other mediums, as well. In 1971, he finally made his play for Hollywood. He and Resnais concocted two film proposals. One was *The Inmates,* and it was to be "a contemporary romantic comedy, based on an intriguing fantasy premise," as Stan put it in a proposal. When humankind starts experimenting with space travel, aliens decide to "remove the cancer" that is our species and "destroy the planet Earth and its inhabitants in order to protect the universe." However, an extraterrestrial female named Dela comes to Earth to see if mankind deserves one last chance and encounters a newspaper columnist named Harry, "a confirmed bachelor, cynical, street-wise and world-weary. He's seen it all and done it all. But he's never seen anyone like Dela before!" Love and fish-out-of-water hijinks ensue. Ultimately, Dela gives up her alien immortality to live a human lifespan on Earth with Harry; moved by her sacrifice, the "galactic confederation" gives humans a stay of execution so we can try to improve ourselves and avoid the apocalypse. The audience was to be left with a message: "The choice is ours!"

Stan and Resnais went further in developing their other movie idea, *The Monster Maker.* For this one, Stan even wrote a screenplay—one of the few times in his life that he'd written a full script for anything—and Resnais was aching to direct it. The story was a curious sort of eco-parable, in which the cast and crew of a low-budget movie get mixed up in an adventure involving a sentient pile of garbage (the environmentalism was Resnais's idea, according to Stan). The action leads the producer, Larry Morgan—in a move perhaps echoing Stan's own aspirations—to abandon his schlocky past and write high-minded material about pollution. "I always wondered how you could bring yourself to keep grinding out such juvenile, unintellectual pabulum," Larry's ex-wife tells him near the climax. "But now, to think of you tackling a worthwhile theme like pollution—to think of you turning your back on commercialism in order to say something that must be said—Oh, Larry—I can't tell you how thrilled—how proud of you I am."

As the script nears its end, a montage depicting New York City's ecological problems plays while a character emits a portentous monologue. He begins, "We deserve no pity, for we have done this to ourselves," and concludes, "In all the world, there can be no greater horror story than this—the story we ourselves have written, the story in which we all must play a part—the final horror story of man's last days upon the planet Earth." According to Stan, a producer bought the script for $25,000. But, in Stan's retelling, the project fell apart when the producer demanded script changes and Resnais, refusing to let Stan's work be insulted like that, walked away from the deal. Whether that's true or not, the script never went anywhere, nor did the proposal for *The Inmates*.

There was one other stab at showbiz in the same period. A recent Yale graduate, aspiring filmmaker, and Marvel diehard named Lloyd Kaufman looked Stan up in the phone book and, in Kaufman's recollection, told him, "I'm a big fan. I wanna make movies." Stan immediately replied, "Come on over." The two met up, and Stan gave Kaufman a recording he'd made on quarter-inch tape—perhaps with that same tape recorder Kirby had seen—in which he'd outlined a movie idea called *Night of the Witch*. It was set in contemporary Salem, Massachusetts, where the titular immortal witch, who survived the Salem Witch Trials, goes on a terror spree. According to Kaufman, Stan wanted her targets to be bad guys, and Kaufman agreed but felt the bad guys should all be real-life evildoers: munitions manufacturers, greedy corporate stooges, et cetera—something Stan was uncomfortable with. "Stan was not political," Kaufman recalls; nevertheless, he "went with it," and Kaufman wrote up an entire screenplay for the film.

At the time, Kaufman was working for a low-budget film-production house called Cannon and, in his recollection, got in touch with a Cannon executive's independently wealthy wife, who read it and optioned it for about five hundred dollars. "I think Stan wasn't a big fan of Cannon," Kaufman recalls, and the sum they'd received was paltry to him. As Kaufman puts it, "Stan, I think, was not happy." Like Stan's work with Resnais, *Night of the Witch* languished. Nevertheless, Kaufman and Stan became close friends, and Kaufman went on to become a legendary schlock-film auteur, cofounding indie-film house Troma in 1974 and going on to make cult classics like *The Toxic Avenger* and *Tromeo and Juliet*. Kaufman tells me he and Stan attempted to get an updated *Night of the Witch* made again in 2014. It didn't work out.

Yet Stan's most humiliating event of the early seventies came not in a film exec's office but rather on one of the most famous stages in the world. Goodman's son, Chip, had concocted a deal with a promoter named Steve Lemberg whereby Lemberg bought the media rights to all of Marvel's characters. Lemberg admired Stan and reached out to him for consultation; the two became fast friends and hatched an idea. Lemberg proposed that Stan make a play for the big time by devising a one-night-only live show at Carnegie Hall. The show would not be a depiction of a Marvel story—no, it was to be a celebration of Stan himself. Stan leapt on board. They took out an ad in *The New York Times* to advertise the event and paid an estimated $25,000 to rent out the space. The plan was to have a series of acts come out and pay tribute to Stan and his great works. On Wednesday, January 5, 1972, the curtain rose. The whole thing was, by all accounts, a disaster.

Some of the acts were performed by Marvel employees: While Thomas's rock band played, secretaries danced in Fantastic Four costumes and artists drew, with Stan in the forefront, reading text aloud. Resnais spoke, as did actor René Auberjonois (much later known for playing Odo on *Star Trek: Deep Space Nine*) and none other than Tom Wolfe, who was an avowed Marvel reader. The tallest man in the world, Eddie Carmel, read a piece and cried due to excitement at being in Carnegie Hall. Jazz musician Chico Hamilton did a set and audience members, bored out of their minds, ripped

A street scene in Botoșani, the city of birth for
Stan Lee's father, Iancu Urn Liber, circa 1902.
(CIVIL BOOKS COLLECTION OF BOTOȘANI)

Stan Lee as
a young boy,
circa 1920s.

From left:
Stan, Jack, Larry,
and Celia Lieber
in the early
1930s.

Stan Lee on a bike as
a teenager. As he put
it in his memoir,
"That bike was my
best friend because it
gave me a feeling of
freedom. So what if
our family didn't have
a car. I finally had
wheels. I could ride
all over the city, go
wherever I pleased.
No kid ever loved
a bike more than
I loved mine."

Joan Lee's modeling photos, circa 1940s.

Stan and Joan Lee relaxing, circa 1940s.

Stan Lee during
his World War II
military service.

Joan Lee
holds JC
Lee, 1950.

Stan and JC Lee at the beach, circa 1950s.

Stan Lee at work, sometime in the 1950s.

Stan Lee and Jack Kirby
at the National
Cartoonists Society,
circa 1965.
(DAVID FOLKMAN)

Stan and Joan Lee,
dressed in costume
for a party,
circa 1960s.

Joan Lee with
glasses, fur,
and cigarette,
circa 1960s.

A page from *Mr. A*, a comics story that was written and drawn by Steve Ditko roughly a year after he left Marvel and was emblematic of his harshly moral politics.
(DITKO ESTATE)

The rarely photographed Steve Ditko at his parents' home in Pennsylvania in the early 1950s.
(DITKO ESTATE)

A promotional signed photo of Stan Lee, produced and sold by Stan Lee through advertisements in Marvel Comics, 1968.

Stan Lee meets with promoter Steve Lemberg, who then held the media rights for Marvel Comics, at the Marvel Comics offices on Madison Avenue, 1971.
(GETTY IMAGES)

A sketch of Marvel superhero the Thing in traditional Jewish garb, drawn by Jack Kirby on a Hanukkah card for a fan in 1975, during Kirby's final residency at Marvel
(DAVID FOLKMAN)

Remembering you at Hanukkah
And hoping you will find
That your holiday leaves many
Special memories behind.

HAPPY HANUKKAH

The Kirbys—

Stan Lee confers with artist John Romita, Sr., while the
two were working on the Spider-Man newspaper strip.

Stan Lee's
handwritten
note to
himself about
a book idea,
circa 1978.

DO NOVEL --
OR SERIES OR SHORT STORIES --
DEPENDING THIS
UNDEFENSIBLE.

I.E.: WAR IS GOOD
CRIME IS NECESSARY
HATRED IS IMPORTANT
MURDER IS ADMIRABLE

(WE KILL EVERYTHING. BUT
WE GET UPTIGHT ABOUT
A SINGLE MURDER.
IT'S BECAUSE OF
FEAR -- WE PROJECT
& IDENTIFY
W/ VICTIM.)

Stan and JC Lee appear together on a Father's Day edition of
Midday with Bill Boggs, 1979 (BILL BOGGS)

Stan Lee is greeted at his personal Rolls-Royce in the Marvel
Productions parking lot by a Marvel employee in a Spider-Man
costume, early 1980s.

JC Lee strikes a pose, circa 1980s.

One of Stan Lee and Jack Kirby's final meetings, at the 1989
San Diego Comic-Con. (SCOTT ANDERSON)

From left: Stan Lee, Joan Lee, Andrea Paul, and Peter Paul at a charity gala in Beverly Hills, California, 1997. (GETTY IMAGES)

The author and Stan Lee meet for the first time at the Wizard World comic-con in Rosemont, Illinois, circa 1998.
(MARGARET ROSS)

Stan Lee and the cast of *Who Wants to Be a Superhero?* at
San Diego Comic-Con, 2006. (GETTY IMAGES)

Stan Lee mugs for the camera with a bottle
of Excelsior, 2007. (DAVID FOLKMAN)

Stan Lee poses in front of Stan Lee.

From left: Larry Lieber, Stan Lee, and Ken Bald at the 2013
Wizard World New York City. (BOBBY MOONEY)

Keya Morgan and JC Lee on the red carpet for the premiere of
The Amazing Spider-Man, 2012. (GETTY IMAGES)

---

up comics and threw them at the stage. Joan and JC read from a self-serious poem Stan had written ("soon to be published in a book of poems of mine," he falsely claimed to the audience) called "God Woke," with JC feigning an English accent. "At one point, at the end of the show, Doctor Doom appears and supposedly takes Stan away," recalled Marvel writer Gerry Conway. "Then Stan's voice comes over the speakers: 'Okay, everybody, if you want me to come back, you have to sing "The Merry Marvel Marching Song."'" And there was deafening silence."

Then, blissfully, the whole affair ended, and Conway went backstage to soothe Stan by congratulating him. "He was sitting on a chair in the middle of the dressing room, and he looked so exhausted and brain-dead," Conway says. "A little kid was talking to him about how excited he was, and he was saying, 'Thank you,' but he looked like a guy who was hit upside the head by a two-by-four."

Soon afterward, Stan took a much-needed vacation and visited Goodman at the latter's condo in Palm Beach, Florida. There, Goodman may have broken some news to Stan: After four decades in the publishing game, he was retiring. The plan was for Chip to take over as publisher of Marvel Comics. "Stan was very unhappy about that," recalls Thomas. "They just didn't get along well and Stan was increasingly restive at that stage." Stan, it seems, executed a plan to seize control and expel the Goodmans from his professional life, once and for all. "Martin had his son working there, and he told Cadence that he wanted the son to be the publisher after he left," Stan would recall late in life. "I said to Cadence, 'If he's the publisher, I'm quitting.'" Rumors were swirling that DC was courting Stan as it had courted Kirby. Stan remained a massive brand name inside the comics industry, and Cadence CEO Sheldon Feinberg had no interest in losing him. So Feinberg made Stan an offer: Stan would now be president of Marvel Comics.

But that wasn't all. He was also being made publisher of Marvel. Chip would be publisher of Martin Goodman's overall company, Magazine Management, meaning he'd still be Stan's boss, but Stan would have far more leeway than he otherwise would have. As Stan later put it, "That was my one bit of revenge." More than thirty years after Stan had first been hired by his cousin-in-law, he was taking the elder man's place. Finally, Stan would have the chance to show how much better he was than his professional father figure. But the opportunity was bittersweet, as it also meant he'd have to give up his writing duties. That was probably for the best. Losing Kirby had been like losing a limb, and he hadn't since garnered the kind of praise he'd had when the two were working together. Indeed, he never would again. Stan's good days as a respected creator of new material were, unbeknownst to him at the time, permanently over.

When Stan left the editor's chair, Roy Thomas was anointed as his successor—"in a kind of half-assed way," as Thomas once recalled. "All I know is, he called me in and suddenly told me he was now going to be the president and publisher of Marvel Comics; the company was going to be a whole separate kind of company, no longer just kind of the tail on the Magazine Management dog; and he was in charge," Thomas tells me. "I was going to be the 'story editor' or something like that. Not editor-in-chief, just story editor." Others would take on various other tasks that Stan had previously busied himself with, but, after some back-and-forth, he concluded that such an arrangement was too complicated. Thomas was named as the head editor and John Romita, Sr., was installed as art director. The new regime was in place.

In an extra-long "Soapbox," Stan informed his loyal followers about what was going on. "I'll finally have the time (after all these years of writing and kibitzing) to devote myself exclusively to dreaming up new exciting projects for the Bullpen," he wrote, "new directions for us to take, new types of mags to produce—both comix and other kinds, and new fields for Marvel to conquer in film, TV, books, and you-name-it-we'll-do-it!" He assured fans that the "Soapbox" columns would continue apace and that he would never leave their lives. His conclusion was chipper: "Hang loose! Face front! Marvel's on the move again! We're pushing Phase Two—and it's all for you!" But for Stan's career, it was really phase three. The first had been his unrecognized toiling until 1961, and the second had been his bumpy, meteoric rise since. In the third, he would no longer write the characters that made his reputation, but he would finally perfect the details of the character that would allow him to stay famous until the end of his life.

6.

CHAFING IN
THE C-SUITE

———

(1972–1980)

STAN'S SUCCESSOR SOON RAN INTO A MINOR CRISIS, AND STAN was the cause. Gerry Conway had been given the task of writing *The Mighty Thor* in Stan's wake, and Roy Thomas was very pleased with the work that had emerged, especially the dialogue. "He was the only person besides Stan and myself that understood the kind of quasi-Shakespearian dialect that Stan had gradually drifted into for Thor, the 'thou's and everything," Thomas recalls. Though Thomas was generally in charge, Stan couldn't quite let go of his old editing instincts: He still mandated that he'd get approval privileges for all the covers of the comics and would occasionally even micromanage interior pages. One day, Stan was reviewing interiors for an issue of *The Mighty Thor* and saw the so-called splash, meaning an initial page designed to dazzle the reader as an introduction. "Stan saw the splash page: a little quiet character standing around or walking around, drawn by John Buscema," Thomas says. "It was way too quiet. And he happened to see Gerry Conway in the hall. So, instead of going to me as his editor and saying, 'I'm not happy, it's a little too quiet, this and that,' which is what he would ordinarily do, he just grabs Gerry and says, 'This is no good. This is no good.'"

The gentle Conway was shocked. "I spent the next two or three hours after Gerry came out of the office persuading him not to quit *Thor,* if not the whole company," Thomas says. "And Stan couldn't understand that. I said, 'Look, you're the publisher. You're the guy who created this whole thing and the publisher on top of it. You come down like a ton of bricks on somebody, they're not going to look on it as just 'Do better next time.' They're going to look on it as 'My whole future is in jeopardy here' or something. You've got to act through me a little bit more, or you're going to scare people away." Thomas emphasizes that this happened only once and that Stan took his advice to heart. Nevertheless, it demonstrates two key facts about this new stage of Stan's life and career: One, Stan was standing at the base of a difficult learning curve due to his executive status, and two, that status would make his relationships with creators even more tense and complicated.

Stan had plans, ones that Goodman would never have considered. He swiftly abandoned the role of president, because he couldn't stand worrying about charts and numbers, but he embraced his publisher title with gusto. He reached out to novelists Anthony Burgess and Kurt Vonnegut about contributing work to Marvel, as well as to Czechoslovakian dissident playwright Václav Havel, of all people. None of them bit, but he had better luck with a fellow DeWitt Clinton grad, the great cartoonist Will Eisner, with whom he corresponded about developing a new magazine. It appears that the men wanted it to be a flippant mix of real news and ambitious satire. A few memos between the two of them, outlining some ideas for the periodical, survive at the Stan Lee archives. Among the proposed topics: "PORNOGRAPHY" ("Pornography is no longer interesting so what's next??"); "HIJACKING: THE CURRENT STATE OF THE ART" (including "advertisement by tourist bureaus of poor countries who can't get tourists any other way—'Come to beautiful Conga, we have accommodations . . . Hijack your next plane to our country'"); "BLACK COUNTRIES WITH ANTI-WHITE POLICIES" ("Funny sequence about whites [British maybe?] in a sort of white ghetto"), and, most eyebrow-raising of all, "SHALL WE LEGALIZE RAPE?" ("With the new liberation of women—with the new standards of sexual relations the old laws and does their criteria have to be changed—What about women raping men? What about homosexuals?"). It, like the celebrity collaborations, never materialized.

However, other publications did emerge from Stan's edicts. There was *FOOM,* a fan-oriented periodical about Marvel (its title was an acronym for "Friends of Ol' Marvel"), containing exclusive features and interviews. The Comics Code Authority had relaxed its standards on depictions of horror stories, so Stan decreed that black-and-white comics magazines with titles like *Vampire Tales* and *Monsters Unleashed* be produced. There were attempts to capture women and minority readers: *Master of Kung Fu* depicted an Asian American Bruce Lee type; *Red Wolf* showed the travails of a Native American hero; *Night Nurse* and *Shanna the She-Devil* vied for female eyeballs (with limited success); and, seeing the box-office success of movies like *Shaft* and *Sweet Sweetback's Baadasssss Song,* Stan said Marvel should have its own blaxploitation hero, leading to the creation of a jive-talking, Harlem-based, money-minded superhuman named Luke Cage. All of these comics bore a new heading on their title pages: STAN LEE PRESENTS. Even when he wasn't doing anything to directly create a given comic book, his name still came first in the credits.

But you didn't need to look inside a comic to find him. Stan was even more ubiquitous than he had been during his late-sixties heyday, blitzing through interviews and appearances at a lightning pace. There he was in one of the hippest magazines in the country, *Creem,* starring in a cover story about Marvel: "The present comic book scene is largely the work of this Stan Lee, Publisher and former Editor of Marvel," it declared before quoting him as saying, "I think you're going to find in the next year or so that Marvel is going to come out with a lot of things that will take people by surprise." Stan finally made a movie debut of sorts, narrating portions of Alain Resnais's impressionistic art-house film *L'An 01* ("The Year 01").

Above all, he was milking his popularity on college campuses for all it was worth. It seemed he'd appear at any school, anywhere: famed institutions like Notre Dame or University of Texas at Austin one day, lesser-known locales like Nassau Community College or Montana State University the next. Posters at the schools almost invariably described him as the supreme individual of his accidental medium: THE RENAISSANCE MAN OF THE AMERICAN COMIC STRIP, read one; STAN LEE, CREATOR OF MARVEL COMICS, read another. One letter from a student requesting an appearance spoke of how the student wished to "expose the unbelievers" to the "wonders" of Marvel and vowed, "We recognize the place of your mags in the realm of literature."

Stan's schedule for these appearances could be frenzied: One itinerary in the archives shows him appearing at seven schools over the course of just two months, with a featured spot at a comics convention and time on a Canadian late-night show sprinkled in. He signed with a lecture-coordination agency called the American Program Bureau, which put together promotional materials touting his genius: a one-sheet text biography recounting the origin and evolution of Marvel (Jack Kirby was nowhere to be found and Goodman wasn't mentioned by name, only as "someone else" who used to run the company) and a goofy comic strip in which a superheroic Stan was envisioned as "Speaker-Man," flying to the rescue of program directors ("Simply *give* them what they want—let the *king* of the *comic-books* be your next speaker!" he shouted). If you went to see Stan live, you got a glimpse of his new look: Gone was his beard, replaced by a mid-thickness mustache "that my wife liked," as he would later recall; fake salt-and-pepper hair was placed atop his bald dome (a toupee most of the time, though he experimented with hair plugs); and he had his glasses tinted to protect his eyes from the sun. These elements would, as it turned out, be a large portion of the visual presentation that would become iconic for his brand. His rapport with the public had never been stronger.

At the same time, his connections with creators back home at

Marvel were ever more tenuous. He was particularly difficult for Conway, a star writer who endured a number of Stan's whims and rebukes. The most infamous incident involved the tragic death of a bombshell blonde. Conway had been teamed up with Romita on *The Amazing Spider-Man,* and at one point in late 1972 or early 1973, the topic of juicing sales with a shocking story was raised by the editorial team; Thomas, though, has claimed the idea didn't originate with Stan. "Roy Thomas had said, 'We're thinking of killing Aunt May,'" Romita recalls. "Said they wanted to test the fandom, so we're gonna have to kill somebody." Conway and Romita weren't sold on the choice of victim—as Romita puts it, "If you kill Aunt May, you're gonna have one less burden on Peter Parker's personal life." So the creative duo met at Conway's apartment to hash out alternative ideas. Conway and Romita each claim to be the one that landed on the ill-fated winning candidate: Gwen Stacy, one of Peter's love interests.

Marvel wasn't historically much of an abattoir—characters generally stayed alive, no matter the dangers they faced, making this a major departure from the norm. "Stan was the publisher, and any big idea had to pass with his approval," Conway says, and he insists that he got the green light from Stan to move forward with the tale. And so, in early 1973, Marvel published a two-part story known as "The Night Gwen Stacy Died," in which supervillain the Green Goblin tosses the woman off a bridge. Spidey shoots webs at her legs, and although it's left ambiguous whether the fall or the web-induced whiplash kills her, she's dead as a doornail by the end. Fans were furious. As Conway puts it, "Stan found himself in positions at various colleges where he was doing speaking tours of being asked constantly, 'How can you kill off this beloved character?'"

So Stan started telling people that he'd been out of town when the death warrant was signed and that he had nothing to do with the story. Even decades later, Stan stuck to that story; in a 1998 interview, he said, "I think [Conway] was quoted somewhere as asking me whether he could kill her off and I said yes. I don't remember that and can't believe I would have." Conway remains miffed about the situation but gets why it went down the way it did: "Stan doesn't like controversy," he told me a few years before Stan died. "He's a guy who likes to be liked. He likes to be friendly. He doesn't want to create stress and be the subject of stress."

Right around the same time, Stan informed Conway that Marvel had signed a deal to make a toy car for Spider-Man and that the writer had to introduce the vehicle in the comic. The ridiculousness of a high-flying web-slinger driving through New York City traffic drove Conway nuts, leading him to write the story such that two loathsome businessmen develop the car and ask Spidey to drive it— one of the gents looked an awful lot like Stan, and his business card bore the real-life address of Marvel Comics.

The situation at that address disintegrated further when the ghosts of Stan's corporate maneuvering came back to haunt him. In 1974, Chip Goodman's contract with Cadence ran out, and Sheldon Feinberg chose not to renew it. Stan, as a result, became the publisher of Magazine Management as a whole—he truly was the new Martin Goodman. But the old Martin Goodman, along with Chip, soon made the decision to strike back and attempt to destroy the company the elder man had created. That summer, they formed a new publishing company, Seaboard Periodicals, which had a comics arm named Atlas, leading historians to refer to it as Atlas/Seaboard. The Goodmans started to hunt for top-tier talent, promising creator-friendly incentives that they never would have considered while running Marvel: high page rates, ownership of original artwork, even—astoundingly—creator ownership of characters. The mainstream press caught wind of the new venture and wrote about it in terms befitting a clash of titans: "Other, smaller comics publishers have tried to challenge the Big Two (notably the Charlton line), but they have never had the expertise (and incentive) represented by Atlas," wrote a reporter in the *Philadelphia Daily News*. "The new company might well be the Marvel of the 1970s." In the industry, Atlas/Seaboard gained a nickname: "Vengeance, Incorporated."

People who had worked at or currently worked at Marvel, including Conway, Ditko, and even Stan's own brother, Larry, joined the Goodmans' enterprise. Larry had been deeply dissatisfied with Stan—it was around this time that he asked Stan for work and got that comment from an editor that Stan didn't consider Larry to be part of his family. Larry recalls taking lunch with Goodman and getting a confidence boost. "Martin gets angry: 'That son of a bitch, why doesn't he give you some work?'" Larry remembers. So Larry went to Stan and said he was thinking of jumping ship. "He says to me, 'Well, I guess you've got to go over there and give [Goodman] the work, but I'd rather you didn't write for them. But I guess I can't ask you to do that,'" Larry says. "The guy's got millions! I can't pay my rent! And he's telling me not to write for them!" Indignant, Larry made a rare stand against his brother and went to Atlas/Seaboard.

Stan sensed that Marvel was in trouble and put together an impassioned two-page letter that he sent to his freelancers, urging them not to work for other companies, though it was clear that the Goodmans' firm was the one he was primarily concerned about. Paragraph three was somewhat astounding in its grandiosity, comparing the Jewish Goodmans to Hitler:

> Unfortunately, the fact that we're big, the fact that we're solidly financed, and the fact that we're ethically responsible actually acts against us. It's like Nazi Germany and the Allies in World War Two. Hitler, being a dictator and having no one to answer to, could do as he wished whenever the mood struck him, and could make the most extravagant promises to his captive people, while being completely heedless to the consequences. The U.S. however had to move slowly, following firmly established principles of law and government. Marvel, like the Allies, simply cannot counter-react with impetuous pie-in-the-sky offers and promises.

Stan listed Marvel's virtues: rising pay rates, health and life insurance for the most loyal freelancers, exposure through a nascent co-publishing venture with Simon & Schuster, and a possible future with bonuses and the return of original artwork for creators. "Furthermore, no company has a greater respect for the creative person than Marvel," Stan wrote. "It was this writer who founded ACBA, for the purpose of bringing new stature to the artisans in our field. It was this writer who first instituted the practice of prominent credits to erase the former anonymity of editors, artists, writers, and letterers." He concluded with a staccato plea of dubious veracity: "Marvel has never lied to you. Marvel never will. Stay with us. You won't regret it."

As it turned out, Stan needn't have worried all that much—Atlas/Seaboard was poorly managed and folded after just a few months. Stan and Martin Goodman were estranged all the way until Goodman's death in 1992, and the former would often denigrate the latter in interviews as the years wore on. Near Stan's own death, he did an onstage interview where he was particularly blunt about the relative without whom he would never have had a career. In recounting the origin story of Spider-Man, he said Goodman had been initially skeptical about the character—that part Stan had said many times before—but punctuated the anecdote by saying, "I got to do the kind of books I wanted to do, not the kinds of things that moron wanted." The audience laughed and cheered, but Stan didn't crack a smile. "As you can tell," he said, "I was not his biggest fan."

Thomas had dutifully echoed Stan's anti-Goodman sentiment during the Atlas/Seaboard imbroglio, telling freelancers that their future work would be in jeopardy if they defected to Marvel's former owner. But soon, he, too, reached a breaking point. As the story goes, there was a fateful meal between Stan and DC chief Carmine Infantino around the middle of 1974. According to Thomas, the two publishers discussed the fact that freelance artist Frank Robbins had been going back and forth between their companies and misrepresenting his page rates in order to drive the price up. "Stan told me, 'Carmine and I made an agreement that from now on he can call here and get our rates, and we can call there and get his,'" Thomas recalls. This was, of course, price collusion—a serious financial crime. "I thought about it and I wrote Stan a memo saying I just didn't think that was right," Thomas says. "I don't know if it's even legal and it certainly isn't something we should be doing, and I won't enforce it." Thomas's situation at Marvel had already been a bit tenuous of late: He'd been clashing with Stan's successor as president, a man named Al Landau. Thomas says he would push for more creator rights and Stan would initially agree with his protégé, but then Stan would back down once Landau pushed back. "By becoming publisher, [Stan] had gone from being creative force to total company man, which was what he wanted—but I didn't want to follow him along that path as I had before," Thomas said.

So when the alleged collusion incident occurred and Thomas handed Stan the memo objecting to it, Stan suggested that maybe the memo was really a letter of resignation. "And I said, 'Well, you know, if you want it to be,'" Thomas recalls. At the last minute, Stan changed his mind—he didn't want to fully lose the wunderkind who had served him so well, so they hammered out a deal whereby Thomas would step down as head editor and instead write comics that Thomas himself would edit, reporting only to Stan as publisher. A power vacuum had been created and chaos ensued, with a mad scramble to find a new head editor, and the process led to Gerry Conway getting screwed yet again. According to Conway, Stan had previously made him a promise: "Stan told me, 'Well, Ger'—in the kind of friendly, glad-hand sort of way Stan has—'if it ever worked out that Roy leaves the company, we want you to take over as editor.'" But when Thomas did, indeed, leave his post, Stan divided the role in two and gave the color comics to writer Len Wein and the black-and-white ones to another writer, Marv Wolfman. To add insult to injury, not long after the new regime was installed,

Stan decreed that Gwen Stacy had to come back, and Conway was stuck with the awkward task of undoing his own work. He painstakingly crafted a tale that split the difference by introducing a *clone* of Gwen, but, according to Conway, when Stan saw the published story, he said, "This doesn't really work, does it?" When I ask Conway for his general estimation of Stan, he pauses for a moment and replies, "He's a *good* guy. He's just not a *great* guy."

That comment is revealing. Talk to anyone who worked for Stan in his days as publisher and they'll tell you something similar, or at least allude to it. His employees and freelancers were aware of his shortcomings, but many of them also admired his strengths: his work ethic, his tenacity, his geniality. "He had a very dynamic personality, he was always on the go, he was always working hard," recalls Jim Salicrup, who worked as a teenage messenger in the Marvel offices in the seventies and later became an editor. "There was a friendly vibe in the bullpen in that, even though he was clearly the boss, he was Stan. Everyone was on a first-name basis. He would go out of his way, just like if he was at a convention, to treat everyone as well as he possibly could. He didn't just whiz in and just go to his office. If he saw ya, it'd be"—here, Salicrup launches into a pitch-perfect impression of Stan's voice—"'Abe! How are ya? How ya doin'? I gotta run, Sol wants this . . .' and he'd be on his way." That friendliness, however brief, was key, Salicrup thinks: "People could look at it as being manipulative, but he had to make the people working with him be as happy to do it—to enjoy it as much as he was enjoying it—as possible." One has to remember that such cheer, bonhomie, and praise stood in stark contrast to that of many other editors that the staff and army of freelancers dealt with in the cutthroat comics industry. "Up until Stan, their treatment was 'Here's your check; go away,'" Salicrup muses. "And with him, it was like 'Yeah, he actually knows I have some talent and he saw what I did there.' . . . I think they would just enjoy that kind of appreciation that they'd never had before."

This personable approach was miles away from Goodman's aloofness, but in other dimensions, Stan was turning into Goodman more than he'd ever admit. For one thing, as we've seen, he had become a relentless trend-chaser, imitating whatever was popular in comics and pop culture at large. But for another thing, in the realm of magazines, he was churning out piles of low-grade, derivative content in an effort to grab eyeballs on the newsstand. He helmed a weird *People* knockoff called *Celebrity,* which employed Joan Lee as a contributing editor and couldn't quite decide what time period it was in. For example, the November 1976 issue featured strange takes on current events, including an astrologer's horoscope predictions about that fall's presidential election and a Cindy Adams–penned gossip column that accumulated dull data points (e.g., "Over some beautiful food and gorgeous music at the Monsignore I learned that the Empress of Iran is a licensed helicopter pilot and so I figured why should I know this and you shouldn't—right?"), but the cover story was about Old Hollywood actor Mae West, who hadn't been even remotely relevant in decades, and there was an interview with erstwhile gangster Mickey Cohen, who'd been out of the crime game for twenty years.

Even more stuck in the past was another of Stan's magazine creations, *Nostalgia Illustrated,* which would profile performers of the vanished black-and-white era, like actor John Garfield and diminutive performer Johnny Roventini. The general-interest mag *Pizzazz* never quite connected with the youth it was aimed at—for example, the first issue awkwardly tried to cash in on *Star Wars* mania by showing a photo of robots R2-D2 and C-3PO with an overlaid dialogue bubble reading "It's Darth Vader with the ultimate weapon . . . *a can opener!*" And perhaps the weirdest of them all was *Film International,* a magazine mostly dedicated to risqué and outright pornographic movies that doubled as an excuse to throw *Playboy*-esque parties where Stan could be photographed alongside celebrities. However, he could never quite get the top tier of talent for them: A print spread about the party for the mag's 1975 debut announced the presence of names that have since become obscure for the average American: Cornel Wilde, Bob Radnitz, Dimitra Arliss, Ray Bolger, and the like.

Stan had one victory in the mainstream publishing market, but it consisted mostly of comic-book content. In 1974, he scored a minor coup when the venerable book publisher Simon & Schuster released *Origins of Marvel Comics,* a compilation of classic Marvel stories with accompanying text from Stan about how the characters were created. Kirby and Ditko featured prominently in the form of effusive praise from Stan for their drawing abilities, but it was staunch in its assertion that Stan was the progenitor of each and every piece of intellectual property. Just as important as the book itself was the publicity blitz that accompanied it, with Stan appearing in dozens of broadcast spots and print stories. In them, Stan would attempt to legitimize comics, even as he privately stewed in irritation with the medium and industry. "Suppose Michelangelo were alive today and suppose Shakespeare wanted to collaborate with him on a comic strip," he told *Women's Wear Daily,* in a thought experiment that he'd go on to repeat ad infinitum over the ensuing decades. "Would the product of their collaboration be any less important because it was just a comic strip?"

None other than the esteemed author Ray Bradbury provided further legitimization with a *Los Angeles Times* review of the book, albeit a slightly undermining one: "I have been accused on several occasions of being anti-intellectual. I plead guilty to the charge," Bradbury wrote. "I would gladly draw and quarter pretend liberals who wind up being reactionary conservatives against rockets and space travel. And now, with Stan Lee's book 'The Origins of Marvel Comics' in my hands, I realize I have one more to add to the list: intellectuals who don't understand comic strips, never read the stuff and advise against it." The book was a sales success and was followed by three sequels in as many years: *Son of Origins of Marvel Comics,*

Bring on the Bad Guys, and *The Superhero Women.* Such success in bookstores must have been gratifying, but the fact was that it was all still about superhero comics, an ecosystem Stan wanted out of.

While Stan was attempting to garner acclaim in the mainstream, he also made a stab at increased relevance by entering the world of the undergrounds. The year 1974 saw the debut of a Marvel series that was as fascinating as it was short-lived: *Comix Book.* Note well the "x" in the place of the "cs": Ever since the late sixties, the term "comix" had been adopted by creators who produced outré, experimental, provocative, and often-obscene comic books that were targeted at adults and sold in head shops and other offbeat venues instead of traditional newsstands. The comix revolution had produced cult superstars like R. Crumb, Art Spiegelman, Trina Robbins, Kim Deitch, Gilbert Shelton, and Spain Rodriguez, and one of the leading publishers of their work was a Wisconsin-based independent businessman named Denis Kitchen.

Kitchen had been a Marvel fan since he'd started picking up *The Fantastic Four* and *The Amazing Spider-Man* as a teenager in the mid-sixties: "They were a breath of fresh air because I had dutifully read all comic books, including DC, but I always found DC comics of that era really boring and predictable, while what Stan did was truly fresh," he tells me. In 1969, when Kitchen published an underground anthology called *Mom's Homemade Comics,* he boldly sent a copy to Stan and was shocked to receive a reply. "Your mag was really funny—I enjoyed every page," Stan wrote. "In a way, I envy you . . . it must be a blast to just let yourself go and do whatever tickles your funnybone."

The two struck up an unlikely correspondence in the ensuing years, with missives bouncing back and forth between the backwater underdog kid and the big-city Establishment veteran. In 1972, shortly after Stan became publisher, he asked Kitchen to meet him in New York, where he presented the lad with an off-the-wall idea: What if Marvel published its own underground-comix series, with Kitchen acting as editor? They couldn't get it past the Comics Code

Authority, so Stan said it could come out as a magazine. "I don't think he really thought undergrounds were going to take over and supplant Marvel, but there was an energy there," Kitchen tells me. "What he was always good at was spotting trends and then, frankly, mimicking trends." Kitchen was intrigued but skeptical.

Eventually, the underground icon agreed to the endeavor but demanded that the contributors be allowed freedoms that were entirely off-limits to Marvel's existing creators: return of original artwork, near-total creative freedom, and ownership of their creations. Stan was reluctant on all counts, so they worked out compromise measures: Original artwork would be returned; copyrights would initially be owned by Marvel but eventually revert to creators; and they could be somewhat outrageous but were barred from depicting full-frontal nudity, the word "fuck," or off-color parodies of Marvel superheroes. As Kitchen puts it, "He broke some rules, thinking, *These hippies go in a separate box*."

Tensions rose as the series developed: There were fights over content, and Stan, ever cautious, started to waffle on how much he wanted Marvel and his own name to be associated with the finished product, eventually telling Kitchen that it would be published without a Marvel insignia and that he, Stan, would ambiguously be credited as "Instigator." The first issue of *Comix Book* debuted in October of 1974, but it ended up having only four subsequent installments, despite (according to Kitchen) decent sales. It was plagued by one big problem: There seems to have been tremendous resentment from longtime Marvel creators over the freedoms and privileges awarded to the *Comix Book* contributors. "I'm convinced they killed it over the political feedback he was getting from the regular bullpen," Kitchen says. "It's a small industry and, at some point, some of those older guys working for Stan said, 'What the fuck are you doing, giving these hippies a better deal than you're giving us?' And Stan didn't have an easy answer. He thought it was a lock-box they would never see, which was naïve on his part." Once again, despite his friendly nature, Stan couldn't quite bring himself to favor workers' rights over corporate priorities, and he paid a price as a result. What's more, he was about to enter a surprising chapter in the greatest labor–management dispute of his career.

KIRBY HAD THOUGHT HE'D find salvation at DC. Instead, he found only disappointment. He'd started out with something revolutionary—an epic, ongoing, cosmic saga chronicled in four interlinked monthly series: *Superman's Pal Jimmy Olsen, Mister Miracle, The New Gods,* and *The Forever People*. The latter three were entirely based on characters of his own creation. Together, they bore the cryptic title of "The Fourth World," and the initial plan was for him to launch them before handing them off to others and acting as a kind of creative director. However, there had been a thicket of snags: DC wanted Kirby to stay on as writer/artist of all four, a turbulent comics market hurt sales, editorial interference resulted in aborted storylines and redrawn artwork, and Kirby's idiosyncratic scripting style alienated many readers. In subsequent decades, his Fourth World characters—most notably the supervillain Darkseid— would become world-famous DC staples, with an Ava DuVernay-directed New Gods movie in development since 2018. But at the time, the company was tepid on these figures.

After about a dozen issues of each title, DC canceled the line and forced Kirby to come up with unrelated comics, which he dutifully did, only to face further skepticism from the higher-ups and the public. According to Mark Evanier—by then ensconced for years as Kirby's assistant and confidant—a breaking point came in 1975, when DC was running into dire financial straits and word came down that Infantino was being fired (Evanier also claims DC made overtures to Stan about replacing Infantino, but nothing came of them). Kirby's contract was coming up and, as Evanier puts it, "Jack realized at that point that he was not going to get a good deal out of DC and—to use a *Titanic* analogy—he didn't want to go down with the ship." Stan had repeatedly spoken and written about his affection for Kirby, even going so far as to occasionally publicly declare that he'd love to work with his erstwhile partner again.

And so, when word got out that Kirby was about to potentially be a free agent, Marvel made him "not a good offer, but a safer offer," as Evanier puts it, and he accepted. However, he would stay away from any of his sixties series and would, instead, do a new series called *The Eternals,* helm an adaptation of the film *2001: A Space Odyssey,* take over *Black Panther,* and return to his old warhorse, *Captain America*—with sole credit as writer and penciler on everything. When I ask Kirby's other assistant, the California-based Steve Sherman, whether Kirby was nervous about working for Stan again, he replies, "No. As long as Stan knew what the deal was, Jack was fine with it, 'cause he was here and Stan was back in New York, so he didn't have to see him."

On March 22 through 24, 1975, Marvel convened its own comics convention, the Mighty Marvel Convention, at New York City's Hotel Commodore, and the centerpiece of the event came on the second day. During a panel about the Fantastic Four, Stan announced a surprise guest: the so-called King of Comics himself. Kirby walked onstage to thunderous, shocked applause, and Stan informed the crowd that Kirby was returning to his old stomping grounds. "Whatever I do at Marvel," Kirby declared, "I can assure you that it'll electrocute you in the mind!" Stan corrected him: "*Electrify,* Jack! *Electrify!*"

One of the great paradoxes of Kirby was the degree to which he could be polite, even friendly, to Stan in spite of their differences, and an astounding artifact in the Stan Lee archives reveals that fact. At some point after the surprise Kirby appearance on the convention floor, elder artist C. C. Beck picked up a guitar, and Stan, Kirby, and Neal Adams joined him for a joyful jam session, which a fan captured on tape. "You've all heard of the Beatles," Stan says near the beginning, giggling. "Here, we have the Cock-a-roaches!" They launch into boisterous renditions of kitschy oldies like "Clementine," "Pistol Packin' Mama," "Praise the Lord and Pass the Ammunition" ("Can't ya hear Sgt. Fury singin' this?" Stan shouts), and "Dixie." Kirby sings a solo a cappella snippet of the theme song written for Captain America on the old Grantray-Lawrence cartoon. At the eleven-minute mark, they even start bellowing "The Merry Marvel Marching Song," although even Stan can't quite remember the words past the first few lines. Everyone's chuckling, everyone's chummy; all is right in the world.

However, as it turned out, Kirby was no happier back at Marvel than he had been at DC. Stan wasn't the direct problem this time—he had virtually no involvement with Kirby's comics and even reportedly stood up for Kirby on a few occasions when the editorial leadership questioned the King's creative decisions. That questioning happened a lot—although Kirby's artwork was still explosive and visionary, he ignored changes his characters had undergone in recent years, and his declarative and stilted dialogue felt enormously out of place in the Marvel stable of the time. Fans regularly wrote in to complain, and creators grumbled about how Kirby had lost his touch.

Meanwhile, Stan was ever more visible in the world, happily accepting credit for being a genius. In 1976, he gained a new status in advertising when his visage appeared in not one but two mass-market ads for non-comics products. There was a thirty-second TV spot for the Personna Double II razor, featuring Stan in the Marvel offices, speaking directly to the viewer: "There's no finer shaving system made," he said. "I may create a whole new character: Personna Man!" The other promo was a print ad for apparel brand Hathaway, which depicted Stan standing in front of a wall of comic-book covers, with the following text below: " 'When you create superheroes, people expect you to look like one. I wear Hathaway shirts.' *Stan Lee, Originator of Marvel Comics*." Kirby, who may well have been the actual originator of Marvel Comics and was, at the very least, the co-originator, was nowhere to be found. Roughly the same goes for an instructional book Stan published with artist John Buscema, called *How to Draw Comics the Marvel Way:* Despite the fact that the "Marvel Way" was essentially the Kirby Way and that the book was chock-full of Kirby panels, Kirby's name was barely mentioned in it.

There were other reasons for Stan to be proud as the decade wore on. He signed a contract with Harper & Row to write his memoir, leading to that revealing autobiographical outline. He also got to taste success in a medium he'd once tried to escape to: newspaper comic strips. January 1977 saw the debut of *The Amazing Spider-Man* in newspapers across the country, with art from Romita and writing from Stan—at least ostensibly. In fact, despite his writing credit, Stan was just doing the meager dialogue each strip contained, while a succession of Marvel Comics writers came up with the plots—for a fraction of the pay Stan was receiving from the strip's syndicate. It was the Marvel Method multiplied, but no one seemed to mind much. What's more, Marvel scored its first big win in filmed fiction with the November 1977 airing of *The Incredible Hulk,* a TV movie on CBS that was successful enough to garner a sequel and an ongoing show that ran until 1982, giving Stan hope that he might become the Hollywood player he so longed to be. Stan foresaw more big things, telling Marvel's licensing agent in a letter, "Considering the vast influence and appeal Marvel and I seem to have with today's so-called 'youth market,' it seems a shame not to be harnessing this tremendous asset in areas other than the sale of comic books alone."

However, for the most part, those other areas brought only disappointment. Another newspaper strip of Stan's, *Says Who?,* was based on his eternally beloved format of adding wacky captions to existing images, but it was a quickly canceled failure. He sought to sell a pornographic comic strip to *Playboy,* a tongue-in-cheek fantasy saga called *Thomas Swift,* starring characters with names like High Priestess Clitanna and Lord Peckerton and featuring proposed episodes with titles like "Thomas Swift and His Eclectic Sauna" and "Thomas Swift and His Evasive Erection." Romita was supposed to draw that one, too, but the artist grew increasingly nervous about the content—"I don't wanna do stuff that I'm ashamed to show my grandchildren," he recalls telling Stan—and the pitch never came to fruition.

A live-action Spider-Man TV show arrived on CBS and, despite reportedly strong ratings for its premiere, quickly became the object of ridicule for its laughable special effects and lousy scripts. Stan, seeing the criticism lobbed at the show, was remarkably vicious about it in interviews, telling one magazine writer that the writers were "all a bunch of hacks" who "keep writing one bad script after another. So we're either going to have to drop the show or go with bad scripts—I don't know which is worse." On top of all that, he never got around to actually writing his memoir and, missing deadlines, had to scrap the project and return the publisher's advance payment. Stan would mention Marvel movie projects in interviews, but it was all empty bluster and premature promotion—no one in the film industry was biting.

Case in point: According to Evanier, Stan got a Silver Surfer movie optioned by producer Lee Kramer—who was soon to release the famed flop *Xanadu*—and Kramer suggested that Stan and Kirby put their heads together for a story that they could sell. Whatever trepidations Kirby may have had about working with Stan again were apparently assuaged by Stan's assurance that, this time, they would publish the story with Simon & Schuster and hold the copyright on it themselves, meaning a potentially enormous financial windfall and creative credit. And so it was that Stan and Kirby got together for one last, improbable ride, collaborating on a graphic novel—the term was still in its infancy—called *The Silver Surfer: The Ultimate Cosmic Experience*. As always, it remains unclear exactly who came up with the core plot, although letters from Kirby in the Stan Lee archives—always addressed to "Stanley," not "Stan"—indicate that Kirby was trying to leave a paper trail about specific ideas he had along the way. It was published in 1978 to great fanfare in the comics world, but the film adaptation never came to be. Kirby, by that point, was already fed up with this latest stint at Marvel and had decided to let his contract lapse. He left with an anticlimax, heading to the world of animation to do concept work for a new Fantastic Four cartoon on NBC. Despite the fact that Stan was listed as a producer on the series, Kirby, far away in California, never worked with him. Indeed, they never worked together again.

Stan still didn't seem to get what was bothering Kirby. Evanier tells me of a time near the end of the 1970s when he ran into Stan at the San Diego Comic Convention and got into a conversation with him about Kirby. The topic of that infamous 1966 *Herald Tribune* article came up and Stan started talking about how it wasn't his fault that journalists and others gave him full credit instead of acknowledging Kirby—a refrain he would utter many times throughout his life. Evanier couldn't take it anymore. He recalls the following dialogue, which referenced the entertainment duo Dean Martin and Jerry Lewis:

> I said, "At some point in every Martin and Lewis movie, Dean says to somebody, 'Hey, you can't do that to my pal.'" And I said, "Stan, no matter what they do to Jack, it's always *somebody else*. You dive under the desk: 'I'm not responsible for him being screwed, because I didn't screw him personally.'" I said, "When I work with people and I get credit for their work, I go out and I write a letter and I try to correct the record." And I finally said, "I don't understand how you can write superheroes and say, 'With great power comes great responsibility.'" And he got furious at me and didn't speak to me for a year and a half.

Kirby and Evanier weren't the only ones who were at the end of their ropes with Stan and Marvel. In late 1977, Stan dropped a bomb on the bullpen at their annual Christmas party: an editor named Jim Shooter was being promoted to editor-in-chief. Shooter, though beloved by Stan, had profoundly tense relationships with many pros in the Marvel stable, and the announcement was met with stunned silence. Immediately, Shooter and Stan were hit with a wave of criticism over a dire legal matter. As of January 1, 1978, a new federal law took effect that finally clarified what, exactly, work for hire consisted of in the United States. Panicked, Marvel's higher-ups realized they had to get legal agreements from their creators stating that the creators wouldn't try to assert copyrights over their Marvel creations. In the spring, Shooter distributed one-page contracts to that effect, and Neal Adams—in an echo of his conflict with Stan over the ACBA—flew into action. He sent around a mimeograph of the contract with scrawled handwriting on top, reading "DON'T SIGN THIS CONTRACT!! YOU WILL BE SIGNING YOUR LIFE AWAY!! URGENT!!" At the bottom was a call to gather at Adams's studio for a meeting of the laborers. At the assemblage, they discussed the formation of a guild, and some even went so far as to call for an outright union.

However, afterward, Shooter and Marvel president Jim Galton made it clear that anyone who joined such an organization would be sacrificing all their future work at Marvel, and the cries for collective bargaining died down. Most people reluctantly signed the contract. Stan, throughout the entire debacle, was silent. His time in the executive suite had been so much more trouble than it was worth. Hell, he was thinking his entire *career* had been insufficient, even with its dizzying highs. "I wish I had made my move at Marvel twenty years ago, had done the different things earlier. I was stupid—for my first twenty years, I did what my publisher wanted," he told a reporter in 1978. "And I think I should have gotten out of this business twenty years ago. I would have liked to make movies, to be a director or a screenwriter, to have a job like [TV producer] Norm Lear or [TV programmer] Freddie Silverman. I'd like to be doing what I'm doing here, but in a bigger arena." And yet, the gate to that arena remained closed.

IN BOX 53 OF the Stan Lee archives, you can find two folders labeled "Misc Scripts & Notes 1978." One of the folders contains a typewritten document with a handwritten note on top indicating that the text was intended to be submitted to an editor (the name is illegible) at *The New York Times*. Bearing the title "The Great Superhero Turn-On!", it reads like a cover letter for an application to be admitted into the ranks of Hollywood creatives. Stan argues that the hit show *The Six Million Dollar Man* and the era-defining film *Star Wars* were both "undeniably influenced by virtually every fantasy and science-fiction comic strip that's ever seen print" and that, in the immediate aftermath of the *Star Wars* debut, "all of the filmmaking community was beginning to suspect what we at Marvel Comics have known for decades—the public turns on to fantasy." After shouting out the glory of Marvel's superheroes and the success of the Hulk TV series, Stan comes to a conclusion: "The point is—no matter who the characters are, no matter how outlandish their powers or their shtick, if you make them believable, if you can write them realistically, if you can make the audience empathize, then you too can cash in on this suddenly discovered superhero/fantasy fad—this brand new fad which has been going on since Homer gave us the Iliad!" Implicit, of course, is the idea that no one would be better suited to help you cash in than Mister Marvel himself.

Even more intriguing, the folder contains a stack of notepad sheets with Stan's handwriting, all of them depicting various half-cocked ideas he had for projects of one kind or another. One is a book or magazine entitled *Fannies,* which would have "Photos of gals' (+ guys') backsides (candid + posed) (in + out of clothes)." One page is just titles—for books, films? It's unspecified—without descriptions: "Shall We Close the Office on Doomsday?" "The Benefactor." "As American as Apple Pie." "A Day of Fun and Games." Some ideas feel like those of a stoned freshman: "As a gag, an animal (pig?) is nominated for public office. People so fed-up w/regular candidates that he's elected!" "Future. Population growth is out of hand. Govt. has a week each month when people are paid a bounty to murder anyone." "TV + advertising have taken over the world. Sponsors + network chiefs are supreme rulers. Even wars must start during prime time. Everything is done for TV programming."

Some are the barest threads of concepts: "Write an adult, philosophical novel in the form of a children's story." "Write screenplay or story re: guy on subway seeing innocent person being assaulted and afraid to help." "Guy writes a petition for some minor matter—gets people in his apt bldg to sign it—it snowballs—changes his life." One improbably posits, "Mafia takes over govt. Now what? Now they're legit—<u>they</u> have to worry about crime!" Of course, there's a pitch for a publication of captioned news photos, as was Stan's wont. But perhaps most notable is a scrawled concept that reads like a personal fear: "Movie plot—man (executive) loses his job. Was big wheel in company. Now can't get another job. What happens to him—his pride—etc. A slow deterioration."

As the seventies entered their home stretch, Stan may well have felt like he was in a similar deterioration. He was clearly fantasizing about escaping his past and present—note how none of those ideas features a superhero—but he couldn't quite get the respect he so desired. He was initially credited as the writer on a new comic strip about the Hulk, drawn by Larry, but he cared so little about it that he handed the writing duties off to his brother shortly after its launch. He curated a book of factoids for Harper & Row, entitled *Stan Lee Presents the Best of the Worst: A Comprehensive Compendium of the Rottenest Things on Earth,* but it made no dent in the wider culture and failed to establish him as a mainstream author. Nothing was taking off anymore.

Much of his motivation was likely a desire for respect and fame, but he also had to keep up a steady cash flow to sustain the Lee family's expensive tastes. JC had returned from a stint living in London—allegedly the place where she met Eric Clapton and got her abbreviated nickname—and was dabbling in classes at New York City's School of Visual Arts, attending one semester in 1974 and another in 1976 before dropping out. In June of 1979, Stan and JC appeared on a Father's Day talk-show special alongside other celebrities—Don King, Paul Sorvino, John Cullum—and their own children, and when he was asked about his relationship with his only daughter, Stan noted, with no sign of sarcasm, "There are many problems, such as her extreme extravagance, which she shares with my wife." But Stan, too, bore some of the blame for any financial strain: As a profile in *People* pointed out, Stan had taken to wearing "thoroughbred Guccis" and "a conservative Paul Stuart herringbone jacket."

JC, her engagement with Isaac Tigrett broken off, had no job of her own (as she noted on the talk show, "At the moment I'm pursuing an acting career, but it's moving a little bit faster than I can catch it, so I'm still pursuing it") and was entirely living off the largesse of her dad. In her copious free time, JC had taken up odd habits: The Stan Lee archives contain long audiotapes of ambient sound and conversations that she apparently recorded while surreptitiously carrying a tape recorder around. Sometimes you pick up her half of a mundane phone conversation, sometimes she seems to be driving through the city, and one tape is just forty-seven-odd minutes of nothing more than shuffling clothes and the distant hum of a radio.

Stan, sometimes with his family, was regularly commuting to Los Angeles to take meetings and work on a partnership with animation studio DePatie–Freleng. But when he made his rare visits to the Marvel offices in New York, he demonstrated that he was completely out of the loop as to what was going on in the comics he was ostensibly publishing. For example, Marvel's breakout hit of the day was a revamped *X-Men* that featured a team of international heroes, including the Soviet expat Colossus, but when an interviewer asked him about the topic of Russians in Marvel, Stan responded, "I didn't know we had any Russian superheroes."

When he did dive into the comics world, his ideas were increasingly craven and cynical. There were rumors that the producers of the Hulk TV show wanted to create a female Hulk character and leave Marvel out of the deal, so a panicked Stan leapt into action and demanded the slapdash creation of a character named She-Hulk, in order to capture any potential copyrights and licensing fees on such an idea. Similar was the origin of a new character known as Spider-Woman: As Stan told a contemporary audience, he "suddenly realized that some other company may quickly put out" a series with the name *Spider-Woman* "and claim they have the right to use the name." He continued: "And I thought we'd better do it real fast to copyright the name. So we just batted one quickly, and that's exactly what happened. I wanted to protect the name, because it's the type of thing [where] someone else might say, 'Hey, why don't we put out a Spider-Woman; they can't stop us.'"

Stan's vision for the company kept clashing with that of the rank and file. According to writer Chris Claremont, Stan happened to catch a glimpse of a drawing by star artist Dave Cockrum that depicted a character named Ms. Marvel. "She's wearing a long-sleeve shirt and jeans," Claremont recalls. "And Stan looks at it and says, 'Ah! Can't we make her more sexy? Can't we put her in hot pants and a tight, stylish top?'" Claremont and Cockrum bristled—Ms. Marvel was supposed to be a serious-minded Air Force officer, not a wild club kid. "But we had to say this very carefully, because Stan's attitude would be, 'Screw that, we want to sell copies!'" Claremont says. "So we compromised and she basically tied her shirt up into a bikini top, but we kept the jeans. But from his perspective, the suggestions were always practical and from the perspective of 'How do we make the book more accessible? How will we sell more copies?'"

What's more, Shooter's rigid approach to running Marvel's day-to-day operations was causing a serious decline in morale, and Stan never seemed to intervene on behalf of the frustrated staff. Cockrum, fed up, wrote a resignation letter to Stan that declared, "I am leaving because this is no longer the team-spirited 'one big happy family' I once loved working for." Writer Marv Wolfman, equally pissed off, made the shocking announcement that he was defecting to DC, and the move prompted a damning feature in *The New York Times* about chaos at the House of Ideas. In it, an anonymous Marvel writer shot a venomous quote in Stan's direction: "I have the sense that he wants to be like Walt Disney," the writer said. "Comics are sort of beneath him."

Instead of fixing his broken company, Stan was doing things like telling journalists how excited he was for an execrable Captain America TV movie and taking out ads in *Variety* that advertised all the amazing Marvel characters Hollywood could license and exploit. In a letter to Resnais, Stan summed up where his head was at. He was all abuzz in the missive about a tentative deal to do a Silver Surfer movie on which he would serve as "consultant and some sort of associate producer." He noted that his and Joan's apartment had been robbed: "Every bit of jewelry Joanie owned was stolen. And—we're not insured!" But the crime had the effect of deepening his resolve on a crucial point: "It's one of the reasons we'd like to pull up stakes and come out to Los Angeles permanently, if we can."

Yes, the time had come for a change of scenery. Stan had hammered out that animation deal with DePatie–Freleng, and he convinced the Cadence execs to let him run their new joint venture out of an office in the Los Angeles suburbs. He, Joan, and JC sold their residences in New York and flew three thousand miles west for a new lease on life, never to permanently return. He retained the title of publisher as a matter of ceremony and branding but with the explicit understanding that others would actually be handling the comics and magazines. Stan had, in a way, fulfilled the wish he'd harbored since at least the end of World War II: He was finally free from the world of comic books. The time had come to try his hand in showbiz. Like a wish on the monkey's paw, the results ended up being as much curse as blessing.

LOST IN HOLLYWOOD

—

(1980–1998)

"STAN HAD THIS SADNESS," SCREENWRITER RON FRIEDMAN says over brunch at Caffe Roma in Beverly Hills, his Philadelphia accent lilting in the dry heat. "And the sadness was, 'The people that I hope to reach don't value what I've done. And I know I can reach higher, but nobody wants to do that.'" Friedman, long ago transported from the East Coast to L.A. for work, met Stan during the latter's periodic trips to the City of Angels during the 1970s. They initially encountered each other when they'd both been brought to lunch by producer Lee Mendelson, and the two quick-witted Jewish scribes immediately hit it off. "When I said, 'You're the Jewish Walt Disney,' he loved that," Friedman recalls of that first meeting. "He wanted to be liked. He wanted to be admired. That's one of the reasons he loved the spotlight."

In L.A., Stan got that spotlight in certain settings, says Friedman. "The minute Stan moved here full-time, he said, 'Let's have dinner.' So we went to a place called Amici, which was a delightful little restaurant nobody knew, and [Stan and Joan] loved it because paparazzi weren't hanging around." I ask if paparazzi were a regular problem for Stan in those days. "He would be beset, besieged, and befucked," Friedman replies. "I'd be sitting at dinner with Stan and people would go, 'Stan! How *are* ya, baby?' They'd leave and he'd go, 'Who the fuck was that?'"

But even though Stan might be recognized by strangers at a restaurant, he was still something of a nobody in the offices of studio executives. Friedman and Stan became collaborators, pitching Marvel projects and seeing rejections left and right. "He was a person without honor, frequently," Friedman muses. "When I was in meetings with him, his input was discounted. And I watched that moment when Stan would go to get up and yell or cry. But then it was, 'I'm going to eat it and smile.' And that's what he did."

You would be hard-pressed to find a better summary of Stan's first eighteen years in Los Angeles. For the better part of two decades, Stan lived with a mix of fanboy fame and corporate obscurity that left him uncomfortable, then frustrated, and ultimately desperate enough to abandon Marvel as his primary place of employment. In that time, he entered new personal and professional circles, accumulating acquaintances and contacts who both admired and pitied him. Most important, Stan made one particular friend who would go on to fundamentally change his life (and his afterlife), a man with a name so simple and alliterative, you might think it belonged to a Marvel character: Peter Paul.

Our insight into Stan's inner world expands greatly in this period thanks to the advent of the home videotape recorder, a device of which both Stan and Paul were enamored. The picture that comes into focus is one of a man struggling to figure out who he could be in a social web of increasing eccentricity, an industry that had little respect for him, and a company with a decreasing desire to put him to work as anything other than a figurehead. And yet, all the while, he was finally getting to mingle with the celebrities he so wished to be included among and throwing classy fetes in the Hollywood Hills. It was, perhaps, an era of taking one step forward and two steps back.

On June 19, 1980, *The Hollywood Reporter* announced the formation of Marvel Productions. It was to be a company that would generate television content: specials, pilots, and—most important—children's cartoons. Stan would be acting as the creative director, a title that meant little in the way of nitty-gritty tasks and much in the way of leadership and pitching. His task was to further embrace the mass-media ambassador role he had taken on while acting as publisher and to elevate the Marvel brand to new heights on the small screen. Theoretically, he would do the same for cinema, but that was going to be a secondary aim, as the wheels were already turning for television and those gears needed to be greased.

Marvel Productions was an evolved version of DePatie-Freleng, and the titular David DePatie, still in a leadership role as executive producer, was supremely doubtful of the world's appetite for Marvel content and regularly clashed with Stan over the entity's direction. As a result, the vast majority of Marvel Productions' output in the 1980s was, oddly enough, totally unrelated to Marvel's characters. *Muppet Babies; G.I. Joe: A Real American Hero; The Transformers; My Little Pony 'n Friends*—these superhero-free series were their biggest hits over the course of the decade. However, at the outset, they gave Marvel's intellectual property a firm try, with the launch of three superhero series: *Spider-Man, Spider-Man and His Amazing Friends,* and *The Incredible Hulk. Hulk* was never much of a success, lasting only one season; the first two were eventually merged and largely just known to history collectively as *Spider-Man and His Amazing Friends.* There was interest in *Amazing Friends* at NBC, but Stan found resistance from the network and within his own team when it came to the development of the project.

"NBC bought the show, which was great, but they didn't understand the essence of Spider-Man, who is a loner, and they made him have amazing friends," recalls television executive Margaret Loesch, who had befriended Stan during his periodic trips to L.A. in the seventies. "The prevailing attitude in Hollywood was that comics wouldn't translate well to the screen. 'They're too serious, too verbose, too ponderous, too heavy,' et cetera." In order to lighten up Spidey's adventures, NBC ordered Marvel to grant him two pals, the X-Man known as Iceman and a new, female character—created specifically to make the show palatable for girls—named Firestar. Stan was frustrated by the network interference at the time, but he should have been at least slightly grateful for the way things played out, as the show allowed him to make a major and consequential leap into a new role: on-air talent. The idea to have Stan act as narrator for *Amazing Friends* originated with NBC exec Sam Ewing, who hadn't grown up reading comics and therefore had no youthful reverence for Stan but who had been impressed by the man's charisma in pitch and development meetings. "We were doing the casting for the narrator for the show and I said, 'Why don't we use Stan Lee? I mean, it's his characters, it's his comic books—let's use Stan Lee,'" Ewing recalls. "DePatie went absolutely ballistic. He thought this was the worst idea he'd ever heard: 'He's got a New York accent, nobody can understand him,' yada yada yada."

Eventually, Ewing overcame DePatie's objections and Stan was cast in the role, providing the verbal framing for Peter Parker's escapades in his own voice, which was evolving from the solemn tone he'd historically exhibited in public to the street-hawker cadences he would soon become famous for. His narration sequences would typically conclude with a cry of *"Excelsior!"*, further cementing the word as his verbal signature. Stan was closely involved in the writing of the first season, after which he dropped off to work on other initiatives, but the narration continued and was a coup for Stan's personal brand: Countless youngsters of the 1980s would first become familiar with him thanks to his auditory role in *Amazing Friends* and the subsequent narrations and introductions he would perform on other cartoons. It's a direct line from there to his world-famous cameos. Something notable had begun in his life.

At the time, however, Stan seems to have felt only consternation toward the TV industry. By the time of a convention appearance in July 1984, he was publicly denigrating his company's own televised projects. "Those of you who were careless enough to tune in to *Spider-Man* may have seen that he's there with Iceman and with a girl named Firestar as a team of three people," he told a chuckling crowd. "I'll give you a little apology about that, too. The way that it's run in network television, it's like when I was a consultant on a live-action series: You could go to a network and say, 'Hey, we want to do this show, will you buy it?' and the network says, 'Okay, we'll buy it.' But that doesn't mean they'll do it the way you want." In the same speech, he briefly praised Marvel Productions's TV adaptation of the *Dungeons & Dragons* role-playing game but generally railed against the cards that the TV industry had dealt him. A fan asked him why there were such big differences between the comics and the shows, and he replied, "We're not allowed to do it the way we want to." His most cherished goal remained live-action Marvel movies, and he made that clear to his audience, telling them that he was *this* close to closing deals on a Doctor Strange movie by Bob Gale and Robert Zemeckis, the duo behind *Back to the Future;* a Captain America picture by the creators of the then-upcoming film (and eventual bomb) *King Solomon's Mines;* and an X-Men movie written by Roy Thomas and Gerry Conway. Such negotiations never went anywhere.

Right around that time, Marvel Productions hit an inflection point with the arrival of Loesch as CEO. She and Stan got along like gangbusters, and she helped bring the company to new heights with many of the aforementioned non-superhero shows. However, she saw firsthand how little Stan and his intuitions were respected. Sometime in the mid-eighties, Stan walked into Loesch's office, brandishing a videocassette. "He says, 'Maggie, this is our next hit,'" Loesch recalls. He gave her the tape and, a little while later, she watched what he'd found: a Japanese show about spandex-clad warriors battling extraterrestrial beings in balletic fight sequences. "I went over to his office and I said, 'Stan, I looked at that videocassette you gave me and it's interesting and kinda neat, but it's all in Japanese,'" she says. "And he said, 'Did it matter?' And I said, 'Not exactly, because it was fascinating, all those crazy characters.' Stan said, 'Maggie, we oughta develop it, it'll be a great show!'" The idea was to incorporate that footage with new, English-language content as framing devices, and Loesch authorized the creation of a sizzle reel to take to all three networks for presentations alongside Stan.

They flopped. "One network exec pulled me aside, away from Stan's earshot because she didn't want to offend Stan, because I'd given Stan all the credit," Loesch remembers. "She says, 'Margaret, how could you show me this? You're the executive producer behind *Muppet Babies,* an Emmy award–winning show! How could you show me this garbage?'" After that failed pitch, Loesch and Stan went to get one of his favorite meals, milkshakes and hamburgers— Stan loved junk food, despite Joan's constant protestations that he should eat healthier. "We licked our wounds, and we were really embarrassed because they embarrassed us by their reaction," Loesch says. "Stan said, 'We weren't wrong, Maggie. This is just typical. This is what I've faced my whole life.'"

As it turned out, another producer got his hands on the Japanese show, called *Super Sentai,* and developed an American adaptation a number of years later. It was called *Mighty Morphin Power Rangers,* and it was one of the biggest children's hits of the nineties. Speaking of eventual hits that found only rejection at the time: Stan was also big on pitching an Ant-Man TV show. "Stan kept saying, 'He's a man! Who's an ant! An *ant!*'" Loesch recalls with a laugh. Despite the fact that an Ant-Man movie would go on to make more than half a billion dollars in 2015, no one was biting in the eighties. "Stan wasn't rude to people, but he would say to me when they left the room, 'I don't understand why they don't have any imagination, I don't understand why they can't understand what I'm saying,'" Loesch says, adding that he had become something of a cynic when it came to all matters of the world. "It's not that he felt hopeless, but he felt skeptical that we keep repeating the same mistakes," she muses. "And he really threw up his hands many times and said, 'I don't know what's gonna happen. I don't feel good about the direction we're going in.'"

Stan was used to being disrespected in television and film, but he'd always been able to rely on the fact that he retained an aura of grandeur in the world of comic books. That changed in the eighties. After a decade of lackluster leadership at Marvel and a prior decade of taking credit for things he didn't do, Stan's demons were finally starting to catch up to him in public. An opening shot across the bow came in a letter printed in *The Comics Journal* in the summer of 1980, written by a disgruntled former Marvel writer and childhood adorer of Stan named Steve Gerber. Gerber was in the midst of an aggressive legal battle with Marvel over the ownership of his Marvel character Howard the Duck, and he was not the sort of man who pulled punches. "Stan was responsible for a massive infusion of creativity into the industry twenty years ago," Gerber wrote in the letter, "but he is also the man who, under the protective umbrella of Marvel company policy, has robbed Jack Kirby, Steve Ditko, and others of the credit due *them* as creators for those same twenty years." Few outside hardcore comics circles had heard such accusations against Stan. It would not be the last time they heard them.

Kirby had finally had enough of staying clammed up or vague in his accounts of his collaborations with Stan. The King of Comics had decided to ally himself with Gerber in the latter's war against Marvel, even going so far as to contribute art for free to *Destroyer Duck,* a comic of anti-Marvel agitprop that Gerber had put together to fund his legal proceedings. In a 1982 interview, when asked about Gerber, Kirby went on an unprecedented rant against his former place of employment. He called Marvel's comics "ads for toys" and said its corporate structure made it such that only "second-rate" ideas could succeed. Then he started to talk about Stan, and though he claimed the two of them had gotten along—"We were very good friends"—he was blatant in his claims about creative credit. "And, my God, I came up with an army of characters!" Kirby declared. "I wrote them all. Well, I never wrote the credits. Let's put it that way, all right? I would never call myself 'Jolly Jack.' I would never say the books were written by Lee." He even took credit for creating Spider-

Man, something virtually no one in the public had ever even suspected.

Just a few months later, Kirby spoke to Will Eisner for the latter's magazine *The Spirit* and was similarly straightforward. He told of creating Marvel's superhero stable: "I had to regenerate the entire line," he said. "I felt that there was nobody there that was qualified to do it. So I began to do it. Stan Lee was my vehicle to do it." He laid out the dark secret of the Marvel Method, which was that he was the one actually crafting the plots. "Stan Lee wouldn't let me fill in the balloons. Stan Lee wouldn't let me put in the dialogue. But I wrote the entire story under the panels," he said, referring to his narrative margin notes. "I never explained the story to Stan Lee. I wrote the story under each panel so that when he wrote that dialogue, the story was already there. In other words, he didn't know what the story was about and he didn't care, because he was busy being an editor." It's hard to overstate how much of an impact these sorts of statements had among people who took comics seriously. Previously, you had to have dug pretty deep and made some wild extrapolations to believe that Stan wasn't the primary writer on the classic Marvel stories. Now, here was the only other man in the room when the books were hashed out, telling the world that Stan had virtually nothing to do with what was put on the finished page. Kirby was a trusted and venerated figure—in no small part due to the cult of personality Stan had built up around him—so his words carried substantial weight.

Much of this saber-rattling came as a result of a legal push on Kirby's part to get back the voluminous library of original art that he had generated for Marvel over the years. He wasn't a poor man, but he certainly wasn't wealthy, and his deteriorating health made the sale of those valuable pages vital to his future financial plans. Marvel was ruthlessly stubborn in its efforts to keep that handover from happening. Other artists were getting their artwork back, but the company was nervous about Kirby asserting legal ownership over the characters, and Marvel allegedly used his artwork as leverage to coerce him into signing any potential rights away. In 1984, he was reportedly presented with a special four-page agreement demanding that he relinquish those sorts of claims if he wanted to get the art back. However, then–chief editor Jim Shooter makes a different claim, saying that Kirby was given the standard release letter for original art and instead demanded a special document that would give him ownership of the characters. Whatever the case, nothing was signed, and Kirby and Marvel were at a stalemate: "I wouldn't cooperate with the Nazis," Kirby was quoted as saying, "and I won't cooperate with them." Kirby kept pushing his case, telling an interviewer in 1985, "I always wrote my own story no matter what it was. Nobody ever wrote a story for me. I created my own characters. I always did that. That was the whole point of comics for me."

That same year, an ad in *Variety* promoted an upcoming film adaptation of Captain America (it would go on to stay in development hell for years and get U.S. distribution on only video and cable), which read in part "Based on Stan Lee's Marvel Comic Strip Character." Infuriated, Kirby and his attorney demanded that Marvel revise the copy. Subsequently, Kirby started to publicize his fight to get the original art. In interviews with various publications, especially *The Comics Journal,* he would declare that Marvel was stonewalling him, and commentators would accuse Stan of standing idly by while the House of Ideas screwed their uncompensated ideas man. "They don't give a shit," Kirby told the *Journal.* "I feel adamant; I feel like I've contributed a lot when people really needed me, and there's a hell of a lot of ingratitude. It smells like garbage."

What was Stan's response to this full-frontal assault? For the most part, it was condescension. "Well, I think that Jack has taken leave of his senses," he told an interviewer. "Jack was at home drawing these monster stories, until the day I called him and said, 'Let's do the Fantastic Four.' I think Jack is really—I don't know what to say. I don't want to say anything against him. I think he is beginning to imagine things." Another interviewer asked if Stan could explain what Kirby was talking about in all these comments about creative credit. "No, I really don't know what he's talking about," Stan said. "But I don't know much of what Jack is talking about these days. I mean, when I listen to these things he says, I just feel I'm listening to the mouthings of a very bitter man who I feel quite sorry for. I don't know what his problem is, really."

Such comments served only to further tick Kirby off. In an interview, he compared Stan to the weaselly, nefarious Sammy Glick in Budd Schulberg's *What Makes Sammy Run?* and, when asked whether he'd ever work with Stan again, he was indignant: "No. No. It'll never happen. No more than I would work with the SS," he said, before referencing an apparent incident in which he spoke with members of the Nazi paramilitary force during combat in World War II. "There's no way I could reach the SS. I tried to reach them. I used to talk with them and say, 'Hey, fellas, you don't believe in all this horseshit.' And they said, 'Oh, yes, we do.' They were profound beliefs. They became indoctrinated. And Stan Lee's the same way. He's indoctrinated one way and he's gonna live that way. He's gonna benefit from it in some ways and I think he'll lose in others."

Mostly, Stan was losing. He projected a triumphant image in his many press appearances, talking about a litany of classy live-action projects that he deemed to be right around the corner: *Rocky*'s Carl Weathers starring in a Luke Cage movie, a Daredevil TV show written by Oscar-winning Stirling Silliphant, Tom Selleck as Doctor Strange, an X-Men movie, a Human Torch movie, a Spider-Man movie done by Roger Corman, Angela Bowie as Marvel superspy the Black Widow—the list of projects never seemed to stop, nor did they ever materialize. There's a whole folder in the Stan Lee archives filled with Stan-penned movie and TV treatments based on other Marvel characters—Nick Fury, the Sub-Mariner, Doctor Doom— none of which came to anything. Meanwhile, Stan was working on pitches for his own, non-Marvel projects, some of which survive in the archives.

For example, he wrote an outline for a picture called *Decathlon 2020,* about a future world where life "is much too violent, death too imminent for man to enjoy the sports that thrilled him decades ago. Football, Soccer, Prize-Fighting, Hockey, Basketball, they're far too tame for us in the year 2020. But one thing isn't tame . . . The De-cathlon 2020!" In that event, "athletes have one objective—to kill their opponents! The games don't end until only one man remains alive and the others are all dead! The survivor is acclaimed as the world's greatest hero. There are no other rules." If you find this a little derivative of 1975's *Death Race 2000,* you aren't alone, and there were no takers for the proposal. On the opposite end of the tonal spectrum, Stan developed a pitch for a children's-book series, to be titled either *Creepies, Beenie,* or *Gnorman Gnat,* which would star a "hilarious, heart-warming bevy of bugs." It, too, was a dead end.

The multimedia projects that did come to fruition were, by and large, duds. Stan went on the publicity trail to hype up a 1986 film about Gerber's somewhat-famous Howard the Duck character, but as soon as it flopped, he didn't hesitate to denigrate it in public. Marvel was sold off by Cadence to film production and distribu-tion house New World Pictures in November 1986, but even being employed by a movie company didn't get Stan out of his Holly-wood rut.

His comfort seems to have come from his social life. Living first in tony Beverly Hills and then the high-class "Bird Streets" of the Hollywood Hills, Stan and Joan would throw and attend dinner party after dinner party, with Stan grinning and reciting Irish lim-ericks while a drunk Joan belted out old chanteuse standards. For-mer TV-network executive Lynn Roth was one of the Lees' neighbors and attended many a fete with Stan and Joan in the early eighties. "If I had to draw a picture of it, it would be Joan with a glass in her hand, and everybody's head tossed back in laughter," Roth recalls. "Joan drank these martinis, and she was very much like, *Ahhhh, dahhhling!* They were so much fun. That's the word I would use. They were in love, and they were fun." That was largely what Stan and Joan's social life seemed to consist of, says Roth: "Eating and partying. Telling jokes, laughing, ranting about politics. I think their desire to have a good time was contagious and pervasive." Valerie Friedman, wife of Ron Friedman—and herself an Englishwoman—has a similar estimation of what it was like to socialize with Joan. "We would go out to dinner, get pretty much drunk—I don't drink, actually, which she found very annoying—and she would sing outrageous songs to me or tell me outrageous jokes, trying to sort of break me down and maybe have me join her," Valerie recalls with a smile. "She would be outrageous." In 1987, Joan published an erotic novel called *The Pleasure Palace,* which, according to sources close to them, Stan likely either ghostwrote or got someone else to ghostwrite as an expression of his love and devotion.

Producer Sonny Fox was a perennial presence at Stan and Joan's parties and also had regular lunch meetups with Stan, finding him to be an overwhelmingly generous soul. For instance, Fox recalls turning seventy and Stan being unable to attend their birthday party but sending Fox seventy signed comic books instead. "That was Stan," Fox muses. "He wasn't going to say, 'I'm sorry, I can't.' He had to do it with a flourish. And he knew what would make me amused." Home movies from the era survive in the archives, and many of them look like a vision of paradise, with the ex–comics writer and his charismatic wife luxuriating on their veranda overlooking L.A. alongside giggling, beaming pals.

There's a person who doesn't show up in the videos of those chummy affairs: JC. She had her own social life, built largely around the bungalow Stan bought her on Rosewood Avenue, not far from his own residence. There, she would raise dogs and compose artwork: massive painted tapestries that incorporated abstract imagery into text taken from news reports—she called them "newscloths"—as well as hand-constructed wood objects, many of them crucifixes. She would throw pot-hazed parties at her home and invite a motley crew of offbeat Angelenos. Photographer Harry Langdon met her during her travels in the art world and was immediately fascinated by her and her work. "She was a consummate painter, artist, and assemblage-person," he recalls. "We had a lot of fun, smoked grass, some drinking—a very uncomplicated, very bohemian existence."

Langdon was especially stunned by the newscloths and started hanging them as decoration at his studio. "I said, 'Gee, JC, these things are worth a fortune,'" he says. "But they were her products as an artist and she never wanted to sell any of them, she just wanted to display them." He recalls her selling one tapestry for roughly $50,000, only to immediately regret it. "She was kinda disappointed, as though she gave birth to something and wanted it back," Langdon says. "The story goes that she paid the purchaser for the painting and bought it back."

JC enjoyed festivities with her parents on a somewhat regular basis, as evidenced by the many videos of holiday parties and casual daughter–parent hangouts in the archives. There's one that Stan filmed of his daughter standing by the poolside, featuring her attempting to tell a confusing story involving buying moon cookies at a bakery and prompting an exasperated Stan to eventually interrupt her by saying "Say good night, Gracie." A tape labeled "Xmas '86" takes us inside a Christmas party where Joan and JC seem like the best of friends, breaking into various carols together while Stan films and JC's devastatingly handsome, deer-in-headlights fiancé—a man identified only as Don, with whom things would not last— looks on. At one point in the '86 Christmas film, JC gives her father expensive cologne, prompting him to declare, "I, who use three-dollar Old Spice! This girl probably spent eight million dollars on some toiletry that won't make any difference to me." Joan receives an assortment of bizarre items, including the top of an urn, a large statue of a pig, and a watch shaped like a Volkswagen Beetle—all of which she adores. In that video and others, JC flourishingly addresses her father as either "Daddy" or "Living Legend," always preening for the camera.

However, there are hints of darkness in the relationship between JC and her parents here and there in the tapes. In one, taken after Joan's sixty-fifth birthday party, Joan tells the camera, "Today, on my sixty-fifth birthday, I am very angry with my daughter." She doesn't get into detail, but she sounds deadly serious. More apparent is the tension between Stan and JC. Stan regularly cuts his daughter off, never seeming terribly interested in what she has to say and often chastising her for showing off. In one video, JC declares, "Daddy is very pensive, 'cause Mother yelled and he doesn't like Mother yelling. Because in his life with Mother, there is no yelling. But when I come into the picture? When I come into the picture . . ." she trails off, her meaning implicit. Stan and JC seem to have been especially tense on the matter of the latter's own levels of talent and success. As she cryptically puts it in one video's conclusion, "All right, I'm turning off the camera, and listen, world, eat your heart out, 'cause he's my dad and I'm still the number-one fan, regardless of what he says. 'Cause I'm the gene and I'm the one who totally gets it. Just 'cause I'm not the success with the money, it doesn't mean I don't get it." At one point in another video, we see JC lying on top of Stan in a chair; the scene opens with the conversation *in medias res,* but it's nonetheless evocative.

"Honey, you take things as they come," Stan tells JC.

"I want help," she replies.

He doubles down: "That's like me, I take things as they come, that's part of the greatness of being."

She sounds utterly downtrodden as she mumbles, "But I'm *not* great."

And therein lies one possible factor in the growing toxicity between Stan and JC, at least according to Langdon. "I said, 'JC, what does your father think of these creations?'" he recalls. "And she said, 'Y'know, he's always disappointed.' I think he wanted her to be more of a Salvador Dalí, or someone with that creativity." Langdon continues: "I got a feeling that she always wanted to gain her father's approval as an artist. That she was a worthwhile creator-person and that he would stand behind her in that regard." Yet Stan firmly saw himself as the only thing standing between JC and destitution. "JC was the worry of their lives," recalls Loesch. "Stan was always concerned about his daughter and always was trying to help her and make her happy. It was always a challenge."

MAY 7, 1989, BROUGHT a quiet milestone for Stan: the first of his many onscreen cameos. That evening saw the airing of a TV-movie sequel to the old NBC live-action series *The Incredible Hulk*, entitled *The Trial of the Incredible Hulk*. Directed by star Bill Bixby, it featured a silent Stan as a member of the jury in the titular trial. While the Hulk rampaged through the courtroom, Stan sat there, looking dismayed and increasingly terrified. (For what it's worth, Kirby had him beat by a mile: The show's creators had put the King in an episode as a police sketch artist a decade prior.) Stan said nothing in the scene, but the chance to finally put his face on a screen delighted the sixty-six-year-old former comics maven. Just a few months later came an appearance as himself on *Muppet Babies*, followed by the premiere of the first theatrical movie to feature a Stan cameo, Larry Cohen's 1990 comedic thriller, *The Ambulance*.

The film follows a comic-book artist played by up-and-comer Eric Roberts as he attempts to pin down a conspiracy involving a mysterious ambulance, and Stan was selected to play Roberts's comics-editor boss. Cohen and producer Robert Katz were Marvel fans and, having discussed previous projects with Stan that never came to anything, Cohen called Stan directly and asked him to join the production. Stan enthusiastically agreed and came to the set by himself, without an entourage, only to find that he was less than famous with the cast and crew: "Most of them didn't know who he was," Katz recalls. Stan filmed another cameo as a professor in a zero-budget vampire thriller called *Jugular Wine: A Vampire Odyssey* at the behest of his assistant, Shaun Irons, who was friends with the film's auteur, Blair Murphy. "He was a blast and very funny," Murphy says. "He walked out and said, 'I'm one-take Lee, that's what they call me!' That's how he'd perform: We'd give him the line, he'd say it with great enthusiasm, and that was it."

Even if Stan found some joy in his appearances in these movies, there was little to rejoice about when it came to his company's overall cinematic output. Celebrity financier Ron Perelman bought Marvel's parent company, New World, in 1989 and saw the company's comics fortunes turn around, but he and underlings like Stan couldn't stop Marvel from putting out clunker after clunker in the film department. A schlocky Dolph Lundgren vehicle ostensibly about Marvel vigilante the Punisher (a Gerry Conway and John Romita, Sr., creation of the seventies, though Stan had granted him his moniker) barely followed the premise of the comics and hobbled along to a direct-to-video release in the States. The same miserable fate awaited a Captain America movie starring, of all people, J. D. Salinger's son, Matt. Marvel's reputation in Hollywood had only gone downhill since Stan ventured out West. However, the wheels kept turning, there were more efforts to get features made, and there was at least one big-name filmmaker who came tantalizingly close to legitimizing the whole Marvel enterprise.

Stan made contact with James Cameron, director of hits like *The Terminator* and *Aliens,* and the two met up to discuss Cameron producing an X-Men film with his partner, Kathryn Bigelow, in the director's chair. Ecstatic and nervous, Stan brought X-Men writer Chris Claremont to the meeting to help him make his case. According to Claremont, it seemed as if an agreement to do the movie was imminent when Stan accidentally scuttled the whole effort. "Stan said the magic words: 'I hear you love Spider-Man,'" Claremont recalls. "And Cameron's eyes just went, *Whoa!*" Abruptly, Stan and Cameron were talking about a Spidey movie, not one about the merry mutants. "And Cameron goes, 'I'll write it, I'll direct it, the best guys will be in it!'" Claremont says. "And everyone else in the room, we're just watching the X-Men shrivel." It proved to be a strategic mistake. Although Stan would get mileage for years afterward by talking up Cameron's involvement in the development of a Spider-Man picture (the two got so close that Stan and Joan even had Cameron over to one of their Christmas parties), the movie rights to the web-slinger were hopelessly more convoluted than those of the X-Men, and Cameron eventually gave up in the face of all the legal wrangling.

To make matters worse, Perelman started selling off parts of New World, prompting a nervous Stan to set up a personally owned side project in the form of a VHS series called *The Comic Book Greats*. Stan acted as host, inviting comics artists young and old to sit in a studio and talk shop, then draw on camera, all while Stan riffed and vamped. He'd come a long way since that failed 1968 talk-show pilot: He was polished, energetic, witty, and very much comfortable in the grinning persona he'd developed since he left active writing duty at Marvel. The contrast between his smooth delivery and the awkward dourness of lots of his interview partners—many of them vastly more revered than Stan within the comics industry—emphasized the degree to which Stan's charisma had nonetheless made him the face of that industry. However, there were little moments where Stan hinted at his own shortcomings. At one point in a video with Timely and *Mad* veteran Harvey Kurtzman, who had long harbored a certain degree of resentment toward Stan, Stan suggested that they move to the drawing board. "Just like old times," Kurtzman said, a hint of exasperation in his voice. Stan chimed in: "Just like old times: You do the work and I'll take the credit!" Kurtzman didn't laugh.

Meanwhile, Stan was desperately trying to take any shred of credit he could for the one area in which Marvel Productions was finding success: children's cartoons. By the dawn of the nineties, that success was entirely driven by shows about non-Marvel characters. "The thing you have to realize is, you couldn't *give* comic books away in those days, as far as properties," recalls animation writer John Semper, who worked with Marvel Productions back then. "Hollywood, TV, Saturday-morning cartoons? 'Not interested.' So, consequently, nobody really cared about Stan." Finally, a breakthrough came when Loesch left Marvel to run the Fox Kids division of TV network Fox in 1990, giving her the opportunity to do business with her former employees. With guidance from new Marvel Productions chief Rick Ungar and toy executive Avi Arad (the company he co-ran, Toy Biz, had signed a major deal with Marvel), Loesch got the green light for an X-Men animated series.

Stan proved himself largely useless when it came to that franchise, though, having not paid attention to its comics since he stopped editing them in the early seventies. When show writers Rick Hoberg and Eric Lewald met with Stan to discuss their ideas for the animated series, "We realized that *he didn't know the characters we were talking about* for the show," Hoberg later said. When the show went into development, Stan tried to be involved but found himself largely sidelined. "He didn't talk too much in those meetings, because there were too many people in the room," Arad recalls. "But he would nod his head when he liked something and go side to side if he had some doubts." At one point, Stan attempted to insert himself as one of the stars of the show. "He wanted to narrate and introduce [the show] and have it be, in effect, *Stan Lee's X-Men,*" Lewald recalled. As Hoberg put it, "Luckily, it didn't work out that way. I don't think he really had any idea of what we were talking about at that point."

Soon afterward, a Spider-Man cartoon went into development at Fox Kids, as well. Arad wanted Stan to be involved in that one, since Spidey was Stan's signature character, but Stan appears to have been reluctant. "At that time, animation was not terribly interesting to him," recalls Semper. Stan offered notes and guidance on the first thirteen episodes of the show, but even then, he wasn't producing his best material. Semper recalls Stan coming to him one day and saying, "We should do the Spider-Man diaries: It begins with Spider-Man saying, 'I'll never forget the day I fought the Green Goblin. . . .'" Semper was disappointed with his childhood idol. "I said, 'The problem with that is we know he's alive and well, so there's no suspense.'"

The one bright spot for Stan's animation career came in a subsequent two-season cartoon block about miscellaneous other Marvel characters, called *The Marvel Action Hour,* the first season of which was written by Stan's pal and collaborator on various failed Marvel-movie pitches, Ron Friedman. At Friedman's behest, Stan was made the narrator of the show, doing live-action introductions to every episode. "I wanted him to do the intro specifically because there were so many characters in every episode, and that's very difficult for any kid to connect with any one of them," Friedman says. "So I wanted some unifying force. That was Stan." Marvel's corporate higher-ups still saw him as a unifying force, too—in 1994 he signed a new lifetime contract, albeit with his role largely confined to promotional appearances and interviews, which continued to come out in a steady stream.

One of the key problems Stan faced in Hollywood was that, as Marvel film agent Don Kopaloff later put it, "It was like Laurel and Hardy without Laurel." Stan was there and, yes, he was recognizable, but he was deprived of the human creative force that had powered so much of Marvel's success: Kirby. The latter had made an uneasy settlement with Marvel that returned hundreds of pages of original art to him while not forcing him to relinquish creative credit, but many pages remained unaccounted for (there were even rumors that Stan had them squirreled away in a storage locker somewhere), and Marvel was hardly tempted to grant that credit to Kirby in public. Other than his occasional sniping in the press, Stan had entirely sat out the Kirby–Marvel battle and certainly didn't defend the man without whom he likely wouldn't have become famous.

"I believe he could have done more for Kirby," says Shooter, the former Marvel head editor. "Same for Ditko, same for others. But he kept his head low. He didn't want any danger to himself. He didn't want to be on the wrong side of any issue. He didn't fight for them. And he could have. He was Stan Lee. He had super-clout. He could have gotten a lot of things done." But to get those things done wasn't in Stan's nature, says Shooter: "Stan just wasn't a fighter." It's unclear what Kirby thought of Stan after all the decades of fighting and stolen credit. On the one hand, he gave interviews like the 1989 one for *The Comics Journal* that yielded so many blistering quotes. But according to Kirby's assistant and friend Steve Sherman, Kirby didn't let the rage expressed in any given interview overpower him. "Once the interview was done, he forgot he'd even done it," Sherman says. "It didn't weigh that heavily on him, really."

On February 6, 1994, Kirby died of a heart attack in his home. Reports differ as to what his final interactions with Stan were. A comics journalist caught up with Kirby at a convention in 1986, and the King told him he'd shaken hands with Stan the previous day but that he remained bearish on his former partner:

> I can't understand why there's a struggle over who did what, 'cause Stan and I know. Nobody else knows. If Stan would only come out of his hiding place and tell the world, everything would go great. It isn't obscure. He knows it, and I know it. There won't be a resolution. People don't change. They can't change. Sometimes it's too late. You just go on being what you are. Human beings go on being human beings. I can predict everything that Stan will do. I know I can't change Stan. He says his piece, and I say mine. I could shake hands with Stan till doomsday and it would resolve nothing. The dance goes on.

On the other hand, the two men ran into each other at the 1989 San Diego Comic-Con, and, as one eyewitness remembers, "They warmly greeted each other and embraced and were chatting it up like long-lost friends." Shooter recalls an incident at a Marvel party attended by Stan and Kirby near the end of the latter's life, where the two were "really getting along" and each offered to entertain the other at his home; Stan allegedly then proposed that they work together, and before Kirby could answer, his wife, Roz, snarled out the words, "Bite your tongue." Stan used to say he ran into Kirby at San Diego Comic-Con in 1993 and that Kirby told him, "You have nothing to reproach yourself about, Stan." Kirby's other assistant and biographer, Mark Evanier, vehemently rejects that latter account. "That convention story—that absolutely did not happen," he says. "They had some civil conversations, they talked to each other, but Jack was never going to feel he hadn't been wronged."

When the Kirby family was preparing their patriarch's burial, Evanier says, Stan was understandably concerned that he wasn't going to be welcome at the funeral. Evanier assured him that Roz would welcome him. "Anyway, Stan came; he sat in the back," Evanier tells me. "A couple of people who attended later told me that they scowled at him a lot. And a few people I think said some things to him later, like, 'Aren't you ashamed?'" As soon as the ceremony was over, Stan made a beeline for the exit, and Evanier ran after him as Stan hopped into his Volkswagen Rabbit, adorned with a license plate reading MARVELCMX. Days later, according to Evanier, he called Stan and discussed the incident. "He said, 'God, I wish I'd stayed. I thought I wasn't welcome. I didn't feel welcome there,'" Evanier recalls. "And I said, 'Stan, if you want to show some feelings for the Kirbys, why don't you guys give Roz a pension? It's small change for you guys. It's not gonna come out of your pocket.' And he said he'd look into it. It happened. I don't know how much he had to do with it, but it did happen; she got a pension." For the next decade and a half, the dispute between Stan and the Kirby family would lie dormant. But even as one toxic relationship wound down, another one, just as consequential for Stan's life, was building up.

STAN WOULD LATER SAY under oath that he met Peter Paul in the early 1990s, when Paul was working with the male model known as Fabio and Fabio was seeking to play Thor in a movie, but that was a demonstrable falsehood. They met in 1989, when Paul needed someone who could reach the youth. Back then, Paul was in charge of the American Spirit Foundation, a vaguely philanthropic organization he'd formed that year alongside famed actor Jimmy Stewart. Their inchoate goal was to, as the organization later put it, "enlist the entertainment industry's leadership, creativity, and resources in developing and applying creative solutions to critical challenges facing America." "One of the objectives was to use the entertainment industry's resources to help youth at risk," Paul recalls, and that meant finding someone who had pull with kids.

Paul had once worked with Muhammad Ali as an adviser and fixer; Ali had introduced him to Michael Messer, composer of the hit song "The Greatest Love of All"; and Messer introduced him to Stan. "I never read comic books when I grew up," Paul says. "I started researching Stan and it became clear that he was an ideal candidate for the position, because he had a unique ability to reach adolescents who weren't responsive to communicating with adults in any other forum. And he was intrigued with the idea of being the chairman of a foundation that Jimmy Stewart founded. Stan was a celebrity-geek." Paul tapped Stan as chairman of the foundation, a role whose primary tasks were to pique the interest of young people who loved Marvel and to take on the honor of presenting an award from the foundation to ex-president Ronald Reagan at their inaugural gala, something Stan did with aplomb. "And that led to a relationship from '89 to 2001 in which we found each other as kindred spirits," Paul says. "I was kind of adopted by him and Joan." At one point, the adoption seems to have almost gone on the path to being literal: "In the early part of the relationship, he asked if I would date his daughter, and I went out with her once," Paul says with a laugh. "And I told him there wasn't enough money in the universe for me to continue dating her."

Although much of what Paul says about his life seems outlandish, there is plenty of documentary evidence that the bit about becoming extremely close with the Lees was very much the truth. In the archives, there are tapes shot by Paul of Stan and Joan, carousing and conversing with Paul and his wife, Andrea. "I used to spend Friday nights, generally, with them, most of the time," Paul says. The two couples would begin their evenings together with drinks on the second floor of Joan and Stan's home. "She would make hors d'oeuvres and they would drink a lot," Paul tells me. I counter that it must have been Joan drinking, as Stan reportedly hardly touched alcohol. Paul chuckles. "He had his share," he says. "She got nasty and she would berate him, and she would say the most embarrassing things to him, and he would smile. It was amazing how he would let her abuse him."

In one tape from 1996, we see a soused Joan holding court before the rest of the quartet on the then-hot topic of African American Vernacular English, then known as "Ebonics." Joan was against using it in schools. "Education has not taught these black children how to speak!" she cries. Nevertheless, she admits there were some positives to the way black people talk: "I can understand that they have a rhythm," she says. "We're living in a daft, crazy, insane world, but there is a rhythm to the black people, back to the ghettos of their grandmothers." Stan tries to chime in: "All I'm saying is, black people have always had their own way of speaking, but to start teaching Ebonics—" and then Joan cuts him off to keep ranting. "If you'd listen and stop being Stan Lee . . ." she says, trailing off as she struggles to hold her train of thought. However, the two were clearly still very much in love: They talk at length about how they have a secret language of nonsense words (e.g., "kitchamonga" and "donka") that they use only with each other.

The video cuts to everyone having dinner, served by a Tibetan domestic worker. Stan and Paul riff on obscene pun names—"Imma Hoar," "Fuque Yu," and so on—before Paul goes on about his friendship with Muhammad Ali and Stan talks about his correspondence with mentalist Uri Geller. They joke that the Pauls' soon-to-be-born child might be named Stan Lee Paul. At one point, Stan says, "You can know Peter for a million years and each time you see him, you learn something new about him. You're the most amazing guy in the world. You really are." It's clear that the Lees and the Pauls were tightly bound, although JC was a peripheral figure. Paul says Stan and Joan acted as godparents to one of the Pauls' daughters, and the night of the christening, everyone went to JC's house for dinner. "JC couldn't tolerate the fact that, number one, we were married," Paul says. "She didn't like that, and she didn't like the fact that we had a child and her parents were doting on the child." In his telling, JC berated them so much that Andrea, the new mother, left in tears. "And they were embarrassed," Paul says. "They didn't socialize with JC very much as a result."

When the Lees and the Pauls weren't having dinner parties, they were scheming about bigger and better prospects for Lee—and, implicitly, for Paul, too. Stan was eager to go along with it all, never passing up the opportunity to hobnob with the famous people Paul knew. In the early nineties, Paul helped to advance the career of Fabio by being his manager, aiding in his transformation from a simple model to an icon across multiple mediums. In the spring of 1995, Paul brought Stan to Fabio's birthday party at the home of actor Whoopi Goldberg, no doubt aiming to let Stan press the flesh and accomplish some networking. A video of the event lingers on the gaiety of the soiree, then cuts to Stan sitting at his desk in the New World building, staring into the camera and recording a video message for Goldberg. "Hiya, Whoopi!" he says. "It was great meeting you at the party, Fabio's birthday party. And you may remember, we were talking about me perhaps coming up with some concepts for you to play a superheroine. You wanted a superpower. Well, I thought of three little ideas."

He then launches into his pitches for her alter egos, presumably to be used in a movie. First up is the Femizon, a waitress who drinks a concoction made by an eccentric nutritionist and gains supernatural strength. Next there's Chastity Jones, the offspring of an alien father and a human mother who possesses the ability to be sexually irresistible to men ("It's a power any woman would want!" he declares). Finally there's Baaad Girl, the child of a woman impregnated by Satan who is tasked with bringing souls to hell yet defies her father's orders and falls in love with the human race. Nothing came of the pitches, but Paul says he was doing those kinds of linkups for Stan all the time, introducing him to Steven Spielberg, Ron Howard, and other luminaries. According to Paul, he tried over and over again to "liberate" Stan from Marvel: "I went around to every studio head in 1997, '98, and I spoke with everybody, Bob Daly over at Warner Bros., Bill Mechanic at Fox, [Michael] Eisner at Disney," he says. No one was interested. As Paul puts it, Stan "was effectively relegated to a broom closet at New World and wasn't doing anything productive."

That was the truth, more or less. Marvel was in tumult and Stan was getting left by the wayside. The comics market had collapsed in 1995, driving Marvel into Chapter 11 bankruptcy the following year, which led to Arad and his Toy Biz partner, Ike Perlmutter, taking control of the whole company. Perlmutter treated Stan like a useless anachronism and, while Arad respected Stan's creativity, he understood that Stan's presence at Marvel was more of a contractual courtesy than anything else.

"Stan was kind of a minister without portfolio at that point in his career," says Shirrel Rhoades, who became Marvel's executive vice president during this era of chaos. "He would sometimes send us ideas, but they weren't always the greatest ideas. . . . I think he was, I sensed, frustrated that he didn't have enough to do and was out of the creative process." Rhoades recalls a particular anecdote that sums up the interactions between Stan and the suits of the time, which he says happened during a meeting that included Rhoades, Stan, Arad, and Marvel chairman Scott Sassa. Stan reported that he'd been talking with actor David Schwimmer, of *Friends,* and that Marvel should do a project with him. "And the general consensus around the table was that David Schwimmer had no charisma and was a little bit derided," Rhoades recalls. "And Avi and Scott, with Stan sitting between them, they agreed we shouldn't do anything with Schwimmer. They reached over and high-fived each other over his head."

Stan dipped his toe into Marvel's comics every now and again. On one occasion, it led to acclaim: He did a two-part Silver Surfer story with legendary French artist Moebius in 1988–89 that remains beloved to this day. But the rest of it was failure all around. He thought it might be fun to introduce a new superhero based on a real person, ideally someone Hispanic, to appeal to that demographic, and was linked up with a model named Jackie Tavarez. Together, they conceived of a singer-turned-crimefighter named Nightcat, whose civilian identity was none other than Tavarez herself. She appeared in a Marvel comic and even recorded an accompanying album of Nightcat-themed songs, but every aspect of the endeavor landed with a thud and it was quickly consigned to the dustbin of history.

Speaking of dustbins: Stan had been kicking around an idea for a comic about a superpowered garbageman from the future named Ravage. Somewhere around the turn of the nineties, Marvel editor Tom DeFalco made a radical suggestion for it. Steve Ditko had, improbably, been doing freelance work for Marvel for a few years (though he always refused to draw Spider-Man or Doctor Strange), and DeFalco thought it might be time to get the band back together. He tasked editor Jim Salicrup with recruiting Stan and Ditko to collaborate on Ravage. Stan was an easy sell; Salicrup expected Ditko to be more of an uphill battle, but the editor was surprised by the way the reclusive artist received the summons when they spoke at the Marvel offices in New York. "I said, 'Stan Lee's working on a new character and he's interested in having a meeting to work it out with you,' and there was a silence," Salicrup recalls. "All I could imagine was Steve with a thought balloon over his head reading, *I knew he'd come crawling back.* He didn't say anything like that. Instead, it was just, 'Okay, yeah, when do I come in?'"

The meeting was arranged, and Stan flew back to the city of his birth to meet up with one of his greatest partners. "It truly was a mutual-admiration thing, where Stan maybe laid it on a little bit thicker, but you could tell that Steve had respect for this guy, was interested in possibly working with him again," Salicrup says. "Stan did his pitch for his futuristic garbageman character, and Steve didn't insult it, he was totally polite about it." However, they reached an impasse: Stan wanted a gritty vision of the future, but Ditko wanted the world they created to be positive and hopeful. "Stan could see it wasn't going anywhere and he figured he didn't want to waste time because he's so impatient, so he figured, go for broke," Salicrup says. "So he asked Steve, 'Why don't we just do a Spider-Man graphic novel? One last Spider-Man story, you and me. We'll make a fortune! It'll be great!' And Steve responded—again, professionally and politely—turning him down, saying, 'I just could never care about Spider-Man as much as I did back then. I just can't do it.'" They said their goodbyes, and that was that. Everyone went away from the meeting empty-handed. Ravage eventually saw publication as *Ravage 2099*, done via the Marvel Method with writer/artist Paul Ryan, but it was a flop, and Stan left after just a few issues.

In the mid-nineties, Stan concocted an idea for a whole new line of comic books, dubbed Excelsior Comics, starring characters he created—with indisputable credit this time—and produced by writers and artists he would oversee. "I'm launching a new comic book line next year named EXCELSIOR COMICS!" he declared in one of the many online chat-room interviews he did in the early days of the World Wide Web, sometimes under the AOL screen name "Smilinstan" (his personal email address was COMBKMAN@aol.com). In that aforementioned chat, he then threw Marvel's controversial practices of the time—dizzying continuity, morally gray ultraviolence, publishing comics with a multitude of collectible "variant" covers—under the bus: "Promise: one cover per mag—readable stories—real heroes—dastardly villains—lots of action—and hopefully you'll be able to even understand what's going on without reading 100 previous issues!" he typed.

He recruited top-flight talent to work on the project, including up-and-coming writer Kurt Busiek. Stan and Busiek had a meeting, and the latter's joy at being called to work with the legendary Stan Lee quickly melted into dismay. "The character he wanted me to work on was called Omega, and the character was possibly an angel who was cast down to Earth, but Stan never wanted to confirm that one way or the other," Busiek recalls. "My impression—to be slightly less than complimentary at this point—was that this was around 1995 and Stan's sense of the industry had caught up to about 1986." There was widespread concern among the creators tapped for Excelsior Comics that the whole enterprise was dead on arrival. "The stuff didn't feel modern, and it also didn't feel on-brand for Stan," Busiek recalls. "When the writers would talk when Stan wasn't there, we were concerned that this line was going to seem old-fashioned, but not old-fashioned in a way that people would associate with Stan creating stuff like it's the 1960s again."

Nevertheless, they didn't feel that they could speak up. In Busiek's recollection, when he expressed his concerns to Stan's deputy editor for the project, Rob Tokar, Tokar replied, "This is Stan's line, this is what he wants to do, and we can't really say, 'Stan, you're wrong.' If anybody's earned the credibility to do this, it's Stan, and he's gonna do it his way." Gradually, Busiek heard less and less about Excelsior. "My impression was that the line was not going to be a success," he says, sadness in his voice, "and when it finally got terminated, I was a little relieved." Given Stan's declining reputation in the comics world, it was little wonder that *The Comics Journal* ran an entire 1995 issue about his checkered career, featuring essays with headlines like "The Two Faces of Stan Lee" and "Once and for All, Who Was the Author of Marvel?" (Spoiler alert: Their answer wasn't "Stan Lee.")

There were tiny glimmers of hope in other mediums. In the mid-nineties, Stan made contact with a tech entrepreneur and screenwriter named Larry Shultz, and the two put together a side company called Lee–Shultz Productions, to develop multimedia projects together. The U.S. copyright office lists seventeen Lee–Shultz Productions ideas, with titles like *Cougar, Ninja Man, Scarlet Ninja, Vindicator,* and *Un-humans.* One pitch survives in the Stan Lee archives: *Decoy,* billed as "A One Hour Erotic Action Series Like None Ever Seen on TV Before." The premise induces more than a few cringes now:

A street-wise, kick-ass, uninhibited woman—who knows she's one hot, desirable "babe" and isn't shy about using her voluptuous body and all her feminine wiles to get what she wants—utilizes colorful make-up, a variety of wigs, fake accents, sexy costumes, theatrical body language, and her own personal brand of street-fighting martial-arts skills to become an undercover *DECOY* for an ultra-secret government agency which undertakes "impossible" missions that lie beyond the scope and jurisdiction for normal law enforcement agencies.

None of these Lee–Shultz projects were ever produced. Stan had slightly better luck with a novel series he sold to publisher Byron Preiss, called *Stan Lee's Riftworld*. The quasi-comedic concept involved a comics artist at a Marvel pastiche who encounters an interdimensional rift between his world and a world populated by superheroes. Despite the branding in the titles, these novels were written by an author named Bill McCay, who says his interactions with Stan consisted of "an hour with him signing books" at San Diego Comic-Con. The series was supposed to last for six installments but was canceled after just three. Stan scored a tender and verbose cameo as himself in *Mallrats,* the sophomore effort from superstar *Clerks* auteur Kevin Smith, but the film was a box-office bomb. Stan kept getting lifetime-achievement awards in comics circles and was the subject of a retrospective documentary on the A&E Channel's *Biography* series, but he didn't want to be remembered for the past; he wanted to be relevant in the present.

In the summer of 1998, as Marvel was restructuring after its bankruptcy, Stan's contract was terminated (a later lawsuit brought by JC against Marvel said he was fired, but that may just be a matter of semantics). When he went to meet with Perlmutter about getting a new one, the latter reportedly told him he could come back with a two-year deal that paid him only $500,000 a year—a significant reduction from what he'd been paid previously, and a paycheck that could easily stop after the two years were up. It wasn't nearly enough to keep up with Joan and JC's expensive habits and the lifestyle he himself had grown accustomed to. "And he cried on my shoulder, literally," Paul recalls. "He said, 'What do I do? I can't live on $500,000 and two years. I don't know what to do. I said, 'Hire a lawyer.' He refused. He wouldn't spend the money to hire a lawyer. He was like that. He had an attitude about lawyers." But where Stan saw a brick wall, Paul saw a newly opened door. If Stan was no longer going to be an employee of Marvel, that meant he could do whatever he wanted. Stan wanted to be a superstar. If Marvel couldn't give that to him, maybe Paul could.

Paul had an idea. It was a dangerous one, more dangerous than either man could have predicted. It would rupture both their lives and launch Stan into the final stage of his time on Earth, one in which he'd experience the most dizzying highs and most horrific lows of his entire existence. Stan was about to become a brand.

GET RICH
QUICK

"He asked to cross the Jordan,
and he asked to see the Holy Land.
The first request would not be granted,
but his second request would be granted.
God did not want to let Moses go
out empty-handed."

—Daat Zekenim

8.

THE GREAT EXPERIMENT

(1998–2001)

TO HEAR HIM TELL IT, PETER PAUL WAS A CON MAN BY AGE thirteen—though he'd never use that term, of course. Growing up in Miami, he had a fascination with historical documents and wanted to see if he could get his hands on a few of them. "I started a front organization called Americans Seeking Knowledge—ASK was the acronym—and I represented the youth of America," Paul tells me, far beneath the vaulted roof of his Florida living room. A half smile then crawls up the side of his silver-bearded face. "But I have to say that that was a bit of a fabrication, because I was the only member of the organization." He would send letters to venerable men and women of the world—great artists, decorated warriors, heads of state—and ask them for artifacts. "I became friendly with Karl Dönitz, of all people," he tells me, referring to the Nazi admiral and war criminal who became führer of the Third Reich after Hitler's suicide. "Dönitz, for some reason, liked our correspondence, and he started sending me these voluminous handwritten stories in German about his career." Not content with the Axis, Paul also apparently became close with the Allies: "I would correspond with Douglas MacArthur, and he would send me signed Japanese surrender documents," he says.

In his capacity as head of ASK, Paul says, he developed a friendly correspondence with John F. Kennedy's secretary, Evelyn Lincoln, while Kennedy was president. As the story goes, one day in the early 1960s, the boy was on a trip with his stepfather—Paul was born Peter Eisner but had his Jewish surname stripped from him by this loathed husband of his mother—that took them to Washington, D.C. Paul cold-called Lincoln to see if he could get an audience with JFK. She said the president couldn't make time that day but could do so the next. "My stepfather, who was jealous of my precociousness, said he couldn't wait an extra day," Paul recalls. Furious, the lad snuck away to visit the Executive Office Building, just west of the White House. "I had taps on my shoes, and I was walking down the hall, and I ended up in Lyndon Johnson's office," Paul claims. "So I met him, and as a result I got involved . . . That's what started my involvement in politics."

But when it comes to that political involvement, perhaps even more important than LBJ was Salvador Dalí. According to Paul, while he was a law student, he started dating a Danish woman and got her a job as a flight attendant so he could fly for free. "And the first day that I had flight privileges, I go to New York, go to the St. Regis, and Dalí happened to be there," Paul says. "I went up to him and said I'd like to commission him to do an etching for the bi-centennial of the Declaration of Independence. So we started talk-ing about that. And I knew the way that it would start with him was to employ him, because he loved money. And I didn't have any money at the time. We started negotiating his contract to do an etching." Astonished, I point out that he was conning Salvador Dalí. "I wouldn't call it conning," he says, "because I had every intention of getting the money."

Paul says he insinuated his way into Dalí's retinue, flying back and forth from New York every weekend, and quickly developed an admiration for the old man: "I really marveled at the way he'd built a life in which he was able to use surrealism to have an extraordinary existence." At another point in the conversation, we're discussing

Paul's multiple felony convictions in the seventies, which he claims stemmed from secret missions he was performing on behalf of the U.S. government in the global struggle against communism. I ask him why he would abandon his successful legal career and comfortable status as an up-and-coming Miami entrepreneur to do such things. Fingers tented, he laughs and says, "I think it was, maybe, I had been the protégé of Salvador Dalí for a while, and it was just . . ." He trails off, then starts up again: "The notion of the surreal being incorporated into political action, for whatever reason."

"Surreal"—yes, that's a good word for what it's like to listen to Peter Paul tell his life story. Who knows how much of it is true? The most astounding stuff is unverifiable, or at least very difficult to conclusively disprove. It all comes out in such an overwhelming torrent that it's a challenge to keep track of it all. Russian mobsters, Iranian nuclear officials, Nicaraguan death squads, Cuban counterrevolutionaries, Brazilian arsonists: These are the sorts of people who populate his self-professed personal chronicles. Yet despite all that potential bullshit and his shady background, Paul is enormously charismatic and intimidating, the sort of man who could alternatingly charm and bully you into starting a business with him. And that's exactly what Stan Lee did in 1998. Stan Lee Media—often referred to in lawsuits and criminal cases as SLM—was supposed to permanently change Stan's life, and it certainly did, for better and very much for worse.

So, about those felony convictions. Paul had three of them prior to the founding of SLM. The first two came at the same time in 1979, in the wake of a breathtaking scandal that was dubbed the "Cuban Coffee Caper" by the Florida press. In short: Paul, who had left his stepfather's law firm to oversee the development of a World Trade Center in Miami, was caught trying to bilk the Cuban government in an elaborate scheme involving the fraudulent sale of three thousand metric tons of coffee, worth roughly $8.75 million. He and his co-conspirators had purchased a freighter to ship the beans and planned to sink it and claim the cargo had been lost at sea.

Paul contends that he was doing all of this at the government's behest and that Castro was already "buying black-market coffee, re-
packaging it as Cuban coffee, selling it to the Russians at three times
the market value, and pocketing the money himself. . . . So the idea
was, if we could expose that he was screwing the Russians, chances
are that they might get pissed off at him for doing that, right? And
we could expose them internationally for doing that. I accepted and
was tasked with the oversight and direction of that sting." Separate
but simultaneous to that, Paul says, there was an operation to fight
Castro that used drugs as currency, "and the people that worked on
[the coffee project] under me included a guy who himself was involved in cocaine transactions." According to Paul, that gentleman
prompted the second felony charge. "One night, to get himself out
of it, he came to my garage, within the pretext of putting coffee
samples in the middle of this transaction," and placed a bag of cocaine there, Paul says. "Thirty minutes later, a SWAT team comes
and pulls the bag out. I'd never even opened it."

Once Paul was arrested and charged with attempted fraud and
cocaine possession, he was forced into silence about what really happened, he says: "I couldn't defend myself without exposing a lot of
the other activities that were going on." Instead, he pleaded guilty
and told the judge that he suffered from "hypomania," which
couldn't be properly treated in prison. He was sentenced to three
years for the java and eight years for the coke, but he ended up serv-
ing only forty months.

Years passed, and Paul claims he got back into the covert-
operations game, this time for Ronald Reagan's "kitchen cabinet" of
informal advisers, who he says liked him because of his fierce patriotic streak. He went to Canada in 1983 and says he did so to help
former Watergate burglar Frank Sturgis in a scheme to financially
aid the right-wing Nicaraguan Contras "by selling stories in advance
to German magazines," which for unspecified reasons involved him
traveling to the Great White North. While crossing the border, he
used the identification card of a dead man who, according to him,

was the brother of a fellow covert operative. Whatever the reasoning, this misrepresentation of his identity was a violation of his parole, and he was sent back to prison.

Nevertheless, when he was released, he got back into the good graces of the American elite, working with celebrities like Muhammad Ali and Buzz Aldrin as a kind of manager and eventually getting tapped for the gig running the American Spirit Foundation, which led him to Stan. This is a greatly simplified version of the story of Peter Paul's pre-Stan decades. When he talks about those early years, he also talks about adventures that brought him into contact with a litany of intense individuals: Supreme Court justice Warren Burger, Colombia-based CIA agents, actor Ian McShane, Gestapo chief Heinrich Müller (who disappeared at the end of World War II but whom Paul claims he found living in the mountains of Peru), eventual Donald Trump lawyer Marty Raskin . . . The saga never stops and probably merits a book of its own.

Paul claims Stan knew about the felonies early on in their friendship. "He couldn't believe it," Paul recalls. "Like I'd do with anything I say, I showed him all the facts and everything about it. He didn't care. It didn't affect our lives." So when Paul came to Stan with a business proposal after the termination of his Marvel contract in 1998, nearly a decade into their friendship, enough trust had been built that Stan was eager to hop into bed with him. The proposal was simple. As Stan once put it, "He said, 'Hey, Stan, now you're free! Lemme build a company.'" Paul would oversee the creation of an entertainment firm in which Stan would generate new story and character ideas that would then be brought to life in the growing ecosystem of the World Wide Web. "My intention, from the outset, with Stan was to use the Internet for what it was intended: to be a global medium for exchange and ultimately of entertainment," Paul recalls. Like many companies in the dot-com boom, they would probably operate without profits for a while, but the plan was to eventually land major deals with top-flight talent that would generate cash in the form of film adaptations, licensing agreements, and other endeavors. However, in order to get the whole thing started, Paul needed to formally get Stan on board.

Paul legally registered a company called Stan Lee Entertainment, Inc.; on October 15, 1998, he presented Stan with an employment agreement (printed, for some reason, in Comic Sans font) that would make Stan chairman, publisher, spokesman, and chief creative officer of that company. The key point for all future problems came in section 4(a) of that agreement, which stated that Stan would forever assign to the company "all right, title and interest I may have or control, now or in the future" to all the characters and concepts he held any rights to, as well as his name and likeness and verbiage like "Excelsior" and "Stan's Soapbox" (though he had the option to let Marvel conditionally use such phraseology). Such a wide-ranging agreement was, as Paul puts it, "not usual, but it's not exceptional, either." More important, Paul says he had done research and found that the legal ambiguities of Marvel in the early sixties meant Stan, in fact, actually owned all of the characters he claimed to have created there, meaning this new company would own them. Paul says he planned to make a move on Spider-Man et al. eventually but that Stan didn't want to do so right away out of residual loyalty to Marvel. Stan signed the document.

Simultaneously, Stan was in negotiations with Marvel to establish a new contract with them, and, on November 17, they signed a deal whereby Stan would continue to act as a figurehead for Marvel in exchange for $810,000 a year, with annual raises capping at $1 million, pensions for Joan and JC, $125,000 a year for the still-ongoing Spider-Man newspaper strip, stock options, and a 10 percent cut of Marvel's film and television profits. He was even allowed to compete with Marvel, should he so choose. However, there was also a clause that would prove problematic in the future: He signed away to Marvel "forever throughout the universe all right, title and interest solely and exclusively which you may have or control or which you may have had or controlled" to the characters he claimed to have created in his work for them. In Marvel's eyes, this meant an extra layer of reinforcement in the foundations of their edifice. In Paul's eyes, that clause would one day be useless to Marvel, because Stan had already assigned those Marvel properties to his new company a few weeks prior. But Stan was desperate for Marvel's money and respect, Paul says, and thus made this misleading agreement anyway. They would lie in wait until the time was right, according to Paul, and one day take over all those world-famous figures.

In the meantime, they had their own enterprise to set up, and Stan couldn't believe how quickly things were moving. "It's all in the formulative stage now and it's happening so fast that I can hardly follow it," he wrote in a letter to a friend in December 1998, "but the guys who are running the business part of the deal seem to be very optimistic as they keep making what they call 'strategic alliances' with other companies." The newly dubbed Stan Lee Media quietly opened its doors at the web address stanlee.net (stanlee.com had already been claimed by an unrelated person) and, more concretely, at a building occupied by other Paul-controlled companies in the Los Angeles suburb of Encino. They initially had three employees and just $1 million in seed money, but, as a message on the backs of the promotional materials they distributed put it, "In case nobody told you, we're taking over the world."

Stan misleadingly assured any worried fans that he was still a Marvelite, through and through: "Nothing short of an H-bomb could tear me from the company I love," he wrote in a "Soapbox" column for Marvel. "I'm just setting up my own website, in my spare time, for the fun of it. Come and visit when we officially open in August, but no matter what—Marvel rules!" Eager to raise cash on the open market without having to go through the rigamarole of issuing an IPO, Paul—who, due to his felony convictions, couldn't legally be an officer of the company and instead was listed as a "consultant"—executed the corner-cutting enterprise of a reverse merger with an existing company in order to become publicly traded. Their stock symbol became "SLEE." The merger seemed to be a successful strategy, at least in the beginning: On the first day of trading, the price per share shot up 40 percent, to nine dollars.

Some of this initial success likely had to do with the media blitz that Paul sent Stan on in the early going, which portrayed Stan—who was pushing eighty—as an energetic visionary and the firm as a sure bet of the dot-com boom. Stan would talk to anybody and was quoted everywhere from venerable outlets like *The Wall Street Journal* to trade magazines like *Animation World* and low-rent geek websites. "I've been in comics, radio, television, animation, movies, and now the Internet," he told *The New York Times*. "When I got into comics, it was the early days of the industry, and it was all new. . . . Here's another chance for me to get in at the beginning," he said to *Time* magazine. He presented an air of wild optimism: As he put it in one interview, "If the characters and stories prove popular, we've no reason to think that they won't spin off into interactive games, into movies, television, Saturday morning animated shows, T-shirts, everything." To a lesser extent, Paul hit the interview circuit, too, but his verbiage often descended into jargon. For example: "We're an umbrella to harness other global-branded entertainment groups to develop strategies that integrate the best use of the Internet with rich content to enhance off-line promotions, marketing, and activities." When Paul was asked by an interviewer what he wanted the company to look like five years down the line, he was bluntly grandiose: "I think this will be the successor to Disney as a global lifestyle-brand content creator, producer, marketing and distribution company."

While all this was going on, Stan suddenly saw a conflagration from his past that he had to put out. He'd done an interview with the magazine *Comic Book Marketplace* just before SLM materialized, in which he'd claimed credit for writing that famous scene from *The Amazing Spider-Man* #33 where Spidey lifts a pile of rubble off himself through the strength of his moral convictions. A furious Ditko, who hadn't communicated with the press since the late sixties, emerged from the shadows and wrote a letter to the editors pointing out that the story had been his idea. Just a few months after that, *Time* ran an article that referred to Stan as the sole creator of Spider-Man. Ditko, livid, wrote them a letter, as well: "Spider-Man's existence needed a visual concrete entity," he wrote. "It was a collaboration of writer-editor Stan Lee and Steve Ditko as co-creators." Stan claimed he then called Ditko to hash the matter out. "I saw it meant a lot to him," Stan later recalled. "So I said, 'Fine, I'll tell everybody you're the co-creator.' That didn't quite satisfy him." Stan and Paul huddled to hammer out their official response. "We discussed the fact that it seemed to be a little controversial, and why feed a controversy?" Paul recalls. "What difference does it make? We know [Stan's Marvel artists] played a role in this. If they want to be co-creators, that's fine. At the time, as long as Stan was credited as *a* creator, that satisfied the requirements for his [creative] rights to be maintained."

So Stan and Paul issued an open letter, published in August 1999 on SLM stationery for anyone to see, in which Stan declared, in part, "I have always considered Steve Ditko to be Spider-Man's co-creator." This failed to satisfy Ditko, who put out a pamphlet in which he made a compelling point about the presence of Spidey, whom he visually designed, on Marvel's official documents: "Check Marvel's stationery, mailing labels. *Which* creation is *used?* Word or art? Name or costume?" And he pointedly added, " 'Considered' means to ponder, look at closely, examine, etc., and does not admit, or claim, or state that Steve Ditko is Spider-Man's co-creator."

That may seem like a pedantic distinction, but Ditko turned out to be on to something: In subsequent years, Stan made it clear that his use of the term "co-creator" was a purely formal effort, one that he didn't truly believe in. As he put it while describing Ditko in his autobiography, "I really think I'm being very generous in giving him 'co-creator' credit, because I'm the guy who dreamed up the title, the concept, and the characters." Even after the open-letter incident, an intra-office memo from the Stan Lee archives shows Stan billing himself as "the creator of Spider-Man, the X-Men, the Incredible Hulk, and all the other franchisable characters that have stood the test of time for so many decades." Nevertheless, when it came to public-facing verbiage, 1999 is when "co-creator" entered the lexicons of Stan and his promoters, never to leave. Ditko and Stan remained unreconciled all the way through Ditko's death in the summer of 2018, just a few months before Stan's own demise. To the very end, Ditko refused interviews but kept churning out comics and essays, many of them about the ways in which Stan and Marvel had wronged him.

Back at the turn of the millennium, the Spider-Man dispute didn't seem to matter much, as Marvel was still struggling to prove that it had any juice left in the marketplace and Stan was mostly talking up his newest properties—some developed in partnership with Paul—instead of those of his past. These characters and scenarios were to play out first in animated cartoon "webisodes" rendered in the then-cutting-edge technology of Macromedia Flash, with the aim of transporting them to other mediums after they'd taken off. The centerpiece property was a saga set in cyberspace known as *The 7th Portal*. In it, a young video-game beta-tester named Peter Littlecloud encounters a computer-based gateway to another dimension, populated by champions and monsters. The noble Izayus (voiced by Stan) warns Peter of the danger posed by the sinister Lord Mongorr, who has conquered six other realms and is looking to make Peter's universe his seventh. Peter and his friends soon find themselves doing battle in the digital world, where they are granted superpowers (most of them generic, although Peter's was the odd talent of having super-powerful breath). SLM had its eyes on an array of international markets and, as a result, young Peter's cohort were assembled from all over the world—Germany, Brazil, Japan, India, South Africa—and bore slightly awkward superhero monikers like Conjure Man, Imitatia, and the Streak.

High technology permeated the SLM roster, as further evidenced by another new property, *The Accuser*. That one starred a disabled lawyer whose wheelchair was capable of turning into a robotic battle suit—and more than a few people pointed out that Daredevil had been a lawyer and Iron Man had had a machine outfit, perhaps betraying that Stan didn't have as many original ideas as he'd like to think he did. Another property was *The Drifter,* a story about a gritty cyberpunk loner from the future who came back in time to do battle with an evil corporation, but whose knowledge of things to come caused him to be written off as insane. There were cartoons about a mischievous copy of Stan called Stan's Evil Clone. A Merry Marvel Marching Society-esque fan club for SLM called SCUZZLE (short for Searching Cyberspace for Unknown Zoological Zygomorphic Living Entities) was established.

Most intriguing of all, SLM signed a deal with superstar boy band the Backstreet Boys to create a series called *The Backstreet Project,* in which a spaceship crashes near one of their concerts and the alien inside bestows upon them magic crystals that grant them superpowers—martial-arts expertise, top-flight marksmanship, what have you. The Boys then defend the earth from invasion as the so-called Cyber Crusaders. On top of all that, Stan signed a deal with longtime rival DC Comics to create strange alternative versions of that company's flagship characters in a comics series co-produced by SLM, cumbersomely entitled *Just Imagine Stan Lee Creating the DC Universe.* Whatever you thought of the quality of Stan's ideas in this period, one had to admit that they were cascading into production at a clip unseen in nearly forty years.

The staff expanded at an astounding rate, too, ballooning to roughly forty people within a matter of months. Over time, Paul found a CEO in former Columbia Pictures studio head Kenneth Williams, an executive vice president in the form of a longtime business associate named Stephen Gordon, and a COO named Gill Champion, who had a mysterious past in the entertainment industry. Most bizarre of all, *Zorro, The Gay Blade* star (and friend of Stan's) George Hamilton was hired as the company's president. The collective expansion led to a gradual takeover of the Encino office building— employees regularly complained about the permanent presence of drywall dust in the air. For the first time since the fifties, Stan had an honest-to-God bullpen of creatives at his beck and call, furiously working to churn out the content that the company so desperately wanted to push on stanlee.net in order to drum up enthusiasm.

Stan and Paul took meetings with Hollywood bigwigs in which they chatted up movie adaptations of their newly minted intellectual property—in fact, there's a fascinating video in the Stan Lee archives that Paul shot of a lunch meeting between the two of them and *The Godfather* auteur Francis Ford Coppola. They discuss Coppola working on a *7th Portal* film, although Coppola seems primarily interested in grilling Stan about the origins of his classic Marvel properties. Stan dismisses those properties blithely at one point: "I would've kept doing them, but I suddenly realized, I don't own these, I'm not getting any royalties, and I figured, the hell with it, let 'em pay my salary, and that was it," he says. "And I stopped coming up with new ones after meeting Peter. Now I wanna start it all over again."

However, his ownership of these new properties wasn't so simple, either: They were, per the terms of that fateful contract, owned by Stan Lee Media, which he had a massive share in but wasn't coterminous with his own self—something that would come back to bite him later. So, too, would the company he was keeping. Movie producer Mark Canton met regularly with Stan and Paul about the prospect of making that *7th Portal* movie, and even came to a tentative deal at one point, but Canton had his doubts about Paul. When I ask Canton about his memories of Paul, he diplomatically replies, "[Stan] was working with some people that felt not-solid by my standards," and adds, "I certainly felt that Stan Lee had, in his life, people that inserted themselves so he needed them."

Stan was hardly worried about any of that on February 29, 2000. That balmy night brought the glitzy launch party for the *7th Portal* web-cartoon series at Hollywood's Raleigh Studios, streamed in low resolution through Internet connections around the world. Famed TV host Dick Clark emceed the gala, which attracted figures ranging from actor James Caan to former TV Hulk actor Lou Ferrigno. There was a strange performance from a man who dressed as an extraterrestrial and played synthesizers without touching them, followed by a rollicking number performed by Jerry Lee Lewis. Larry King piped in a message of support to "one of the true American innovators, Stan Lee"; a similar one from James Cameron featured the filmmaker calling Stan "a one-man, walking, talking Big Bang Theory in action." Chaka Khan did a song. There was a satellite simulcast of an audience watching in Japan. A beaming Paul spoke of how *The 7th Portal* "signals a new era for the Hollywood creative community—we are all now the true pioneers of a totally interactive, participatory, and instantaneous global medium." Stan, uncharacteristically clad in stylish head-to-toe black, gave a brief address, and Dick Clark noted that "Stan the Man" was "soon to be known as Stan the Brand."

There was one slightly ominous moment at the end of the live broadcast, when Champion, Gordon, and other SLM higher-ups presented a token of their gratitude to Paul. "Without your vision and your leadership, we wouldn't be here tonight," Champion said before giving Paul a large placard on which Paul's face was superimposed over that of *7th Portal* supervillain Mongorr, in the form of a WANTED poster. It ended up being more appropriate than it seemed at the time, as the whole evening may well have been the celebration of an unlawful act. It would later emerge that writers Steven Salim and Jesse Stagg claimed to have approached Stan in the nineties about a never-realized project called *Jason and the Cybernauts,* which followed almost the exact same setup as what would be *The 7th Portal,* and that Stan and Paul ripped off their idea. They would go on to sue years later, and a settlement was reached that paid them $200,000 and allowed them to snatch up the rights to *The 7th Portal* should they choose to do so. That would prove to be the least of Stan and Paul's concerns when it came to SLM and its impact.

However, as of mid-2000, the company was continuing to rise at a rocket's pace, its share price climbing ever upward. The fuel was a copious amount of cash—one estimate said the company spent more than $20 million in the first year of its existence. But it seemed to be paying off in the short term: When *The 7th Portal* launched, SLM was capitalized at around $300 million in the market—nearly $100 million more than the market cap for still-suffering Marvel. "I thought we had some money in the company and—whether it was Peter's idea or mine, but the point is—we both discussed, 'Gee, wouldn't it be something if we could actually buy Marvel?'" Stan said years later in sworn testimony regarding Paul. "I remember I said, 'I hope it can be a friendly takeover.'" There was another potential buyer for the House of Ideas: Michael Jackson. The international icon, long a fan of Marvel Comics, came to visit the SLM offices, videotaped by Paul. In the tape, an awed Jackson watches as Stan signs posters for him and his friends. "He strikes a nerve in every human," Jackson says of Stan. "He is the psyche of our youth. And I grew up watching his comics, and it just tickles me so much to know that we are talking and working and planning to do something together. It's like a dream come true." According to a former SLM employee, at one point in Jackson's visit, Jackson told Stan he was thinking of buying Marvel. "If I buy Marvel," Jackson asked, "you'll help me run it, won't you?" to which Stan reportedly replied, "Sure, I'll be here."

There were similar meetings with other musical stars. Mary J. Blige was going to be converted into a superhero in the mode of the Backstreet Boys, whose Cyber Crusader alter egos were now populating kids' meals at Burger King in the form of cheap plastic giveaway toys. There was even a dialogue between Stan and Wu-Tang Clan rapper RZA about pursuing some sort of mutual entertainment endeavor. When asked about being associated with the lyrically violent and oft-offensive Wu crew, Stan replied, "If they're popular with young people, I don't mind being associated with them. Maybe in our own way, we can turn them away from gangsta rapping." In other words, no goal was too lofty in those days. Stan was kept quite busy with all of these encounters, as well as interviews, daily sessions with his teams of creatives, and long periods of signing piles of posters and promotional items at Paul's behest. A former employee suspects that, when Stan grew tired of the signing, he would let Paul forge his signature on the remaining items; another ex-staffer recalls Stan doing a mass-autograph session and asking, genuinely befuddled, "Who are all these for?"

That sort of confusion was, it seems, deeply ingrained at SLM. Speak to former employees of the company and they'll generally tell you a few things: The content being made was of questionable quality, none of them had any clue what the overall corporate direction was, Stan was as charming and energetic as ever, and they were all either suspicious or terrified of Paul. "To this day, I don't understand the full dynamic of Stan Lee Media," recalls Mark Evanier, who, despite having been Kirby's assistant, had known Stan professionally and personally for decades and was hired to supervise a group of animators. "I used to walk around that office and say 'We don't sell anything. We have no product. We have nothing.' There was always a deal pending for us, *7th Portal* or a *Drifter* line or something else, but the deals never materialized." In Paul, Evanier saw a man he couldn't trust: "Every time I shook hands with him, I wanted to bathe in tomato juice," he recalls. "Peter Paul's office, you'd sit there and you're surrounded by 'Look at all the fancy people I've met.' There's Muhammad Ali's boxing gloves and photos of Peter with everybody. He would just hit you with 'name drop, name drop, name drop,' and how connected he was." Stan, too, frustrated Evanier in their creative meetings: "He was shooting everything down," Evanier says. "Nothing was good enough, because nothing was the new Silver Surfer."

This combination of discomfort with the leadership and the gumming-up of the creative works was endemic. Stan's pal Ron Friedman was brought in as vice president of development and content and immediately took a dislike to Paul, whom he now calls an "absolute swine" before noting that many of the other staffers were no better. For example, he says he once met Paul's "money man" and was appalled by what he heard from him. "Peter Paul said, 'This guy witnessed the suicide of Salvador Allende,'" Friedman recalls, referring to the much-disputed 1973 death of the Chilean president. "I said, 'You witnessed the suicide of Salvador Allende?' He says, 'Better than that, *I shot the fucker*. I was with the CIA and I shot the fucker.' So I'm thinking, *Who are these people?*" A former high-level employee who asked to remain anonymous for fear of legal trouble says at least one other high-level employee would come to work drunk "every day."

Writer Buzz Dixon was brought on board as creative director and abruptly promoted to vice president for creative affairs. The grandiosity of the corporate vision at SLM astonished him, and not in a good way. "They thought somebody in Mumbai would pay them money to set up an office in Mumbai, where they would take characters and develop them for India," he recalls. Dixon thinks Paul was a "flippin' sociopath" who had no idea how to manage the empire he'd built: "It seemed like anyone who would ask Peter Paul concrete questions about 'How are we gonna make money off all of this?' made him nervous," he says. Stan, too, would drive Dixon nuts. Take, for example, their discussion of that Mumbai idea: In the planned stories for the Indian market, Stan wanted to call the city by its British imperial name, Bombay, and Dixon pointed out that that wasn't the preferred nomenclature anymore. Stan was insistent that they stick with Bombay. "And it could not penetrate to Stan that if you want to sell something to the Indian audience, you have to find out what they want," Dixon says. Stan seemed similarly out of touch to his receptionist, Holli Schmidt: "He'd say stuff like 'Come take a letter,' and wanted to know if I knew shorthand," she recalls with a laugh. When I ask what she made of Paul, there's a long pause before she simply says, "I thought he was a bit aggressive."

Such aggression seemed necessary for the kind of growth the company sought. That growth would feed Stan's ego, but it would also keep him financially afloat. One highly placed employee I spoke to grew close with Stan and suspected that Stan, despite being worth millions on paper thanks to SLM's stock price, was so desperate for liquid cash that his judgment was distorted. "Joan would spend every penny [Stan] would make," the employee says. "I mean, from what I had heard, she was easily spending fifty thousand a month on crap. She would go to auctions, jewelry stores, antiques stores. She had a problem." Joan wasn't alone: "JC was a problem, too. I remember he bought her a house in, like, 2000, and somebody helped him to raise the money for that. He took cash and he bought her a house. He would do everything for his kid." Paul remembers Joan possessing unusual habits when it came to money. "She used to bury diamonds all around the property," he says, referring to Stan and Joan's home. "She had this thing about diamonds, and she was constantly buying diamonds. She had a fixation on diamonds."

Although money was coming into Stan's wallet, even he reached a point where he realized that his future probably wasn't as bright as it had seemed just a few months prior. In the first quarter of 2000, SLM posted a revenue of just $296,000, against a net loss of $5.4 million. The Stan Lee archives contain a pair of what appear to be email messages that Stan sent to the SLM leadership. The first is eyebrow-raising: He laments that SCUZZLE is "dying on the vine" and suggests juicing interest for the ostensibly kid-oriented site with some T&A: "Just like there's a 'Playboy's Playmate of the Week,' let's have a 'Scuzzle Sweetie of the Week,'" Stan wrote. "Or 'Scuzzle's Most Adorable Agent of the Week!' Or 'Scuzzle's Grooviest Girl-Friend of the Week,' or 'Scuzzle's Coolest Chick of the Week' or 'Scuzzle's Most Exotic Enemy of the Week.' You get the idea." He notes that "we must play up a cartoon and some features that involve Wrestling," proposes features with names like "Maggie the Model," "Supermodels from Hell!", "Melanie's Modeling School," "Bikini Betty, the Peach of the Beach," "Stan's Bikini Babe of the Week," and—in an echo of projects past and projects yet to come—he pitches "Hysterical History," in which "interesting photos" of historical figures will be selected "so I can add whacky dialogue balloons."

Even more remarkable is a message that Stan penned for his fellow SLM higher-ups, which begins with a blunt sentence: "I just had an epiphany—Our website <u>stinks!</u>" It goes on to describe a litany of ways in which SLM was dropping the ball. "Think about it—what are we offering to make anyone come to our site—and, even if they do come, why would they want to come back????" he wrote. "I logged on myself last night; after a few minutes I got bored and went away!" The list of complaints went on and on: "We're trying to be all things to all people—but our target audience—the hip, teenage fans, aren't getting what they want." "7th Portal is a disaster. Even if The Accuser and The Drifter are better, two weeks is too long a wait between episodes. Nobody cares that much." "And there's too much 'Stan Lee' all over the place. You don't see Walt Disney splattered all over—or George Lucas—or anyone. I think using my name and image so much is a case of overkill." And yet, in the face of these issues, Stan saw only chaos at the upper echelons. "Another problem is—who the hell is responsible for things???" he wrote. "I feel like the little kid in that fairy tale who yells out, 'But the Emperor is wearing no clothes!' Everyone's working around the clock, doing a million things to our site, but we all seem to be too busy to notice that the site's a bomb!!!"

The message is also notable for the fact that it suggests Stan wasn't exactly in the know about the deepest inner workings of the company that bore his name. According to those who worked with him, that appeared to be the case. "If you think of it in levels, Peter was the first level, Stan was on the second level, I was on level three, and the artists were on five or six," Buzz Dixon recalled. "I think there were wheels within wheels that Stan may not have been aware of."

PAUL LONGED TO BRING greater prestige to SLM, prestige on the level of past achievements like the American Spirit Foundation. So he set his sight about as high as it could go. Despite his history of loyalty to Republican political operatives, he decided he wanted outgoing president Bill Clinton to act as a global ambassador for

SLM after leaving office. Perhaps unsurprisingly, he had an inroad toward that goal. Years before, Paul had met and worked with an avowed con artist named Aaron Tonken, who had made a name for himself by befriending Hollywood celebrities and corralling them into glitzy fundraising galas. Tonken—who began his memoir with the sentence, "In a land of moral imbeciles, I knew I could be king"—eventually ingratiated himself with the Democratic Party establishment, helping an associate of convicted-felon financier and Clinton friend Marc Rich throw high-end fundraisers. When Paul decided to get in bed with the Clintons, he reached out to his old friend Tonken, who informed him that he'd been invited to a small, $30,000-to-$55,000-per-plate dinner with Bill and Hillary Clinton in Los Angeles. Paul and Tonken got into the event and made contact with the president and first lady and, in the ensuing weeks, ties grew between the Tonken–Paul brain trust and Hillary's campaign to become the next senator from New York. It was decided that Paul would enter the fundraising arena.

He started to throw elite events for the Democrats in 2000's pivotal election: a fundraiser for Al Gore at the Beverly Hills Hotel (Stan got to present a poster featuring a superhero-ified Gore character called the Silicon Surfer), a Hillary fundraising lunch at top-flight restaurant Spago (Dionne Warwick sang, something Paul says cost him $25,000, and Stan got to sit right next to Hillary), and a sunny afternoon tea party for two hundred Hollywood donors (video of it shows Hillary thanking Peter, Andrea Paul, Stan, and Joan by first name, something that must have electrified Stan). Hillary visited the SLM offices—animators were abruptly pulled off their projects to hastily assemble a welcome video in which an animated Stan quipped about creating a superheroine named Super Senator and Lord Mongorr intoned, "I shall rule everything. Except New York. I hear you've got a lock on it." Photos were taken of the grinning Clintons posing alongside the Pauls. At these events, Paul laid out parts of his curious past in direct conversations with Hillary, including mentioning that he was involved in anti-Castro activities and that he once ratted out Carter administration budget director Bert Lance. "I mean, I wasn't hiding anything," Paul says. "I was testing her to see how far I'd go with her." If there was any effective vetting going on, surely Hillary and her campaign would have been aware of his felonious past. But either they did an incompetent job, consisting of a quick online search for Paul's name (as a Clintons' lawyer would later claim), or they weren't bothered enough by his criminal convictions to avoid associating with him.

Whatever the case, it was decided that Paul and Tonken would throw their biggest shindig yet. The plan was to organize a Hollywood send-off for Bill that raised money for Hillary. The arrangements were hastily made and, on August 12, 2000, the 1,300-person tribute fundraiser took place on a $30 million estate. It was a massive undertaking, but it was initially a screaming success for all involved. "The Hollywood Gala Salute to President William Jefferson Clinton" was officially identified as a production of SLM, and Stan and Joan got to sit next to the two Clintons, with Paul and his wife on their opposite flank. Diana Ross belted out "Ain't No Mountain High Enough," Cher cheekily confessed that she didn't vote for Bill but sang "If I Could Turn Back Time" as a plea for forgiveness, and Bill cried as he listened to singer/songwriter Melissa Etheridge say he had partly inspired her to publicly announce that she was gay. Eventually, Bill spoke to the assembled members of the donor class, spouting platitudes about brighter futures: "The kind of chance we have today to build a future of our dreams for our kids maybe, maybe, comes along once in a lifetime," he said. "Nothing stays the same. So thanks for the honor, thanks for the memories you gave me tonight, but don't stop"—a pause—"thinkin' about tomorrow." Paul later told a reporter, "It was the apogee of my career." Everyone went home feeling like a winner.

The feeling was fleeting. Three days later, *Washington Post* gossip columnist Lloyd Grove wrote in his column that one of the gala's producers, Paul, was a convicted felon and rhetorically asked, "Is Hillary Clinton soft on crime?" Paul wrote Grove an open letter in which he laid out the secret anti-communist reasoning for his previous jail time, convincing few. The next day, Grove wrote that Federal Election Commission records put Paul down as a donor of $2,000 to Hillary's campaign, the legal maximum for individuals. The campaign announced that it was giving the check back, but no mention was made of a key fact, says Paul: He'd spent $1.176 million of his own money on the gala, which was both a violation of election laws and an amount significantly larger than the $401,419 cost that the campaign had reported to the FEC.

That last fact had yet to come out when Bill and Hillary sent separate thank-you notes to Stan and Paul that weekend; Bill's to Stan was handwritten and read "Thanks so much for the wonderful event—I loved it and am very grateful for the boost it gave Hillary's campaign." But as word spread in Hollywood and the Beltway that Paul was who he was, his name became toxic, and an invitation to the final state dinner of the Clinton presidency was rescinded. Paul, to this day, insists that he and Bill had already come to an agreement that the latter would act as a global spokesperson for SLM, so the distancing that the Clintons were carrying out infuriated him. But, as it turned out, he didn't have much time to worry about a welched deal. He had more-pressing concerns.

What came next remains a matter of great dispute between Paul and, well, virtually everyone else. As 2000 wore on, the dot-com bubble was rapidly contracting, putting SLM in a perilous position. Paul and his team secured a deal with a bank to get $2.2 million in short-term financing, with the catch that the stock price had to stay above $1—something that seemed possible, given that it had been trading between $7 and $9 per share most days. But, on November 27, 2000, a few days after Thanksgiving, the price plummeted to $3 a share. The next day, it fell to $1.75. Investors panicked and sold like crazy, dropping the stock price to 13 cents—far below that $1 bank threshold. The financing was cut off, throwing the company into a sudden, horrifying panic. SLM staffer Scott Koblish would later speak about seeing nervous creatives during those shocking days: "You could hear them calling out the tumbling stock price in the bullpen area. And as loud as the panic was downstairs, there was a tremendous silence coming from upstairs." Soda delivery stopped, after the delivery man let it be known that he hadn't been paid in months. Paul flew to Brazil—he claims it was to shore up his other major company, a language-education firm called Mondo English, but prosecutors would later say it was to escape what he knew was coming. One day, employees were sent emails informing them that they were fired, only for the company to announce that it was a computer mistake and that no one was being terminated. Yet.

Rock bottom arrived on December 15. "We went home one night and then came in the next day and, somehow, overnight, everything had changed," says former SLM staffer Dana Moreshead. Emails went out informing the company's roughly 140 employees that there would be a meeting at 2 P.M. in the bullpen. "The computer guys burned copies of their Napster songs and the Flash files of what we did on the shows so we could keep something for our portfolios," said Koblish. "They were shut out of the system at 4 P.M." But by 4 P.M., everyone had already been told that they were getting fired. Kenneth Williams had informed the assembled group of employees that they were all out of a job and that the company was shutting down operations. "It was a crushing blow to Stan," recalls Dixon. Koblish later said Stan literally collapsed when he heard the news. By sheer coincidence, a life-size Spider-Man statue was being delivered to the offices that day, and employees had to somberly construct it from its constituent parts and present it to the devastated man whose name was on the building. "I remember being in his office and he was pretty sad and he was crying," recalls Schmidt, the receptionist. "He kissed the top of my head and said, 'I'm so sorry.'"

As Stan started individually calling newly fired people on the phone to apologize, matters only got worse. On January 2, 2001, the rump SLM entity, by now employing only Stan and a few execs, announced that it was being looked at by the Securities and Exchange Commission. Investigators were curious about why the SLM stock had so abruptly dropped off a cliff and said they found alarming evidence of fraud at the top levels of SLM. Here's where the dispute comes in: The federal government, an auditor hired by SLM, and multiple former SLM execs have gone on the record to say they learned that Paul had built the company on fraud; Paul claims everything he did was perfectly legal and that it was Williams, Stephen Gordon, and a "cabal" of others that sought to take SLM down to plunder the assets.

The details would require more space than this narrative allows, but, in short, Paul and Gordon were accused of inflating the price of the company's stock through a variety of methods, such as lying to the press and hiring a Wall Street analyst to plug the company in bogus research reports. Subsequent to that, according to the charges, Paul and Gordon opened accounts at Merrill Lynch and, using SLM stocks as collateral, borrowed millions of dollars on margin—thus converting their stock into instant cash without disclosing it to investors. They allegedly then used shell companies to invest more than $2 million of the borrowed money into SLM, providing the illusion that the companies were independent entities betting big on the endeavor. Gordon's brother, a broker at a branch of Merrill Lynch, stood accused of facilitating the transactions and getting $340,000 in off-the-books payments. They were also accused of trying to save the company by writing checks from empty accounts (Paul maintains that the accounts weren't empty, per se, because they were based on SLM stock), a process known as check-kiting. On top of all that, there was an accusation that Paul and Gordon were buying back their own shares of SLM through two co-conspirators to boost the stock price. When the stock-buyback scheme ran out of cash, so the allegations go, the share price declined and a brokerage firm that had loaned Paul money made a margin call that dumped more than 170,000 shares. It was that final act that triggered the stock collapse and all that came after.

The Department of Justice indicted Gordon and Paul, though the latter was still in Brazil. Stan was investigated but cleared of wrongdoing and has always pleaded ignorance: "I have absolutely no idea who paid for what at any time in our company," he said in sworn testimony a few years later. But the anonymous high-level SLM staffer I spoke to was senior enough to have known the wheels within wheels at the company and is adamant that Stan lied to investigators and prosecutors. "One thing about Stan is he knew everything that was going on, but he always played the dummy," the employee says. "His game was 'Oh, I'm just a simple old man that really doesn't understand what's going on, but Peter will help you out.' . . . He was a nice man, but it was very apparent that he was playing this innocent, didn't-understand-what-was-going-on type of guy." Paul, on the other hand, was picked up by Interpol in Brazil and detained in what he says was called "the Corridor of Death," a stretch of jail where people had been burned alive a few months earlier and where, he claims, he was cellmates with an al-Qaeda terrorist. As with so much associated with Peter Paul and Stan Lee, objective truth is elusive, and bombast drowns out any potential contrition.

The men had much in common, and those similarities had drawn them together for nearly a decade and a half. But they would never meet again in their lifetimes, and the wounds they inflicted on each other only festered. According to Paul and his wife, Stan and Joan never once reached out to make sure that Paul's family was doing all right, despite the fact that they ostensibly had nothing to do with whatever happened at SLM. Stan never liked to talk about the period from 1998 to 2001. Years later, when he commissioned a comics-format memoir based on his prose one of a few years prior, the writer of the comic, Peter David, wrote out multiple pages' worth of narrative about SLM. David was told by Stan's people to excise them entirely. All that was left and approved was an anecdote about meeting the Clintons and a single panel in which a resentful-looking cartoon Stan muses, "Also around then I was talked into starting up an *Internet* company. Seemed like a good idea at the time. It wasn't. It ended badly and the less said the better." This was wishful verbiage on Stan's part, as there was and would still be much left to say about Stan Lee Media and its impact on his life.

But, in the meantime, there was still money to be made. Stan quickly formed a business alliance with three fellow SLM refugees, and the quartet started concocting a plan for a new venture. It was to be one that portrayed itself as the quiet, workaday alternative to SLM, free of Paul's brashness and hubris. As it turned out, that new enterprise picked up its own allegations of extensive fraud, but SLM would always remain Stan's most visible professional embarrassment by a length and a mile. Paul would eventually return to Stan's life at a distance, but their friendship, which had brought both men to fairy-dust riches, was permanently, irrevocably ceased. All that was left was a stinging reminder of the dangers of Wall Street froth, style winning out over substance, and the impulse to cut corners. Stan had been able to taste the sky, but, after all was said and done, he'd rarely been lower to the ground.

9.

SPOTLIGHT
AND SHADOW

———

(2001–2017)

———

WHEN I ASK JUNKO KOBAYASHI ABOUT THE ALLEGED CRIMES she witnessed or committed while working for POW Entertainment, Stan's second post-Marvel company, it isn't long before she starts crying. It's not the first conversation I've had with the former chief financial officer of POW, but it's the one that the previous two were leading up to. After some initial chatter, I dive into the locus of my questioning: a concise signed declaration from a private investigator named Becky Altringer in which Altringer enumerates various misdeeds that Kobayashi allegedly confessed to her, many of them involving POW executives Gill Champion and Arthur Lieberman. It's serious stuff, with lines like "Kobayashi stated that she has a large amount of evidence to prove illegal activities were conducted by Arthur Lieberman and Gill Champion," "Kobayashi stated that she had been guilty of altering some documents and bookkeeping records when she was working for Stan Lee Media and POW Entertainment," "Kobayashi stated that she was in possession of illegal bookkeeping records that could cause Lieberman and Champion to go to prison," and "Kobayashi stated that she lied under oath in regard to Peter Paul's criminal case because Arthur Lieberman threatened her."

Over the phone, I describe the document to Kobayashi and ask her if she stands by what she's recorded as saying. She admits that she spoke with Altringer, then says she can't speak to the veracity of the document unless it's notarized. "I'm going to tell you right now," she says, "to have to go through all this stuff again, and have to go back and take the time to look through stuff that I had back then, it's going to kill me." She tells me the situation isn't fair, that the burden of proof shouldn't be on her. "I've been so cooperative with you, and now you're telling me that I have to defend myself on something that apparently I did illegally?" she says, her voice rising. She denounces POW: "To have to defend myself on something that I didn't believe in, I feel that that's really unfair to me. I left because I didn't believe in POW." Then she changes her mind and says she won't respond even if I get the notarization. "I just can't take it," she says, her voice quivering. "It's too much. It was a lot for me to handle at that time. I just don't want to go through it now, again. I'm over it. I'm really over it." She finally cracks into a sob. "I can't deal with this," she cries. "I just can't deal. This is not cool. I never did anything illegal. . . . I just can't do this. Please."

Such is the legacy of Stan's final attempt to achieve professional success. Ostensibly a humble shop dedicated to gifting the world with new gems from the mind of the man who made Marvel, POW was mired in accusations of criminal activity. It stands accused of routinely ripping off investors, lying to shareholders, entering the stock market through an illegitimate merger, and committing bankruptcy fraud, among other misconduct. Reports differ as to how much Stan knew about what was going on, but even if he was out of the loop, his decision to *stay* out of the loop and remain uninterested in his own company's dealings—especially in the wake of the Stan Lee Media debacle—does not speak well of him. Perhaps his neglect meant he ultimately had no problem with the commission of crimes, so long as the company kept filling his coffers with relatively easy money, as one lawsuit claims.

That may also be the reasoning behind a number of relationships that bloomed for Stan in the period between the death of SLM and another death, which would prove even more devastating. One by one, people of unstable morals entered Stan's life, promising him fame and riches, so long as he didn't ask too many questions about how the sausage was being made—and didn't worry too much that he, too, might be getting bilked by them. What's more, members of Stan's inner circle say JC lost all control in this stretch of time, allegedly going so far as to physically attack her parents.

And yet, in a stunning contrast, while Stan became mired in the grime of his private world, his public image shone brighter than ever. As the Marvel brand ascended—first gradually, then rapidly— to the heights Stan had dreamed of, he was allowed to bask in its reflected glory, his face plastered on the big screen in cameo appearances that made him recognizable around the globe and swiftly solidified his status as a cultural icon of the upper echelons. However, he had to grapple with the fact that he could never be as famous as the characters he claimed to have created, nor would he directly enjoy the fruits of this cinematic success in financial terms. As Stan grinned for the peoples of the world, his own world was rotting from the inside.

POW was, in many ways, a kind of life raft from the sinking of SLM, formed by four of its survivors. One was Kobayashi, a chipper, serious-minded accountant who had served as the chief auditor for SLM since the early days and had been one of the first to uncover Peter Paul's alleged financial malfeasance. Another was Gill Champion, a "personable guy," in the words of Kobayashi, as well as the chief operating officer of SLM and someone with a past in sales and entertainment that no one seemed to know much about. Champion produced two soft-core pornographic films in the 1970s; then, according to him, worked as a co-producer on the Paul Newman vehicle *Fort Apache, The Bronx;* was head of production for a company that developed *The Boys from Brazil* and *The Shining*; and went on to act as CEO of a merchandising company called American Cinema-Stores, which, as Champion puts it, "sold retail merchandise at movie theaters and other venues." There are less-savory aspects of his past: One man claimed Champion met him in the eighties and that Champion lied about being a producer of the Academy Awards, took $250,000 of the man's money to produce video projects, then never actually created the videos and ran off with the cash—a move that Champion would later be repeatedly accused of pulling off at POW. (Champion tells me over email that he has no memory of the man or the incident.)

There was Arthur Lieberman, a lawyer who had interacted with Marvel in the seventies while representing the owners of licensed Marvel character Conan the Barbarian. He later did legal work for Dow Chemical, and then represented Stan in his 1998 contract negotiations—Peter Paul says it was his idea to hire Lieberman for that—before working more extensively with SLM. Lieberman was a hefty man with a big personality that could turn on a dime. "You knew when Arthur was in the room," says a friend named Alan Neigher. "Booming voice, amazing laughter, as funny as anybody I've ever met." But, as Kobayashi says, "He was a shark." Lieberman and Stan formed a close relationship—"almost like a father and son," according to Neigher—and, as Kobayashi puts it, "A lot of people thought of him as a real son of a bitch, and he kind of was. But what I appreciate about him: He fought fiercely. So if he felt like somebody was doing some injustice to Stan, he fought. He fought *hard*." In a lesser role was Mike Kelly, a stern and quiet man who had been Stan's assistant through Marvel for years, helping him with editorial and administrative tasks, and who retained that Marvel role but also began working on the POW payroll.

And finally there was Stan, a man gutted by the loss of SLM, the endeavor that was supposed to be his crowning achievement. For a few months after SLM ceased production and fired nearly everyone, CEO Kenneth Williams made some desperate attempts to tell the press that the company would get back on its feet, but it was clear to everyone else that nothing like that was in the offing. On January 30, 2001, Stan and Lieberman sent a letter to Williams alleging that SLM had breached its contract with Stan, thus freeing him to leave, but that he would also "continue to perform services to the company to assure the equitable distribution of assets to creditors and stockholders" and would waive his rights to challenge the 1998 assignment of his intellectual property to SLM. Just a few days later, SLM filed for bankruptcy. The humiliating process of mass liquidation of property began. "I led this whole crazy paring-down thing and I had everybody going to all the production areas, because we let everybody go and there weren't very many people left," Kobayashi recalls. "So everybody rolled up their sleeves. We started emptying out desks, we started putting everything into boxes, we started moving the computers and figuring out stuff we needed to keep. Literally, I had people running up to me like 'Should we keep this? What do we do about this? What is this one worth?'"

Stan initially put on a slightly happy face for the public, telling interviewers that the company was trying to restore itself, but even he couldn't keep up the façade for very long, and in June he formally left the company. That same month, Paul and three others were indicted for various financial crimes relating to SLM. Although there was still a legal entity named Stan Lee Media, Inc., its unpaid sole employee for the next six years was Kobayashi, whose role was confined to the legal and financial complications of dismantling a company. By any rubric, it was an ignominious end for the first stage of the SLM saga.

Yet Stan still held out hope for a brighter tomorrow. Along with Champion, Lieberman, and Kobayashi, he concocted a new company that was to be called POW Entertainment, sometimes styled with an exclamation point after "POW," an acronym ostensibly standing for "purveyors of wonder," although that unpacked version of the name was hardly ever used. The company was launched as a limited-liability corporation in November, its sole stated goal being to leverage Stan's creativity to launch new pieces of intellectual property that bore his name. However, the POW crew also had their eyes on some existing properties, namely SLM's *The Drifter,*

The Accuser, Stan's Evil Clone, and—most important of all—the rights to Stan's name, likeness, and trademarked slogans. In order to get them, they engaged in transactions that were suspicious at best and criminal at worst. That same month, Stan and his cohort formed a company called QED Productions, LLC, and by April of 2002 they were working to divert the SLM properties to it. The bankruptcy court approved the sale of those properties to a Stan-controlled entity that was slated to be called SLC, LLC—however, for whatever reason, POW moved the properties to QED instead, in an apparent contravention of the approved plan that a judge would later find to be unlawful. (When I ask Champion about the QED sale, he defers to a lawyer named Chaz Rainey, who tells me, "There should be no doubt at this point that POW is the sole owner of Stan Lee's writings since he left Marvel and is furthermore the sole owner of Stan Lee's name, likeness, and related publicity rights. He explicitly assigned these rights to POW in no fewer than seven different documents over a period of seventeen years.")

What's more, Kobayashi, the only employee of SLM and also the newly minted CFO of POW, was self-dealing: Instead of adhering to her duty to SLM's remaining shareholders to try to get the firm back on its feet, she was actively working to plunder the old company for her new one. No one in the wider public seemed to be paying attention to any of this, and POW started garnering a certain degree of positive press for its first few steps. They announced a first-look deal with MGM and Bruce Willis's Cheyenne Enterprises to make three movies: *The Femizons* (perhaps a callback to Stan's old pitch to Whoopi Goldberg), *The Double Man,* and *Nightbird*. None of them came to fruition, but another endeavor did.

In the SLM period, Paul had set Stan up with celebrity biographer George Mair to work on a memoir, and on May 7, 2002, *Excelsior!: The Amazing Life of Stan Lee* finally saw the light of day, closing a loop that had begun with Stan's failed attempt at an autobiography in the seventies. The book was largely self-serving, contained numerous falsehoods, reinforced Stan's legend, and elided anything for which he might be found to be at fault. Roughly six pages were dedicated to the still-throbbing wound of SLM, and all the blame was laid at Paul's feet, with Stan merely lamenting that he himself was such a "trusting guy." As it wound down, the book declared that "if any form of today's entertainment can reach the public, there's no way that POW! and I won't be a part of it," and concluded with the following claim: "It's all so different from the first time I started working in comics, when I figured I'd hang with it for a while until I got some experience and then I'd go out and get into the real world. I think I just might be ready now. Excelsior!"

Whatever good press *Excelsior* might have brought was immediately overshadowed by a further legal entanglement. Since Stan signed his 1998 contract with Marvel, the company had, at long last, scored three hits at the box office: 1998's *Blade,* 2000's *X-Men,* and 2002's *Spider-Man.* Although Stan had nothing to do with creating these films, his contract stipulated that he would receive 10 percent of Marvel's profits on its film and television projects (though not any portion of the licensing fees). And yet, on June 17, an article in *The Times* of London had revealed a shocking claim: Stan hadn't been paid for any of the pictures. "Oh, no, I haven't made a penny," he told the reporter, adding that viewers of *Spider-Man* "read that the movie will make half a billion dollars so they figure I'll get about a third of that, but no." He said it didn't matter much to him: "I try not to look at yesterday. I try to look ahead." Similarly, he appeared in a profile on CBS television and, when asked if he felt "screwed" by Marvel concerning the profits, he simply replied, "I try not to think of it." However, he either had a change of heart or was goaded into one by someone else: Just a few weeks after the CBS segment aired, Stan filed a $10 million lawsuit against Marvel with the aid of Lieberman, claiming that Stan's contract had been violated.

The suit sent shock waves throughout the media: How could Stan be suing the company that he made and that, in turn, made him? It was, as one news commentator put it, "like Colonel Sanders suing Kentucky Fried Chicken." The suit also made public Marvel's

1998 contract with Stan, thus allowing everyone to see that he was being paid $1 million a year for doing virtually nothing and, more important, that Marvel had previously kept the details of the contract secret from their shareholders, raising suspicions about the whole process. Paul and his allies have a specific conspiracy theory about the whole situation, which is that Marvel knew the intellectual-property claims in the 1998 contract were rendered void by SLM's prior contract with Stan, that Marvel's garbled legal situation in the sixties meant Stan might actually have had copyrights over the Marvel characters he claimed to have created, and that SLM thus held those copyrights now. In other words, there's a strong possibility that Marvel thought their rights were in ambiguous territory and were terrified of what Stan might choose to do.

However, within a few months, discussion of the suit died down and the biggest headline for Stan was the arrival of a new character, the last one with any notable brand-name recognition that he would ever be associated with. At a party, Stan encountered the brother of supermodel/actor Pamela Anderson, who was then playing the lead role on an action TV series called *V.I.P.* Stan, as was his wont, sought to ingratiate himself by offering to turn Pamela into a fictional character. The brother and Stan worked out an idea for a crusader with an exotic-dancer civilian identity and the libidinous code name of Stripperella. Stan was invited to the set of *V.I.P.* and he and Anderson hit it off: "I loved the idea," she recalls, adding, "Stan is brilliant. Very creative," and noting that they disagreed only on one thing: "Stan wanted nudity. I didn't."

However, there really wasn't anything to the idea as of then, just the name and the vague notion of a woman who fights evil and takes her clothes off in public. Nevertheless, POW, Anderson, and Stan sold *Stan Lee's Stripperella* as an animated series to cable network TNN. The actual task of creating the show was left not to Stan but rather to the two showrunners of the children's TV comedy series *All That,* Heath Seifert and Kevin Kopelow. As Kopelow recalls, "They called us and they go, 'Hey, we have a meeting. We want to hook you up with Stan Lee. You guys are creative and funny. We want to do a show called *Stripperella* with Stan Lee. Pam Anderson is the voice.' We're like 'What else do you know about it?' And they go, 'It airs June 26.'" Seifert and Kopelow were a little confused. As Seifert recalls it, "I go 'Is she a crimefighter, or is she a spy, or a superhero?' And they're like 'It's up to you guys!'"

The duo shrugged and decided on a tonal direction for the show: "We looked at it as a really great opportunity to do absurdist humor—this non sequitur, fun, campy thing," Seifert says. "We were doing something way, way out of Stan's comfort zone. So he kind of put the reins in our hands and said, 'Let's see what happens here.' We went out and wrote this pilot and it was really out there." The pilot introduced Erotica Jones, exotic dancer by night and secret agent by later at night, and pitted her against a villain named Dr. Cesarean, who is injecting supermodels with implants that make them obese. "Stan really thought it was funny," Seifert says. "And we appreciated that, that he had this sense of humor." Seifert and Kopelow wrote out scripts for the first season at a lightning clip, with virtually no input from Stan, although they say they had lunch with him (and, occasionally, Champion) nearly every day to get approvals and chat about life. They found Stan to be "super creatively supportive," as Seifert puts it.

The first season premiered on June 26, 2003, and garnered mild praise from a handful of critics for its tongue-in-cheek ribaldry. However, it got a scathing review in the *New York Post,* which declared, "It makes for desperately sad television," and the production was marred by a bizarre lawsuit. A Florida-based dancer named Janet Clover claimed that she'd once spent hours doing a private show for Stan and told him about how she led a double life as a philanthropist on the side, which she claimed led to his idea for the dual-identity Stripperella. The case went nowhere, but neither did the show: It was canceled after just thirteen episodes and, by then, had cemented itself as an object of ridicule for Stan's detractors, who still point to *Stripperella* as proof of Stan's creative shortcomings.

If Stan had doubts about his own abilities, he certainly didn't let them show. In fact, POW was presenting an image of the octogenarian Stan as a creative powerhouse, capable of churning out a wealth of ideas that could be converted into lucrative entertainment properties. However, POW's primary product was announcements. Throughout the last decade and a half of Stan's life, POW flooded the press with news about an overwhelming number of deals and projects that had emerged, Athena-like, from the head of Stan. There was *The Forever Man,* a movie to be made in partnership with a production company called Idiom and written by a newcomer named Luke McMullen. "It has to do with crime and punishment in the not-too-distant future and a unique way of punishing people who are menaces to society," Stan said in a statement, adding that he came up with the story in two days. "It's a concept that hasn't been seen before, with tremendously interesting villains with unique powers." At San Diego Comic-Con, he announced *Hef's Superbunnies,* a cartoon series produced in coalition with *Playboy* and its figurehead, Hugh Hefner, who told reporters he and Stan "go back a long ways." There was to be a TV show made with production company DiC Entertainment called *Stan Lee's The Secret of the Super Six*. There was even discussion of making a superhero comic starring Beatles drummer Ringo Starr. None of these projects ever saw the light of day, and media outlets hardly ever followed up on them to find that out, simply moving on to the next cheery declaration of POW's intent.

The headlines may have been more skeptical if they knew about the alleged skulduggery occurring behind closed doors. POW, unable to come up with a hit, was desperate for cash and sought to do a version of what SLM had done: engage in a reverse merger to get on the stock exchange. The difference here was that POW would not be publicly traded as its own company but rather as a subsidiary of an existing, publicly traded firm, which POW would have a controlling stake in. Eventually, the POW leadership set its sights on a small entertainment company called Arturion, also known by its stock designation, ARUR, and in the autumn of 2003 approached its president, Valerie Barth, as well as its shareholders, about a merger. "The concept of having the company instantly launched to the top of the entertainment industry with an Icon like Stan Lee at the helm was a dream for the shareholders of ARUR," a minority shareholder named Ron Sandmann would later assert in a sworn legal statement as part of a lawsuit against POW. Curiously, Sandmann claimed that he hadn't heard about the SLM meltdown. "None of us knew anything of Stan Lee's former company Stan Lee Media Inc. as we all still assumed that he was Mr. Marvel and was the creative force behind the Marvel Empire," he wrote. "The main concern from the Arturion shareholders was to make sure that POW had 'In The Can' finished product that could potentially get the company cash flowing without having to come up with the huge outlay for development cost."

According to the statement, POW won the shareholders over by stating that they had firm control over many of SLM's properties, including animated shorts that were already completed and ready to debut, and by providing what Sandmann called "assurances that there was no litigation or pending litigation, and that POW owned the non disputed exclusive rights to the Stan Lee name and brand." Indeed, according to the statement, POW released a memo to Arturion shareholders saying, in part, "There are no operations in SLM and it does not have any working relationship, association or dealings with POW other than POW having acquired the right to distribute most of SLM's intellectual property, subject to an agreement to pay SLM royalty out of any revenues received from such intellectual property."

Those were questionable claims. For one thing, POW had, if the bankruptcy court's analysis is to be believed, unlawfully obtained the SLM properties in the bankruptcy proceedings, making its grasp on those properties tenuous at best. For another, not only did SLM have a relationship with POW, but SLM was being run out of the offices of POW by Kobayashi, who answered to Lieberman, Champion, and Stan. What's more, according to Sandmann's statement, there were still roughly 1,800 SLM shareholders who had yet to be compensated for the sale of their assets to Arturion. (Chaz Rainey, the lawyer working with POW, tells me it's "not unheard of for some members of a company's management to be on both sides of an asset sale" and emphasizes that "from a practical perspective, where the company is truly bankrupt [i.e., insolvent], shareholders have almost no rights at all.") When the merger occurred and the press pointed out that Stan Lee's business acumen was tainted by the SLM scandals, Arturion's stock plummeted, leading Sandmann and Barth to reportedly confront the POW crew at its offices. The pair's agenda was to make things right by buying SLM's remaining assets and compensating SLM's shareholders, but Lieberman shot back with a statement that "floored both Ms. Barth and myself," as Sandmann put it: "Mr. Lieberman said that they wanted the judge to believe there are no assets and they wanted to make sure that Stan Lee Media Inc. was dissolved"—in other words, more bankruptcy fraud. According to the suit, Lieberman then allegedly bragged that "Stan Lee does whatever he tells him to do and what we witnessed is that Arthur Lieberman completely dominated the control of [SLM] and POW." If Sandmann is to be believed, then Stan Lee's second company was as shadowy as his first.

A few months after the merger, the first book-length biography of Stan was released, Tom Spurgeon and Jordan Raphael's *Stan Lee and the Rise and Fall of the American Comic Book*. If the Arturion shareholders read it, they would not have been pleased, given that the slim volume contained skepticism about Stan's creative claims at Marvel. Stan had agreed to be interviewed for it and, near the end of the tome, one could find yet another quote from him about how he wished he'd been successful in a bigger venue: "I didn't have any big compulsion to write comics. It was a way of making a living," he said. The authors asked him whether he'd trade all of his achievements in comics in order to be famous for those other imagined endeavors. "It's a question that there is no answer to, because I'll never have a chance," Stan said. "God isn't coming and saying, 'Do you want to start again?' If he did, I don't know, I might . . . I might be interested in trying again." And yet, in a way, he was already getting his shot at big-time showbiz fame.

STAN SPENT MORE THAN twenty years of his life struggling to get Marvel properties turned into big-screen hits, and he had to deal with the fact that their first one came only after he had handed the reins to others. Back in August of 1998, while he was in the midst of watching his full-time contract with the House of Ideas get tossed in the shredder, New Line Cinema released *Blade,* an adaptation of a vampire-hunting Marvel Comics character who had originated in the horror-steeped days of the early seventies. There had been discussion of giving Stan a cameo as a police officer, but, per director Stephen Norrington, "schedules couldn't be reconciled and we were unwilling to move days and plans around to fit in with him, so it was never executed." The film was a surprise smash and, within a few months, the long-stalled X-Men movie was greenlit by executives at Twentieth Century Fox, with the film to be directed by Bryan Singer and co-written by writer/actor David Hayter, Singer, and producer Tom DeSanto. While the feature was being shot in 1999, the filmmakers decided they wanted Stan on set for a cameo.

DeSanto contacted Stan, who, in DeSanto's retelling, said he felt uncomfortable doing it, because he assumed Marvel didn't want to work with him, probably due to his status as the face of a competing corporation. "Stan," DeSanto recalled saying, "you *are* Marvel." With Stan convinced, schedules were worked out for him to head to a beach in Malibu and play a hot-dog vendor who witnesses a mutant emerging from the water. DeSanto said Stan's arrival was like Jesus descending from the heavens, with a crowd of geeks from the cast and crew assembling around him. When the cameras rolled, Stan merely had to react and had no dialogue to speak, prompting him to tell DeSanto afterward, "Next movie, how about you give me a line?" Although it was not technically Stan's first Marvel-movie cameo—that honor must forever go to *The Trial of the Incredible Hulk*—it was the beginning of something momentous for his life and legacy.

Over the course of his remaining years, as the success of the emerging Marvel movie franchises propelled the brand to the highest echelons of Hollywood success, Stan would become the most famous he had ever been, thanks to his Hitchcock-like presence in the vast majority of these cinematic adaptations. When director Sam Raimi was filming the next Marvel picture, *Spider-Man*, Marvel Studios chief Avi Arad demanded that Stan have another cameo, to which Raimi—a longtime geek who had met Stan in the past—responded, "No. I know Stan, and he can't act." In Raimi's recollection, Arad retorted, "I want him in the movie. We did it for *X-Men*, we're doing it here." Raimi acquiesced and ended up filming two cameos for Stan: one a wordless appearance in which he saves a little girl from falling debris, and the other a scene in which he tries to sell sunglasses to Peter Parker, saying, "Hey, kid, would you like a pair of these glasses? They're the kind they wore in *X-Men*." The latter was cut from the final product, once again leaving Stan as an unobtrusive dog whistle for superfans who recognized him. *Daredevil* in 2003 brought yet another wordless cameo, but that same year also saw the release of the Ang Lee–directed *Hulk*, which gave him his first speaking role in a finished cut: He and former Hulk actor Lou Ferrigno play guards at a research center, with Stan telling Ferrigno that security needs to be "beefed up" there.

The trickle became a flood: By the end of his life, Stan had appeared in more than forty Marvel films, and either he or his likeness showed up in more than a dozen episodes of Marvel television shows. You could find him playing a librarian, a psychiatric patient, a beauty-pageant judge, a general in World War II, lookalikes for Hugh Hefner and Larry King, a FedEx deliveryman, an extraterrestrial barber, even a strip-club DJ. As the years went on, filmmakers started to treat these cameos with sanctity, making sure Stan was highly noticeable so the increasingly Marvel-aware moviegoing public could cheer, then point to the screen and whisper his identity to their out-of-the-loop friends. The impact of these appearances on Stan's personal brand was massive. Marvel movies—especially the unified Marvel Cinematic Universe, which launched with 2008's *Iron Man*—have been the most successful Marvel products in history and have put Stan's face in front of eyeballs the world over, cementing his status as an icon for literally billions of people.

By all accounts, Stan reveled in his cameo appearances. Filmmakers recall people crowding around Stan to express their adulation whenever he appeared on set—a far cry from his near-anonymous day with *The Ambulance* in the late eighties. But, in classic Stan fashion, he always wanted the cameos to be bigger. As Anthony Russo, co-director of multiple Marvel films alongside his brother, Joe, recalled to me, "He just wanted more lines." Take, for example, his appearance as a museum guard in 2014's *Captain America: The Winter Soldier*. "So we had the shot set up for him and he had a very simple line, but he kept throwing in other lines," Anthony says. "But at the end of the day, we had to sorta focus it. But to see the fact that he had that level of passion and enthusiasm, where he just wanted to keep going and he wanted more, he just wanted to find more and more, that was amazing."

Additionally, Stan nearly always attended the red-carpet premieres of these films, getting to pose for photos next to cinema's biggest stars and be interviewed as the man who started it all, the *sine qua non* of the Marvel experience. He dutifully attended the pre-show spectacles, but Stan's eventual business manager, Keya Morgan (more on him later), says Stan had no affection for what he was watching. "Stan hated superhero films," Morgan recalls, noting that Stan probably watched only two or three all the way through. Stan's bodyguard, Gaven Vanover, backs up this assessment: "As soon as we made it to the end of the red carpet," he says, "it was, 'Let's get outta here.'"

Stan ventured into other universes, as well, doing voiceover appearances in animated POW projects and assorted other cameos for non-Marvel flicks. You could see him as a cop in Kevin Smith's *Yoga Hosers,* a wedding guest in *The Princess Diaries 2: Royal Engagement,* even as himself in the DC Comics animated film *Teen Titans Go! To the Movies,* which poked fun at the very idea of Stan Lee cameos. No gig was too small for him, if he was your friend: He appeared in at least three movies made by the proud schlock merchants of Troma Entertainment, the company run by his old writing partner Lloyd Kaufman; and his final cameo came not in a Marvel picture but rather in the micro-budget *Madness in the Method,* helmed by Kevin Smith associate Jason Mewes. In retrospect, there were two great leaps forward for the Stan Lee brand: the self-promotion of the sixties and the cameo appearances of the new millennium. Although the latter would have been impossible without the former, Stan went to his grave having to contend with the fact that he finally became a worldwide legend mostly thanks to the mercy of movers and shakers who weren't him.

The question, as always, was how to leverage his brand. Stan was paid peanuts for the Marvel cameos, and although he was given executive-producer credits for those movies, it was a purely ceremonial title with no financial rewards. But salvation came in the form of a stout man with a torrid past. Throughout Stan's many decades of attending comics conventions, he had typically earned little to no money for his appearances, simply using them to bask in the adulation of his admirers and promote whatever he was working on at the time. But that all changed in the aughts, when, according to subsequent court filings, Stan met a security guard at San Diego Comic-Con named Mac "Max" Anderson. The dates and circumstances of their initial conversations are unclear, and Anderson declined to do an interview with me, but over the course of the next few years, Anderson built a bond with Stan that was jointly based on Stan's almost fatherly love of Anderson and Anderson's remarkable ability to generate liquid cash for Stan. The core of Anderson's business strategy lay in conventions: Under Anderson's guidance, Stan started charging upward of one hundred dollars per autograph and thousands of dollars for onstage appearances. According to multiple people in Stan's inner circle, Anderson would give Stan his fees in cash, which Stan would then use for his own expenses and the even larger expenses of his wife and daughter.

Stan grew very close to Anderson and paid him for his efforts, but there are also allegations that Anderson was stealing money and personal memorabilia from Stan. What's more, Anderson had a dark personal life. According to reports in *The Daily Mail* and a later lawsuit brought against Anderson by JC, Anderson served jail time for a 2002 incident in which he beat up his wife. As in the case of Peter Paul, it's unclear when Stan learned about the assault conviction, but it didn't upset him enough to sever ties. It also appears that Stan looked the other way when Anderson was convicted of abuse again and served probation in 2010, this time for choking and hitting his son with a belt. Anderson, who had to undergo court-mandated counseling, would later claim to be repentant and a changed man, but rumors of his violent tendencies never stopped circulating. Nevertheless, the two were inseparable for years, with Max acting as Stan's bulldog and protector in an array of personal and professional situations around the world. "He loved Max," recalls Kevin Smith, who interacted with Anderson on multiple occasions. "And Max loved him. And Max really took care of him."

While Stan was building his brand on the glory of his past work, his creative endeavors in the present were going nowhere. Everything POW produced was a failure of one form or another. A children's book called *Stan Lee's Superhero Christmas,* a direct-to-video movie called *Stan Lee's Lightspeed,* an online comics series called Stan Lee's Sunday Comics, a series of animations you could view on Sprint-enabled mobile phones cumbersomely named Stan Lee POW! Mobile—all of these were promoted with giddy excitement in press-release quotes from Stan and/or Champion; all were abject disasters in the marketplace. The process of creating these products could be bizarre, rocky, and slipshod. For example, in the mid-aughts, the Sci-Fi Channel signed a deal with POW to make a movie called *Stan Lee's Harpies,* but, as with *Stripperella,* the title was literally all the creative direction that the initial deal consisted of. The task of actually creating a concept and writing a script was handed to Stan and a screenwriter named Declan O'Brien. According to O'Brien, the pair landed on an idea to do a comedic horror film about mythical harpies and O'Brien wrote a screenplay, but the production company "turned it into a piece of shit," making it a self-serious slog. As O'Brien remembers, Stan told him, "Look, Dec, I gotta take my name off this, but you should keep yours on it because you need more credits, kid." It was released and entirely a flop.

Not long after that, Stan arrived at the idea of rebooting *Stripperella,* this time as a lightly comedic but mostly earnest action-adventure comic. Artist Anthony Winn was hired to do it via the Marvel Method, and though he loved working with Stan, the comic landed with a thud. "POW had potential, but, to be honest, I felt like they didn't put the investment into the right places," Winn says. He recalls there being discussion of hiring a staff of creatives at POW: "They could've had a bullpen at one point, and I was supposed to be the equivalent of an art director there, but they didn't end up doing that and they just kind of dropped the ball."

Much of the time, the projects announced in those press releases would be stuck in showbiz limbo. Take, for example, that Ringo Starr endeavor. First it was announced as a comic; then came an announcement about a DVD film that would spin off into other media. At one point, comics writer Scott Lobdell was brought on to work on it and found chaos. He wrote a script for a movie musical that left space for original songs from Starr, and, in a meeting with Starr and Stan, the pair of celebs told him they loved it. However, Starr's manager felt that Lobdell was micromanaging what Starr would have to compose, and Lobdell was fired. Then, about six months later, he was rehired and asked by POW to start from scratch. "Then they said, 'We spent all the money on the first script, so we only have about three thousand dollars for you to write this one,'" Lobdell recalls. It was a pittance, but Lobdell loved Stan and did it anyway. "I never knew what happened after that," he says. The project quietly dissolved into the ether.

It's not unusual in the entertainment business for ideas to come to nothing, but there may have been more to the fact that POW's products were either chintzy or nonexistent. In fact, there are accusations that that wasn't a bug but rather a feature. Consider the tale of Gar Lester's werewolf movie. Lester was a low-level Hollywood agent and childhood Merry Marvel Marching Society member. In his telling, he happened to run into Stan on a Los Angeles street around 2005 and convinced him he had an idea for a movie starring one of his clients that would knock Stan's socks off.

They took a meeting with Champion present, in which Lester presented the concept: a movie about a superpowered werewolf, tentatively titled *Werewolf*. "You can always sell werewolves and vampires," Lester recalls Stan saying. Champion allegedly informed Lester that Lester would have to put up $150,000 in order to get the film done, which he did. "We had some scripts written that were not great, by amateur writers," Lester recalls. "I'd put my life savings in. We kept in touch, and I thought Gill was being nice to me. But Gill Champion, as I look backward, was a thorn in every single thing we did. He got his $150,000 and it was like 'Okay, I'll just lead you on.'" Years passed and no progress was made on the movie. "Gill would postpone everything," Lester says. He adds that there was interest from actors Christopher Walken and Ray Liotta about appearing in the picture, because they wanted to work with Stan, but there wasn't anything to present to them. "Every time, Gill turned everything down," Lester says, and he believes that was by design, that the whole thing was a scheme for POW to pocket the money. "I believe in my heart that he had no intention of moving forward," he says.

Lester indicates that he held the intellectual-property rights over the idea, so when POW was later sold to a Chinese conglomerate named Camsing, he was shocked to find that his rights had been included in the sale without his consultation and, to boot, he hadn't earned anything from the transaction. He felt he couldn't win in a lawsuit against the firm and resigned himself to losing all that money and time. When I ask Champion about all this, he doesn't exactly deny it: "Gar Lester was a financier for the development of a project and a good friend of Stan's, and we spent several years trying to develop that film with him," he says. "But, when Camsing brought in new management in 2017, I was largely shut out of that process. But I think they decided not to move forward or something." "It's a shame," Lester says. "Stan was the nicest guy in the world, and I really believe that Gill Champion screwed him. Gill Champion made a living off of Stan."

However, Stan may not have been as much of a naïf as Lester thinks. A production company named Valcom entered into an agreement with POW to create various entertainment projects that never materialized and would later allege in a lawsuit that POW's whole plan had been to get financing money from Valcom and hold on to it without actually spending anything to make the projects happen. What's more, the suit said that "the statements made by defendant Lee on behalf of defendant POW! were intended to mislead plaintiff" and that Lee "knew that the statements were in fact false." POW countersued and the case was settled. "Even if I could remember the settlement terms, I'm sure they were confidential," Champion says, and when I ask about this suit and the Sandmann one, he declines to respond in detail but does add, "People say all sorts of crazy stuff in litigation." That may be, but suspicion lingers, bolstered by the vague-but-startling claims Kobayashi would allegedly later make about illegal bookkeeping and other financial crimes in this period.

If all of this unlawful activity was, indeed, occurring, Stan was either participating in it or neglecting to take enough of an interest in his own company to find out about it. He certainly had his reasons for sticking with the POW crew, though his victories with them were always tainted by long-term defeat. It seemed that Stan had scored a win in early 2005, when the judge presiding over his case against Marvel for the movie and TV profits ruled in Stan's favor. Soon afterward, Marvel quietly settled with Stan and, although the terms of the settlement remain secret, it appears that he received a $10 million payout in exchange for relinquishing all claims to any Marvel characters and forgoing the profit-sharing portion of the 1998 contract. Lieberman had masterminded the settlement and reportedly pushed Stan to accept, and $10 million surely seemed like a lot of money to Stan at the time. But in the long run this was an unspeakable strategic error: Marvel would go on to earn billions of dollars on its films in subsequent years, meaning Stan could have earned far more than his payout had he not given up his stake.

In the meantime, POW scored a minor success with a reality series on basic cable called *Who Wants to Be a Superhero?,* in which Stan would evaluate real-life people who came up with heroic alter egos and had to prove themselves through feats of strength and virtue, with the prize being a comic book starring the winner. It lasted two seasons and had a short-lived spin-off in Britain, then faded into the mists of television history, but it was enough of a proof of concept that POW was able to follow it up with a three-season reality show, *Stan Lee's Superhumans,* in which a host would meet people with unusual talents and, in short framing segments, talk to Stan about them. Although the shows didn't resonate in the wider world of pop culture, Stan's personal brand kept rising: The cameos were increasingly plentiful; in 2007, *The Atlantic* magazine named him the twenty-sixth most influential living American; and in 2008, he was presented with the National Medal of Arts by President George W. Bush. POW was kept afloat by a first-look deal that it signed with a Disney affiliate named Silver Creek Pictures, by which POW would receive $2.5 million a year, and there was an announcement that Disney would produce three Stan-branded movies: *Nick Ratchet, Blaze,* and *Tigress*—none of which were ever released.

However, Disney didn't give up on the partnership—indeed, they doubled down on their investment, much to POW and Stan's benefit. An insurance broker and former SLM investor named Stanley Compton had formed an acquaintance with Stan and Champion and also happened to be friends with a Disney exec. All of a sudden, he had a revelation in his sleep. "One night I had a dream," Compton recalls. "In the dream, I thought, *Wow, POW needs capital, and Disney is always looking for content*. I woke up that morning and I said to my daughter, 'I'm gonna sketch out this idea of why they might need each other and go talk to POW about it.'" POW was, of course, interested, and Compton brokered a deal whereby Disney would purchase a 10 percent stake in POW for $2.5 million. However, a lawsuit from POW shareholders would later allege that "rather than use these proceeds to fund POW!'s operations, Lee, Champion, and Lieberman used the funds to repay 'loans' made by them to the Company, as well as pay themselves certain portions of purported 'deferred compensation'" and that "proceeds were used to increase the salaries of Lee, Champion . . . and others."

Just a few months prior to the announcement of the POW–Disney deal, and perhaps in part inspired by the negotiations that led to it (as Compton suspects), Disney had bought Marvel for $4 billion—or perhaps the POW deal was to keep Stan from interfering in the Marvel deal. Whatever the case, when the massive Marvel sale was announced on August 31, 2009, Stan's dream from the sixties of turning Marvel into the next Disney came true, but it was bittersweet for the man who claimed to have created the intellectual property that was the foundation of the deal. Although Stan's 1998 contract would continue to be honored and he'd get a steady salary of $1 million a year from Marvel, the actual owners of the company enriched themselves beyond his wildest dreams. He'd had his chance to buy the company and blew it, and now he had to watch from the sidelines as cash was showered upon people who had done what he had failed to do: truly take Marvel to the top.

That said, within weeks, there was a problem with Disney's purchase of Marvel, one that threatened to scuttle the whole affair and very publicly sully Stan's reputation. Jack Kirby's family issued dozens of so-called copyright terminations, claiming that Kirby had created the Marvel pantheon; that, given the vagaries of the legal situation in the glory days, he was their actual owner; and that the Kirby estate was now taking them back from Marvel and its licensees. Marvel leapt into action and sued the Kirbys, setting off a pitched legal battle.

Stan recorded at least two depositions with Lieberman at his side, one on May 13, 2010, and another on December 8 of that year, and although the full testimony remains under lock and key, the portions that were released in public filings were notable for a few reasons. For one thing, although Stan firmly maintained that he came up with the core concepts and main characters, he openly said that insofar as secondary figures went, "Jack would often introduce a lot of new characters in the stories"—a subtle admission that a lot of the creations from the Marvel Age of Comics were not co-creations at all but rather the brainchildren of Kirby. Second, he hewed to the company line about his 2002–05 lawsuit, saying the question of whether he owned the characters "wasn't part of the dispute" and that he had always believed the company owned his work.

Some of the testimony in the other depositions was vicious: Kirby's son, Neal, was asked about the basis on which he estimated that Kirby must have created Iron Man; his response was "I have the basis that I know my father's creativity versus Mr. Lee's creativity, and Mr. Lee was an excellent marketer, he was an excellent manager, excellent self-promoter. I honestly don't believe he had any creative ability."

Another curious item in the depositions came from none other than Larry Lieber, who was called to testify in favor of Marvel. Larry had had a rough go of it in the preceding decades: He'd married and lost his wife to cancer, then entered into a long-term relationship with a woman he called his life partner, who died of an unidentified illness. He lived a lonely existence in his studio apartment in Manhattan, barely scraping by and—similarly to his brother—regretting the fact that he'd spent his career doing comics instead of writing a novel or being a mainstream visual artist. His relationship with Stan had grown paradoxical. In a professional sense, they were closer than they had ever been: In 1986, Larry had taken over the art duties on the Spider-Man newspaper strip at Stan's generous behest and continued to do that as the years wore on. Although Roy Thomas had, uncredited, taken over the writing duties on the strip around the turn of the millennium, Stan would still call Larry up after Larry had turned his artwork in to Mike Kelly and dictate whatever corrections he wanted. As such, Stan and his brother were in regular communication a few times a week, but it was always clipped and impersonal. "He used to call me from the office and say, 'You've got ten minutes, and you never know when I'll call you again—when you least expect it,'" Larry recalls.

Beyond those professional calls, the two hardly spoke. Larry hates flying and rarely came out to see his brother and Joan in California, and when Stan came to New York, he often avoided Larry altogether. Once, Stan attended New York Comic Con and didn't tell Larry he'd be there, so Larry and his life partner, Lynn, just watched a stream of his appearance on the computer. I ask him if that incident hurt and he replies, "Yes, of course. It hurt me for Lynn. I was used to it, but it hurt me for Lynn." I ask why; he says, "Because I thought she would have been proud to be there, and she was being denied this. They never once . . . Joan never once called to say hello to her." So when Marvel wanted Larry to do a deposition in favor of the company's claims against the Kirbys, he was skeptical, but Stan told him a Marvel loss in the case could mean the cancelation of the Spidey strip, thus ending Larry's main source of income. "I really don't know if it was pressure," he says, "or if he was just thinking of me and telling the truth. I don't know his motive." I ask if Stan ever, in all his life, told Larry that he loved him. Larry's answer is blunt: "No."

IN NOVEMBER OF 2010, Stan could be seen in a barely noticed cameo on television, this time as himself. The reality series *Hollywood Treasure* aired an episode in which host Joe Maddalena obtains original artwork from the Kirby-drawn *Fantastic Four* #12 and brings it to Stan at San Diego Comic-Con to confirm its veracity. In a backstage area, he meets Stan, who's wearing a POW Starter jacket and sitting near a watchful Gill Champion. "You had something to do with this book," Maddalena says, after which Stan barks, "I wrote it!" Stan flips through the pages in awe and takes care to note that some of the marginalia was written by him, not Kirby. "Y'know, it's funny," he says. "Historians always write about Jack's notes. They never write about the notes that I put in, because I'd always erase them once the strip was done." His appearance is brief, but after it's over, Maddalena adds a tantalizing tidbit that emerged during a conversation with an unnamed associate of Stan's. "I said, 'Does he have any artwork?'" Maddalena recalls on camera. "[The associate] goes, 'Boxes and boxes in the garage.' I said, 'What do you mean, garage?' He goes, 'Storage units full.' I said, 'Well, supposedly I've heard him say he doesn't have anything.' The guy said, 'Storage units full of artwork.' He goes, 'He has no idea what he has. He's never looked at it.'" Stan had never previously mentioned such a collection, raising questions about what could be in it—and whether any of it was being held from the public in service of ulterior motives.

Far more eyebrow-raising were the behind-the-scenes dealings at POW around the time of the TV episode's airing. Lieberman and Champion had decided that, in order to raise further funds, they wanted POW to go fully public on its own, not just as a subsidiary of Arturion. Kobayashi, who had seen the dysfunction at the company firsthand, was vehemently opposed. She felt that Stan "was not aware of most of the daily activities or what documents were being signed," as she would later say, and she feared a repeat of the disaster that was the publicly traded SLM. "I had enough," she says. "And they said, 'Nope, we're gonna go public. We don't care. You're going to be the CFO of a public company.' I said, 'No, I'm not.'" She opted to leave POW and, with Stan's blessing, form the Stan Lee Foundation, a nonprofit charity dedicated to literacy and education that has proceeded to barely do anything over the course of its existence other than raise money (one fundraising effort involved selling branded bags of coffee that were purportedly the exact blend Stan enjoyed every morning) and declare its intention to perform good works in the future.

POW was hardly more effective. As of 2010, when it was preparing to go fully public, the company was hanging on by a thread, relying on the investments from Disney and spending an enormous amount of its money on executive compensation. According to court filings, Stan was making $300,000 per year, enjoying fully paid-for first-class travel, a sedan limousine, deluxe hotels, and an agreement that he'd make $125,000 for doing nothing if diminished health were to make him unable to perform his duties. Far more lucrative was an alleged agreement from that year that said Stan would eventually be paid $1,132,500, with Lieberman getting an additional $1,195,416. Taken against the paltry amount that POW was raking in from sales and outside investment—revenue in 2009 was a microscopic $113,306—POW's compensation was allegedly accounting for an astounding 715 percent of revenue.

These compensation agreements were yet another example of self-dealing, as well: Stan, Champion, and Lieberman controlled POW's board of directors, meaning they were authorizing their own access to these large sums of money without any independent oversight. In their first SEC filing, on December 10, 2010, the company said fully 97 percent of its revenue was coming from one customer, presumably Disney. The company also confessed in the filing that Stan himself was a risk, given that the entire company was built on his brand and that they'd lose investment money if he were to become incapacitated, which was highly probable, what with his failing senses and an ailing heart that now required a pacemaker. To make matters worse, shareholders Sandmann and Barth, after hiring private investigator Becky Altringer to investigate POW, gathered information and filed their suit a few months later.

Meanwhile, Stan and his cohort were still out on the promotion trail, touting the amazing initiatives they were preparing to unveil. One such effort was a partnership with comics publisher BOOM! Studios, whereby Stan would create new superhero characters that would then be written and drawn by others. Veteran comics writer Mark Waid was in charge of this new imprint and hastens to point out that Stan was no absentee landlord. Although it may have seemed to the outside world that the aging Stan was blithely allowing his name to be slapped on any damn thing, Waid says Stan was intimately involved in the creation and editing of the comics. He tells of meeting with Stan to show him a rough draft of an upcoming issue, which the latter read with consternation. "He got to the end of it and said, 'I can't have my name on this,' and my heart sank," Waid recalls. He got revisions, and Stan enthusiastically endorsed the finished product—but Waid has never forgotten Stan's unwillingness to brand something he didn't like. That said, the BOOM! line was not long for this world, getting canceled after just a few issues of each comic.

This was par for the course. A plan for a multi-medium superhero epic called *Stan Lee's Mighty 7,* in which Stan himself was a lead character who guided a team of super-beings, managed to limp to a direct-to-DVD animated movie (the motley voice cast included Jim Belushi, Sean Astin, Mayim Bialik, and Red Hot Chili Peppers bassist Flea) and a few issues of a comic, but the film was a dud, and the comic ended on a cliffhanger after a handful of issues. A partnership with actor and former California governor Arnold Schwarzenegger to create a project called *The Governator* was announced, then quietly put on the shelf after Schwarzenegger caught media heat for an affair. A plan to create a line of superhero mascots for the National Football League fell through, so POW turned to the National Hockey League and got the green light, but the low-rent characters—

including a number of Marvel rip-offs, such as Black Panther looka-like the Panther, for the Florida Panthers—were loudly mocked upon their debut. An official Stan Lee YouTube channel debuted and produced hardly watched junk such as "Stan's Rants," a series where Stan would look at the camera from his office and talk about things that bothered him ("What is it with these bottles of water?" he asked in one). A project that would produce concerts at military bases, called Stan Lee's POW!er Concert Series, was announced and briefly came into existence before being quietly shuttered. There was even a Stan Lee Signature Cologne—for just $24.99, you could get a bottle of fragrance that smelled of "bergamot, ginger, white pepper, basil, and violet and features layers of cedar, vetiver, and musk accords." Few did. Nothing was sticking.

To make matters even more dire, Arthur Lieberman died in May of 2012, leaving the company without its most ferocious leader. Sandmann and Barth settled their suit that same month, but only because they had exhausted their funds for legal expenses. They had an additional grievance: Footage they'd shot for a documentary was allegedly stolen from them and used for a different documentary, *With Great Power: The Stan Lee Story,* which was another bit of ob-scurantist mythmaking and had been released to little fanfare. Nev-ertheless, that myth was alive and well. The documentary opened with footage of a cavalcade of celebrities—Seth Rogen, James Franco, Ringo Starr, Nicolas Cage, Samuel L. Jackson, Kevin Smith, and many more—talking about what Stan meant to them, and their enthusiasm was shared by the increasingly large audience for Mar-vel's big-ticket products.

The cameos continued apace, and Stan even briefly returned to Marvel's comics to plot and dialogue a short story about the Fantas-tic Four celebrating Hanukkah with the Thing, who had recently been made canonically Jewish. It was the only time Stan ever dipped into storytelling about Judaism or Jewishness, and it was sweet, if a little odd: The story ended with Gentiles Reed and Johnny opting to wear the Jewish head coverings known as *kippot* as they walk down the street, something more than a little disrespectful to a Jewish sensibility and perhaps the result of Stan not knowing much about the ways of his ancestors.

Even with all these professional highs and lows, there is reason to believe that work and fame weren't Stan's primary concerns during this period. His primary concern, it seems, was his daughter. JC had further lost control over herself, regularly getting drunk and high on marijuana and engaging in verbally abusive behavior toward her parents and others, according to those who knew her. Brad Herman is a soft-spoken Los Angeles factotum who had gotten his start in showbiz by, of all things, washing actor Burt Reynolds's car. Decades later, he worked his way up to being a business manager and fixer for various Hollywood types, including Stan. His memory is of Stan and Joan being nearly totally occupied with concerns about JC. "The nexus of this is 'What do we do to neutralize the problems with our daughter?'" he says. "And when I say neutralize, I mean literally neutralize the powder keg that was—and is, I assume, still—JC Lee. I mean, she's incendiary. She's a pit bull. She's unmanageable, in my opinion." As he and others recall, JC would have days where she would call her parents upward of fifty times, screaming at them for not giving her enough money or opportunities for coattail-riding fame. Stan was being bled dry by her and Joan.

Larry Lieber remembers occasionally working up the courage to tell Stan over the phone that Stan needed to stop doing conventions, because he was too old and frail. "He'd say, 'They offer me too much, I couldn't turn it down'; other times he would tell me, 'I need the money,'" Larry tells me. "Once, I said, 'What do you need it for?' And he said, about his wife and his daughter, 'They spend money. My wife spends a lot, and my daughter's even worse.'"

Herman hesitates to diagnose JC with a specific condition but says she's "not well and has not been well for a long time." Alan Duke is a Georgia-born freelance reporter who had once worked for CNN and got involved with the Lees after reporting on Stan, subsequently becoming friends with JC. According to him, she could be fun to be around but was also deeply delusional. In his recollection, she decided she wanted to record a Christian children's song called "Little Baby Jesus." "Anybody famous involving musicians, she'd tell 'em about this song," he says. "It was totally a dead-end vanity thing." According to Duke, when musicians Macklemore and Ryan Lewis scored a hit with their song "Thrift Shop," JC became convinced that they'd stolen it from her, because she had once met an unrelated person who was also named Ryan Lewis and had discussed music with him. "It didn't make sense," Duke says.

In 2013, Duke and JC drove to Las Vegas to see a comedy show and, according to him, she started heckling one of the comedians while she was drunk and stoned. Duke confronted her outside and recorded audio of their exchange, in which you can hear JC screaming at him, "I'm the fucking talent. You respect me or you walk, because none of you respected me and you don't respect me." Duke says the incident prompted Stan to exile him from the inner circle. Then came the alleged assault. According to Herman and Duke, on March 16, 2014, Stan and Joan celebrated JC's sixty-fourth birthday early at their home and, for the occasion, gave her a new Jaguar automobile. However, they had leased it instead of buying it, and this apparently enraged JC. Herman claims to have been present as JC physically attacked her parents. According to him, JC grabbed Joan by one arm and shoved her against a window, at which point Stan screamed, "I'm going to stick you in a little apartment and take away all your credit cards!" and "I've had it, you ungrateful bitch!"

In Herman's account, JC then took Stan by the neck and slammed his head against his chair's wooden backing. There are harrowing photos, now available on Duke's website, of Joan showing enormous deep-purple bruises to the camera, which Herman claims were taken on the scene after the alleged attack. Duke, upon seeing the photos years later, took them to the LAPD, but when the cops came to Stan and Joan's house to investigate, the couple told them no abuse had occurred and the case was dropped. (I asked JC, through her attorney Kirk Schenck, for her response to these allegations and others but did not receive a response.)

And all the while, Stan was still financially supporting JC. She was, eventually, the owner of two houses in L.A. and an apartment in San Francisco, although she also regularly stayed at the Chateau Marmont hotel in L.A. "Stan was the enabler for JC, who is a terrible person," says Valerie Friedman, Stan and Joan's friend. "And he enabled her all along to be that person. Joan was the one that stood up and said, 'No, I'm not buying you that $28,000 handbag' or whatever. Stan would always cave." Stan and Joan, constantly worried about their daughter, even went so far as to pay another Hollywood hanger-on, a man named Jerry Olivarez, to keep JC occupied—to act as a "babysitter" for her, in Duke's words.

However, Olivarez proved to be a liability in and of himself. He persuaded Stan to help him start a company called Hands of Respect, which ostensibly sought to promote cooperation and understanding between white and black people in America; the avowed plan was to sell pins showing a black hand shaking a white hand and to put the money toward community initiatives. Stan dutifully promoted Hands of Respect in the press and on his social-media accounts, but as it turned out, it was a for-profit company that donated no money whatsoever and just pocketed the cash. When a blogger revealed this state of affairs, the company stopped advertising its operations. (Olivarez tells me that "when the dust settles," he'll restart operations.) Very little good was coming from the direction of Stan and Joan's only progeny.

It was also during this period that the Lees became close with another person of dubious moral character, a mysterious gentleman who goes by the name Keya Morgan. Morgan's past is shrouded in mist. He claims to be of Jewish descent, born and raised in New York City—in fact, in Peter Parker's native neighborhood of Forest Hills, Queens—by a psychologist mother named Faith Morgan and, as he puts it, "four or five" different stepfathers. Court filings and police reports have listed his legal name as Keyarash Mazhari, but he tells me Keya Morgan is his actual birth name and that the other moniker is merely a common misunderstanding due to the fact that one of his stepfathers had the surname Mazhari.

He's a consummate wheeler-dealer, having apparently made a considerable amount of money by collecting, selling, and licensing memorabilia of Marilyn Monroe and Abraham Lincoln, even going so far as to claim that Barack Obama was in touch with him about Lincoln paraphernalia. He claims to have been close friends with Donald Trump, Jr., even saving the heir's life during a night of drunken revelry in New York City long ago—and the younger Trump, indeed, enthusiastically retweeted Morgan on Twitter on multiple occasions before his father became president of the United States. Along those lines, Morgan claims he has been in touch with the elder Trump in the past, and when I meet him he shows off an issue of a defunct Trump-owned magazine that published a long feature on Morgan's memorabilia enterprises. He appears, from photos, to have been close with Buzz Aldrin and with Leonardo DiCaprio's father, George. Crucially, Morgan claims he was best friends with pop star Michael Jackson—though he produces no evidence of this claim, despite constantly showing off photos of himself with other celebrities he's met—and that Jackson introduced him to Stan in the aughts.

However, Alan Duke vehemently argues that this is a lie. According to him, he was the one who introduced Morgan to the Lees sometime after 2010, after writing a profile of Morgan for CNN (a profile that, astoundingly enough, appears to have contained the first-ever published quotes from the widow of JFK assassin Lee Harvey Oswald, who said she was in touch with Morgan during his memorabilia exploits). According to Duke, once he'd put Morgan in touch with the Lee family, Morgan glommed onto JC and the two became close—an alliance that would prove to be massively consequential for Stan in the future.

And, all the while, another figure lurked in the background: Peter Paul. His saga since the collapse of SLM had been a rocky and complicated one. After being shipped from Brazil back to the United States in September of 2003 (he claims he'd long wanted to go back and make his case but had been barred from doing so), he pleaded guilty in the SLM case in 2005, although he now claims he did so under duress while being pressured by representatives of Bill and Hillary Clinton. Indeed, the Clintons became a debilitating obsession for Paul. He sued them for welching on their backroom deal to have Bill represent SLM and misrepresenting his contributions to Hillary's campaign, and he was locked in litigation for years with the help of conservative legal group Judicial Watch, whom he also later sued for not following through on promises made to him about the case. He was sentenced to ten years in prison in 2009, although he ended up getting out early and living back in his birth state of Florida, alongside his wife and their children.

During all this, from behind the scenes, he was helping to coordinate a series of legal attacks on POW, Marvel, and Stan. An obscure group of SLM investors had reconstituted the company as an employee-less legal entity and, over the course of the late aughts and throughout the next decade, issued a dizzying array of lawsuits. The details get confusing, but the essence is simple: This zombie SLM claims it is the rightful owner of Stan's name, likeness, and slogans; owner of all the SLM properties that POW purchased in the questionable bankruptcy proceedings; and, most daring, owner of all the Marvel Comics characters that Stan claimed to have created. At various points, media outlets had to scratch their heads and puzzle through how it could be that something called Stan Lee Media was suing Stan Lee. One federal judge, finding himself deep in the morass, unloaded on all parties in a 2011 hearing: "This has become—and not just today, but over time—an unbelievable mess. I mean, it almost is an embarrassment," he said, adding that "the case has become so entangled that it raises more questions than are easily answerable; and what it doesn't come close to doing is addressing what otherwise would be a rather straightforward dispute."

Though Paul was not the only person behind these suits, he admits to me that he was involved in them and that he thinks they were just and necessary. "The end game," Paul says, "was to recover the rights that were rightfully owned by the shareholders of Stan Lee Media that Stan ignored and ultimately defrauded. And he did it for his own benefit." I ask him how he thought the world would embrace a Stan Lee Media that not only didn't employ Stan Lee but was actively in opposition to him. "I was open to discussion," he says. "The point was, it wasn't his right anymore. I mean, either you have laws or you don't." I point out that many would look at Paul as the bad guy for attacking a beloved figure like Stan and that that would diminish a theoretically reborn SLM. "My experience in life is, people will make opinions based on a variety of reasons that have no basis in reality," he says. "I've long since lost the concern of what people think."

Speaking of public images, Marvel and Stan just barely avoided a complete disaster for both of their reputations. By 2014, the Kirbys' legal battle had been kicked up higher and higher in the American legal system, thanks to a series of appeals, and it had reached the point where the Supreme Court was preparing to consider whether or not it would hear the case. It seemed that the world was on the verge of the public spectacle of an ugly fight over the Marvel Universe at the highest levels of the judiciary—one that Disney very well could have lost, which would have thrown the entire Marvel enterprise into complete chaos and set a precedent for creators' rights that could shake the entire entertainment industry. But, at the last minute, on September 26, 2014, Disney settled with the Kirbys for an untold but surely enormous sum of money, along with the assurance that Kirby would get credit alongside Stan in movie adaptations of his work—something that, shamefully, had not always occurred previously. The Lee–Kirby dispute would never flare up again during Stan's lifetime. But new, even more painful controversies awaited him.

A FEW THINGS WENT wrong at the Los Angeles Convention Center in the last weekend of October 2015, during Stan Lee's Comikaze Expo. POW had reached a deal with the preexisting Comikaze comics convention a few years earlier to put Stan's branding on it, but this time around, Stan was off his game. At his handful of events and press conferences, he was mostly his old, witty self, bounding across the stage with a vigor unheard of for most ninety-two-year-olds and telling versions of the same anecdotes he'd been telling for fifty years. But there were revealing moments in which he faltered.

At a panel about POW's upcoming projects, Champion introduced Stan by calling him "the Father of the Superhero," they bantered for a few seconds, then Stan blurted out, unprompted, "And the name of the movie is *Arch Angel!*" A pause of confusion. Champion turned to Stan, in front of the crowd, and said, "No, no, we changed it to *Arch Alien!*" Stan slapped himself on the forehead and entered his familiar street-preacher mode: "*Arch Alien!* I was just testing him to see if he was paying attention," he said. "I'll say it again: *Arch Alien!* And you're wondering what it's about. We will not leave you in too much suspense. We'll give you a few hints. But we're not gonna tell you the whole story, because there has never been a superhero-type story like this one, which involves the whole cosmos comin' together." (*Arch Alien* never materialized.) At a small press conference, Stan and filmmaker/businessman Terry Dougas announced a joint children's book called *Dragons vs. Pandas,* and Stan at one point couldn't remember its title. Elsewhere in that conference, Stan said of Dougas, "No, he's great to work with. He does all the work, I take all the credit. You couldn't have a better arrangement!"—a remarkable joke to make, given Stan's past transgressions.

Stan spent hours upon hours at the convention sitting in a booth, giving autographs that a massive line of fans had paid for (for an extra fee, you could get the signature "certified" with a piece of paper), with a grin plastered over his face, one that betrayed few signs of genuine happiness. Next to the signing booth was something called the Stan Lee Mega Museum, which was a strange spectacle. It featured row after row of memorabilia that was in some way related to Stan. There were myriad awards Stan had won over the years, as well as movie props and special drawings comics artists had made for him. Some of the items in the Mega Museum were only tenuously connected to Stan—in another surprising and unwitting embrace of his enemies' characterization of him, he displayed dozens of recent Marvel comic books he'd demonstrably had nothing to do with, all signed by Stan and, therefore, presented as objects of admiration. What the museumgoers were unaware of was the fact that this museum would one day prove controversial, given that Max Anderson would later be accused by JC of taking items in it from Stan's possession unlawfully. Though the fluorescents shone brightly in the convention hall, the shadows stretched long.

Stan was still working and pitching, but the situation had grown somewhat pathetic. POW had the closest thing to a hit that they'd had since *Stripperella* in the form of the graphic-novel adaptation of his memoir, called *Amazing Fantastic Incredible: A Marvelous Memoir,* written by Peter David and drawn by artist Colleen Doran. But it was the exception that proved the rule: Project after project, deal after deal, was announced and either led to something unnoticeable or nothing at all. In 2016, Keya Morgan and Stan devised a multimedia franchise idea that they called *Nitron* and brought it to a producer named Michael Benaroya. Morgan and Benaroya are reluctant to give details about what it is, as they still expect it'll get made, but Morgan tells me, "Nitron is a planet, and—nobody's heard this ever before—it's filled with crystal and silver and it's a beautiful, magnificent world that's in Andromeda."

When Stan and Morgan met Benaroya, the producer was working on a different property, one adapted from an as-yet-unreleased
comic-book idea called *Blood Merchant,* which centered on a man
who deals blood to vampires and works for a vampire mafia. He
asked if Stan might be willing to give it a blurb or some other impri-
matur. "He didn't want to take credit for or present any character he
hadn't much involvement with," Benaroya recalls. "He thought it
might be cool but wanted things done differently." Stan read the
comic draft and offered a note: Why was there a mysterious introductory scene about someone other than the main character?
Shouldn't they start right at the core narrative? "I tried to say 'This
will come back later, and we think it's important and cool to start
way back in this piece of the story,'" Benaroya says. "He just looked
at me and he said, 'I've been doing this a long time, I think I know.'"

Eventually, Benaroya suggested that Stan come up with his own
idea that they could work on. Morgan and Stan presented him with
Nitron, he hopped on board, and the trio made splashy announcements in Hollywood trade publications about how great this upcoming masterwork was going to be. Though Benaroya tells the
story with pride, it's something of a sad scene: a ninety-three-year-
old celebrity forced by financial desperation into a situation where
he's offering notes on a gruesome and trashy comic book that
doesn't fully exist, yet has already been optioned because of a
comics-adaptation bubble in the industry; then pitching another
low-rent idea that would never make any significant progress during his life.

To make matters worse, Stan had to deal with me. I wrote a profile of him that was published in *New York* magazine's arts and culture site, *Vulture,* in 2016, and its skepticism about Stan's creative
credit stalled a deal that Stan and Morgan were hammering out with
magician David Copperfield. According to Morgan, Stan was furious about my piece, and Declan O'Brien remembers emailing Stan
about it and getting a response of "Thanks, Dec. Ain't nothing to do
but ignore them."

Meanwhile, POW was admitting to the SEC that it was on the verge of collapse, unable to make up for its constant losses, and it became clear to Gill Champion that the time had come to scrap their business strategy. Around 2015, they quietly began to shop the company around to potential purchasers, and in late 2016, thanks to a consultant named Rick Licht, they finally found one: a Chinese media company called Camsing. POW terminated its registration with the SEC as a publicly traded company on March 15, 2017, which shareholders believe was an attempt to end SEC scrutiny of the company in time for what was to come.

According to a later class-action lawsuit—which POW disagrees with on a blanket level—POW "disseminated a materially false, misleading, and incomplete proxy statement recommending that POW! shareholders vote in favor of the Merger." The proxy statement allegedly said all shareholders were on board with the merger, when, if the lawsuit is correct, it was really just Stan and Champion's decision, made over the shareholders' objections. "Moreover," the suit goes on, "Lee and Champion did not hire a banker to shop the company to prospective buyers, nor did it receive a fairness opinion regarding POW!'s true value. Rather, Lee and Champion either hired Licht, or at least agreed to have POW!'s shareholders pay his so-called success fee, and did very little more."

The suit alleges that Stan and Champion misrepresented the cost of the merger, charged the shareholders for the transaction expenses, never provided them with accurate numbers about share value, and that, in general, "Champion and Lee engaged in a sham process focused entirely on obtaining additional benefits for themselves, all the while still receiving their proportional share of the Merger Consideration and shifting the cost of the additional benefits onto POW!'s disinterested shareholders." (Champion declined to comment on the suit, due to the fact that it was ongoing, but hastened to point out it was not technically POW that was being sued, just its directors as individuals.) No one in the wider public knew it at the time, but behind the breathless quotes that POW and Camsing execs distributed to the press was yet more evidence of impropriety and mismanagement.

A layperson may have assumed that, as of July 2017, Stan would be taking a victory lap. A new Spider-Man movie, *Spider-Man: Homecoming,* was about to be released. It was yet another mega-hit Marvel flick about a character Stan was credited with creating, it featured yet another Stan cameo (he played a New Yorker who sees Peter Parker confronting a neighbor), and, perhaps most significant, it further ensconced the Marvel Cinematic Universe as a global leader in entertainment. The MCU was a construct that had by then earned enough money to match the GDP of a small country, and it was built on Stan's notion from the sixties of an interwoven and addictive shared universe. Stan had walked so movies like *Homecoming* could run. But when it hit theaters, he had more important things to worry about: His wife was dying.

Joan had been in poor health for months and finally suffered a stroke that sent her to the hospital, where she perished a few days later, on July 6. It was a devastating blow to Stan, who had loved his wife passionately and monomaniacally. There was no funeral. Valerie Friedman called Stan twice to offer hers and Ron's condolences and check in on him, and he told her how devastated he was and how little he wanted to live. Concerned, Valerie called a third time but noticed something startling: "The phone was cut off," she says. Ron drove to Stan's home to be sure he was okay. "There was a guy standing there," he recalls. "I said, 'I'm here to see Stan.' 'No, you can't come in.' 'Why not?' 'You can't come in.'" Befuddled and frightened for his friend, he went home and tried to figure out what was going on.

10.

DISINTEGRATION

———

(2017–2018)

———

"**W**E WERE THE MERCENARIES,**" SAYS JONATHAN BOLERJACK,** a Southern lilt in his voice. "And if anyone wants to deny that or wants to act like they were doing it for an altruistic reason, they're liars." The thirtysomething runs a hand through his voluptuous brown hair in the unpitying light of the Jacob Javits Convention Center during the 2019 New York Comic Con. He's talking about Stan's inner circle in its final days, a period in which Stan was beset by characters of questionable moral fiber—including, by his own admission, Bolerjack himself. He worked for Max Anderson and was thus regularly around Stan in the latter's waning years. "When I first started, I was a fanboy, and when you ask a fanboy, 'Hey, would you like to hang out with Stan?' anyone is going to take that opportunity," Bolerjack says. "And then, over time, you start to become part of the entourage. Just like violence, you get used to it and it desensitizes you. It becomes normalized." He continues: "None of us were special people. We didn't have college degrees. We could not be more average. And in a lot of ways, we could not be more undeserving. It was luck. You have to remember that. Everyone wants to act like they had some special skill. And none of us had skills like that."

I ask him why, if he and his cohort didn't have special skills, they were able to get so close to one of the most lauded writers of the past century. "I guess the one skill you needed was to be a really good bullshitter," he says with a smile. "That's what you needed to get in. You needed to know either how to kiss ass or bullshit your way into something. But also—it's like anything else—nepotism. Someone liked you." And if you could get Stan to like you, too, it seemed like the rewards were ripe for the plucking. "Stan is actually a really good divining rod of what kind of human you are," Bolerjack says. "Because when you get access to Stan and that kind of money and power, what happens with you and what you do with it is who you are as a person."

There is no way to sugarcoat Stan's final act. From the minute Joan died until his own passing sixteen months later, he was beset by malign forces that sought to extract maximum value from an ailing and depressed man in his nineties. With the notable exception of Bolerjack, all those who surrounded him in those last days will tell you that they alone were the only person who truly wanted what was best for Stan and struggled nobly to fight off the parasites.

While it is certainly difficult to ascertain the truth of who the abusers were, all we see in this period are the consequences of their abuse. There are voluminous recordings, most of them made quasi-surreptitiously by Keya Morgan, of Stan sounding agitated and miserable to a shocking degree, screaming at his daughter and issuing paranoid rants about impending attempts on his life. There were public statements from Stan that identified one person or another in the inner circle as Satan incarnate, typically someone who he would earlier or later on describe in public as his only true friend. There were multiple incidents involving the police, as well as a $1 billion lawsuit. Friends and colleagues struggled to get in touch with, then to liberate, Stan, but to little avail. When death finally came for the ninety-five-year-old man, legal documents had been revised, money was funneled away, and his eulogizers generally chose to excise the unsavory details of the most recent period from their tributes. But to ignore what happened in this last stretch is to avoid hard truths while failing to see where Stan's legacy is headed.

It appears that Joan's passing set off a power struggle, but it was one that had been brewing for a while. The core quintet in Stan's life—Max Anderson, Jerry Olivarez, Keya Morgan, JC, and JC's lawyer and friend, Kirk Schenck—held one another in contempt to one degree or another, and although they were occasionally willing to form alliances, they were typically ones of convenience that only existed until they didn't. It seems, based on the way events played out, that these players had all been looking to oust one another already. Once the fiercely loyal and often brash Joan could no longer act as a bulwark and Stan, hit hard by her death, sank into a listless depression, everyone rushed to fill the vacuum. Initially, it seems that a coalition of Morgan and JC—who were, as one insider puts it, "thick as thieves"—set out to rid themselves of Anderson and Olivarez as well as a set of professionals who had been loyal to Stan and his interests for years. His accountant was fired at Morgan's behest and replaced with, oddly enough, Vince Maguire, brother of *Spider-Man* star Tobey Maguire, who was given access to reams of Stan's personal financial paperwork. His longtime housekeeper and gardener were reportedly fired, too. Morgan also appears to have changed Stan's phone number and essentially made himself Stan's interlocutor for the rest of the world.

And, perhaps most ominous, Morgan at some point installed audio recording devices in Stan's home (he claims with Stan's consent) and started taping virtually everything that happened there. By Morgan's own admission, he typically didn't inform visitors that they were being recorded but instead relied on a sign near the entrance saying the premises were under surveillance. Morgan and JC, with Schenck's help, were attempting to take over Stan's life to the fullest extent possible, ostensibly because they believed Anderson and Olivarez were bad actors who meant Stan ill but also probably because there were personal advantages to be had for them.

For JC, the draw was simple: She wanted money. Stan and Joan had set up a trust that would dole out an allowance to JC after their death, rather than give her all of Stan's money at once, the alleged logic being that they didn't want the profligate spender to blow all of her cash quickly and end up homeless. Schenck was the son of *NCIS* creator George Schenck and an attorney with a background in personal injury and entertainment law—he had once represented POW—as well as a sideline as a low-tier Hollywood hustler (he claims on his official biography that he was in some way involved in producing and/or distributing the ABC television series *Wife Swap*). He was in for the ride with JC, as was Morgan, who claims that he only wanted to protect Stan but whose motives remain suspicious. "Keya had some alternative plan to somehow capitalize on this," suspects one insider who spoke anonymously for fear of litigation. "Otherwise, why would he be there with a ninety-five-year-old man who basically slept all day and have to deal with JC screaming at him all day long? There's no reason why anyone would stay in that situation if there wasn't some sort of payoff."

Meanwhile, out in public, Stan was back on the road almost immediately after Joan's death. It was somewhat bizarre to see. There he was, just eight days later, at Disney's D23 convention, which featured a historic occasion. Disney had decided to award its Disney Legend title to the two men who made Marvel, Stan Lee and Jack Kirby. Neal Kirby, Jack's son, who had been so vicious in his criticism of Stan back in the lawsuit days, accepted the award on his late father's behalf, and he and Stan remained silent about all past disputes in their speeches. It was remarkable: Here were two men from warring camps, essentially signing a peace treaty in one of the most consequential artistic disputes in global popular culture.

There was more reason for the wider public to think things were still on track, given that POW projects continued to come out or be announced: A Stan-involved anime series called *The Reflection* premiered in Japan, and a group of Chinese firms announced that they were forming a movie studio that would develop five POW projects (POW had been doing a lot of deals in the Pacific Rim in recent years). More convention appearances were announced and followed through on. Other than perhaps wondering why Stan was out on the publicity trail when one would expect him to be grieving, you would think everything was hunky-dory. But behind closed doors, it seems, Stan was being pushed into being a public face during what he wanted to be a period of mourning. After all, money was at stake. "He did *not* want to do conventions anymore," says Bolerjack. "He didn't like traveling long distances. He didn't want to stay overnight at hotels. He was very clear about it. It wasn't like it was a secret. If you were in the inside, you had heard him say it." I ask why he was doing the cons, then. Bolerjack is blunt in his reply:

> Because Stan is easily malleable. If you want Stan to do something and you know Stan, it takes about four sentences to get it. Stan felt very guilty. Not that Stan necessarily knew that we were nobodies, but he knew that people depended on him for a living. He knew that people didn't have skills that would keep them up when Stan retired. That was a way you leaned on him, if you wanted to. Stan would've given you his house in ten minutes if he liked you. He was a generous, trusting man that was easily exploited.

On August 7, Stan reportedly signed a declaration, presumably at Morgan's behest, stating that Anderson and Stan had been splitting proceeds from the Mega Museum fifty–fifty and, more important, that Anderson specifically had its contents only on loan. Then things went quiet for a few months. Stan's few close friends, such as the Friedmans, continued to wonder what had happened to Stan and what was going on in his Hollywood Hills home. What they didn't know was that a massive transaction, one of allegedly illegal provenance, was in the works. On October 4, a $300,000 check was written from a Stan-owned shell company to Olivarez's Hands of Respect, with the word "loan" written in the memo line. Olivarez has maintained that it was an honest loan from Stan, but in December, Stan and Morgan reported to the police that it was a forged check. Just a few days later, an audit of Stan's accounts revealed that there had been an $850,000 withdrawal to buy Olivarez a condo near Stan's home, which, similarly, Olivarez says was a consensual transaction but that Stan and Morgan reported to the authorities as a matter of forgery and theft. On top of that, it turns out Olivarez had, legitimately or illegitimately, gained power of attorney over Stan.

When Morgan went to the media about all of this, Olivarez was summarily exiled from the inner circle, never to return. And yet, in the midst of all this, the air of public normalcy remained. On December 28, Anderson threw Stan a small surprise birthday party with twenty to thirty people at a steakhouse in Beverly Hills. Kevin Smith was in attendance and reports that Stan was in seemingly good spirits. Stan and Smith had been discussing having Stan appear in one of Smith's upcoming movies and, according to Smith, Stan asked him, "When are we shooting?" to which Smith replied, "We're getting closer, I promise." However, there were hints that something was amiss. JC was sitting next to Smith, and he'd long despised her for her avarice and attempts to use Stan's fame to burnish her own image. Right after he said the shooting was coming soon, JC chimed in right away to say, "He's not doing it unless I'm in it." Smith, furious, wished Stan a happy birthday and walked away.

Something was up. Bolerjack says he saw Stan at the end of December 2017 and "he was Stan: He was amazingly agile and whatnot and mentally all there. And then I saw him January 2 and he was different. A completely different person. Something happened. He was never the same after that." Bolerjack speculates that Stan may have had a stroke, but he presents no evidence of this. He continues: "I raised my concern to some of his healthcare people and I was just ignored. Nobody took it seriously. He was also much more malleable. He had no resistance at all at that point."

There are few people who will speak on the record about what was going on in this period, but when one of them does, it's always shocking. Take, for example, private investigator Paul Katz. He had been in contact with Morgan in the past, due to a tangential connection to Marilyn Monroe that had led Morgan to film him for an as-yet-unreleased documentary about the late starlet. He'd long found Morgan to be an oddball ("We'd be on the phone and he'd say, 'I can't talk right now, Travolta's on the other line,'" Katz says), but a relatively harmless one. One day, "He calls me out of the blue and says, 'How would you like to possibly work for Stan Lee?'" Katz recalls. Katz said he was intrigued and accepted an invitation to meet at one of JC's houses. Things got strange. "Keya told me I had to dress up in a nice suit and especially have my fingernails clean, because she's picky about that," Katz says. "Then I put my finger in my mouth for one second and she starts to talk about dirty nails for half an hour. I'm getting frustrated. She pulls two thousand dollars cash out of her bra, in twenty-dollar bills. She hands it to me and says, 'Help me with these people. I wanna know what this Jerry [Olivarez] is about. We want our power of attorney back' and stuff."

Katz agreed to do it. "Keya said he's doing this out of the kindness of his heart, that he loves these people and wants to look out for them," he says. "I thought, *That's great, because someone stole their power of attorney*." But the situation started to unravel for Katz when he was told to come to a meeting at the office of Tom Lallas, an attorney representing Stan. Katz arrived and was shocked to see Olivarez enter the room, too, which was highly unusual for a case of this sort: "I'm like, *What the fuck?* I was not happy about that at all." He was ready to leave when Morgan allegedly made a proposition. "Keya took me outside and said, 'Look, we gotta get this power of attorney back, and if you and I work together, *you and I* can get that power of attorney in our name!'" Katz says. "I said, 'If that's something you're going to do, that's your business. I have no desire to have their power of attorney.'"

On top of that, Morgan—who regularly tells people that he's making millions of dollars in big movie deals—allegedly demanded 10 percent of Katz's fee from JC because Morgan had helped with the case. "I said, 'You just told me how you make twenty million, forty million dollars, and that you're doing this out of the kindness of your heart,'" Katz recalls. (When I ask Morgan about Katz's allegations, he doesn't exactly refute them, but does say Katz is "a loser" and "an absolute nobody" who "never met Stan" and met JC only "once at her house, and she paid him $4000 in cash and bought secret bugs and recording devices to plant in Stan's house," though Morgan says he didn't allow them to do so.) Furious, Katz spoke to Lallas after the meeting and got his help in writing up an official statement about what he'd seen, then cut off contact with Morgan. Katz recalls telling Lallas, "You should hire protective services, because something's very wrong here."

That observation was starting to be shared by Stan's fans in the public. A bombshell dropped on January 9, 2018, when the *Daily Mail* published a story accusing Stan of groping and demanding oral sex from nurses in his home and claimed the unnamed nursing agency planned to sue Stan. Just two days later, the same media outlet declared that, the previous April, Stan had sexually assaulted a masseuse—later identified as a woman named Maria Carballo—in Chicago. Stan's camp vehemently denied the claims. Although we should consider these stories very seriously, given their moral weight, there are three complicating factors. For one thing, the nursing agency never ended up taking the legal action they'd been reported to be considering. For another, Carballo went through two law firms with her own suit before disappearing, making it difficult to directly ascertain anything about her or her accusations. On top of that, multiple people in Stan's world, including Bolerjack, suspect that the sexual incidents were impossible, given Stan's age and frailty.

It is, of course, entirely plausible that all the alleged misconduct occurred, but that information of it was leaked in order to stage a hit job. After all, the collateral damage in each story was to Morgan's rival, Anderson: The road manager was accused of allowing the Chicago assault to happen, and the first article also revealed Anderson's past as an abuser of his wife and son. What's more, Morgan seems to have a history of feeding stories to the particular *Daily Mail* writer who wrote those items, though Morgan dismisses him as "some reporter" among the "over 100 reporters who called me while I was with Stan." When I've spoken to Morgan, he has regularly talked about how Anderson used to arrange "whores" for Stan to have sexual contact with while they were on the road and claims he has recorded proof, which he has never produced for me. He also tells me he believes the sexual allegations were "perfectly calculated by Max and orchestrated by him once Stan kicked him out" and that "the fact [Carballo] also sued Max is just a red herring and misdirection."

Whatever the case, the heat was now on Anderson. It appears that Anderson made a last-ditch play to turn the tide by prompting Stan to sign a legal declaration that enumerated the ways in which his home life had disintegrated into chaos and pointed the finger at Olivarez, Morgan, Schenck, and JC, adding that JC was mentally unbalanced and insolvent. That may not have been all: I was provided with footage of a woman, allegedly one of Stan's nurses, sobbing to JC and others as she recounts how Anderson offered her $50,000 to make false statements about JC. Whatever efforts he made or didn't make, they were not enough. On February 15, the LAPD and Adult Protective Services were called to Stan's home to investigate allegations of battery, theft, and elder abuse on the part of Anderson. Morgan later said he was the one who made the call. Another obstacle had been removed, and Morgan was firmly in control of the life of Mister Marvel.

HERE IS THE SORT of person Keya Morgan is. For one thing, if he thinks it will benefit him, he contacts you constantly. There were periods in the researching of this book where he was reaching out to me by phone or text every day, ranting about his side of the story, declaring his absolute innocence, and bragging about all the famous people he knows. He often says he was just on the phone with Robert De Niro or Al Pacino and talks about how close he is with any number of movie stars. Which brings me to another trait—his utter lack of humility. I never heard him once apologize for anything or admit fault in any way, and he instead blames the people around him for causing all the trouble. He swears he was the only one who was looking after Stan, and it does seem to be true that he was at least taking Stan to doctor's appointments, as evidenced by his possession of numerous shockingly intimate photos of Stan in medical settings.

That gets at Keya's unsettling, exhibitionistic approach to talking about the man he claims to have loved so much: He'll show you oodles of images of private things, like Stan looking miserable and old on a hospital bed, or lists of the pills Stan was taking at the time, or even medical charts revealing the problems Stan was facing with his heart. Morgan is also an avid user of Twitter, regularly going on rants there to defend Michael Jackson from rape charges and rail against the "fake news" that has been written about him by reporters, many of whom he says he's going to sue and destroy. On occasions when he suspected that I might be planning to quote negative claims about him, he would say that such an act would be unfair in the same way that it would be unfair if he told people that I rape children. And yet, as if actively trying to undermine himself and his claims of virtue, he once called me with an entirely unethical, possibly illegal proposition. "I have a friend who cloned Stan Lee's hard drive," he told me over the phone. "He wants to know how much it would be worth to you." I declined the offer and scratched my head as I wondered who would say such a thing to a reporter in an on-the-record conversation.

I got in touch with Morgan shortly after Stan's death, but it took him nearly a year to get around to meeting me. He'd promised early on that we would convene in New York City "when it gets warmer there"—and well into a balmy summer, he was still saying that. I had largely given up when he reached out in September 2019 to say he wanted to meet me in the Los Angeles area to play me recordings that he said would exonerate him. We arranged a meetup in October at an Italian chain restaurant in an L.A. suburb, and he told me he would be bringing an armed bodyguard "because I've never met you." After the appointed hour had passed on that day, Morgan texted me to inform me that we had to move to another location because the restaurant wasn't safe. He brought an armed bodyguard, Gaven Vanover, who had previously worked for Stan, and Vanover arrived at the restaurant to escort me to the still-unnamed second location. As we walked across the strip mall, I asked Vanover why we were moving. "Security reasons," he said. "Just security reasons."

We arrived at a steakhouse and sat down, making small talk for a few minutes before Morgan arrived, clad in sunglasses and a dark suit and bearing a laptop and a pile of books and magazines. He didn't bring a lawyer, which I found remarkable, given that he was preparing to stand trial for elder abuse toward Stan. As it turned out, he wanted to begin our meeting by proving his bona fides. He went through the publications, pointing out how each one mentioned him in some way, usually just as a licensing credit for an image of Lincoln or Marilyn that was published somewhere or other. Some of them had interviews and features that bolstered his image, but none of them seemed to have anything like concrete background details on him. Morgan told me not to believe anything I read in journalist Alan Duke's CNN profile of him. He was reluctant to discuss anything about his personal biography, avidly changing the subject whenever I asked for specifics.

Finally, he flipped open his laptop and started playing me some recordings of Stan and his associates, allegedly recorded with Stan's permission, but I must admit that the things Stan said on them were so shocking and unlike his public persona that I have to imagine the elderly man had forgotten about the recording equipment, if indeed he ever knew about it in the first place. The edited files were all plucked from the "thousands and thousands of hours" of recordings of Stan that Morgan constantly claims to have, and what I heard on them chilled the twelve-year-old geek in me.

The vast majority of the twenty recordings he played for me dealt with Stan's relationship with his daughter. That relationship was revealed to be one of horrifying dysfunction. Again and again, I heard recordings of Stan either screaming at his daughter and begging her to leave him in peace or him musing to others about how difficult it was to be her father. The recordings contain no context, so we are left with, to borrow the words of T. S. Eliot, a heap of broken images. "Tell her to go fuck herself, I'm so mad at her" he tells Morgan when discussing JC at one point. In another tape, Morgan relays a phone message from JC about how she loves her father, and Stan replies, "Fuck, she doesn't know what love is" and "I don't need to be upset every fucking time she calls." In another, JC accuses Stan of "fucking Linda," likely referring to his nurse, Linda Sanchez, and Stan bellows, "Get outta my house!" In another, JC yells, "What have you done for your daughter?" and "You stopped my credit cards!" Stan tells JC she's screwing up as an artist, saying, "I want you to do things I can put up in a gallery. Then I'd be proud of you." Stan accuses JC of having bipolar disorder; JC tells Stan she hates him for not supporting her idea for making a comic about the FBI; Stan says JC "always makes me wanna kill myself" . . . The examples of discord, difficult to listen to, go on and on.

It is within this category that some of the most troubling audio exists. On a number of occasions, I heard Stan making racist, homophobic, and misogynist remarks either to or in discussion of JC. "I think you're the dumbest white woman I've ever known!" he screams at her in one (to which she replies, "Fuck you, Stan"). In another, Stan talks to Morgan about JC and says she's "supposed to be an attractive lady," but instead she's "like the worst lesbian you can imagine." At one point, JC tells Stan she's going to adopt an African American baby (something that others in the inner circle say became a brief obsession for her), and Stan grunts back at her, "The hell you want a *black* baby for?" These words are no doubt alarming to Stan's ardent admirers, who have long made him out to be a champion of progressive, or at least liberal, values of tolerance and equality. Indeed, I know of only one other hint at Stan being overtly racist: a story told by an obscure African American cartoonist named Cal Massey about working with Stan in the early 1950s, in which Massey claims Stan paraphrased a pre–Civil War minstrel song called "Massa's in de Cold Ground" at him as an intimidation tactic. It reads as follows:

> I walked into the room and Stan said, "Massey's in the cold, cold ground." I sat down and he said, "Messy Massey." Then I got up and started to leave, when Stan asked me where I was going. I said, "I thought New York had grown past this sort of thing. Have a nice day." . . . Stan was making a play on the lyrics of a song from the South that was written during slavery times, and I didn't like it. He explained that to me, saying, "I just wanted to see what kind of character you had."

However, other than that memory, one struggles to find examples of accusations of easily identifiable bigotry when it comes to Stan. His worshippers and corporate partners have lionized him as a bold man who shares the values of the present-day consumer, but perhaps he was more a child of the 1920s than is comfortable to sit with.

Another prominent category of recordings that Morgan plays for me were related to Max Anderson. There were multiple audio files of Stan telling Morgan that he thinks Anderson, now that he's been ousted from the inner circle, will come back to his home and take lethal revenge. All the while, Morgan energetically eggs these fears on. In one tape, Stan says of Anderson, "He's just crazy enough to do anything," and worries about Anderson coming back to the house for retribution. "Do you have a gun with you?" he asks Morgan, who says no. Stan then launches into a lurid imagined scenario in which Anderson breaks into Morgan's car using the butt of a gun, before adding, "I should have a gun, too . . . Can we buy a couple?" Later, Stan says of Anderson, "He'd wanna not only kill us but torture us," and, "We don't know how he's planning to get us, but he's planning," and, "He would think nothing of killing you or me." To that latter point, Morgan adds, "He has no value for human life." Morgan also talks to Stan about how he thinks Stan needs to move into a high-security condominium to escape from Anderson—an act Morgan later tried to carry out and for which he subsequently caught accusations of abduction. For what it's worth, others told me Anderson didn't seem like much of a threat but that Morgan and Schenck would, to further their interests, tell Stan that Anderson was dangerous and was attempting to take control of Stan's house. The kidnapping charge was dubious, because Stan had definitely consented to the move, but the question is whether that consent was in any way informed.

Then there is the final category of recording, which I assume Morgan played in order to evoke sympathy for his good deeds: files in which Stan says he's miserable and on the verge of death. "If I died today, that's fine with me," Stan says in one recording. "There's nothing that excites me anymore." Morgan tells him that such an attitude is "selfish" and that "we need you." Stan is unmoved, adding, "I don't enjoy being old," and, "It's no fun. It's just . . . I'm existing." After about five hours, Morgan and I said our farewells. I'd spent years researching Stan, but I was still shaken by what I had heard him say. Taken as a whole, the recordings I'd just devoured were a harsh reminder of the fact that a person's true self will always be just beyond the biographer's grasp.

STAN'S SHIP SAILED FURTHER into the storm. The aforementioned former nurse of Stan's, Linda Sanchez, filed a legal declaration containing startling claims about Morgan, Schenck, and JC. They were the sorts of things one hopes to encounter only in overwrought TV dramas. To wit, here were some of the allegations about JC:

JC is constantly verbally abusive toward her father, Mr. Lee. She yells at him, attempts to intimidate him, and screams terrible, abusive things at her father, which causes his blood pressure to rise daily. For example, JC will yell and scream at her father whenever they are together or on telephone conversations, will try to make him feel guilty about JC's problems, will say things like "you are the reason my life is so f_cked up." JC inflicts emotional distress on Mr. Lee by trying to manipulate him and make him feel guilty . . . Recently I heard JC specifically say "I am the Queen" and "I'm taking over the Tiara" . . . Mr. Lee has also stated that he believes that his daughter JC needs a psychiatric evaluation and to be put in a hospital or institution, because JC is also "not normal." Shockingly, I once heard JC tell her father, "I would put you in a mental institution faster than you would put me into an institution." . . . JC frequently refers to Mr. Lee's money as "My money" . . .

It went on and on. Sanchez attested to being intimidated by Schenck, and there were vivid descriptions of physical abuse ("I understand that JC has placed her feet on Mr. Lee's face when JC was drunk or high on drugs"), deception ("Morgan forcefully has tried to convince Mr. Lee that Mr. Lee does not own the Lee home"), depression ("Mr. Lee has told me privately that he is giving up, after this daily harassment, and that he believes he has nothing left to live for but to 'go to sleep' and 'die' "), and suspicion ("Mr. Lee has told me, among other things, he does not trust Morgan, does not like Morgan, Morgan is a dangerous person, and Mr. Lee wants Morgan out of his life and out of the life of his daughter, JC, as well"). There was an accompanying set of statements from Mike Kelly, Stan's assistant, detailing claims about how Morgan had taken control of Stan's professional and personal lives by keeping him away from the POW offices and being omnipresent during any interaction Kelly had with Stan, not allowing the latter to speak about his situation privately. It also detailed a trip Morgan and JC took at night to the POW offices, without prior notification or approval, during which they took a series of boxes, the contents unspecified. Just to make things even more bewildering for Stan, $1.4 million allegedly went missing during a bank-wire transaction, according to Morgan and JC, although no culprit was identified, and police once again arrived at Stan's home to investigate (nothing came of the allegation). It started to appear to anyone paying attention that Stan's world was beset by both totalitarianism and chaos at once.

As if that weren't confusing enough, the public also had to deal with dubious communications from Stan. Morgan had a habit of recording iPhone videos of Stan speaking directly into the camera about his life, typically in terms that venerated Morgan and damned everyone saying Stan was in trouble. It is worth quoting one video in full, to get a sense of the strange transformation Stan seemed to have undergone into a hoarse, tired man given to paranoia and profanity. The rambling address is to unnamed recipients, likely the media:

Hi, this is Stan Lee, and I'm calling on behalf of myself and my friend Keya Morgan. Now, you people have been publishing the most hateful, harmful material about me and about my friend, Keya, and some others—material which is totally incorrect, totally based on slander, totally the type of thing that I'm gonna sue your ass off when I get a chance. You have been accusing me and my friends of doing things that are so unrealistic and unbelievable that I don't know what to say. It's as though suddenly you have a personal vendetta against me and against the people I work with. Well, I want you to know I'm gonna spend every penny I have to put a stop to this and to make you sorry that you've suddenly gone on a one-man campaign against somebody with no proof, no evidence, no anything, but you've decided that people are mistreating me and therefore you're gonna publish those articles. I'm gonna get the best and most expensive lawyers I can and I want you to know, if you don't stop these articles and publish retractions, I am gonna sue your ass off.

Another example worth quoting in full is a video in which Stan defends Morgan in words so intense that one cannot help but be suspicious of them:

Hiya, heroes. This is Stan Lee with an urgent message for you. Of course, every message I have is urgent. And it's come to my attention that a lot of people at a lot of companies are claiming to be partnered with me, to work with me, and this is not true. I have no partner other than Keya Morgan, and he represents me and he is my partner in most of everything I do. So, if ever you wanna get in touch with me, you've gotta contact Keya. Not the various lawyers and companies and people who seem to hang around and whenever somebody wants something, they say, 'Oh, yeah, I represent Stan Lee.' They don't. Keya Morgan is the only one. Now, you may not like him, and he's a very strange guy, because he represents me, but he's very good at what he does. And he's the guy to contact if you want anything that has to do with Stan Lee. Of course, you can contact me, too, but it's usually a little bit easier to find him. Now, having said all that, I wanna wish you all well and end with, *Excelsior*.

Morgan also recorded private videos that took on the same format, which he regularly sent to me over the course of our initial communications. They're eerie and chilling, and there are those who have accused these videos of being something akin to hostage tapes, with the speaker coached in what to say before the camera starts rolling. There is no direct evidence of this, but if the rest of the accusations are true, it would hardly be surprising. Take, for example, a video in which Stan speaks to someone he addresses as "Doctor" (Morgan tells me it was a psychiatrist he was trying to contact) about how he thinks JC needs to be institutionalized. "She's schizophrenic; she's got paranoia," he says. "I have tried, for many, many years, starting when we lived in New York, to get her help, and never could find any. And every year, every day, she just grows worse and worse and worse." He goes on: "She is making threats, she wants to be part of our company, she wants to write for us—all sorts of demands. And she knows nothing about anything. She is totally oblivious to the way the world works."

And yet the wider public didn't really have much of a clue what was happening. Stan was still going to conventions—only now, for the first time in over a decade, without Anderson. But he was starting to cancel appearances here and there, allegedly due to a bout of pneumonia. POW didn't let on that there was any division between the two of them and kept touting all its Stan-related projects, but he was no longer doing much promotion of anything. In addition to facing reports that he was a prisoner in his own home, Stan had to contend with the fact that his health was failing, and he needed full-time nursing care. A high-end and discreet nursing service had been in charge of Stan's daily needs, with Sanchez in the lead, but that situation got complicated on February 28, when—who else?—the *Daily Mail* reported that Stan had been getting sexual favors from nurses and getting inappropriately close to Sanchez.

Whoever was going after Sanchez was soon drowned out by the echo of an atom bomb: On March 10, freelance journalist Mark Ebner published a story at the *Daily Beast* about Stan's situation, with the attention-grabbing headline "PICKED APART BY VULTURES": THE LAST DAYS OF STAN LEE. Ebner is a slow-spoken, cheekily self-described "hippie burnout" who has written books about true crime, much of it celebrity-related. He had received a tip from an insider he still declines to name about all not being well at the House of Lee. Ebner had no special affection for comic books, superheroes, or Stan, but he followed the trail anyway and was shocked by what he found. In the piece, readers learned of JC's avarice, Morgan's shady past, Olivarez's alleged theft, and the general mayhem in the Lee camp. It was the first time a wide swath of people had heard about just how bad things were for the ninety-five-year-old Marvel legend. It would not be the last.

Another public shock arrived after Morgan took Stan to the Silicon Valley Comic Con on April 8 and set him up for his autograph session. Bystanders took cellphone video of Stan signing, and it quickly went viral in geek circles. The footage showed a near-passed-out Stan struggling to hold his pen and having to be told by a looming, dark-suited, and bowler-hatted Morgan that his name was spelled S-T-A-N L-E-E. More bad news was unveiled on the very same day the video hit the Internet: Kevin Smith had received a plea from a desperate Anderson to save Stan from Morgan and JC, and Smith reached out to a contact at *The Hollywood Reporter,* leading to an April 10 investigative article by reporter Gary Baum, headlined STAN LEE NEEDS A HERO: ELDER ABUSE CLAIMS AND A BATTLE OVER THE AGING MARVEL CREATOR. It was another parade of woes. The general accusations from the *Daily Beast* article were present, as were strange new tidbits, such as the reporting of rumors that Stan "hid millions in cash all over his property."

On that same day as the release of the videos and the article, a post was published in a geek-oriented news blog called Bleeding Cool, in which JC told a reporter she was planning to start a chain of submarine-sandwich restaurants based on Stan. Stan appeared to beat back the accusations of elder abuse in the following few days by issuing phone videos, shot by Morgan, of statements about how everything was copacetic and that every ill report was to be ignored. On April 13, Stan (and, implicitly, Morgan) sued Olivarez for theft and fraud, including a scheme by which Olivarez had allegedly sought to obtain samples of Stan's blood for use in a comic-book promotion without Stan's permission.

The "diabolical and ghoulish scheme," as the suit framed it, involved Olivarez getting blood drawn from Stan's body, having someone mix it chemically with ink, then using that ink to make stamps on Black Panther comics—sold at a premium, of course—at a Marvel exhibition in Las Vegas. (Hands of Respect's own website confirmed all of that, but said it had Stan's "full support" for the project; when I ask Olivarez about the fracas, he says the suit and media coverage did not accurately describe the situation, but declines to elaborate on his side of the story.) Just a few days later, Stan was grinning on the red carpet for the mega-blockbuster *Avengers: Infinity War,* Morgan at his side. It was hard to know what to believe, but it certainly seemed that Stan had gone through the looking glass into a world that no longer made sense.

Friends and fans were horrified by what they were reading in the papers and their inability to get in touch with Stan. "As some other pros have already said, something is going on with Stan Lee," Peter David, the comics writer, said on his blog. "His personal assistant, Max Anderson, has been fired and is being kept away from having any contact with Stan, who recently was in poor health fighting a bout with pneumonia. All of the reportage seems to be coming from Stan's 'camp,' although the identity of those in the camp is a bit debatable." Others worried in silence, feeling impotent: "It was disgusting," says former Marvel Studios chief Avi Arad, who claims to have gotten in touch with Stan during this period. "When he was telling me what was going on, I said to him, 'You know, no one can help you with that, because there are so many parasites around you, it's like getting rid of cockroaches.' And it was hard on him, because he didn't have anybody whom to trust. He was a people-believer."

Superstar comics artist and toy entrepreneur Todd McFarlane, who had long enjoyed a friendship with Stan, stopped by the house to check on the nonagenarian and reported that things weren't so bad. According to McFarlane, "we talked about things like his growing up in New York, his love of comics, his even bigger love of his late wife, Joanie, and how he was doing healthwise. He told me that getting old kind of sucked but said, 'What are you going to do?'" That said, McFarlane reported that Stan's overwhelming sentiment was one of resignation and that he told the younger man, "I just wanna be with Joanie." Larry feared for his brother, as well: Around this time, he received a cryptic call from Stan in which the elder brother sounded weary, almost near death, and told him, "Larry, you're the only one I can trust."

An astute reader will notice that one entity has been largely missing from this story. Its name is POW Entertainment. The company released a statement on April 12, explaining their previous silence by claiming they had "respected [Stan's] privacy as he deals with the upheaval within his personal management and life" but that "we feel we must add our voice to the legion of fans and creatives who are speaking out," and they concluded by declaring, "Your thoughts matter, please find it in your heart to Speak Up For Stan!" But if they were making concrete efforts to save him, those efforts remain invisible. Instead, POW plowed ahead, announcing a movie based on one of Stan's old projects from the seventies, *The Virtue of Vera Valiant,* as if nothing was amiss. Two days later, it became clear that something was going wrong between Stan and his ostensible place of employment: Stan's Morgan-appointed lawyer announced that Stan was suing POW for an astounding $1 billion over allegedly unlawful assertion of his name and likeness rights. It appears that Stan was, indeed, no fan of POW by this point. Morgan sent me candid, unstaged-sounding recordings in which Stan rants about how "in fifteen years, POW never made one movie, and I've been with 'em all that time and could never understand how we could not have had at least one deal in a decade and a half."

However, one never knows with Morgan's recordings, and the same goes for whether the lawsuit was actually his initiative rather than Stan's. POW was certainly suspicious and issued a statement in which they said, "The allegations are completely without merit," and "In particular, the notion that Mr. Lee did not knowingly grant POW! exclusive rights to his creative works or his identity is so preposterous that we have to wonder whether Mr. Lee is personally behind this lawsuit." To make matters even weirder, Stan's social-media presence started to sound a lot more like Morgan than like Stan, with tweets being issued that denounced "fake news" like the *Hollywood Reporter* article, that said his Facebook and Instagram accounts had been hacked, and that praised industrialist Elon Musk.

If POW was failing to pick up the ball and most of Stan's friends felt powerless, the same couldn't be said for a small handful of Stan's colleagues and admirers. In the spring of 2018, Manhattan-based writer/artist Neal Adams—Stan's old sparring partner in the Academy of Comic Book Arts days—concluded that enough was enough. Whatever his differences with Stan over the years, he loved the man and couldn't bear to see him mistreated. "We only hoped, those of us out here, that that aggravation didn't institute the potential for Stan's death," Adams says of the chaos that was being reported. "Those of us who were on the outside, we couldn't interfere directly. . . . It was difficult for us to reach out to him. We knew that some of the people out there were not good, and we knew that the police officers were briefly looking at this as a domestic matter that they could basically brush aside." Writer/editor Clifford Meth was similarly concerned when he tried to email Stan. "Keya Morgan called me," Meth says, "which meant Keya Morgan was reading his email. He tried to hire me to do publicity for Stan, but really it was publicity for Keya and his relationship with Stan." Meth and Adams felt stirred to action, so they set out to save Stan. Meth had worked for New York State assemblyman Dov Hikind and reached out to the elected official, who made calls to help the group get in touch with the Los Angeles district attorney's office and the LAPD.

Their efforts may have played a part in what came next. In circumstances that remain murky, Morgan called 911 twice, on May 30 and 31. Morgan says that, in both cases, he was attempting to stop suspicious visitors to the house from hurting Stan. In the first instance, Morgan claimed, Stan was being shaken down by three armed individuals who were demanding money, which led to cops

arriving and arresting the men, although later legal filings and a police report claim that the visitors were, in fact, cops doing a welfare
check on Stan at the behest of Adult Protective Services. The very
next day, Morgan called 911 again, this time claiming that, as he told
the dispatcher, "We have someone who is being very threatening
and being very aggressive and we want him to leave the house," and
that the individual was armed. The subsequent police report countered that the man was one of Stan's Morgan-picked bodyguards,
who had simply arrived to verbally confront Morgan over a nondis-
closure agreement that Morgan had demanded he sign. Lawyer
Robert Reynolds—who had been hired by Morgan after answering
an ad Morgan put up on Craigslist—says he was present in the house
for a meeting with Stan to determine how he was doing when the
second call occurred and a SWAT team and police helicopters descended on the celebrity's residence. Reynolds says nothing like
Morgan's account of events actually occurred and that "it was a
pretty dramatic evening, I'll say."

The day after that, the police interviewed Stan at his home, and
he told them Morgan and JC were great and taking fine care of him.
Along those lines, Morgan released another video of Stan, this one
featuring him praising Morgan and calling him his best friend. Another followed on June 10, in which Stan said Morgan was his sole
business partner and business manager. For understandable reasons,
the public and authorities were not swayed by any of this, and, when
combined with the efforts of Adams and his cohort, matters came to
a breaking point. On June 11, Morgan was arrested and charged with
filing a false police report in regard to the 911 calls. A temporary restraining order on Stan's behalf (and, oddly, Larry's, although Larry
tells me he never asked to be included) was issued against Morgan.
As it turned out, Morgan would never see Stan again. "At that point,
I didn't keep track of it, because it seemed like things had been made
a little bit better," recalls Adams. "But the major problem was not
solvable. It kind of went down from there."

———

ENDING UP IN THE CARE of one's child is generally seen as a natural outcome of a life well lived, but it is unlikely that Stan knew peace once his daughter was calling the shots in his life. Stan's existence grew quieter for the remainder of his days, insofar as there were no more visits from the cops or notarized statements attesting to Grand Guignol circumstances. But based on all we know about Stan's relationship with JC, from testimony and his own recorded words, we can only assume that his hours were still privately hellish. As a source close to the Lees says, JC is "very fear-based" and prone to verbal violence. "It'll be something simple," the person says, "like 'Oh, I forgot to pick up the milk,' and suddenly this whole avalanche of 'You're a terrible person and you're just trying to use me!' That kind of thing will happen. It's incredibly hard to be around. It's incredibly toxic." In the background was the supporting cast: the nurses; a housekeeper; Schenck; and Bolerjack, Stan's body-man, who had somehow outlasted his former employer, Anderson, and whom Stan universally referred to as "Hairspray," due to his voluminous locks. The new arrangement in place, JC succeeded in getting the inheritance trust broken, meaning she'd get all of Stan's money upon his death. On June 18, JC released a video to Bleeding Cool in which she and Stan presented an air of familial harmony and wished the viewer a happy Father's Day.

A further image of peace was projected in July, when Stan dropped the lawsuit against POW. POW continued to announce Stan-related projects: There was an online comic strip called *Backchannel,* co-written by Stan, and the opening of the first-ever Stan Lee Shanghai Comic Universe convention in China. However, the convention's title was merely ceremonial, not denoting Stan's presence, and on August 5, Bolerjack told Bleeding Cool that Stan was no longer going to do public signings. Stan and POW released a statement saying someone had seized control of his social-media accounts previously, but that he had reclaimed them. A statement was released to Bleeding Cool in which Stan was said to condemn Morgan, claiming the videos in which he'd appeared were "hostage videos." He also accused Morgan of stealing from him and asserted that JC and Schenck were taking good care of him. There were no outward signs of dysfunction anymore, but it was hard to believe the situation had wrapped itself up so neatly.

That veneer of normalcy seemed to peel back in Stan's return to the public eye. For months, Morgan had been attempting to get his vengeance by feeding a reporter allegations about JC: stuff about abusing her parents, trying to take her father's money, even hurting the multitudinous dogs she kept as pets in her homes. When Schenck caught wind of the story, he made an end run to edge it out by fostering his own story via Ebner, the freelancer who'd written such an excoriating exposé in the *Daily Beast*. Ebner arrived at Stan's home and found a kind of awkward Potemkin village inhabited by an armed security guard known only as Kane, a nurse, Bolerjack, and Schenck. Ebner spoke with Stan, JC, and Schenck for about an hour, and the transcript as released wasn't explosive, but it was certainly eerie. Ebner reported Schenck pulling him aside to say, "The closest thing I can say is that [Stan and JC] have a Kennedyesque relationship. They yell at each other sometimes, but she is the love of his life, and she has gotten a bad rap."

Stan feebly attempted to dispel rumors of filial rage: "There really isn't that much drama," he said. "As far as I'm concerned, we have a wonderful life. I'm pretty damn lucky. I love my daughter. I'm hoping that she loves me, and I couldn't ask for a better life." However, he also seemed weak and confused at times, at one point muttering, "I couldn't want a better daughter . . . Want a better daughter . . . A sweeter girl . . . A nicer girl . . . Loving . . . Sorry about my voice . . . And I am . . . So, I'm only saying, I don't know that much . . . When you asked me . . . How I would feel before that . . ." then trailing off. Meanwhile, JC and Schenck were egging him on to sound cheerful and telling Ebner that everything was now in its correct place, while JC made ambiguous accusations that the

Church of Scientology was somehow involved in the poor treatment of her father. Few who paid attention were convinced that all was right in Stan's world. It was, as it turned out, the last interview Stan ever did.

It was also around this time that two figures from the past had last shots at reuniting with Stan. Peter Paul had been watching all of the chaos from across the continent at his home in Florida. He and JC got in touch and, according to Paul, she once spoke to him while Stan was in the room with her. "She was saying to him she wanted him to talk to me, but he wasn't ready," he recalls. Right around then, Stan had one more visitor, a man who had had a tumultuous relationship with him but who ultimately forgave and embraced him: his protégé, Roy Thomas. They had a friendly conversation and reminisced about the creation of Spider-Man, Martin Goodman doubting him, and the hagiographic, oversize coffee-table book about Stan's life that Thomas had just published at Taschen. Thomas had a picture taken of the two of them. Roy is smiling, and Stan looks like hell, but he's smiling, too. "I think he was ready to go," Thomas later said. There would be no more visits from old friends.

Two days later, on November 12, 2018, according to an insider, Stan collapsed in his home while his bodyguard and nurses were present. An ambulance was summoned and he was taken to Cedars-Sinai Medical Center, where he was pronounced dead from cardiac arrest due to congestive heart failure and respiratory issues. Less than a day after news of his death went worldwide, JC appeared on the television show of online ultra-tabloid *TMZ* to enthusiastically talk about how she was going to soon unveil a new superhero that she and her dad had created (though insiders say it was just her), called Dirt Man. That same day brought an announcement from Camsing, POW's parent company, saying that fans shouldn't worry, because plenty of Stan Lee products and projects were still on the horizon.

Keya Morgan has suggested to me that JC was in some way responsible for Stan's death, whether by attacking him or by simply berating him to the point where the stress caused his heart to give out. In addition, in the immediate wake of Stan's death, someone was sending text messages to journalists, including Alan Duke, that claimed Stan was murdered (Duke suspects Morgan was sending them, though Morgan denies this). I have seen no evidence of foul play, and my source tells me that, if anything, Stan's death was "anticlimactic." That said, JC did not allow an autopsy and, in a violation of Jewish law that Jack Lieber would have hated, Stan was swiftly cremated. Though POW released a statement claiming there was a "private closed ceremony" to send him off, multiple people tell me there was no such thing and that the atmosphere around JC remained chaotic.

We cannot know how Stan felt as he entered oblivion, but Bolerjack, who knew Stan's lifestyle better than most by the end, says we shouldn't worry too much about how he went out. By the final few weeks, "He did what he wanted every day," Bolerjack recalls. "It wasn't a lot. He didn't want to do a lot. That's what he wanted, was just to do nothing, to sit and think and talk about things and rest and sleep. What a ninety-five-year-old man wanted to do." After a life that spanned nearly a century—a tapestry of triumph and tragedy, of enormous dreams and disappointing realities; a stretch of time in which a man could watch the world become unrecognizable and know he had some not-inconsiderable part in making it thus; an existence that went through a denouement of agony and discord—after all that, Stan may have found a way to rest and deem that life good enough. "I tell everyone that asks," Bolerjack intones with a smile, "Stan died a free man."

PETER PAUL SAYS JC told him. "She said that, of all the people she called to tell that he passed," he boasts to me, "I'm the only one that was visibly upset about it." I express surprise that he was on the short list of people JC wanted to contact; that there was that level of intimacy between a Paul and a Lee. He bristles. "As much as I've been vilified, she knows that I was the best thing that happened to him," he tells me. "Because without my intervention, what do you think Marvel would have done with him?" He then falls down a rabbit hole of self-justification and financial minutiae: "There would have been a two-year contract; Perlmutter would have screwed him to the floor," and so on.

Even now, Paul has a plan for Stan's future. He's convinced that his zombie SLM is the true master of Stan Lee's name, likeness, and slogans, thanks to the 1998 contract situation. Through the mouth of his business partner, former Marvel VP Shirrel Rhoades, he has quietly announced a plot to create a Stan Lee movie studio in China. He even helped JC craft a lawsuit against Camsing, announced in the summer of 2019, that alleges the corporation is not the true owner of those lucrative trademarks. It's actually not beyond the realm of possibility that Paul's dream may come true. The Chinese government seems to have a vendetta against its native Camsing, having begun the process of prosecuting it for massive alleged corruption in early 2019, so they may be receptive to anyone trying to dismantle it. It could well be that the future of Stan's mythos on the other side of the world will be controlled by someone whom he had denounced repeatedly and avoided contact with.

Even more astounding, Paul still loathes the man whose brand he hopes to profit from. As the moon glints off his outdoor pool, he sits at his kitchen table and tells me he doesn't think Stan or Joan had a heart. I ask him to clarify. "Just evident by the way they treated their daughter and the way that they were able to completely dissociate themselves from the issues that their goddaughter encountered," he says, referring to Paul's own daughter. "He has a history of throwing people under the bus, and that was a big bus that he had no problem throwing me under."

I propose an analogy: "It sounds like you're saying you want to do what Disney has done with Walt Disney, which is they don't talk about him anymore."

Paul nods. "I wanted to turn Stan into a lifestyle brand," he says.

"Kind of divorced from who he really was," I say.

Paul nods again. "It's irrelevant. It's what he did."

JIM SHOOTER WAS DEVASTATED when he heard. "About thirty friends of mine sent emails and called me and stuff, and for the next several days all I did was do little interviews and tributes and things and get calls all the time," the intimidatingly tall former Marvel editor-in-chief tells me, his broad back bent forward like a tilting rock formation. We're in the tiny apartment of a friend of his, near his own home in New York's Rockland County. He has brought multiple bound albums containing an astounding quantity of Stan-related mementos: photos featuring the two of them, letters Stan sent to him, a drawing featuring their two offices in the seventies, and so on. We spend hours going through the albums, page by page, the craggy-faced Shooter providing commentary all the way. Shooter is a pariah these days. His time at the helm of Marvel in the seventies and eighties was marred by near-perpetual conflict with his creators. Like Stan, he had grand visions for how the company should reinvent itself, but his iron will and flinty micromanaging ticked off writers and artists to no end. In many ways, he was Stan without the charm—and, as such, was living proof of how crucial Stan's charm was to his success. Shooter burned every bridge in his tenure at the House of Ideas and subsequent independent comics endeavors. He has little to show for his years of labor other than an endless stream of stories, lots of them about how he was wronged by others (a common refrain, for whatever reason, among men Stan grew close to), but many about seemingly every interaction he and Stan ever had. He is hated, but he treasures the love Stan bestowed upon him. Occasionally, Shooter still gets invited to conventions, and it was at one in 2016 that he had his final encounter with Stan. Shooter says he waited hours for the thinning-out of a line of fans who'd paid for photos with Stan the Man. The crowd dispersed and

Stan heartily greeted his old pal. "He got up, because he'd been sitting all day, and he says, 'I am so tired,'" Shooter recalls. He goes on:

> And I say, "I don't blame you. Even just sitting there, it's gotta be grueling." So we sit there and we talk for a while. I hadn't seen him for years, but we picked up like it was before. We got along so well. At a certain time every night, Stan would return to his hotel room and call his wife. So the helpers are like, "Stan, you gotta get on the cart, we gotta go." And he said, "No, wait! We have to have a picture! I want a picture with Jim!" So they're saying, "Get on the cart, we can do it tomorrow!" And he says, "No! We're taking a picture! I want it printed out now, and I'm going to sign it!"

Shooter chuckles at the memory. "Stan was good at that," he says. "He made you feel good." He starts pausing between sentences to compose himself. "Stan was another father to me," he says. "He was my father in the business. I'm using this line in a piece I'm writing for Roy Thomas. Roy said, 'Would you write a tribute to Stan?' And the first thing that occurred to me is, every word I write is a . . ." He halts, then, after a single gentle sob, he continues: ". . . is a tribute to Stan."

LARRY LIEBER WAS ALONE in his microscopic Manhattan apartment, as he is wont to be these days, when he got the news. He had finished his decades-long run as the artist for the Spider-Man newspaper strip in September 2018 and had nothing to do most of the time. He was dabbling in fiction—he'd typed out a short story based on his experiences with a woman he'd loved and had started a novel—as well as pondering a memoir. Occasionally, old pros from the comics industry would have lunch with him at the diner at the end of his block. Every once in a while, Marvel would invite him to New York screenings of their movies. He couldn't understand the stories in the damn things, though—you had to see and remember all of them to track anything. He largely spent his time watching old movies on cable, reminiscing about his youth and the way things used to be.

It was against this backdrop that he got a call from a reporter asking him to comment on his brother's death. It was the first Larry had known of the event—JC and her cohort had neglected to inform him. Two thoughts occurred to him. The first was one of relief for Stan: "He'd been spared his daughter, who could drive anybody, from what I gather, nuts," Larry says. But the second thought was more troubling: "I think to myself, what am I . . ." He trails off. "I mean, everyone I know is going. Gone. And I thought, *did* I lose him? Can you lose somebody you never had? Did I ever have him?" He pauses. "I don't know."

Larry never got to bury his brother, but in a way, he already had, long before. He's old. He has books to write. He doesn't care about all the lawsuits and criminal investigations and everything else that has followed in the wake of Stan's death. Let the crazies obsess over all that. He's tired. It's time to move on. After hours of conversation, the winter sun having long since abandoned the sky above New York, Larry attempts to sum up his feelings about his brother. "What's the famous line from—you probably know of it—*The Man Who Shot Liberty Valance*?" he says to me, then recalls it: "When the legend becomes fact, print the legend."

ACKNOWLEDGMENTS

I'T'S A CLICHÉ TO POINT OUT THAT WRITING A BOOK IS A TEAM effort, but I have learned that people say it because it's true. The list of people without whom this book wouldn't have been possible, or would at least have been significantly worse off, is quite long, but I'll try to get to a few of them.

Perhaps the most important individual here is my colleague and former editor at *New York* magazine, David Wallace-Wells. It was he who sauntered over to my desk in the late summer of 2015, plopped down an advance galley of Stan Lee's *Amazing Fantastic Incredible: A Marvelous Memoir,* and said I should "do something" with it. Grandiose thinker that I was, I figured he meant a profile of Stan, so I raced to set up interviews and begin my research. When I came back to David a week later and told him what I'd gathered so far, he informed me that he'd meant I should write a short book review. Oops. But rather than stifling my efforts, David encouraged me to keep going. Under his expert editorial guidance, we were able to build out the longest and most talked-about piece I had ever written as of its publication in February of 2016. Which brings us to the other person who acts as a *sine qua non* here: this book's editor, Will Wolfslau. He read that profile and, after Stan died in November of 2018, contacted my wonderful and dogged agent, Ross Harris, to ask if I'd be interested in writing a full biography of Stan. I almost refused, having no idea how to write a book, but after one meeting with Will about what he was looking to do, I was giddy with excitement at the prospect of working with him. He has been a guiding light and a venerable resource ever since.

I also would have well and truly been up the creek without a paddle if I had not had a fantastic group of research assistants helping me manage the chaos of the researching and editing processes. The first one I teamed up with was Barbara Bogart, who did all the scanning of the thousands of pages of documents I needed from the Stan Lee archives at the University of Wyoming. I had only five days to get the material, and without her, I would have gotten to only a small fraction of what I ended up obtaining. Next came two others: Britina Cheng and David Odyssey. Both of these wonderful creative minds were kind enough to do the numbing task of transcribing interviews that I didn't have time to transcribe myself, as well as performing other miscellaneous tasks. Britina also acted as the book's fact-checker, which is a truly brutal task that saved my butt on more than a few occasions. Mitra Moin provided great translation help when I was dealing with French-language sources. Maria Mădălina Irimia did research for me in Romania and helped this book become what is, I believe, the first English-language publication to recount the Botoșani pogrom of 1890. Dan Jurca and Fadia-Alexandria Hîrțan did additional research in Romania, where Dan uncovered Stan's father's birth record, which was enormously helpful. Speaking of translation: Martin Swant interpreted a bevy of financial reports for me, and Ryan Pollock of Sher-Tremonte LLP searched various professional legal databases and filings and presented his findings in terms even a fool like me could understand. Lara Rabinovitch, Daniel Soyer, and Deborah Dash Moore all gave me important context on what Jewish life was like in Romania and New York in the first half of the twentieth century. Meryl Schumacker of We Go Way Back navigated parts of the genealogical-research world that I didn't know how to find and came back with some gold. And Rae Binstock did the painstaking work of formatting the notes section, for which I will be forever grateful. I must mention one other person, who wasn't a research assistant: Filmmaker Nat Segaloff was kind enough to provide me with raw interview footage he shot of Stan and various people associated with him for Stan's 1995 episode of A&E's *Biography* series.

There are three figures who provided vital assistance and also happen to be characters in this book. One is Keya Morgan, who was exceedingly generous in giving me contact information for key players in Stan's life, as well as crucial documents and recordings. Another is Peter Paul, who provided piles of documents and hours of video footage relating to both Stan's and his own legal troubles. Finally, there is private investigator Becky Altringer, who gave me invaluable information about a number of individuals and organizations from the final third of Stan's life.

A number of comic-book scholars provided hefty shoulders for me to meekly stand upon. Sean Howe inspired me to get into comics journalism after I read his book *Marvel Comics: The Untold Story,* and he helped me get in touch with a number of comics professionals. Mark Evanier was of tremendous help by both acting as a source and giving me glimpses at his research and Rolodex. Patrick Ford and Michael Hill's unendingly rigorous digging on behalf of the cause of Jack Kirby illuminated nooks and crannies I otherwise might not have explored. Jordan Raphael and the late, great Tom Spurgeon both offered guidance on how to approach Stan as a biographical subject. It weighs heavily on me that I'll never get to know what Tom, who died in late 2019, would think of this book.

I must thank the American Heritage Center at the University of Wyoming for their generosity in letting me peruse and use their phenomenal archives. I must thank my wonderful family, both immediate and extended, for their support and encouragement. I must also thank the insightful and incisive cohort of friends and colleagues who read the book and gave their thoughts, especially the journalist S. I. Rosenbaum. That last person happens to be my beloved life-partner, and writing this volume would've been a hell of a lot less fun without her.

NOTES

W HEN DRAWING ON INTERVIEWS CONDUCTED BY OTHER PEOPLE, I have used past-tense verbs of attribution (e.g., "said"); when drawing on my own interviews, I have used the present tense (e.g., "says"). This is to reduce the need to cite my own interviews in the book's Notes section. Therefore, if you see a present-tense verb for a quotation, assume it was from an interview I conducted. The sole exception is the Overture section, which could read properly only if everything was in past tense.

When citing the release dates of comic books, I have not used the dates emblazoned on their covers. Throughout their existence, comic books have traditionally been given "cover dates" that are anywhere between one and three months past the actual date of release on stands. This is an old magazine-publishing trick: If you put a date in the future on the finished product, it looks new to a buyer even after it's been out for a while. Frustratingly, few records survive that detail exactly when those releases happened, so I have opted to date them vaguely—e.g., "early 1940" or "around the summer of 1963," and so on.

OVERTURE

3 **eastern Romania, containing just over 110,000:** Hugo Grother, "Map of population distribution by citizenship (not ethnicity!), according to the 1899 census," 1907, shaded map, Zur Landeskunde von Rumänien, Halle (accessed April 15, 2019), https://ro.wikipedia.org/wiki/Fi%C8%99ier:Rumania_citizenship_1899.JPG.

3 **people, roughly 6,800 of them:** Radu D. Rosetti, *Roumania and the Jews* (Bucharest: I. V. Socecu, 1904), p. 3.

3 **Vaslui held not only its ear to the ground, but its breath," recalled:** M. E. Ravage, *An American in the Making: The Life Story of an Immigrant* (Rutgers University Press, 2009), ebook.

6 **the cheapest of them cost:** "Kevin Smith & Friends Present: Excelsior!" *Legion M* (accessed February 7, 2020), https://legionm.com/stantribute.

7 **Months later, an even higher-profile tribute:** Lily Olszewski, *Celebrating Marvel's Stan Lee,* ABC television (December 20, 2019).

9 **This was, apparently, a favored phrase:** JC Lee, Stan Lee's Love Story: *"It's All About Love!"* (Klein Graphics, 2015), ebook.

13 **"the Homer of the twentieth century":** For example, Jean-Marc Lainé, *Stan Lee, Homère du XXe siècle* (Copenhagen: Fantask, 2016).

PART ONE EPIGRAPH

15 **Of what import:** Jack Kirby and Stan Lee, *The Fantastic Four* #49 (New York: Canam Publishers Sales Corp., 1961), p. 2.

CHAPTER I

17 **The pogrom that Stan Lee's father survived:** Maria Mădălina Irimia, "The Pogrom of Botoșani" (unpublished article, November 26, 2019), typescript.

17 **the evening of Tuesday, September 11, 1890:** For those who point out that September 11 wasn't Yom Kippur on the Gregorian calendar, we must offer a reminder that Romania was still on the Julian calendar as of 1890.

17 **likely numbering just below sixteen thousand:** Andrei Corbea-Hoisie, "Botoșani," trans. Anca Mircea, *The YIVO Encyclopedia of Jews in Eastern Europe,* https://yivo encyclopedia.org/article.aspx/Botosani.

17 **were wrapping up their observance:** Irimia, "The Pogrom of Botoșani."

18 **Gray-eyed, brown-haired:** "World War I Draft Registration Cards, 1917–1918," registration state: New York, registration county: New York, roll: 1786973, draft board: 169, Provo, Utah, Ancestry.com Operations, Inc.

19 **with the surname Pesica:** Ancestry Team, "For You Comic Fans: Stan Lee's Family Tree (Autographed)," Ancestry.com (November 8, 2013), https://blogs.ancestry.com /ancestry/2013/11/08/for-you-comic-fans-stan-lees-family-tree-autographed/.

19 **as long ago as the days of Roman antiquity:** Carol Iancu, "Jews in Romania, 1866–1919: From Exclusion to Emancipation," *Eastern European Monographs,* 449 (August 2008), 18.

19 **On Iancu's father's side:** Ancestry Team, "For You Comic Fans."

19 **found themselves in the principality of Moldavia:** Iancu, "Jews in Romania," 19.

19 **His bride was Estera Malca Leibovici:** Ancestry Team, "For You Comic Fans."

19 **on the afternoon of September 21, 1886:** There are conflicting records about the date of Iancu Urn Liber's birth. When he registered for the draft in the United States during World War I, he listed his birth date as August 15, 1885; when he registered again during World War II, he listed it as September 15, 1885; his posthumous Social Security record lists it as September 15, 1886; however, the birth records for Botoșani reveal his birth as occurring at around 3 P.M. on September 21, 1886. See "Botoșani County Archives," National Archives of Romania (last modified January 31, 2020), http://arhivelenationale.ro/site/directii-judetene/botosani/.

20 **On the one hand, Jew hatred:** Iancu, "Jews in Romania," pp. 13–67.

20 **The 1878 Treaty of Berlin, authored by:** Lara Rabinovitch, " 'The Gravest Question': Romanian Jewish Migration to North America, 1900–1903," PhD diss. (New York University, 2012), 28–77.

21 **Reactionary pamphlets:** Iancu, "Jews in Romania," 131–132.

21 **A gathering with the straightforward official title:** Ibid., 139–140.

21 **"It is immaterial in which country":** Ibid., 128.

21 **And what of his mother? Celia:** Ancestry Team, "For You Comic Fans."

21 **resided in Vaslui county, possibly:** The Romanian genealogist whose services I retained uncovered a document from one of his contacts that posited Celia's birth as

occurring in Perieni, but she certainly later lived in Huşi, and it's eminently possible that Huşi was her place of birth, as well. Further research—ideally from someone with expertise in Romanian Jewish matters—is needed to pin this fact down. Dan Jurca, email to Abraham Riesman (October 31, 2019).

22 **Huşi was smaller than Botoşani:** Theodore Lavi, "Husi," trans. Ziva Yavin, *Encyclopedia of Jewish Communities in Romania,* vol. 1 (1969), https://www.jewishgen.org /Yizkor/pinkas_romania/rom1_00114.html.

22 **Romanians had, through stigma, violence, and legislation:** Iancu, "Jews in Romania," 110–126.

22 **in astounding numbers:** Samuel Joseph, "Jewish Immigration to the United States from 1881 to 1910," PhD diss. (Columbia University, 1914), 93.

22 **Although their numbers:** Rabinovitch, "'The Gravest Question,'" 17–18.

22 **a ship known as the *Majestic:*** The arrival record is largely illegible; although "Zanfir" and "Sofie" can be read, the other first names under "Solomon" are hard to make out. We may assume Celia was among them, perhaps under a different birth name that was Anglicized as "Celia." See "New York, Passenger and Crew Lists (including Castle Garden and Ellis Island), 1820–1957" (1901), serial: T715, 1897–1957, microfilm roll: 0245, line: 18, p. 137, Provo, Utah, Ancestry.com Operations, Inc.

23 **he took his clan to 4th Street:** "New York, State Census" (1905), state population census schedules, election district: A.D. 10 E.D. 17, Manhattan, New York County, p. 21, New York State Archives: Albany; Provo, Utah, Ancestry.com Operations, Inc.

23 **who had arrived in 1900 and later wrote:** M. E. Ravage, *An American in the Making: The Life Story of an Immigrant* (Rutgers University Press, 2009), ebook.

23 **The family entered the hat-making business:** Larry Lieber, personal interview by Abraham Riesman (New York, N.Y., July 1, 2019).

24 **the Romanian Jewish exodus, only showing up:** "Lieber, Jacob," Liberty Ellis Foundation (accessed February 7, 2020), https://www.libertyellisfoundation.org /passenger-details/ czoxMjoiMTAyMjczMTYwODk2Ijs=/czo5OiJwYXNzZW5nZ XIiOw==.

24 **on the *Nieuw Amsterdam,* he came:** We Go Way Back blog, "Client Report—Stan Lee" (commissioned report, December 2, 2019), 11.

24 **He had been trained in Romania:** Jacob Lieber entry, SS *Nieuw Amsterdam* Passenger Manifest (August 6, 1906), p. 76, line 5; Microfilm Serial: T715, 1897–1957; roll 0749 (New York, N.Y.), Ancestry.com, New York, Passenger and Crew Lists (including Castle Garden and Ellis Island), 1820–1957, Provo, Utah, Ancestry.com Operations, Inc. (2010).

25 **By 1918, Jack was living:** "World War I Draft Registration Cards, 1917–1918," registration state: New York, registration county: New York, roll: 1786973, draft board: 169, Provo, Utah, Ancestry.com Operations, Inc.

25 **Jack already had family in the United States:** We Go Way Back blog, "Client Report."

25 **that branch of the family:** One of Stan's cousins on the Leiber side was none other than Gerson Leiber, a much-loved sculptor, painter, and lithographer—and husband of handbag designer Judith Leiber. They appeared to have had no contact or relationship with Stan. See the We Go Way Back blog, "Client Report."

25 **the year 1920 found:** 1920 United States Federal Census, census place: Manhattan Assembly District 18, roll: T625_1220, p. 3A, enumeration district: 1292, Provo, Utah, Ancestry.com Operations, Inc. Original data derived from "Fourteenth Census of the United States 1920," NARA microfilm publication T625, roll: 323 (Chicago City), Record Group 29, Bureau of the Census, Washington, D.C., National Archives.

25 **in the spring of 1920:** Records differ as to the specific date of their wedding: The New York marriage registry says it was April 26, but a research report from Ancestry

.com says May 5. See "Index to New York City Marriage Licenses, 1908–1929," Reclaim the Records.org. Also see Ancestry Team, "For You Comic Fans."

25 **at 777 West End Avenue:** Danny Fingeroth, *A Marvelous Life: The Amazing Story of Stan Lee* (New York: St. Martin's Press, 2019), ebook.

26 **he said in 1977:** David Anthony Kraft, "The *FOOM* Interview: Stan Lee," *FOOM*, vol. 1, no. 17 (March 1977), 8–9.

27 **And a dive:** Jordan Raphael and Tom Spurgeon, *Stan Lee and the Rise and Fall of the American Comic Book* (Chicago Review Press, 2004), ebook.

27 **Stan begins:** George Mair, *Excelsior! The Amazing Life of Stan Lee* (London: Boxtree, 2003), 5–6.

28 **his marriage was turbulent:** Mair, *Excelsior,* 7.

29 **the boys' cousin (and wife of the eventual publisher of Marvel Comics, Martin Goodman), called:** Raphael and Spurgeon, *Stan Lee.*

29 **Stan told an interviewer in 2014:** David Hochman, "The Playboy Interview with Stan Lee," *Playboy* (November 12, 2018), https://www.playboy.com/read/stan-lee -playboy-interview.

30 **Jean Goodman said Celia was:** Raphael and Spurgeon, *Stan Lee.*

30 **Stan would eventually write:** Stan Lee, "Stan Lee autobiography—Excelsior! (outline)" (1978), Box 127, Stan Lee Archives, University of Wyoming, American Heritage Center.

30 **as they decamped much farther north:** "List of Registered Voters for the Year 1924," *The City Record* (October 16, 1924), ReclaimtheRecords.org.

30 **packed up again and moved:** Fingeroth, *A Marvelous Life.*

31 **The dramatis personae for these dreaded meetups:** Larry Lieber, personal interview by Abraham Riesman (New York, N.Y., July 1, 2019).

31 **"My one celeb relative":** Stan Lee, "My Bio-Auto-Ography," Box 97, Stan Lee Archives.

31 **Most important, there was the aforementioned cousin:** Larry Lieber, personal interview by Abraham Riesman (New York, N.Y., July 1, 2019).

31 **Newspaper comic strips were an early love:** Mair, *Excelsior,* 12.

32 **"Sunday night, we listened to":** Fingeroth, *A Marvelous Life.*

32 **"Errol Flynn was my god":** Matt Atchity, "Five Favorite Films with Stan Lee," *Rotten Tomatoes* (July 23, 2009), https://editorial.rottentomatoes.com/article/five -favorite-films-with-stan-lee/.

32 **"At every meal at home":** Mair, *Excelsior,* 9.

32 **"Some of the books I most enjoyed":** Ibid., 12.

33 **"At the end of each book":** Stan Lee, "Stan the Man & Roy the Boy: A Conversation Between Stan Lee and Roy Thomas," interview by Roy Thomas, *Comic Book Artist #2* (Summer 1998), transcript, https://www.twomorrows.com/comicbookartist/articles /02stanroy.html.

33 **Stan eventually made it explicit, saying:** "Interview with Stan Lee," *Zinezone* (October 6, 2008), https://web.archive.org/web/20081006090009/http://www .communitybridge.com/zz/zones/arts/literature/comics/lee/interview2.html.

34 **"He would entertain the class with humorous and exciting:** Mair, *Excelsior,* 10.

34 **"It made my early years hell":** Lee, *Excelsior* outline.

34 **"Though it may seem like a trivial thing:** Mair, *Excelsior,* 10–11.

34 **"A real depressing time for me":** Ibid., 11–12.

34 **"I never believed in religion":** Raphael and Spurgeon, *Stan Lee.*

35 **"My father insisted I be bar mitzvahed":** Fingeroth, *A Marvelous Life.*

35 **"When I rode it, in my imagination":** Mair, *Excelsior,* 10.

36 **Whatever was in the water:** "DeWitt Clinton High School: Notable Alumni," Wikipedia (last modified January 9, 2020), https://en.wikipedia.org/wiki/DeWitt _Clinton_High_School#Notable_alumni.

37 **I was one of the first to subscribe:** Mair, *Excelsior,* 17.

37 **According to Stan, Jack once owned:** Lee, *Excelsior* outline.

38 **he wrote advance obituaries:** Mair, *Excelsior,* 15.

38 **"I could never understand what":** Fingeroth, *A Marvelous Life.*

38 **He said he did paid acting work:** Mair, *Excelsior,* 18.

38 **"I didn't hate being in school":** Fingeroth, *A Marvelous Life.*

38 **The yearbook for his DeWitt Clinton graduating class:** 1939 DeWitt Clinton High School Yearbook (Bronx, N.Y., 1939), 64 (accessed February 7, 2020), https://www .classmates.com/yearbooks/DeWitt-Clinton-High-School/259?page=0.

39 **He would tell of climbing a painter's ladder:** Fingeroth, *A Marvelous Life.*

39 **his yearbook entry summed up a philosophy:** *Fingeroth, A Marvelous Life.*

39 **In Stan's retelling, around the time he graduated:** Edward Lewine, "Housing History: Sketching Out His Past," *The New York Times (*September 9, 2007), https:// archive.nytimes.com/query.nytimes.com/gst/fullpage-9D03E3DB1E3AF93AA3575 AC0A9619C8B63.html.

39 **he briefly attended:** Raphael and Spurgeon, *Stan Lee.*

CHAPTER 2

40 **publishing imprint initially known as Timely Comics:** Stan Lee, interview with Nat Segaloff (circa 1995).

41 **answering an ad in the paper (sometimes):** Stan Lee, "History of Marvel Comics (first draft)" (1990), Box 5, Folder 7, Stan Lee Archives, University of Wyoming, American Heritage Center.

41 **he'd updated his official line:** George Mair, *Excelsior! The Amazing Life of Stan Lee* (London: Boxtree, 2003), p. 21.

41 **Before the comic book, there was:** Gerard Jones, *Men of Tomorrow: Geeks, Gangsters, and the Birth of the Superhero* (New York: Basic Books, 2005).

43 **obtaining a job at a company that put them out:** Stan once wrote, in an unpublished chapter from a book on the history of Marvel, that he had come across *Captain America Comics* #1 "by some strange quirk of fate" and even joined the fan club that it advertised. But this seems highly unlikely as an account of events, given that he was almost certainly already working for Timely when that issue came out. See Lee, "History of Marvel Comics (first draft)," Stan Lee Archives.

44 **Moses Goodman was born to:** These paragraphs on Martin Goodman's personal and professional history are drawn from Blake Bell and Dr. Michael J. Vassallo, *The Secret History of Marvel Comics* (Seattle: Fantagraphics Books, Inc., 2013), sections throughout Chapter 1.

47 **"we'd fight all the time," Kirby would remember:** This paragraph on Jack Kirby's upbringing is drawn from Mark Evanier, *Kirby: King of Comics* (New York: Harry N. Abrams, 2017), Chapters 1 and 2, https://books.google.com/books?id=oxcuDwAAQ BAJ&newbks=0&hl=en.

48 **Simon allegedly brainstormed:** Joe Simon, *Joe Simon: My Life in Comics* (London: Titan Books, 2011).

49 **This two-fisted paragon:** Joe Simon and Jack Kirby, "Case No. 1. Meet Captain America," *Captain America Comics,* no. 1 (Timely Publications, March 1940).

49 **John Goldwater was one such cynic:** Simon, *My Life in Comics.*

49 **"I don't really know why he was there":** Ibid.

50 **"Robbie had a sister named Celia Lieber":** Ibid.

50 **"Mostly we had Stan erasing the pencils":** Ibid.

50 **"interfering with my work," Kirby later said:** Will Eisner, *Will Eisner's Shop Talk* (Milwaukie, Ore.: Dark Horse Comics, 2001), pp. 208–209.

51 **"We never became very friendly":** Mair, *Excelsior,* 29.

51 **"One day I made his life," Simon wrote:** Simon, *My Life in Comics.*

51 **It began *in medias res:*** Stan Lee, "Captain America Foils the Traitor's Revenge," *Captain America Comics,* no. 3 (Timely Comics, March 1941), 18.

52 **"Being only seventeen at the time":** Mair, *Excelsior,* 26.

52 **"and slyly changed the 'y' to a second 'e'":** Jordan Raphael and Tom Spurgeon, *Stan Lee and the Rise and Fall of the American Comic Book* (Chicago Review Press, 2004), ebook.

52 **"Alas, I never did write that novel":** Danny Fingeroth, *Disguised as Clark Kent: Jews, Comics, and the Creation of the Superhero* (London: Bloomsbury Academic, 2008), 10.

53 **The very next issue of *Captain America Comics:*** Stan Lee, "Captain America and the Bomb Sight Thieves," *Captain America Comics,* no. 4 (Timely Comics, April 1941).

53 **"Captain America and the Bomb Sight Thieves," followed by one:** Stan Lee, "The Story behind the Cover," *Marvel Mystery Comics,* no. 21 (Timely Comics, May 1941).

53 **The first-ever published Stan Lee comics story:** Dr. Michael J. Vassallo, "Stan Lee (1922–2018)—The Timely Years," Timely-Atlas-Comics blog (December 8, 2018), https://timely-atlas-comics.blogspot.com/2018/12/stan-lee-1922-2018-timely-years.html.

53 **In it, an anthropomorphized spirit:** Stan Lee, "Jack Frost," *USA Comics,* no. 1 (U.S.A. Comic Magazine Corp., April 1941).

54 **Afterward came comics stories:** Vassallo, "Stan Lee (1922–2018)."

55 **One more notable bit of career foreshadowing:** Stan Lee, "Marvel Get-Together," *Marvel Mystery Comics,* no. 25 (Timely Comics, September 1941).

55 **it wasn't superhero fiction's first crossover:** Bill Everett, "The Human Torch and the Sub-Mariner Meet," *Marvel Mystery Comics,* no. 8 (Timely Publications, April 1940).

55 **Simon and Kirby, in Simon's account:** Simon, *My Life in Comics.*

56 **"they quit Timely a few months after":** Mair, *Excelsior,* 29.

56 **he first chose his brother Abe:** Dr. Michael J. Vassallo, interview by Abraham Riesman (March 7, 2020).

56 **the contents page of *Captain America Comics* #12:** Stan Lee, ed., *Captain America Comics,* no. 12 (Timely Comics, January 1942).

57 **In his 1978 autobiography outline:** Stan Lee, "Stan Lee autobiography—Excelsior! (outline)" (1978), Box 127, Stan Lee Archives.

57 **As bosses go, Martin was pretty much okay:** Mair, *Excelsior,* 25.

58 **"Martin's mandate was":** Ibid, 31.

58 **"Everybody felt Stan was wonderful":** Vince Fago, "'I Let People Do Their Jobs!': A Conversation with Vince Fago—Artist, Writer, and Third Editor-in-Chief of Timely/Marvel Comics," interview by Jim Amash, *TwoMorrows* (November 2001), https://www.twomorrows.com/alterego/articles/11fago.html.

58 **"He was good-natured but strict with his editing":** Dr. Michael J. Vassallo, "Allen Bellman: The Interview," Timely-Atlas-Comics blog (March 25, 2012), https://timely-atlas-comics.blogspot.com/2012/03/allen-bellman-interview.html.

59 **"And shortly after the war started":** David Anthony Kraft, "The *FOOM* Interview: Stan Lee," *FOOM,* vol. 1, no. 17 (March 1977).

59 **"I think I could have gotten a deferment":** Danny Fingeroth, *A Marvelous Life: The Amazing Story of Stan Lee* (New York: St. Martin's Press, 2019).

59 **Stan only enlisted on November 9, 1942:** World War II Enlistment Records, "Stanley M. Lieber," Enlistment Records 1938–1946 (College Park, Md.: U.S. National Archives & Records Administration, 2002).

59 **In that gap, the only way in which:** Vassallo, "Stan Lee (1922–2018)."

59 **"my parents were worried about me":** Mair, *Excelsior,* 32.

60 **"I used to go to penny arcades in New York and shoot":** Ibid.

60 **Timely artist Dave Gantz would later recall:** Raphael and Spurgeon, *Stan Lee.*

60 **According to Stan, his father:** Lee, "Stan Lee autobiography."

61 **"I couldn't believe it":** Mair, *Excelsior,* 35.

61 **The official military manual:** There are conspiracy-minded amateur comics historians—none of whom would share any of their evidence with me, but all of whom insisted they had some—who contend that the Signal Corps was cultivating Stan for postwar use as an asset in mass-media manipulation through the massively popular comic-book medium. These individuals claim that much of what came next in Stan's professional life was dictated by Cold War psychological operations designed to bolster belief in American might and right. A close contact of Stan's tells me Stan once spoke vaguely of doing favors for the U.S. government in the past. We must take such claims with a shaker's worth of salt, but if such a relationship indeed existed, it likely would have seen its inception here. See United States War Department, *Military Occupational Classification of Enlisted Personnel,* TM 12-427 (Washington D.C.: U.S. Government Printing Office, 1944), 53.

62 **increasingly bouncy products:** Stan Lee, Peter David, and Colleen Doran, *Amazing Fantastic Incredible: A Marvelous Memoir* (United Kingdom: Gallery Books, 2015), 23.

62 **"Officer-in-charge asked me to write slower":** Lee, "Stan Lee autobiography."

62 **Off we go, into our office yonder:** Lee, David, Doran, *Amazing Fantastic,* 24.

62 **So successful was this effort:** Mair, *Excelsior,* 41.

62 **He claimed to have drawn:** Lee, David, Doran, *Amazing Fantastic,* 28.

63 **His commanding officer:** Mair, *Excelsior,* 39.

63 **He bought his first car:** Lee, "Stan Lee autobiography."

63 **He spoke of dating:** Fingeroth, *A Marvelous Life.*

63 **She gets a brief mention:** Lee, "Stan Lee autobiography."

63 **"girl I was really serious with":** Fingeroth, *A Marvelous Life.*

63 **Though Kiye may have been the most relevant:** Joan Schenkar, *Talented Miss Highsmith* (United Kingdom: Picador Paper, 2011), 212–213.

64 **And all the while, in his off-hours:** Lee, David, Doran, *Amazing Fantastic,* 25–26.

64 **"I was just three years older," he told:** Fingeroth, *A Marvelous Life.*

CHAPTER 3

65 **In his autobiography outline, the first item:** Stan Lee, "Stan Lee autobiography—Excelsior! (outline)" (1978), Box 127, Stan Lee Archives, University of Wyoming, American Heritage Center.

65 **Elsewhere in the Lee archives:** If Cerf and Stan corresponded, there appears to be no extant evidence of it in Cerf's voluminous archive of papers at Columbia University, and Cerf's biographer, Gayle Feldman, says she knows nothing about the two men being in touch. Perhaps it was all done in person or over the phone—Stan always loved charming people in real time. See Stan Lee, "Speech to Third General Session of the AASA, Summer Convention" (1979), Folder 5, Box 10, Stan Lee Archives.

66 **seemed to trust Stan:** Vince Fago, " 'I Let People Do Their Jobs!': A Conversation with Vince Fago—Artist, Writer, and Third Editor-in-Chief of Timely/Marvel Comics," interview by Jim Amash, *TwoMorrows* (November 2001), https://www.twomorrows.com/alterego/articles/11fago.html.

66 **Writer Daniel Keyes:** Daniel Keyes, "A Timely Talk with Daniel Keyes," interview by Will Murray, *Alter Ego* 3, no. 13 (March 2002), p. 92.

67 **"Stan was a very jolly guy, always like a kid":** Danny Fingeroth and Gene Colan, "Gold and Silver Memories," in *The Stan Lee Universe,* Danny Fingeroth and Roy Thomas, eds. (Raleigh, N.C.: TwoMorrows Publishing, 2011), 23.

67 **"In this immediate postwar period of late 1945":** Dr. Michael J. Vassallo, "Stan Lee (1922–2018)—The Timely Years," Timely-Atlas-Comics blog (December 8, 2018), https://timely-atlas-comics.blogspot.com/2018/12/stan-lee-1922-2018-timely-years.html.

68 **The bullpen now held dozens:** Dr. Michael J. Vassallo, interview by Abraham Riesman (February 8, 2019).

69 **The first took the form of a cover story:** Jess Zafarris, "Stan Lee's 1947 Guide to Writing and Selling Comics," *Writer's Digest* (November 12, 2018), https://www.writersdigest.com/online-editor/stan-lee-1947-guide-to-writing-and-selling-comics.

69 **The second and more revealing stab at mainstream success:** Catalog of Copyright Entries. Third Series: 1947. United States: Copyright Office, Library of Congress, 1947, https://www.google.com/books/edition/_/QD4hAQAAIAAJ?hl=en.

70 **Never before have you read a book:** Stan Lee, *Secrets Behind the Comics* (Akron, Ohio: Famous Enterprises, Inc., 1947), 4.

70 **It presented, in comics-panel form:** Ibid, pp. 62–68.

71 **"I became one of the best-informed people":** George Mair, *Excelsior! The Amazing Life of Stan Lee* (London: Boxtree, 2003), 50.

71 **Ironically, or perhaps hypocritically:** Dr. Michael J. Vassallo, "Stan Lee (1922–2018)—The Timely Years," Timely-Atlas-Comics blog (December 8, 2018), https://timely-atlas-comics.blogspot.com/2018/12/stan-lee-1922-2018-timely-years.html.

71 **his cousin Morton Feldman at the latter's hat company:** Danny Fingeroth, *A Marvelous Life: The Amazing Story of Stan Lee* (New York: St. Martin's Press, 2019).

71 **"And I remember it very clearly":** Joan Lee, interview with Nat Segaloff, circa 1995.

71 **Archetype from his childhood:** Stan Lee, interview with Nat Segaloff, circa 1995.

72 **"He said, 'Hello, I think I'm going to fall'":** Joan Lee, interview with Segaloff.

72 **There was a slight snag:** Mair, *Excelsior,* 67–68.

72 **It was December 5, 1947:** We Go Way Back blog, "Client Report—Stan Lee" (commissioned report, December 2, 2019), 2.

72 **and Celia was, as Stan put it:** Mair, *Excelsior,* 69.

72 **recalls Larry. On December 16:** "Celia Solomon Lieber," Find A Grave (February 7, 2020), https://www.findagrave.com/memorial/194676277/celia-lieber.

73 **"When my mother died":** Mair, *Excelsior,* 71.

73 **refused to be a single parent:** Fingeroth, *A Marvelous Life.*

73 **Stan wrote that Joan took:** Mair, *Excelsior,* 71.

74 **sequels or great acclaim:** Jeet Heer, "There's Money in Comics," Comics Comics blog (August 25, 2010), https://comicscomicsmag.com/?p=5223.

74 **"The funny thing is, I never was a comic-book reader":** Stan Lee, "Events and appearances—Orlando Theme Park opening with Francis Ford Coppola" (November 1999), Box 157, Stan Lee Archives.

74 **"Being the ultimate hack":** Mair, *Excelsior,* 57.

74 **for better or worse:** Vassallo, "Stan Lee (1922–2018)."

74 **The oft-told story:** Sean Howe, *Marvel Comics: The Untold Story* (New York: Harper Perennial, 2013).

75 **There's also speculation:** Vassallo, interview.

75 **April 18, 1950:** Joan and Stan Lee, "Correspondence" (1973–74), Folder 4, Box 12, Stan Lee Archives.

75 **saw the birth by cesarean:** Stan Lee, "Events and appearances (Marvel Mania Grand Opening, New World Office, Stan Lee dinner with Peter Paul)" (1996–1998), Folder 1, Box 84, Stan Lee Archives.

75 **in an interaction with Eric Clapton:** Stan Lee, "a biography of J.C. LEE" (undated), Box 97, Stan Lee Archives.

75 **someone that writer/director Kevin Smith:** Kevin Smith, interview by Abraham Riesman (July 23, 2019).

75 **a person Stan himself would refer to as:** This quotation comes from an unpublished and undated private recording of Stan speaking to JC in his final years, which was recorded by Keya Morgan.

75 **Her life was controversial from the start:** Larry Lieber, interview with Abraham Riesman (December 27, 2018).

76 **Three years later:** Mair, *Excelsior,* 74.

76 **"We called her Jan":** *With Great Power: The Stan Lee Story,* directed by Terry Dougas, Nikki Frakes, and Will Hess, 1821 Pictures (United States: 2010).

76 **"It was the first, and most heartbreaking":** Mair, *Excelsior,* 74.

76 **When he and Joan were filmed:** *With Great Power,* Dougas, Frakes, and Hess.

77 **"And not only did my doctor tie them off":** Ibid.

77 **As Joan put it:** Fingeroth, *A Marvelous Life.*

77 **There's old footage:** The American Heritage Center (AHC) reached out to Stan around the late 1970s and he started donating his effects in the early '80s. The donations continued on a rolling basis all the way through 2011, at which point, for whatever reason, Stan and Joan stopped sending them. Stan used to say he was convinced to go with the University of Wyoming because the AHC also houses the archives of comedian Jack Benny. See Kathryn Mayers, "UW holds tight to Stan Lee collection," The Branding Iron blog (November 28, 2018), https://www.uwbrandingiron.com/2018/11/28/uw-holds-tight-to-stan-lee-collection-2/.

77 **Wintertime shots of Joan:** Stan Lee, "Home movies, 1950s (video recording)," Box 164, Stan Lee Archives.

77 **Perhaps it's all retrospective assessment:** Lee, "Stan Lee autobiography."

78 **" 'Well, what do you do?' " he recalled:** *With Great Power,* Dougas, Frakes, and Hess.

79 **like critic John Mason Brown, who called:** John Mason Brown, "The Press: Code for the Comics," *Time* (July 12, 1948), http://content.time.com/time/magazine/article/0,9171,804769,00.html.

79 **On March 19, 1948:** "The Psychopathology of Comic Books," *Association for the Advancement of Psychotherapy* (symposium), (March 19, 1948).

80 **Just eight days later, *Collier's* magazine:** Judith Crist, "Horror in the Nursery," *Collier's* (March 27, 1948).

80 **Dr. Fredric Wertham. Born in Germany:** David Hajdu, *The Ten-Cent Plague: The Great Comic-Book Scare and How It Changed America* (New York: Farrar, Straus and Giroux, 2009).

80 **The *Collier's* article:** Crist, "Horror in the Nursery."

80 **A May 9, 1948, article:** Fingeroth, *A Marvelous Life.*

81 **crusade in the beginning:** Vassallo, interview.

81 **"To me, Wertham was a fanatic":** Mair, *Excelsior,* 92.

81 **There's just one problem:** Jordan Raphael and Tom Spurgeon, *Stan Lee and the Rise and Fall of the American Comic Book* (Chicago Review Press, 2004).

81 **The closest thing to a contemporary broadside:** Vassallo, "Stan Lee (1922–2018)."

82 **Timely was put in the hot seat:** United States Senate, "Juvenile Delinquency (Comic Books)," *Investigation of Juvenile Delinquency in the United States* (Washington, D.C.: U.S. Government Printing Office, 1954), https://archive.org/stream/juveniledelinque54unit/juveniledelinque54unit_djvu.txt.

83 **"No drawing should show a female indecently":** Ibid.

83 **Stan later recalled that:** Howe, *Marvel Comics.*

83 **"Founded by Irving Forbush":** Mair, *Excelsior,* 106.

84 **After the mass firings of 1949–50:** Raphael and Spurgeon, *Stan Lee.*

84 **"I remember the dark day":** Mair, *Excelsior,* 94.

84 **"It was the toughest thing I ever did in my life," he later said:** Hajdu, *The Ten-Cent Plague.*

84 **"I was like a human pilot light":** Mair, *Excelsior,* 94.

85 **he wrote in his autobiography outline:** Lee, "Stan Lee autobiography."

85 **Joan would later tell an interviewer:** Joan Lee, interview (undated), Box 190, Stan Lee Archives.

85 **He would occasionally mention:** Stan Lee, *Origins of Marvel Comics* (New York: Simon & Schuster, 1974), 10.

85 **Additionally, he had periodically:** Vassallo, "Stan Lee (1922–2018)."

85 **In the middle of the decade:** All the below information about Stan's comic-strip career, unless otherwise noted, comes from Ger Apeldoorn's essential article on the topic: Ger Apeldoorn, " 'Get Me Out of Here!': Stan Lee's Thankfully Fruitless Attempts to Escape Comicsbooks (1956–1962)," *Alter Ego, vol.* 3, no. 150 (January 2018): 21–54.

87 **His name was Joe Maneely:** Vassallo, interview.

87 **So it only made sense:** Apeldoorn, " 'Get Me Out of Here!' "

88 **A publicity push:** Danny Fingeroth and Roy Thomas, "Who Is Stan Lee?" in *The Stan Lee Universe,* Danny Fingeroth and Roy Thomas, eds. (Raleigh, N.C.: TwoMorrows Publishing, 2011), 7–8.

88 **Nevertheless, despite a few major papers:** Apeldoorn, " 'Get Me Out of Here!' "

89 **The death also resonated:** Steve Sherman, interview with Abraham Riesman (January 24, 2019).

89 **Stan got Timely artist Al Hartley:** Apeldoorn, " 'Get Me Out of Here!' "

91 **Little is known about his early life:** All the below information about Steve Ditko's biography, unless otherwise noted, is drawn from Blake Bell's essential *Strange and Stranger: The World of Steve Ditko* (Seattle: Fantagraphics Books, Inc., 2016).

91 **avoided all the trappings of fame:** Ibid.

92 **Since his brief stint:** Lieber, interview.

93 **"Stan said he wanted":** Larry Lieber, "A Conversation with Artist-Writer Larry Lieber," interview by Roy Thomas, *Alter Ego, vol.* 3, no. 2 (Autumn 1999), 20.

93 **"I said, 'Stan, I'm not a writer.' ":** Danny Fingeroth and Larry Lieber, "Gold and Silver Memories," in *The Stan Lee Universe,* Danny Fingeroth and Roy Thomas, eds. (Raleigh, N.C.: TwoMorrows Publishing, 2011), 22.

93 **The years since Kirby's 1941 departure:** All the below information about Jack Kirby's career in the 1940s and '50s, unless otherwise noted, is drawn from Mark Evanier's *Kirby: King of Comics* (New York: Harry N. Abrams, 2017).

95 **Here is how Kirby, in a 1989 interview, recalled:** Jack Kirby, "Jack Kirby Interview," interview with Gary Groth, *The Comics Journal,* no. 134 (February 1990), http://www.tcj.com/jack-kirby-interview/.

95 **In a 1998 interview, his response:** Stan Lee, "Stan the Man & Roy the Boy: A Conversation between Stan Lee and Roy Thomas," interview by Roy Thomas, *Comic Book Artist,* no. 2 (Summer 1998), https://www.twomorrows.com/comicbookartist /articles/02stanroy.html.

97 **"he had no assistants," Larry would recall:** Lieber, "A Conversation with Artist-Writer," 19.

97 **Goodman's magazine arm, recounted:** Drew Friedman, "An Interview with Drew Friedman," interview with Kliph Nesteroff, WFMU's Beware of the Blog (August 8, 2010), https://blog.wfmu.org/freeform/2010/08/an-interview-with-drew-friedman .html.

97 **"Things had started getting really bad":** Dick Ayers, " 'To Keep Busy as a Freelancer, You Should Have Three Accounts!': A Candid 3-Way Conversation with Golden/Silver Age Artist Dick Ayers," interview by Roy Thomas and Jim Amash, *Alter Ego,* vol. 3, no. 31 (December 2003), 18.

97 **In fact, when one does the math:** Vassallo, "Stan Lee (1922–2018)."

97 **"I was given monsters, so I did them":** John Morrow, *Kirby & Lee: Stuf' Said!* (Expanded Second Edition) (Raleigh, N.C.: TwoMorrows Publishing, 2019), 131.

98 **It was only in May 1998:** Lee, "Stan the Man & Roy the Boy."

98 **He mentioned no other scribes:** Lieber, "A Conversation with Artist-Writer," https://www.twomorrows.com/alterego/articles/02lieber.html.

99 **I wrote the complete story:** Jack Kirby, radio interview with J. Michael Strazcynski

and Larry DiTillio, Mike Hodel's *Hour 25* (April 13, 1990), transcript posted on The Kirby Effect: The Journal of the Jack Kirby Museum & Research Center, https:// kirbymuseum.org/blogs/effect/2015/06/16/interviews/#25.

100 **I wrote the stories:** Stan Lee, "interview, radio stations—KTAR" (April 1987), Box 178, Stan Lee Archives.

100 **Some artists, of course:** Ted White, "A Conversation with the Man Behind Marvel Comics: Stan Lee," in *Stan Lee: Conversations,* Jeff McLaughlin, ed. (University Press of Mississippi, 2007), 6.

101 **"In fact, I was probably":** Mair, *Excelsior,* 31.

PART TWO EPIGRAPH

103 **"I knew for a fact":** Stan Lee, *Origins of Marvel Comics* (New York: Simon & Schuster, 1974), p. 17.

CHAPTER 4

105 *Fantastic Four* #1 **crystallized an art form:** Stan Lee, Jack Kirby, Walter Mosley, Mark Evanier, and Paul Sahre, *Maximum Fantastic Four* (United Kingdom: Marvel Enterprises, 2005), p. 233.

106 **It's a summary of that particular:** Roy Thomas, "A Fantastic First," in *The Stan Lee Universe,* ed. Danny Fingeroth and Roy Thomas, eds. (Raleigh, N.C.: TwoMorrows Publishing, 2011), 15.

106 **"After kicking it around with Martin":** Stan Lee, *Origins of Marvel Comics* (New York: Simon & Schuster, 1974), 18.

106 **In 1997, Thomas told:** Roy Thomas, "Roy Thomas Interview," interview with Jim Amash, *The Jack Kirby Collector,* no. 18 (January 1998), 21.

106 **I didn't discuss it with Jack first:** Thomas, "A Fantastic First," 17.

106 **assistant, Steve Sherman, recalled:** Brian Cronin, "Comic Book Legends Revealed #222," CBR blog (August 27, 2009), https://www.cbr.com/comic-book-legends -revealed-222/2/.

106 **"Stan says he conceptualized":** Jack Kirby, "Jack Kirby Interview," interview with Gary Groth, *The Comics Journal* no. 134 (February 1990), http://www.tcj.com/jack -kirby-interview/.

108 **Droom was introduced in spring 1961:** Larry Lieber and Stan Lee, "I Am the Fantastic Dr. Droom!," *Amazing Adventures,* no. 1 (Atlas Magazines, Inc., March 1961).

108 **around 1965, a journalist asked:** Stan Lee and Ted White, "Stan Lee Meets *[Castle of]* Frankenstein,*" Alter Ego,* vol. 3, no. 74 (December 2007), 8.

109 **"For years we had been producing":** Roger Ebert, "A Comeback for Comic Books," in *The Stan Lee Universe,* Danny Fingeroth and Roy Thomas, eds. (Raleigh, N.C.: TwoMorrows Publishing, 2011), 74.

109 **"Finally, about seven years ago":** Stan Lee, "Legend Meets Legend," interview by Jud Hurd, in *The Stan Lee Universe,* Danny Fingeroth and Roy Thomas, eds. (Raleigh, N.C.: TwoMorrows Publishing, 2011), 80.

109 **In 1972, he spoke to a group:** Jim Panyard, "King of the Comic Books," *The News Journal (*November 20, 1972), 23, Newspapers.com.

110 **"She wondered why I didn't":** Lee, *Origins,* 16.

110 **As he put it while recounting:** Tom DeFalco, *Comics Creators on Fantastic Four* (London: Titan Books, 2005), 8.

111 **I had to do something different:** Kirby, "Jack Kirby Interview."

112 **In 1993, he told an interviewer:** *Prisoners of Gravity,* season 3, episode 13, "Jack Kirby," directed by Gregg Thurlbeck (Canada: TVOntario, aired January 7, 1993).

112 **"When people began talking about the bomb":** A comics researcher who pseudonymously writes as "Tuk" has asserted in his ebook *The Case for Kirby* that Kirby was

referring to a bomb explosion that occurs later in the comic, but this argument feels tendentious at best. See Kirby, "Jack Kirby Interview."

112 **the FF was that, as he put it:** Jack Kirby, "An Interview with Artist-Writer-Editor Jack Kirby," interview with Bruce Hamilton, *The Jack Kirby Collector,* no. 18 (January 1998), 60.

113 *The Fantastic Four* #1 begins: Jack Kirby and Stan Lee, "The Fantastic Four!," *Fantastic Four,* no. 1 (Canam Publishers Sales Corp., August 1961).

114 **the issue written on August 29:** Stan Lee and Jerry G. Bails, "Tell It to the Doctor," correspondence, in *The Stan Lee Universe,* Danny Fingeroth and Roy Thomas, eds. (Raleigh, N.C.: TwoMorrows Publishing, 2011), 35.

114 **"This comic was utterly stark-raving":** Jason Shayer, "1983—Alan Moore's 'Blinded by the Hype,'" Marvel Comics of the 1980s blog (October 3, 2012), https://mar . . . 980s.blogspot.com/2012/10/1983-alan-moores-blinded-by-hype.html.

115 **"There I was at my desk":** Lee, *Origins,* 74.

116 **"I created the Hulk, too":** John Morrow, *Kirby & Lee: Stuf' Said!* (Raleigh, N.C.: TwoMorrows Publishing, 2019), 92.

116 **he cited Stevenson: "What comics were doing":** Will Eisner, *Will Eisner's Shop Talk* (Milwaukie, Ore.: Dark Horse Comics, 2001), 218.

116 **The Hulk I created when I saw:** Kirby, "Jack Kirby Interview."

117 **the name was Larry's idea:** Larry Lieber, "A Conversation with Artist-Writer Larry Lieber," interview by Roy Thomas, *TwoMorrows,* Autumn 1999, https://www .twomorrows.com/alterego/articles/02lieber.html.

117 **Stan would later recall, and, sure enough:** William Keck, "Here Come Marvel's 'Avengers,' and Stan Lee, Joe Simon weigh in," *USA Today* (June 22, 2008), https:// usatoday30.usatoday.com/life/movies/news/2008-06-22-marvel-magic_N.htm.

117 **in summer 1962's *Tales to Astonish* #35:** Jack Kirby and Stan Lee, "The Return of the Ant Man!," *Tales to Astonish,* no. 35 (June 1962), Vista Publications, Inc.

118 **or with Joe Simon going back:** Alex Grand, "Jack Kirby, Co-Creator of the Marvel Universe," Comic Book Historians blog (October 21, 2016), https://comicbook historians.com/jack-kirby-co-creator-of-the-marvel-universe/.

118 **"I kept coming back to the same":** Lee, *Origins,* 178.

119 **"put him in a superhero costume," Kirby said:** Jack Kirby, "Jack Kirby in the Golden Age," interview with James Van Hise, *The Jack Kirby Collector,* no. 25 (August 1999), 11.

119 **Larry was recruited to write a script:** Larry Lieber and Stan Lee, "The Stone Men from Saturn!," *Journey into Mystery,* no. 83 (Atlas Magazine, Inc., June 1962).

119 **he put it in a 2008 interview:** Stan Lee, "Creating The Hulk, Spider-Man and Daredevil," filmed interview with Leo Bear, *Web of Stories* (April 2006), https://www .webofstories.com/play/stan.lee/16.

119 **"Why the name?":** Lee, *Origins,* 133.

120 **According to Joe Simon:** Joe Simon, *Joe Simon: My Life in Comics* (London: Titan Books, 2011).

121 **"*The Silver Spider,*" Kirby said:** Eisner, *Shop Talk,* 217.

121 **some sample pages from Kirby and thought:** George Mair, *Excelsior! The Amazing Life of Stan Lee* (London: Boxtree, 2003), 127.

121 **"I created all those books":** Kirby, "Jack Kirby Interview."

121 **Ditko wrote in an essay:** Roy Thomas, *Alter Ego: The Comic Book Artist Collection* (Raleigh, N.C.: TwoMorrows Publishing, 2001), 56.

122 **a webbed costume of blue, red, and black:** There is a curious addendum to the story of Spider-Man's costume. It appears that, in the early 1950s, a Brooklyn costume manufacturer known as Ben Cooper, Inc., produced a mask that looks eerily similar to that of Spider-Man, complete with oversize eye outlines and webbing, and that bore the words "SPIDER MAN" (no hyphen). It is possible that Ditko lifted his design from the mask or semiconsciously remembered seeing it, although there is no way to

prove this. For more on this, see Reed Tucker, "The Billion-Dollar Spider-Man 'Cover Up,'" *New York Post* (July 14, 2015), https://nypost.com/2015/07/14/did-stan -lee-steal-spider-man-from-a-brooklyn-costume-shop/.

122 **Spider-Man's genesis may be in dispute:** Stan Lee, "Spider-Man!," *Amazing Fantasy,* no. 15 (Atlas Magazines, Inc., June 1962).

123 **It's a story with a very strong theme:** Abraham Riesman, "Comics Legend Brian Michael Bendis on *Guardians of the Galaxy,* Sexism, and Making a Nonwhite Spider-Man," *Vulture* (July 31, 2014), https://www.vulture.com/2014/04/comics-brian -michael-bendis-spider-man-guardians-x-men.html.

123 **"They must consider that":** France, "Constitution of the Republic of France, Completed on the 26th June, 1793, and Submitted to the People by the National Convention," *Collection générale des décrets rendus par la Convention Nationale* 35 (May 1793), 72.

123 **"Where there is great power":** "Commons," *The Parliamentary Debates* CLII, series 4 (1906): 1239, https://books.google.com/books?id=PoM6AQAAMAAJ&lpg=PR840& dq=%22where%20there%20is%20less%20power%20there%20is%20less%20responsibili ty%22&pg=PR840#v=onepage&q=%22where%20there%20is%20less%20power%20 there%20is%20less%20responsibility%22&f=false.

123 **"Today we have learned in the agony of war":** Franklin Delano Roosevelt, "Franklin D. Roosevelt's last message to the American people. n. p., (1945)," https://www .loc.gov/item/rbpe.24204300/.

124 **simply referred to the phrase:** Lee, "Creating The Hulk, Spider-Man and Daredevil."

124 **In December 1962: Newcastle** *Evening Chronicle* (December 24, 1962), 1.

124 **In July of 1963, nearly two years:** *South Shore Record* (July 4, 1963).

124 **series entitled** *You Don't Say!:* Stan Lee, *You Don't Say!* (United States: Non-Pareil Publishing Corp, 1963).

125 **He thought well enough:** Stan Lee, "*You Don't Say! #3*" (1963), Folder 8, Box 48, Stan Lee Archives, University of Wyoming, American Heritage Center.

125 **Stan gave an interview:** Scott Rosenberg, "Still a Marvel: Stan Lee," *The Washington Post* (April 21, 2008), https://www.washingtonpost.com/express/wp/2008/04/21/still _a_marvel_stan_lee/.

125 **"I couldn't forget MG telling me":** Stan Lee, "Stan Lee autobiography—Excelsior! (outline)" (1978), Box 127, Stan Lee Archives.

126 **letters-page section of** *Fantastic Four* **#10:** Stan Lee, "Fantastic 4 Fan Page," *Fantastic Four,* no. 10 (Canam Publishers Sales Corp., October 1962).

126 **Later, he would claim:** Stan Lee and Jack Kirby, "Silver Age Stan and Jack—interview with Mike Hodel, WBAI Radio, March 3, 1967," in *The Stan Lee Universe,* Danny Fingeroth and Roy Thomas, eds. (Raleigh, N.C.: TwoMorrows Publishing, 2011), 164.

126 **"I realized we could build":** Lee, "Stan Lee autobiography."

126 **Take, for example,** *The Amazing:* Stan Lee, "Nothing Can Stop . . . The Sandman!," *The Amazing Spider-Man,* no. 4 (Non-Pareil Publishing Corp., June 1963).

128 **Speaking of the X-Men:** Stan Lee, "X-Men," *The X-Men,* no. 1 (Canam Publishers Sales Corp., July 1963).

128 **"I wanted to do a new team":** Tom DeFalco, *Comics Creators on X-Men* (London: Titan Books, 2006), 8.

128 **"The X-Men, I did the natural thing":** Jack Kirby, "1986/7 Jack Kirby Interview," interview with Leonard Pitts, Jr. (1966–67), The Kirby Museum, https://kirby museum.org/blogs/effect/2012/08/06/19867-kirby-interview/.

129 **whom Stan and Kirby both claimed credit for:** Mark Evanier, interview by Abraham Riesman (February 1, 2020).

129 **"He worked so hard, but":** Danny Fingeroth and Jerry Robinson, "Gold and Silver Memories," in *The Stan Lee Universe,* Danny Fingeroth and Roy Thomas, eds. (Raleigh, N.C.: TwoMorrows Publishing, 2011), 34.

130 **spring 1964's *The X-Men* #6:** Jack Kirby and Stan Lee, *X-Men,* no. 6 (Canam Publishers Sales Corp., July 1964).

130 **"Lee started out early with his self-serving":** Steve Ditko, *The Avenging Mind* (United States: Robin Snyder and Steve Ditko, 2007), 16.

131 **Dick told us how Stan called him:** Barry Pearl, "The Yancy Street Gang Visits Dick & Lindy Ayers," *Alter Ego,* vol. 3, no. 90 (December 2009), 11.

131 **In his autobiography outline, Stan wrote, "Credits for everyone":** Lee, "Stan Lee autobiography."

132 **It's no wonder that, allegedly:** Larry Lieber deposition, *Marvel Worldwide, Inc. et al. v. Kirby et al.,* Filing 65, Exhibit 4 (Justia, Dockets & Filings, Second Circuit, New York, New York Southern District Court, January 7, 2011).

132 **"Well, we have a new character in the works":** Daniel Best, "Marvel Worldwide, Inc. et al. v. Kirby et al.—Stan Lee's FF #1 Synopsis & Jerry Bails," 20th Century Danny Boy blog (April 10, 2011), https://ohdannyboy.blogspot.com/2011/04/marvel-worldwide-inc-et-al-v-kirby-et_10.html.

132 **"In July of 1963 I gifted the world":** Mair, *Excelsior,* 163.

132 **"JACK: SGT. FURY? Is that one of OURS?":** Stan Lee, *Sgt. Fury,* no. 1 (Bard Publishing Corp., March 1963).

132 **"Hey, Jack—do we still publish":** Stan Lee, *Fantastic Four,* no. 30 (Canam Publishers Sales Corp., September 1963).

132 **"He proceeded to tell me how hard":** Steve Ditko, *Outer Limits: The Steve Ditko Archives Vol. 6* (Seattle: Fantagraphics Books, Inc., 2016), 8.

133 **a letter from one John Butterworth:** Stan Lee, *The Amazing Spider-Man,* no. 15 (Non-Pareil Publishing Corp., May 1964).

133 **Stan founded a Marvel fan club:** Sean Howe, *Marvel Comics: The Untold Story* (New York: Harper Perennial, 2013).

134 **He and Goodman worked out:** Stan Lee, "Marvel Super-Heroes Promotional Film Starring Stan Lee 1965," videocassette, Box unknown, Stan Lee Archives.

134 **"I realized that most of our readers":** Mair, *Excelsior,* 153.

135 **We rehearsed in the office:** Sergio Aragonés, "Walk a Little Prouder . . ." News from Me blog (October 12, 2005), https://www.newsfromme.com/2005/10/12/walk-a-little-prouder/.

135 **Entitled "The Voices of Marvel":** "Marvel music—Merry Marvel Marching Society—Voices of Marvel," 1965, Box 188, Stan Lee Archives.

136 **"I preferred that we have PP/S-m ideas":** Steve Ditko, "The Amazing Spider-Man #1," *The Comics,* vol. 12, no. 11 (November 2001).

137 **Stan acquiesced, and issue #18:** Howe, *Marvel Comics.*

137 **"Many readers have asked":** Stan Lee, "The Coming of the Scorpion!" *The Amazing Spider-Man,* no. 20 (Non-Pareil Publishing Corp., January 1965).

137 **"Little by little I noticed":** Mair, *Excelsior,* 170.

137 **"At some point before issue #25":** Blake Bell, *Strange and Stranger: The World of Steve Ditko* (Seattle: Fantagraphics Books, Inc., 2016), 89.

138 **"Painstakingly Plotted and Drawn":** Stan Lee, "The Man in the Crime-Master's Mask!", *The Amazing Spider-Man,* no. 26 (Non-Pareil Publishing Corp., July 1965).

138 **I enjoyed working with Stan on *Daredevil*:** Bhob Stewart and Wallace Wood, *The Life and Legend of Wallace Wood: Volume 1* (Seattle: Fantagraphics Books, Inc., 2016), 248.

139 **First, Stan opened the issue:** Wally Wood, "While the City Sleeps! Part One: The Organization!" *Daredevil,* no. 10 (Olympia Publications, Inc., October 1965).

139 **"Stan had changed five words":** Stewart and Wood, *The Life and Legend,* 248.

139 **"Wonderful Wally decided":** Wally Wood, "Let's Level with Daredevil," *Daredevil,* no. 10 (Olympia Publications, Inc., October 1965).

139 **Marvel's big break came on April 1, 1965:** R. C. Baker, "Spiderman [*sic*] in Forest Hills," *The Village Voice* (July 9, 2018), https://www.villagevoice.com/2018/07/09/spiderman-sic-in-forest-hills/.

141 **"I guess because he figured DC Comics"**: Dennis O'Neill, *The DC Comics Guide to Writing Comics* (New York: Watson-Guptill, 2001), 8.

142 **Stan said Fellini had abruptly called him**: Nat Freedland, "Super-Heroes with Super-Problems," in *The Collected Jack Kirby Collector,* John Morrow and Jack Kirby, eds. (Raleigh, N.C.: TwoMorrows Publishing, 2004), 156.

142 **A few years later, he told another journalist**: Robin Green, "Marvel Comics: Face Front," *Rolling Stone* (September 16, 1971), https://www.rollingstone.com/culture /culture-news/marvel-comics-face-front-185546/.

142 **Other times he said the receptionist**: Pat Jankiewicz, "The Marvel Age of Comics: An Interview with Stan Lee," in *Stan Lee: Conversations,* Jeff McLaughlin, ed. (University Press of Mississippi, 2007), 110.

144 **"I don't plot Spider-Man anymore"**: Freedland, "Super-Heroes," 159.

144 **One such story came out**: Stan Lee and Steve Ditko, "The Final Chapter!" *The Amazing Spider-Man,* no. 33 (Non-Pareil Publishing Corp., February 1966).

145 **In 2005, Stan recalled**: Roy Thomas and Stan Lee, "Stan Lee's Amazing Marvel Interview," *Alter Ego,* vol. 3, no. 104 (August 2011), 9.

145 **"One day I got a call from Sol"**: Steve Ditko, "Why I Quit S-M, Marvel," *The Four-Page Series,* no. 9 (September 2015).

145 **It was right around Thanksgiving 1965**: Morrow, *Kirby & Lee: Stuf' Said!,* 60.

146 **"I was angry over the way he quit"**: Tom DeFalco, *Comics Creators on Spider-Man* (London: Titan Books, 2004), 16.

146 **Word of this epochal event**: Morrow, *Kirby & Lee: Stuf' Said!,* 60.

146 **As if that weren't enough**: Freedland, "Super-Heroes," 159.

146 **Jack's wife, Roz, read the article**: Mark Evanier, "Well-Read Fred," News from Me blog (January 29, 2005), https://www.newsfromme.com/2005/01/29/well-read -fred/.

CHAPTER 5

149 **Presented over the course of issues #48 through 50**: Stan Lee, *Fantastic Four Epic Collection: The Coming of Galactus* (United States: Marvel, 2018).

150 **Stan spoke at Princeton University**: John Morrow, *Kirby & Lee: Stuf' Said! (Expanded Second Edition)* (Raleigh, N.C.: TwoMorrows Publishing, 2019), p. 73.

150 **Just a few weeks later, the magazine section**: Ibid.

151 **"he even writes the stories sometimes"**: Sergio Aragonés, "Well-Read Fred," News from Me blog (January 29, 2005), https://www.newsfromme.com/2005/01/29/well -read-fred/.

151 **"Another Spellbinding Spectacular"**: Stan Lee, "Fantastic Four," *Fantastic Four Annual,* no. 5 (Canam Publishers Sales Corp., November 1967), 1.

151 **The Galactus Trilogy was immediately followed**: Lee, "This Man . . . This Monster!" *Fantastic Four,* no. 51 (Canam Publishers Sales Corp., June 1966).

151 **Right after that came a true landmark**: Lee, "The Black Panther!," *Fantastic Four,* no. 52 (Canam Publishers Sales Corp., July 1966).

151 **"I wanted to create"**: To be fair, Stan said in the same interview, "I created the Black Panther with Jack Kirby some years ago," but his description of the event heavily suggests that he regards himself as the sole creator. See Roy Thomas and Stan Lee, "Stan Lee's Amazing Marvel Interview," *Alter Ego,* vol. 3, no. 104 (August 2011), 38.

152 **"I came up with the Black Panther"**: Jack Kirby, "Jack Kirby Interview," interview with Gary Groth, *The Comics Journal* no. 134 (February 1990), http://www.tcj.com /jack-kirby-interview/.

152 **(emerged at almost the exact time)**: Kirby appears to have also come up with the idea for a black character code-named the Coal Tiger, and a presentation board of this character has survived. Popular lore holds that either Kirby or Kirby and Stan conceived of Coal Tiger and then transformed him into Black Panther, but I have never

seen a primary source confirming this, and Kirby's assistant, Mark Evanier, tells me he has no idea what the Coal Tiger's origins are.

152 **his work. Shortly thereafter:** "The Marvel Superheroes," TV.com (accessed February 7, 2020), http://www.tv.com/shows/the-marvel-superheroes/episodes/.

153 **this work-for-hire arrangement:** Roy Thomas, interview with Abraham Riesman (September 18, 2015).

153 **Kirby allegedly made an attempt:** Abraham Riesman, "The King's Gambit," *Vulture* (November 2017), https://www.vulture.com/2017/11/jack-kirby-fourth-world -steppenwolf-justice-league.html.

153 **Stan would later say Kirby never:** Stan Lee, "Stan Lee Interview," interview with Jon B. Cooke, October 11, 2001, in *The Jack Kirby Collector,* no. 33 (November 2001), 61.

154 **Simon, on the warpath:** Tom Brevoort, "Brand Echh—Sick #48," The Tom Brevoort Experience blog (October 20, 2019), https://tombrevoort.com/2019/10/20 /brand-echh-sick-48/.

155 **more than one hundred publications:** Morrow, *Kirby & Lee: Stuf' Said!,* 62.

155 **appearing regularly on broadcast:** Stan Lee, "Series I. Professional files, 1942— 2011," Stan Lee Archives, University of Wyoming, American Heritage Center.

155 **On one show, he boasted:** Stan Lee, "Barry Gray S.L.," circa 1966, Box unknown, Stan Lee Archives.

156 **"Our rollickin' readers":** Lee, "Stan's Soapbox," quoted in Peter Derk, "The Best of Stan Lee's Soapbox," Litreactor.com (January 21, 2019), https://litreactor.com /columns/the-best-of-stan-lees-soapbox.

156 **"I always say that Jack is the greatest":** Morrow, *Kirby & Lee: Stuf' Said!,* 75.

157 **According to Evanier, Kirby had:** Mike Gartland, "A Failure to Communicate: Part Four," *The Jack Kirby Collector,* no. 24 (April 1999), pp. 12–17.

157 **"creator of the Marvel Comics Group":** Morrow, *Kirby & Lee: Stuf' Said!,* 78.

157 **Advance ads for the FF show:** Ibid., 79.

158 **Stan and Kirby were separately:** Rob Steibel, "Excelsior Fanzine (1968) Kirby & Lee Interviews" (April 13, 2012), The Kirby Museum, https://kirbymuseum.org/blogs /dynamics/2012/04/13/from-mike-gartland/.

160 **He was my boss and sometimes I liked him:** Robin Green, "Marvel Comics: Face Front," *Rolling Stone* (September 16, 1971), https://www.rollingstone.com/culture /culture-news/marvel-comics-face-front-185546/.

161 **An unexpected phone call from my brother:** George Mair, *Excelsior! The Amazing Life of Stan Lee* (London: Boxtree, 2003), 175.

163 **"I don't think my daughter has ever read":** Saul Braun, "Shazam! Here Comes Captain Relevant," *The New York Times* (May 2, 1971), https://www.nytimes .com/1971/05/02/archives/shazam-here-comes-captain-relevant-here-comes-captain -relevant.html.

163 **now in her late teenage years:** Stephen Herring, email interview with Abraham Riesman (November 1, 2019).

163 **After a little while, they opted to sell:** Stan Lee, "Stan Lee autobiography— Excelsior! (outline)" (1978), Box 127, Stan Lee Archives.

163 **JC dropped out of the academy:** Herring, interview.

164 **In spring 1968, Marvel started advertising:** Morrow, *Kirby & Lee: Stuf' Said!,* 83.

164 **In a remarkable coup:** Dick Cavett, "*The Dick Cavett Show:* An Interview with Stan Lee," in *Stan Lee: Conversations,* Jeff McLaughlin, ed. (University Press of Mississippi, 2007), 14–19.

165 **Stan even dreamed of starting a talk show:** Stan Lee, "Other—Stan Lee talk show pilot" (1968), Box 166, Stan Lee Archives.

166 **In June of 1968:** Sean Howe, *Marvel Comics: The Untold Story* (New York: Harper Perennial, 2013).

167 **He received criticism:** Ibid.

167 **and was allegedly modeled:** Ibid.

167 **In *The Amazing Spider-Man* #68:** John Romita and Stan Lee, "Crisis on Campus!," *The Amazing Spider-Man,* no. 68 (Perfect Film & Chemical Corp., January 1969).

167 **Captain America was the next:** Stan Lee, "Crack-Up on Campus!" *Captain America,* no. 120 (Magazine Management Co., Inc., December 1969).

168 **Resnais was a rabid Stan fan and claimed:** Phil Patton and Sharon Shurts, "Alain Resnais: From Marienbad to the Bronx," *The Harvard Crimson* (April 14, 1972), https://www.thecrimson.com/article/1972/4/14/alain-resnais-from-marienbad-to -the/.

168 **For one thing, we learn:** "A. Resnais 5-14-69" (1969), Box unknown, Stan Lee Archives.

169 **"You created and drew":** Morrow, *Kirby & Lee: Stuf' Said!,* 92.

170 **But another provocation came:** Ibid., 96.

170 **That publishing house allegedly screwed Kirby:** Ibid., 70.

170 **DC chief editor Carmine Infantino:** Riesman, "The King's Gambit."

171 **Kirby called Stan from California:** Morrow, *Kirby & Lee: Stuf' Said!,* 101.

171 **In 2001, he was asked:** Lee, "Stan Lee Interview," 61.

171 **In 1969, he and DC's Infantino:** Stan Lee, "Stan the Man & Roy the Boy: A Conversation between Stan Lee and Roy Thomas," interview by Roy Thomas, *Comic Book Artist,* no. 2 (Summer 1998), https://www.twomorrows.com/comicbookartist /articles/02stanroy.html.

171 **"Motion Picture Academy of Arts and Sciences":** Ibid.

172 **we had an awards ceremony:** Ibid.

172 **At a meeting of the group:** Ibid.

172 **"I remember saying to him":** Ibid.

172 **On January 20, 1971:** Gary Growth and Gil Kane, *Sparring with Gil Kane: Colloquies on Comic Art and Aesthetics* (Seattle: Fantagraphics Books, 2018), 288.

173 **First came a May 2 article:** Braun, "Shazam!"

174 **Stan's former secretary:** Green, "Marvel Comics: Face Front."

174 **In a "Soapbox" column:** Stan Lee, "Stan's Soapbox," quoted in Tyler Malone, "Stan Lee, the Would-Be Novelist Who Created Worlds," Lithub.com (November 14, 2018), https://lithub.com/stan-lee-the-would-be-novelist-who-created-worlds/.

174 **For instance, in partnership:** Maren Williams, "*Amazing Spider-Man* Anti-Drug Story Hastened Demise of Comics Code," *CBLDF* (October 27, 2017), http://cbldf .org/2017/10/amazing-spider-man-anti-drug-story-hastened-demise-of-comics -code/.

174 **his friend Harry's pill addiction:** Stan Lee, "The Goblin's Last Gasp," *The Amazing Spider-Man,* no. 98 (Magazine Management Co., Inc., July 1971).

175 **Stan finally chose to enshrine:** JC Lee, "letter to the Social Security Administration" (October 2, 1973), Folder 1, Box 12, Stan Lee Archives.

175 **One was called *Mister Miracle:*** Jack Kirby and Mark Evanier, *Mister Miracle,* no. 6 (National Periodical Publications, Inc., January–February 1972).

175 **Roy Thomas later had lunch:** Thomas, interview.

176 **One was *The Inmates:*** "Inmates" (undated), Folder 7, Box 52, Stan Lee Archives.

176 **was Resnais's idea, according:** James Monaco, *Alain Resnais* (Oxford University Press and Secker & Warburg, 1979).

176 **"how you could bring yourself":** "*Monster Maker* (motion picture script)" (1971), Folder 7, Box 53, Stan Lee Archives.

177 **According to Stan, a producer bought:** Pat Jankiewicz, "The Marvel Age of Comics: An Interview with Stan Lee," in McLaughlin, *Conversations,* 112.

177 **There was one other stab at showbiz:** Lloyd Kaufman, interview with Abraham Riesman (February 27, 2019).

178 **had concocted a deal:** Ibid.

179 **from a self-serious poem:** "Events/lectures—Carnegie Hall—JBL and JCL reading 'God Woke' " (1972), Box 191, Stan Lee Archives.

179 **"At one point, at the end of the show":** Raphael and Spurgeon, *Stan Lee*.

179 **"He was sitting on a chair":** Gerry Conway, interview with Abraham Riesman (September 22, 2015).

179 **Stan took a much-needed vacation:** Howe, *Marvel Comics*.

179 **"Martin had his son working there":** Danny Fingeroth, *A Marvelous Life: The Amazing Story of Stan Lee* (New York: St. Martin's Press, 2019).

180 **"That was my one bit of revenge.":** Ibid.

180 **When Stan left the editor's chair:** Howe, *Marvel Comics*.

180 **Thomas was named as the head editor:** Ibid.

180 **"I'll finally have the time":** Fingeroth, *A Marvelous Life*.

CHAPTER 6

183 **He reached out to novelists:** Sean Howe, *Marvel Comics: The Untold Story* (New York: Harper Perennial, 2013).

183 **A few memos between the two of them:** Stan Lee, "Suggested Subjects and Possible Treatment of Potential Articles" (circa 1973), Folder 1, Box 7, Stan Lee Archives, University of Wyoming, American Heritage Center.

184 **The Comics Code Authority had relaxed:** Howe, *Marvel Comics*.

184 **"The present comic book scene":** Mike Baron, "And Now Spider-Man and the Marvel Comics Group," *Creem* (April 1973), p. 39.

184 **"I think you're going to find in the next year":** Baron, "And Now Spider-Man," 78.

185 **THE RENAISSANCE MAN:** "College publicity" (1966–1977), Folder 5–6, Box 2, Stan Lee Archives.

185 **read another. One letter:** The school was the University of Notre Dame. See Frank J. Barrett, "letter to Stan Lee" (October 25, 1972), Folder 5, Box 2, Stan Lee Archives.

185 **appearances could be frenzied:** Author unknown, "Stan Lee itinerary" (January 8, 1975), Folder 1, Box 7, Stan Lee Archives.

185 **a one-sheet text biography recounting:** Author unknown, "Stan Lee biography for American Speakers Bureau" (undated), Folder 11, Box 4, Stan Lee Archives.

185 **and a goofy comic strip:** Danny Fingeroth and Roy Thomas, eds., *The Stan Lee Universe* (Raleigh, N.C.: TwoMorrows Publishing, 2011), 76.

185 **as he would later recall:** Stan Lee, email correspondence with Abraham Riesman (November 4, 2015).

186 **Thomas, though, has claimed:** Stan Lee, "Stan the Man & Roy the Boy: A Conversation Between Stan Lee and Roy Thomas," interview by Roy Thomas, *Comic Book Artist*, no. 2 (Summer 1998), https://www.twomorrows.com/comicbookartist/articles/02stanroy.html.

186 **And so, in early 1973:** Gerry Conway, "The Goblin's Last Stand!," *The Amazing Spider-Man*, no. 122 (Marvel Comics Group, July 1973).

186 **in a 1998 interview, he said:** Lee, "Stan the Man & Roy the Boy."

187 **Right around the same time, Stan informed:** Howe, *Marvel Comics*.

187 **In 1974, Chip Goodman's contract:** Ibid.

187 **"Other, smaller comics publishers":** Jon B. Cooke, "Vengeance, Incorporated," *Comic Book Artist*, no. 16 (December 2001), https://twomorrows.com/comicbookartist/articles/16goodman.html.

187 **In the industry, Atlas/Seaboard:** Howe, *Marvel Comics*.

188 **Unfortunately, the fact that we're big:** Sean Howe, " 'It's like Nazi Germany and the Allies in World War II': Stan Lee Letter to Freelancers Regarding Competing Publishers, 1974," On Comics blog (January 2, 2016), https://oncomics.tumblr.com/post/136453896890/seanhowe-its-like-nazi-germany-and-the-allies/amp.

189 **Near Stan's own death:** A disclaimer: These quotes may be slightly incorrect, as I'm re-creating them from my notes. I saw video of the event where Stan said them when that video was played as part of the preshow tribute to Stan at New York's New Amsterdam Theatre, but Marvel refused to allow me to review the footage for a fact-check and declined to do their own review of it on my behalf. See Stan Lee, video interview with Joe Quesada, Paley Center for Media (Beverly Hills, Calif., April 14, 2017).

189 **Atlas/Seaboard imbroglio, telling:** Howe, *Marvel Comics*.

190 **"By becoming publisher":** Ibid.

190 **"Stan told me, 'Well, Ger'":** Ibid.

191 **He painstakingly crafted:** Ibid.

192 **He helmed a weird *People* knockoff:** Stan Lee, ed., *Celebrity* magazine (Mae West, Mickey Cohen, Ann-Margret, Jimmy Carter), vol. 2, no. 11 (1976).

192 **"beautiful food and gorgeous music":** Lee, *Celebrity* magazine, 3.

192 ***Nostalgia Illustrated,* which would profile:** Stan Lee, ed., *Nostalgia Illustrated* (June 1975), https://www.pulpinternational.com/pulp/entry/Cover-and-scans-from -Nostalgia-Illustrated-from-June-1975.html.

192 ***Star Wars* mania by showing:** Mike Kelly, "'Wow! That Has Real Pizzazz!': A Look at Marvel's Late 1970s Pop Culture and Humor Magazine," *The Real Stan Lee* (February 14, 2019), https://therealstanlee.com/entertainment/wow-that-has-real-pizzazz -a-look-at-marvels-late-1970s-pop-culture-and-humor-magazine/.

192 **for them: A print spread:** "Film International #1 Marvel Magazine 1975," CGC Chat Boards (posted June 1, 2009), https://www.cgccomics.com/boards/topic/157045 -film-international-1-marvel-magazine-1975/.

193 **he scored a minor coup:** Stan Lee, *Origins of Marvel Comics* (New York: Simon & Schuster, 1974).

193 **"Suppose Michelangelo were alive today":** Howard Kissell, "Comic Books: Not a Laughing Matter to Stan Lee," *Women's Wear Daily* (November 15, 1974), 16.

193 **"I have been accused on several occasions":** Ray Bradbury, "'Origins of Marvel Comics': Even Intellectuals May Like It," *Times-Union* (December 15, 1974), reprint.

194 **"Your mag was really funny":** Stan Lee, "Letter to Denis Kitchen, July 11" (1969), Kitchen Sink Press records, Box 4, Columbia University Library, Rare Book and Manuscript Library.

195 **Stan was reluctant on all counts:** Stan Lee and Denis Kitchen, ed., *The Best of Comix Book* (Milwaukie, Ore.: Dark Horse Comics, 2014), https://www.google.com/books /edition/The_Best_of_Comix_Book/pB9lAgAAQBAJ?hl=en&gbpv=0.

197 **On March 22 through 24, 1975:** Howe, *Marvel Comics*.

197 **"Whatever I do at Marvel":** Danny Fingeroth, *A Marvelous Life: The Amazing Story of Stan Lee* (New York: St. Martin's Press, 2019).

197 **At some point after the surprise:** "Conventions—Conference (Stan Lee, Jack Kirby, CC Beck, Neal Adams, Daniel Reed)" (1975), Box 190, Stan Lee Archives.

198 **That questioning happened a lot:** Howe, *Marvel Comics*.

198 **There was a thirty-second TV spot:** Sean Howe, "Stan Lee for the Personna Double II," The Untold Story blog (September 14, 2012), https://seanhowe.tumblr.com /post/31546334492/stan-lee-for-the-personna-double-ii-lee-shot-the.

198 **"When you create superheroes":** Howe, "Stan Lee for Hathaway shirts," The Untold Story blog (September 10, 2014), https://seanhowe.tumblr.com/post/97136380792 /stan-lee-for-hathaway-shirts.

198 **Roughly the same goes:** John Buscema and Stan Lee, *How to Draw Comics the Marvel Way* (New York: Atria Books, 1984).

199 **He signed a contract:** Jordan Raphael and Tom Spurgeon, *Stan Lee and the Rise and Fall of the American Comic Book* (Chicago Review Press, 2004).

199 **January 1977 saw the debut:** Howe, *Marvel Comics*.

199 **In fact, despite his writing credit:** Jim Shooter, interview with Abraham Riesman (April 5, 2019).

199 **Marvel scored its first big win:** *The Incredible Hulk,* season 1, episode 1, "The Incredible Hulk," directed by Kenneth Johnson (aired November 4, 1977, Universal Television).

199 **"Considering the vast influence":** Howe, *Marvel Comics*.

199 **Another newspaper strip of Stan's:** Raphael and Spurgeon, *Stan Lee*.

199 **He sought to sell a pornographic:** Stan Lee, "Thomas Swift and His Electric Sauna (memo)" (circa 1978), Folder 3, Box 53, Stan Lee Archives, University of Wyoming, American Heritage Center.

200 **despite reportedly strong ratings:** Nicholas Hammond, interview with Abraham Riesman (January 9, 2019).

200 **Stan, seeing the criticism:** Fingeroth, *A Marvelous Life*.

200 **On top of all that, he never:** Howe, *Marvel Comics*.

200 **As always, it remains unclear:** "Misc. correspondence between Stan Lee and Jack Kirby" (1977), Box 55 & 56, Stan Lee Archives, University of Wyoming, American Heritage Center.

200 **It was published in 1978:** Stan Lee and Jack Kirby, "The Silver Surfer," *The Silver Surfer,* no. 1 (Simon & Schuster, 1978).

201 **In late 1977, Stan dropped a bomb:** Howe, *Marvel Comics*.

202 **As of January 1, 1978:** United States Code, "Appendix A," *The Copyright Act of 1976,* Pub. L. No. 94-533, 90 Stat. 2541 (October 19, 1976).

202 **In the spring, Shooter distributed:** Gary Groth, "The Comics Guild," *The Comics Journal,* no. 42 (October 1978), pp. 15–28, http://www.tcj.com/the-comics-journal -no-42-oct-1978/.

202 **However, afterward, Shooter and Marvel:** Howe, *Marvel Comics*.

202 **"I wish I had made my move":** Ira Wolfman, "Stan Lee's New Marvels," *Circus Magazine* (July 20, 1978), 42.

202 **In box 53 of the Stan Lee archives:** Stan Lee, "The Great Superhero Turn-On!"— (unpublished article)" (circa 1978), Folder 4, Box 53, Stan Lee Archives.

203 **Even more intriguing:** Stan Lee, miscellaneous notes (circa 1978), Folder 4, Box 53, Stan Lee Archives.

204 **He curated a book of factoids:** Stan Lee, *Stan Lee Presents the Best of the Worst* (New York: Harper & Row, 1979).

204 **and was dabbling in classes:** Maeri Ferguson (School of Visual Arts), email correspondence with Abraham Riesman (November 11, 2019).

204 **In June of 1979, Stan and JC appeared:** "Eleven Year Old Mira Sorvino, Paul Sorvino, Marvel Comic's Stan Lee and Joan Ceila Lee, Don King," YouTube video, posted by BillBoggsTV (December 18, 2017), https://youtu.be/TMkMKiU8-jM.

205 **As a profile in *People* pointed out:** Barbara Rowes, "Stan Lee, Creator of Spider-Man and the Incredible Hulk, Is America's Biggest Mythmaker," *People* magazine (January 29, 1979), https://people.com/archive/stan-lee-creator-of-spider-man-and -the-incredible-hulk-is-americas-biggest-mythmaker-vol-11-no-4/.

205 **(as she noted on the talk show):** "Eleven Year Old Mira Sorvino," YouTube video.

205 **The Stan Lee archives contain long audiotapes:** "R. Bernstein, December audio recording" (1976), Box 178, Stan Lee Archives.

205 **one tape is just forty-seven-odd minutes:** "December 23 (audio recording)" (1976), Box 178, Stan Lee Archives.

205 **Russians in Marvel, Stan responded:** Eric Leguebe, "Stan Lee Replies to Eric Leguebe," in *Stan Lee: Conversations,* Jeff McLaughlin, ed. (University Press of Mississippi, 2007), 82.

205 **There were rumors that:** Howe, *Marvel Comics*.

206 **licensing fees on such an idea:** "Hello, Culture Lovers: Stan the Map Raps with

Marvel Maniacs at James Madison University," *The Comics Journal,* no. 42 (October 1978), 55.

206 **Cockrum, fed up, wrote a resignation:** Howe, *Marvel Comics.*

206 **"I have the sense that he wants":** N. R. Kleinfield, "Superheroes' Creators Wrangle," *The New York Times* (October 13, 1979), https://www.nytimes.com/1979/10/13/archives/superheroes-creators-wrangle-creators-of-superheroes-wrangle-within.html.

207 **In a letter to Resnais:** Stan Lee, "letter to Alain Resnais, May 23" (1979), Folder 1, Box 14, Stan Lee Archives.

CHAPTER 7

209 **On June 19, 1980:** Sean Howe, *Marvel Comics: The Untold Story* (New York: Harper Perennial, 2013).

210 **the titular David DePatie:** Sam Ewing, interview with Abraham Riesman (August 15, 2019).

211 **"Those of you who were careless enough":** "Stan Lee Speech 7/1/84 Charlotte, N.C. Heroes Con—(video recording)," Box 157, Stan Lee Archives, University of Wyoming, American Heritage Center.

214 **"responsible for a massive infusion":** Steve Gerber, "Letter," *The Comics Journal,* no. 57 (Summer 1980).

214 **In a 1982 interview:** John Morrow, *Kirby & Lee: Stuf' Said! (Expanded Second Edition)* (Raleigh, N.C.: TwoMorrows Publishing, 2019), pp. 126–127.

215 **"I had to regenerate the entire line":** Ibid., 132–133.

216 **In 1984, he was reportedly presented:** Howe, *Marvel Comics.*

216 **"I wouldn't cooperate with the Nazis":** Ibid.

216 **"I always wrote my own story":** Morrow, *Kirby & Lee: Stuf' Said!,* p. 133.

216 **That same year, an ad in *Variety:*** Tom Heintjes, "The Negotiations: Jack and Roz Kirby Interviewed," *The Comics Journal,* no. 105 (February 1986), 53–60.

216 **"Well, I think that Jack has taken leave":** Morrow, *Kirby & Lee: Stuf' Said!,* 146.

217 **"No, I really don't know":** Leonard Pitts, Jr., "An Interview with Stan Lee," in *Stan Lee: Conversations,* Jeff McLaughlin, ed, (University Press of Mississippi, 2007), 92.

217 **"No. No. It'll never happen.":** Jack Kirby, "1986/7 Jack Kirby Interview," interview with Leonard Pitts, Jr. (1966–67), The Kirby Museum, https://kirbymuseum.org/blogs/effect/2012/08/06/19867-kirby-interview/.

217 **He projected a triumphant image:** Howe, *Marvel Comics.*

217 **For example, he wrote an outline:** Stan Lee, "Decathlon" (2000), Folder 10, Box 50, Stan Lee Archives.

218 **On the opposite end:** Stan Lee, "pitch manuscripts" (1984), Folder 10, Box 51, Stan Lee Archives.

219 **Stan likely either ghostwrote:** Anonymous sources, interview with Abraham Riesman.

219 **She had her own social life:** Harry Langdon, interview with Abraham Riesman (November 5, 2019).

220 **There's one that Stan filmed:** "JC Home Movies (video recording)" (undated), Box 164, Stan Lee Archives.

220 **A tape labeled "Xmas '86":** "Xmas '86 (video recording)" (1986), Box 164, Stan Lee Archives.

220 **Joan tells the camera, "Today, on my sixty-fifth birthday":** "JBL 65th BD (video recording)" (1987), Box 164, Stan Lee Archives.

221 **In one video, JC declares:** "JC + Dog" (undated), Box 164, Stan Lee Archives.

221 **As she cryptically puts it:** Ibid.

221 **At one point in another video, we see JC lying:** "JCL, JBL, Don P. 10/27/86 / Party 12/86 (video recording)" (1986), Box 164, Stan Lee Archives.

222 **May 7, 1989, brought a quiet milestone:** *The Trial of the Incredible Hulk,* directed by Bill Bixby (United States: 1989, Bixby-Brandon Productions), TV movie.

222 **While the Hulk rampaged:** Ibid.

222 **(For what it's worth, Kirby):** "Jack Kirby," IMDb (February 7, 2020), https://www.imdb.com/name/nm0456158/.

222 **The film follows a comic-book artist:** *The Ambulance,* directed by Larry Cohen (United States: 1990, Epic Productions, Esparza/Katz Productions).

224 **At one point in a video:** "Comic Book Greats Jack Davis Harvey Kurtzman Stan Lee," YouTube video, posted by CrashLanden (May 15, 2011), https://www.youtube.com/watch?v=rsQa_IHChJY.

224 **Finally, a breakthrough came:** Margaret Loesch, interview with Abraham Riesman (April 2, 2019).

225 **we realized that *he didn't know the characters:*** Eric Lewald, *Previously on X-Men: The Making of an Animated Series* (United States: Jacobs Brown Media Group, LLC), 306.

225 **"Luckily, it didn't work out":** Ibid.

226 **Marvel's corporate higher-ups still:** "Marvel Comics Gives Stan Lee Lifetime Deal," *Los Angeles Times* (April 26, 1994), https://www.latimes.com/archives/la-xpm-1994-04-26-fi-50448-story.html.

226 **"It was like Laurel and Hardy":** Jordan Raphael and Tom Spurgeon, *Stan Lee and the Rise and Fall of the American Comic Book* (Chicago Review Press, 2004).

227 **On February 6, 1994:** Associated Press, "Jack Kirby, 76; Created Comic-Book Superheroes," *The New York Times* (February 8, 1994), https://www.nytimes.com/1994/02/08/obituaries/jack-kirby-76-created-comic-book-superheroes.html.

227 **A comics journalist caught up with Kirby:** Morrow, *Kirby & Lee: Stuf' Said!,* 152.

227 **On the other hand, the two men:** Heidi MacDonald, "A Long Lost Photo of Jack Kirby and Stan Lee Has Surfaced," The Beat blog (November 16, 2018), https://www.comicsbeat.com/a-long-lost-photo-of-jack-kirby-and-stan-lee-has-surfaced/.

227 **"Bite your tongue." Stan used to say:** Howe, *Marvel Comics.*

228 **Jimmy Stewart. Their inchoate goal:** "Home Page," The American Spirit Foundation (January 16, 2013), https://web.archive.org/web/20130116194754/http://www.theamericanspiritfoundation.com/Home_Page.html.

229 **there are tapes shot by:** Paul claims he got an addiction to camcorder documentation thanks to a friendship with TV host Robin Leach, who allegedly turned him on to the hobby.

230 **In one tape from 1996:** "Events and appearances (Marvel Mania Grand Opening, New World Office, Stan Lee dinner with Peter Paul) (video recording)" (1996–1998), Folder 1, Box 84, Stan Lee Archives.

231 **In the spring of 1995, Paul brought Stan:** "Whoopi's Party/Stan's Pitch to Whoopi (video recording)" (1995), Box 164, Stan Lee Archives.

232 **He did a two-part Silver Surfer story:** Stan Lee, Moebius, and Keith Pollard, *Silver Surfer: Parable* (Marvel, 2012).

233 **He thought it might be fun:** Jackie Tavarez, interview with Abraham Riesman (August 14, 2019).

233 **Somewhere around the turn of the nineties:** Jim Salicrup, interview with Abraham Riesman (February 5, 2019).

234 **"I'm launching a new comic book line":** Stan Lee, "interview with various chatroom users" (August 11, 1995), Folder 11, Box 3, Stan Lee Archives.

235 **Given Stan's declining reputation:** *The Comics Journal,* no. 181 (October 1995).

235 **The U.S. copyright office:** "Copyright Catalog (1978 to present)," United States Copyright Office (February 7, 2020), https://cocatalog.loc.gov/cgi-bin/Pwebrecon.cgi?SAB1=Stan+Lee&BOOL1=as+a+phrase&FLD1=Name%3A+All+%28KNAM%29+%28KNAM%29&GRP1=AND+with+next+set&SAB2=Larry+Shultz&BOOL2=as+a+phrase&FLD2=Name%3A+All+%28KNAM%29+%28KNAM%29&GRP2=AND

+with+next+set&PID=AxrG04lTTnu_vG8gAKVtNShkauT4A&SEQ=2013120923113
0&CNT=100&HIST=1.

235 **One pitch survives:** Stan Lee and Larry Shultz, "Decoy" (undated), Box 97, Stan Lee Archives.

236 **In the summer of 1998:** Howe, *Marvel Comics.*

239 **"He asked to cross the Jordan":** *Daat Zekenim,* trans. Eliyahu Munk (Sefaria) (accessed February 7, 2020), https://www.sefaria.org/Daat_Zkenim_on_Deuteronomy .32.52?lang=bi.

CHAPTER 8

242 **Paul was born Peter Eisner:** Peter Paul, email interview with Abraham Riesman (May 20, 2019).

243 **Paul had three of them:** April Witt, "House of Cards," *The Washington Post* (October 9, 2005), https://www.washingtonpost.com/archive/lifestyle/magazine/2005/10 /09/house-of-cards/5aebcde6-a0cb-4e1e-947c-e5facdb54a1a/.

244 **Instead, he pleaded guilty:** Ibid.

245 **"Hey, Stan, now you're free!":** Abraham Riesman, "It's Stan Lee's Universe," *Vulture* (February 2016), https://www.vulture.com/2016/02/stan-lees-universe-c-v-r .html.

246 **Paul legally registered a company:** Peter Paul, "Employment Agreement/Rights Assignment," Stan Lee Entertainment, Inc., signed by Stan Lee (October 15, 1998).

246 **Simultaneously, Stan was in negotiations:** "Employment Agreement," Marvel Enterprises, Inc., signed by Stan Lee, Joan Lee, and JC Lee.

247 **"It's all in the formulative stage":** Stan Lee, "Letters to 'morty'," Folder 13, Box 106, Stan Lee Archives, University of Wyoming, American Heritage Center.

247 **by other Paul-controlled companies:** Jordan Raphael and Tom Spurgeon, *Stan Lee and the Rise and Fall of the American Comic Book* (Chicago Review Press, 2004).

247 **"Nothing short of an H-bomb":** Sean Howe, *Marvel Comics: The Untold Story* (New York: Harper Perennial, 2013).

248 **On the first day of trading:** Raphael and Spurgeon, *Stan Lee.*

248 **"I've been in comics, radio, television":** Reed Abelson, "Outlook 2000: An Epitaph for the 20th Century; A Time of Energy and Enterprise and E-Everything," *The New York Times* (December 20, 1999), https://www.nytimes.com/1999/12/20/business /outlook-2000-epitaph-for-20th-century-time-energy-enterprise-e-everything.html.

248 **"When I got into comics, it was the early days":** James Poniewozik, with Jeffrey Ressner, "Look Up on the Net! It's . . . Cyber Comics," *Time* (February 06, 2000), http://content.time.com/time/magazine/article/0,9171,38788,00.html.

248 **If the characters and stories:** Adweek Staff, "IQ Interactive Special Report: Interview—Marvel Comics' Stan Lee," *Adweek* (May 1, 2000), https://www.adweek .com/brand-marketing/iq-interactive-special-report-interview-marvel-comics-stan -lee-25457/.

248 **"We're an umbrella to harness":** Ibid.

248 **"I think this will be the successor":** Ibid.

248 **He'd done an interview with the magazine:** John Morrow, *Kirby & Lee: Stuf' Said! (Expanded Second Edition)* (Raleigh, N.C.: TwoMorrows Publishing, 2019), p. 164.

249 **"I saw it meant a lot to him":** Howe, *Marvel Comics.*

249 **So Stan and Paul issued an open letter:** Morrow, *Kirby & Lee: Stuf' Said!,* 164.

249 **"Check Marvel's stationery":** Steve Ditko, *Steve Ditko's 32-Page Package* (Bellingham, Wash.: Robin Snyder and Steve Ditko, 1999), 29.

249 **"I really think I'm being very generous":** George Mair, *Excelsior! The Amazing Life of Stan Lee* (London: Boxtree, 2003), 172.

249 **Even after the open-letter incident:** Stan Lee, "Mission Statement" (date unknown), Box 97, Stan Lee Archives.

250 **The centerpiece property:** "7th Portal episode 1 Let the game begin!," YouTube video, posted by Stan Lee Media Studios (April 25, 2016), https://www.youtube.com /watch?v=fcHKwWOHYy0.

250 **That one starred a disabled lawyer:** "Accuser #1 The Accused," YouTube video, posted by Stan Lee Media Studios (April 25, 2016), https://www.youtube.com /watch?v=Dedt6Rath5s.

251 **Another property was** *The Drifter:* "Stan Lee's The Drifter Episode 1," YouTube video, posted by Stan Lee Media Studios (April 25, 2016), https://youtu.be /2sVOUTaOwAo.

251 **There were cartoons about a mischievous copy:** "STAN 2 0 Evil Clone Episode 1," YouTube video, posted by Stan Lee Media Studios (April 25, 2016), https://www .youtube.com/watch?v=XUOuEUV4Qo8.

251 **A Merry Marvel Marching Society-esque fan club:** United States Patent and Trademark Office, "SCUZZLE SEARCHING CYBERSPACE FOR UNKNOWN ZOO-LOGICAL ZYGOMORPIC LIVING ENTITIES KEEPING CYBERSPACE SAFE," Arthur M. Lieberman, 2—Sec. 8, serial no.: 75938712, registration no.: 2446223 (April 24, 2004).

251 **SLM signed a deal:** "The Backstreet Project—Webisode 1 Larger Than Life (Part 1)," YouTube video, posted by The Dark Side Of Backstreet (August 11, 2015), https:// youtu.be/OcHSzdbuuTo.

251 **The staff expanded:** Variety Staff, "Obituary: Stan Lee Media," *Variety* (January 15, 2001), https://variety.com/2001/digital/news/obituary-stan-lee-media-1117792008/.

252 **They discuss Coppola working:** "Events and appearances—Orlando Theme Park opening with Francis Ford Coppola, November (video recording)" (1999), Box 157, Stan Lee Archives.

252 **Stan was hardly worried about any of that:** "Stan Lee Media Hollywood Gala (Betacam SP), February (video recording)" (2000), Box 175, Stan Lee Archives.

253 **writers Steven Salim and Jesse Stagg:** *Steven SALIM, et al. v. Stan LEE, et al.,* no. 01CV3485,202 F.Supp.2d 1122 (United States District Court, Central District, California, April 2, 2002).

253 **They would go on to sue years later:** Civil minutes, *Steven SALIM, et al. v. Stan LEE, et al.,* no. 01CV3485-LGB(Ex.) (United States District Court, Central District, California, March 12, 2003).

253 **one estimate said the company:** Michael Dean, "If This Be My Destiny: The Stan Lee Story Reaches Chapter 11," *The Comics Journal,* no. 232 (April 2001), 10.

254 **"I thought we had some money in the company":** Stan Lee deposition, *Paul v. Tonken,* no. LA 04-12883-EC (United States Bankruptcy Court, Central District, California, February 23, 2005).

254 **"He is the psyche of our youth":** "Spiderman's Stan Lee Meets Michael Jackson— Part 1," YouTube video, posted by GooSEegg (July 20, 2009), https://youtu.be /_fCaBkHk-58.

254 **"If I buy Marvel," Jackson asked:** Michael Dean, "How Michael Jackson Almost Bought Marvel and Other Strange Tales from the Stan Lee/Peter Paul Partnership," *The Comics Journal,* no. 270 (August 2005), 21.

254 **"If they're popular with young people":** Raphael and Spurgeon, *Stan Lee.*

256 **One highly placed employee I spoke with:** This is the same employee as the one who mentioned the drunkard executive.

257 **In the first quarter of 2000:** Securities and Exchange Commission, "Quarterly Report: Stan Lee Media, Inc.," commission file no.: 0-28530, form: 10-QSB (Washington, D.C., March 31, 2000).

257 **The first is eyebrow-raising:** Stan Lee, "memo to undisclosed recipients" (date unknown), Box 97, Stan Lee Archives.

258 **I just had an epiphany—Our website stinks!:** Stan Lee, "memo to undisclosed recipients" (date unknown), Box 97, Stan Lee Archives.

258 **"If you think of it in levels":** Dean, "If This Be My Destiny," 9.

258 **Paul longed to bring greater prestige:** Witt, "House of Cards."

259 **"In a land of moral imbeciles":** Aaron Tonken, *King of Cons: Exposing the Dirty, Rotten Secrets of the Washington Elite and Hollywood Celebrities* (Nashville: Thomas Nelson, 2004).

259 **eventually ingratiated himself:** Witt, "House of Cards."

259 **two hundred Hollywood donors:** *Hillary Uncensored! An American Above the Law,* directed by Neil Cope (United States: Paraversal Studios, 2010), DVD.

259 **"I shall rule everything":** "Hillary Clinton Welcome to Stan Lee Media 6/9/00 (video recording)" (2000), Box 165, Stan Lee Archives.

259 **the Pauls. At these events:** *Hillary Uncensored!,* Cope.

260 **as a Clinton lawyer would later claim:** Witt, "House of Cards."

260 **on August 12, 2000, the 1,300-person:** *Hillary Uncensored!,* Cope.

260 **"It was the apogee of my career":** Witt, "House of Cards."

260 **The feeling was fleeting. Three days later:** Ibid.

261 **Bill's to Stan was handwritten:** Bill Clinton, "correspondence to Stan Lee, Aug. 18" (2000), Folder 12, Box 107, Stan Lee Archives.

261 **Paul and his team secured a deal:** Raphael and Spurgeon, *Stan Lee.*

261 **SLM staffer Scott Koblish would later speak:** Dean, "If This Be My Destiny," 12.

262 **"The computer guys burned copies":** Ibid., 13.

262 **As Stan started individually calling:** *With Great Power: The Stan Lee Story,* directed by Terry Dougas, Nikki Frakes, and Will Hess, 1821 Pictures (United States: 2010).

262 **On January 2, 2001:** Raphael and Spurgeon, *Stan Lee.*

263 **the assets. The details would require:** Ibid.

264 **"I have absolutely no idea":** Lee deposition, *Paul v. Tonken.*

264 **Years later, when he commissioned:** Peter David, interview with Abraham Riesman (November 19, 2019).

264 **All that was left and approved:** Stan Lee, Peter David, and Colleen Doran, *Amazing Fantastic Incredible: A Marvelous Memoir* (United Kingdom: Gallery Books, 2015), 23.

CHAPTER 9

266 **It's serious stuff, with lines like:** When I asked Champion about the alleged bookkeeping and documentation fraud, he simply replied, "I'm not sure what you're implying here"; when I asked him about the claim that he and Lieberman pressured Kobayashi into false testimony, he said, "Wow! That is absurd." See Becky Altringer, unpublished client report, private investigation (April 24, 2021).

268 **Champion produced two soft-core pornographic:** Becky Altringer, unpublished client report, fraud investigation (2011).

269 **There was Arthur Lieberman:** Alan Neigher, interview with Abraham Riesman (July 26, 2019).

269 **For a few months after SLM ceased:** Michael Dean, "If This Be My Destiny: The Stan Lee Story Reaches Chapter 11," *The Comics Journal,* no. 232 (April 2001): p. 13.

269 **On January 30, 2001:** Becky Altringer, research notes, private investigation (2011).

270 **That same month, Paul:** Reuters, "Stan Lee Media Founder Indicted," *Wired* (June 12, 2001), https://www.wired.com/2001/06/stan-lee-media-founder-indicted/.

270 **hardly ever used. The company was launched:** Securities and Exchange Commission, "Annual Report: POW! Entertainment, Inc.," commission file no.: 000-52414, form: 10-K (March 23, 2012).

271 **That same month, Stan and his cohort:** Order Denying Plaintiffs' Motion for Partial Summary Judgment as to Standing [95, 108, 121], *QED Productions, LLC, et al. v. James Nesfield et al.,* CV 07-0225 SVW(SSx) (United States District Court, Central District, California, January 20, 2009). POW denies that the sale was fraudulent: "False Allegations and Unfounded Statements Have Been Made Regarding Stan Lee and POW! Entertainment," *Business Wire* (January 28, 2009), https://www.business wire.com/news/home/20090128006303/en/False-Allegations-Unfounded-Statements -Stan-Lee-POW%21.

271 **They announced a first-look deal:** Rick DeMott, "POW! Stan Lee Reloaded," *Animation World Network* (July 18, 2003), https://www.awn.com/animationworld /pow-stan-lee-reloaded.

271 **In the SLM days, Paul had set Stan up:** Peter Paul, interview with Abraham Riesman (April 16, 2019).

272 **Roughly six pages were dedicated:** George Mair, *Excelsior! The Amazing Life of Stan Lee* (London: Boxtree, 2003), pp. 227–233.

272 **"if any form of today's entertainment":** Ibid., 244–246.

272 **his contract stipulated:** "Employment Agreement," Marvel Enterprises, Inc., signed by Stan Lee, Joan Lee, and JC Lee (November 1, 1998).

272 **And yet, on June 17:** Andrew Billen, "Spidey, Can You Spare a Dime?," *The Ottawa Citizen,* originally printed in the *Times of London* (June 22, 2002).

272 **he appeared in a profile on CBS:** David Kohn, "Superhero Creator Fights Back," *CBS News* (October 30, 2002), https://www.cbsnews.com/news/superhero-creator -fights-back/.

272 **Stan filed a $10 million lawsuit:** Gary Susman, "Stan Lee Sues Marvel over 'Spider-Man' profits," *Entertainment Weekly* (November 13, 2002), https://ew.com/article /2002/11/13/stan-lee-sues-marvel-over-spider-man-profits/.

272 **It was, as one news commentator:** Jordan Raphael and Tom Spurgeon, *Stan Lee and the Rise and Fall of the American Comic Book* (Chicago Review Press, 2004).

273 **At a party, Stan encountered the brother:** Pamela Anderson, interview with Abraham Riesman (October 15, 2015), and Heath Seifert and Kevin Kopelow, interview with Abraham Riesman (August 13, 2019).

274 **The pilot introduced Erotica Jones:** *Stripperella,* season 1, episode 1, "Beauty and the Obese," directed by Kevin Altieri (Network Enterprises—MTV Networks, The Firm, aired June 26, 2003).

274 **The first season premiered:** *Stripperella,* "Beauty and the Obese."

274 **However, it got a scathing review:** Phil Mushnick, "Spike TV—An Exercise in Fertility," *New York Post* (July 6, 2003), https://nypost.com/2003/07/06/spike-tv-an -exercise-in-fertility/.

274 **A Florida-based dancer:** John Wolfson, "Take It Off, Stripper Tells Adult Cartoon's Creators," *Orlando Sentinel* (July 11, 2003), https://www.orlandosentinel.com/news /os-xpm-2003-07-11-0307110390-story.html.

275 **There was *The Forever Man*:** "Stan Lee To Take On 'Forever Man' Next," Killer Movies blog (February 20, 2003), http://www.killermovies.com/f/foreverman /articles/2807.html.

275 **At San Diego Comic-Con, he announced *Hef's Superbunnies*:** Josh Grossberg, "Hef, Lee 'Toon Up 'Superbunnies'," *E! News* (September 8, 2004), https://www .eonline.com/news/48200/hef-lee-toon-up-superbunnies.

275 **There was to be a TV show:** Steve Brennan, "Lee's 'Universe' Expanding with DIC," *Backstage* (July 10, 2003), https://www.backstage.com/magazine/article/lees -universe-expanding-dic-32919/.

275 **There was even discussion:** Associated Press, "Ringo to Become a Comic Superhero," *Today* (January 27, 2005), https://www.today.com/popculture/ringo-become -comic-superhero-wbna6876727.

275 **POW, unable to come up with a hit:** "Declaration of Ron Sandmann," POW! *Entertainment v. Media Dynamics et al.,* no. CVUJ 11-1163, January 3, 2012 (County of Del Norte, Superior Court of the State of California). Posted by Becky Altringer, "Ron Sandmann Declaration," Scribd, June 5, 2017. https://www.scribd.com/document /350433621/Ron-Sandmann-Declaration.

276 **"The concept of having the company":** Ibid.

276 **According to the statement, POW:** Amended Cross-Complaint, *POW! Entertainment v. Media Dynamics et al.,* no. CVUJ 11-1163 (County of Del Norte, Superior Court of the State of California, March 13, 2012).

277 **When the merger occurred:** "Declaration of Ron Sandmann."

277 **If Sandmann is to be believed:** POW denies all of the accusations of crimes and malfeasance.

277 **"I didn't have any big compulsion":** Raphael and Spurgeon, *Stan Lee.*

278 **There had been discussion:** Stephen Norrington, interview with Abraham Riesman (August 5, 2019).

278 **DeSanto contacted Stan:** Joshua M. Patton, "How We Almost Didn't Have the 'Stan Lee Cameo' in Modern Marvel Films," *Medium* (November 15, 2018), https:// medium.com/@JoshuaMPatton/how-we-almost-didnt-have-the-stan-lee-cameo-in -modern-marvel-films-3b4b47e7b953.

278 **With Stan convinced:** *X-Men,* directed by Bryan Singer (United States: Twentieth Century Fox, Marvel Enterprises, 2000).

278 **When the cameras rolled:** "Tom DeSanto Talks about Stan Lee at San Diego Comic-Con 2019," YouTube video, posted by therealstanlee (July 25, 2019), https://www .youtube.com/watch?v=Cwf4tSl5TSc.

278 **"Next movie, how about you give me":** Patton, "How We Almost."

279 **When director Sam Raimi:** Sam Raimi, "Sam Raimi on Pitching a 'Thor' Movie with Stan Lee—and Getting Rejected," *The Hollywood Reporter* (November 14, 2018), https://www.hollywoodreporter.com/heat-vision/stan-lee-wasnt-going-get-spider -man-cameo-director-reveals-1161054.

279 *Daredevil* **in 2003 brought:** *Daredevil,* directed by Mark Steven Johnson (United States: Twentieth Century Fox, Marvel Enterprises, 2003).

279 **release of the Ang Lee–directed** *Hulk:* *Hulk,* directed by Ang Lee (United States: Universal Pictures, Marvel Enterprises, 2003).

279 **Marvel television shows. You could find him:** "List of cameo appearances by Stan Lee," Wikipedia (last modified February 1, 2020), https://en.wikipedia.org/wiki /List_of_cameo_appearances_by_Stan_Lee.

280 **As Anthony Russo, co-director:** Abraham Riesman, "How the Russo Brothers Wrote Stan Lee's Cameo into *Avengers: Endgame,*" *Vulture* (May 2, 2019), https://www .vulture.com/2019/05/russo-brothers-endgame-interview-stan-lee-time-travel.html.

281 **You could see him as a cop:** "List of cameo appearances," Wikipedia.

281 **He appeared in at least five movies:** Lloyd Kaufman, interview with Abraham Riesman (February 27, 2019).

281 **Stan was paid peanuts:** JD Cargill, "Stan Lee Revels in Success of 'Avengers'," *CNN* (May 14, 2012), https://www.cnn.com/2012/05/14/showbiz/movies/stan-lee-avengers /index.html.

281 **But that all changed in the aughts:** Filed complaint, *Joan Celia Lee v. Max Anderson* (County of Los Angeles, Superior Court of the State of California, May 31, 2019).

282 **but there are also allegations:** Ibid.

282 **What's more, Anderson had a dark:** Ryan Parry, "Exclusive: Marvel Creator Stan Lee, 95, Is Accused of Groping Nurses and Demanding Oral Sex in the Shower at His $20m Los Angeles Home—but Says He Is Victim of a 'Shake Down'," *Daily Mail* (January 9, 2018), https://www.dailymail.co.uk/news/article-5250513/Marvel -creator-Stan-Lee-95-accused-groping-nurses.html.

282 **A children's book called:** Stan Lee and Tim Jessell, *Stan Lee's Superhero Christmas* (New York: Milk & Cookies, 2016).

282 **a direct-to-video movie:** *Stan Lee's Lightspeed,* directed by Don E. FauntLeRoy (United States: POW! Entertainment, FWE Picture Company, 2006), TV movie.

282 **a series of animations:** "Vidiator Launches Stan Lee's POW! Mobile on Sprint," *Business Wire* (October 4, 2006), https://www.businesswire.com/news/home /20061004005294/en/Vidiator-Launches-Stan-Lees-POW%21-Mobile-Sprint.

282 **For example, in the mid-aughts:** Declan O'Brien, interview with Abraham Riesman (February 22, 2019).

283 **then came an announcement:** "Ringo Starr, Superhero," *CNN* (January 25, 2005), https://web.archive.org/web/20050126044020/http://www.cnn.com/2005/SHOW BIZ/01/25/showbuzz/index.html.

283 **At one point, comics writer Scott Lobdell:** Scott Lobdell, interview with Abraham Riesman (March 5, 2019).

284 **Lester was a low-level Hollywood agent:** Gar Lester, interview with Abraham Riesman (April 4, 2019).

285 **A production company named Valcom:** Adversary proceeding, *Valcom, Inc. v. POW! Entertainment, LLC, and Stan Lee,* Case 2:07-bk-15984-E (United States Bankruptcy Court, Central District, California, August 23, 2007).

285 **POW countersued and the case was settled:** Stipulation dismissing adversary complaint and counter-complaint, *Valcom, Inc. v. POW! Entertainment, LLC, and Stan Lee,* Case 2:07-ap-01638-E (United States Bankruptcy Court, Central District, California, June 17, 2008).

285 **It seemed that Stan had scored:** Nat Ives, "Marvel Settles with a Spider-Man Creator," *The New York Times* (April 29, 2005), https://www.nytimes.com/2005/04/29 /business/media/marvel-settles-with-a-spiderman-creator.html.

286 **Soon afterward, Marvel quietly settled:** CBR Staff, "Marvel Settles with Stan Lee for $10 Million," *CBR* (April 28, 2005), https://www.cbr.com/marvel-settles-with -stan-lee-for-10-million/.

286 **In the meantime, POW scored a minor success:** *Who Wants to Be a Superhero?,* created by Stan Lee and Scott Satin (POW! Entertainment, Nash Entertainment, 2006).

286 **three-season reality show:** *Stan Lee's Superhumans: Stan Lee's Superhumans,* created by Stan Lee (Off the Fence, History Channel, 2010).

286 *The Atlantic* **magazine named him:** "POW! Entertainment's Founder 'Stan Lee' Voted 26th Most Influential Living American; Breaking News Alert by Stock Information Systems," *Business Wire* (January 10, 2007), https://www.businesswire.com /news/home/20070110005158/en/POW%21-Entertainments-Founder-Stan-Lee -Voted-26th.

286 **POW was kept afloat:** "Annual Report: POW! Entertainment, Inc."

286 **there was an announcement:** Carolyn Giardina, "Stan Lee to Launch Superhero Franchise," *Reuters* (April 16, 2008), https://www.reuters.com/article/film-stanlee-dc /stan-lee-to-launch-superhero-franchise-idUSN1628575220080416.

287 **POW was, of course, interested:** Borys Kit, "Disney Acquires Stake in Stan Lee's POW!," *The Hollywood Reporter* (January 1, 2010), https://www.hollywoodreporter .com/news/disney-acquires-stake-stan-lees-19050.

287 **"rather than use these proceeds":** Verified class action complaint for breach of fiduciary duty, *Richard Norwood v. Stan Lee, Gill Champion, Bick Le,* case no.: 2018-0056 (Court of Chancery, State of Delaware, January 24, 2018).

287 **"Lee, Champion . . . and others":** POW denies these allegations.

287 **Just a few months prior to the announcement:** David Goldman, "Disney to Buy Marvel for $4 Billion," *CNN Money* (August 31, 2009), https://money.cnn.com/2009 /08/31/news/companies/disney_marvel/.

287 **Jack Kirby's family issued:** Sean Howe, *Marvel Comics: The Untold Story* (New York: Harper Perennial, 2013).

288 **one on May 13, 2010:** Stan Lee deposition, *Marvel Characters, Inc. et al. v. Lisa R. Kirby et al.,* case no.: 11-333 (United States Court of Appeals, The United States District Court for the Southern District of New York, May 13, 2010).

288 **and another on December 8:** Stan Lee deposition (December 8, 2010).

288 **For one thing, although Stan firmly:** Stan Lee deposition (May 13, 2010).

288 **Second, he hewed to the company line:** Ibid.

288 **Kirby's son, Neal, was asked:** Neal Kirby deposition, *Marvel Characters, Inc. et al. v. Lisa R. Kirby et al.,* case no.: 11-333 (United States Court of Appeals, The United States District Court for the Southern District of New York, June 30, 2010).

288 **Larry had had a rough go of it:** Larry Lieber, interview with Abraham Riesman (December 27, 2019).

289 **in 1986, Larry had taken over:** "Larry Lieber," Lambiek Comiclopedia (last modified February 11, 2017), https://www.lambiek.net/artists/l/lieber_larry.htm.

289 **Although Roy Thomas had, uncredited:** Roy Thomas, interview with Abraham Riesman (September 18, 2015).

290 **In November of 2010, Stan could be seen:** "Hollywood Treasure—'Comic Conquest,'" YouTube video, posted by multipleverses (November 5, 2010), https://www.youtube.com/watch?v=bgdkpQsSwAc&t=8s.

290 **Lieberman and Champion had decided:** Junko Kobayashi, interview with Abraham Riesman (April 11, 2019).

291 **a nonprofit charity dedicated to:** "Home page," Stan Lee Foundation (February 7, 2020), https://stanleefoundation.org/.

291 **According to court filings:** *Norwood v. Lee, Champion, Le.*

291 **Far more lucrative:** Ibid.

291 **outside investment—revenue in 2009:** "Annual Report: POW! Entertainment, Inc."

291 **POW's compensation was allegedly:** *Norwood v. Lee, Champion, Le.*

291 **without any independent oversight:** POW denies these allegations but does not offer a counter-narrative explaining what happened.

291 **In their first SEC filing:** "Annual Report: POW! Entertainment, Inc."

292 **One such effort was a partnership:** Lewis Wallace, "Stan Lee Unveils 3 New Superheroes at Comic-Con," *Wired* (July 22, 2010), https://www.wired.com/2010/07/stan-lee-boom-studios/.

292 **A plan for a multi-medium superhero epic:** *Stan Lee's Mighty 7,* directed by Ningning Lee (United States: Stan Lee Comics, 2014), TV movie.

292 **A partnership with actor and former:** Andy Khouri, "Stan Lee and Arnold Schwarzenegger Create 'The Governator' [Why]," *Comics Alliance* (March 31, 2011), https://comicsalliance.com/stan-lee-arnold-schwarzenegger-the-governator/.

292 **then quietly put on the shelf:** Andy Heyward, interview with Abraham Riesman (July 23, 2019).

292 **create a line of superhero mascots:** Anthony Winn, interview with Abraham Riesman (February 22, 2019).

292 **but the low-rent characters:** Lia Grainger, "NHL and Stan Lee Give Each Pro Hockey Team Its Own Superhero. We Rate All 30, Including the Lousy 'Maple Leaf.'" *Toronto Life* (February 1, 2011), https://torontolife.com/city/toronto-sports/nhl-and-stan-lee-give-each-pro-hockey-team-its-own-superhero-we-rate-all-30-including-the-lousy-maple-leaf/.

293 **"What is it with these bottles of water?":** "Stan Lee Hates Water—Stan's Rants," YouTube video, posted by MarvelousTV (August 21, 2012), https://www.youtube.com/watch?v=6f5h82f9k8Y.

293 **A project that would produce concerts:** Nicole Gonzales and Monica Garske, "Comic Book Legend Stan Lee Kicks Off Military Concert Series in San Diego," *NBC San Diego* (April 6, 2013), https://www.nbcsandiego.com/news/local/stan-lees-power-concert-series-military-camp-pendleton-gloriana/2101957/.

293 **There was even a Stan Lee Signature Cologne:** Brooke Jaffe, "You, Too, Can Smell Like Stan Lee, Just Like You Always Wanted!," *The Mary Sue* (June 11, 2013), https://www.themarysue.com/stan-lee-cologne/.

293 **To make matters even more dire:** "Arthur M. Lieberman," *The New York Times* (May 4, 2012), https://www.legacy.com/obituaries/nytimes/obituary.aspx?n=arthur-m-lieberman&pid=157454426.

293 **They had an additional grievance:** Confidential source, interview with Abraham Riesman.

293 **The documentary opened with:** *With Great Power: The Stan Lee Story,* directed by Terry Dougas, Nikki Frakes, and Will Hess, 1821 Pictures (United States: 2010).

293 **Stan even briefly returned:** *Marvel Digital Holiday Special,* Joe Quesada, ed., no. 2 (2008).

295 **Duke and JC drove to Las Vegas:** Alan Duke, "Episode 1: Scandal: Stan Lee's World: His Real Life Battle with Heroes & Villains," podcast audio (November 15, 2018), http://stanleesworlds.com/index.php/episode/episode-1-scandal-stan-lees-world-his-real-life-battle-with-heroes-villains/.

295 **According to Herman and Duke:** Alan Duke, "Stan Lee's World: Shocking Evidence of an Unappreciated Birthday," *Stan Lee's World* (November 29, 2018), http://stanleesworlds.com/index.php/2018/11/29/stan-lees-world-shocking-evidence-of-an-unappreciated-birthday-gift/.

295 **JC physically attacked her parents:** Gary Baum, "Stan Lee Needs a Hero: Elder Abuse Claims and a Battle Over the Aging Marvel Creator," *The Hollywood Reporter* (April 10, 2018), https://www.hollywoodreporter.com/features/stan-lee-needs-a-hero-elder-abuse-claims-a-battle-aging-marvel-creator-1101229.

295 **There are harrowing photos:** Duke, *Stan Lee's World.*

295 **Duke, upon seeing the photos years later:** Alan Duke, *Stan Lee's World,* podcast audio (November 29, 2018), https://art19.com/shows/scandal/episodes/17b978be-688d-4452-8ddb-f9a21be6a05a.

296 **supporting JC. She was, eventually:** Joan Celia Lee public records, LexisNexis records search.

296 **He convinced Stan to help him:** Home page, Hands of Respect (2017), https://handsofrespect.com/.

296 **it was a for-profit company:** Jonathan Bourne, "RESPECT," Jonathan Bourne blog (December 11, 2016), http://www.jonathanbourne.com/2016/12/respect-our-intelligence.html.

297 **different stepfathers. Court filings:** Complaint for damages and injunctive relief, *Pete Livingston v. Keya Morgan,* case no.: 1:07-cv-07835-RMB-KN (United States District Court, The United States District Court for the Southern District of New York, September 5, 2007).

297 **and police reports:** Ryan Parker, "Stan Lee's Former Business Manager Arrested on Suspicion of Elder Abuse," *The Hollywood Reporter* (May 25, 2019), https://www.hollywoodreporter.com/news/stan-lees-business-manager-arrested-suspicion-elder-abuse-1213740.

297 **enthusiastically retweeted Morgan on Twitter:** Rich Johnston, "The Bromance Between Keya Morgan and Donald Trump Jr. May Be Over," Bleeding Cool blog (June 12, 2018), https://www.bleedingcool.com/2018/06/12/keya-morgan-stan-lee-donald-trump-jr/.

297 **after writing a profile of Morgan for CNN:** Alan Duke, "Collector Keya Morgan has an Unusual Path to the Stars," *CNN* (November 22, 2011), https://www.cnn.com/2011/11/22/showbiz/celebrity-news-gossip/keya-morgan-fame-series/index.html.

298 **After being shipped from Brazil:** Memo and order, *Paul v. Bragg,* F.Supp.2d (United States District Court, West District of Texas, El Paso Division, August 1, 2011).

298 **he pleaded guilty in the SLM case in 2005:** Judgment of permanent injunction and

other relief against defendant, *Securities and Exchange Commission v. Peter Paul, Stephen Gordon, and Jeffrey Pittsburg,* case no.: 2:04-cv-06613-SVW(SSx) (United States District Court, Central District of California, Wester Division, July 20, 2005).

298 **He sued them for welching:** *Peter Paul v. William Jefferson Clinton,* case no.: BC252654 (United States District Court, County of Los Angeles, June 19, 2001).

298 **Judicial Watch, whom he also later sued:** *Peter Paul v. Federal Election Commission,* case no.: 1:01-cv-02527-RJL (U.S. District Court, District of Columbia, Washington, D.C., December 7, 2001).

298 **He was sentenced to ten years in prison:** Criminal cause for sentencing, *USA v. Peter Paul,* case no.: 2:01-cr-00636-LDW (U.S. District Court, Eastern District of New York, New York, N.Y., June 25, 2009).

298 **One federal judge, finding himself:** Daniel Best, "At Last...The End Of Stan Lee Media Inc vs Stan Lee," 20th Century Danny Boy blog (August 23, 2012), https://ohdannyboy.blogspot.com/2012/08/at-lastthe-end-of-stan-lee-media-inc-vs.html.

299 **By 2014, the Kirbys' legal battle:** Brooks Barnes, "Marvel Settles with Family of Comics Artist Jack Kirby," *The New York Times* (September 26, 2014), https://www.nytimes.com/2014/09/27/business/media/marvel-settles-with-family-of-comic-book-artist-jack-kirby.html.

300 **A few things went wrong:** The information about Stan Lee's Comikaze in 2015 is drawn from my own reporting while attending the event.

301 **Called *Amazing Fantastic Incredible*:** Stan Lee, Peter David, and Colleen Doran, *Amazing Fantastic Incredible: A Marvelous Memoir* (United Kingdom: Gallery Books, 2015).

302 **When Stan and Morgan met Benaroya:** Michael Benaroya, interview with Abraham Riesman (January 25, 2019).

302 **in Hollywood trade publications:** Dave McNary, "Stan Lee Unveils Comic-Book Franchise 'Nitron,'" *Variety* (July 19, 2016), https://variety.com/2016/film/news/stan-lee-comic-book-franchise-nitron-1201817889/.

302 **I wrote a profile of him:** Abraham Riesman, "It's Stan Lee's Universe," *Vulture* (February 2016), https://www.vulture.com/2016/02/stan-lees-universe-c-v-r.html.

303 **POW was admitting to the SEC:** Securities and Exchange Commission, "Quarterly Report: POW! Entertainment, Inc.," commission file no.: 000-52414, form: 10-Q (May 14, 2015).

303 **shop the company around:** *Norwood v. Lee, Champion, Le.*

304 **A new Spider-Man movie:** *Spider-Man: Homecoming,* directed by Jon Watts (United States: Marvel Studios, Columbia Pictures, 2017).

304 **The MCU was a construct that had:** "Box Office History for Marvel Cinematic Universe Movies," The Numbers (February 7, 2020). https://www.the-numbers.com/movies/franchise/Marvel-Cinematic-Universe.

304 **Joan had been in poor health for months:** Keya Morgan, interview with Abraham Riesman (October 12, 2019).

304 **she perished a few days later, on July 6:** Legacy Staff, "Joan Lee," *Legacy* (July 6, 2017), http://www.legacy.com/news/celebrity-deaths/notable-deaths/article/joan-lee.

CHAPTER 10

307 **His accountant was fired at Morgan's behest:** Gary Baum, "Stan Lee Needs a Hero: Elder Abuse Claims and a Battle Over the Aging Marvel Creator," *The Hollywood Reporter* (April 10, 2018), https://www.hollywoodreporter.com/features/stan-lee-needs-a-hero-elder-abuse-claims-a-battle-aging-marvel-creator-1101229.

308 **Schenck was the son of:** "Weddings; Allison Stark, Kirk Schenck," *The New York Times* (January 21, 2001), https://www.nytimes.com/2001/01/21/style/weddings-allison-stark-kirk-schenck.html.

308 **background in personal injury:** Kirk E. Schenck biography, counsel, office of Kulik

Gottesman Siegel & Ware LLP, http://kgswlaw.com/wp-content/uploads/2016/06/Schenck-Bio.pdf.

308 **There he was, just eight days later:** Heidi MacDonald, "Jack Kirby and Stan Lee become Disney Legends at D23," *The Beat* (July 14, 2017), https://www.comicsbeat.com/jack-kirby-and-stan-lee-become-disney-legends-at-d23/.

308 **A Stan-involved anime series:** *The Reflection,* Anime News Network (February 8, 2020), https://www.animenewsnetwork.com/encyclopedia/anime.php?id=19388.

308 **and a group of Chinese firms:** Vivienne Chow, "China's Linking Star Picture to Develop Superhero Projects from Stan Lee's POW! Entertainment," *Variety* (July 26, 2017), https://variety.com/2017/film/news/linking-star-picture-stan-lee-pow-1202506801/.

309 **Stan reportedly signed a declaration:** Baum, "Stan Lee Needs a Hero."

309 **October 4, a $300,000 check:** Mark Ebner, "'Picked Apart by Vultures': The Last Days of Stan Lee," *Daily Beast* (November 12, 2018), https://www.thedailybeast.com/picked-apart-by-vultures-the-last-days-of-stan-lee.

309 **but in December, Stan and Morgan:** Baum, "Stan Lee Needs a Hero."

310 **On December 28, Anderson threw Stan:** Drew Mollo, "Kevin Smith Shares a Video of His Last Time with Stan Lee," *CBR* (December 20, 2018), https://www.cbr.com/kevin-smith-last-video-with-stan-lee/.

312 **A bombshell dropped:** Ryan Parry, "Exclusive: Marvel Creator Stan Lee, 95, Is Accused of Groping Nurses and Demanding Oral Sex in the Shower at His $20m Los Angeles Home—but Says He Is Victim of a 'Shake Down,'" *Daily Mail* (January 9, 2018), https://www.dailymail.co.uk/news/article-5250513/Marvel-creator-Stan-Lee-95-accused-groping-nurses.html.

312 **Just two days later:** Ryan Parry, "Exclusive: Marvel Creator Stan Lee, 95, Faces MORE Abuse Allegations as Hotel Masseuse Says He Demanded Sex and Masturbated in Front of Her but His Lawyer Says It's Another Shake-Down," *Daily Mail* (January 11, 2018), https://www.dailymail.co.uk/news/article-5259559/Stan-Lee-accused-masturbating-masseuse.html.

312 **later identified as a woman:** Hannah Leone and Gregory Pratt, "Massage Therapist Accuses Stan Lee of Marvel Comics of Inappropriate Sexual Behavior in Chicago Hotel," *Chicago Tribune* (April 24, 2018), https://www.chicagotribune.com/news/breaking/ct-met-stan-lee-lawsuit-20180423-story.html.

312 **For another, Carballo went through:** I contacted both firms and both declined to elaborate on what had happened.

312 **The road manager was accused:** Parry, "Stan Lee, 95, Faces MORE Abuse Allegations."

312 **the first article also revealed:** Parry, "Stan Lee, 95, Is Accused of Groping Nurses."

312 **Morgan seems to have a history:** William Gatevackes, "Is the Sad Saga of Stan Lee Entering Its Engame?," Film Buff Online blog (June 15, 2018), http://www.filmbuffonline.com/FBOLNewsreel/wordpress/2018/06/15/is-the-sad-saga-of-stan-lee-entering-its-engame/.

313 **It appears that Anderson made:** Supplemental Memorandum, "Declaration of Stan Lee," *Stan Lee v. Keya Morgan,* no. 18STR004115, July 6, 2018 (County of Los Angeles, Superior Court of the State of California): 30–37.

313 **On February 15, the LAPD:** Ryan Parry, "Exclusive: Cops Are Called to the L.A. Home of Comic Book Legend Stan Lee, 95, to Probe 'Battery' Allegation and Are Seen Quizzing His Bodyguard on the Doorstep," *Daily Mail* (February 15, 2018), https://www.dailymail.co.uk/news/article-5397737/Cops-probe-battery-allegation-Stan-Lee-home.html.

313 **of Anderson. Morgan later said:** Ebner, "'Picked Apart by Vultures.'"

317 **in the early 1950s, in which Massey claims:** "You Have to Earn Your Talent through Discipline," *Alter Ego,* vol. 3, no. 105 (September 2011).

318 **The aforementioned former nurse of Stan's:** Supplemental memorandum of points and authorities in support of request for: (1) permanent elder abuse restraining order against Keya Morgan; and (2) appointment of Tom Lallas as guardian ad litem for Stan Lee in support of EARO, *Stan Lee v. Keya Morgan,* case no.: 18STR004115 (Superior Court of the State of California, County of Los Angeles, Central District, July 3, 2018).

320 **It is worth quoting one video in full:** "Stan Lee Denies Reports of Elder Abuse, Threatens Legal Action," *TMZ* (April 12, 2018), https://www.tmz.com/2018/04/12/stan-lee-denies-elder-abuse-claims-threatens-legal-action/.

321 **Hiya, heroes. This is Stan Lee:** "2018 06 10 IMG_9960," video recording (June 10, 2018).

321 **Take, for example, a video:** "2018 05 28 20.10.59," video recording (May 28, 2018).

322 **he was starting to cancel:** Jon Arvedon, "Stan Lee Canceling Con Appearances Due to Pneumonia," *CBR* (February 28, 2018), https://www.cbr.com/stan-lee-canceling-appearances-pneumonia/.

322 **the *Daily Mail* reported that Stan:** Ryan Parry, "Exclusive: Stan Lee Fires Manager and His Nurse Who Gave Him Naked Showers over 'Plot to Estrange Him from His Daughter and Sole Heir' as Cops Probe Missing Millions and He Battles Pneumonia," *Daily Mail* (February 28, 2018), https://www.dailymail.co.uk/news/article-5428459/Stan-Lees-longtime-manager-fired-honeytrap-claims.html.

322 **freelance journalist Mark Ebner:** Ebner, " 'Picked Apart by Vultures.' "

323 **Another public shock arrived:** Rich Johnston, "Fans Express Concern about Stan Lee at Silicon Valley Comic Con," Bleeding Cool blog (April 8, 2018), https://www.bleedingcool.com/2018/04/08/concern-stan-lee-silicon-valley-comic-con/.

323 **an April 10 investigative article:** Baum, "Stan Lee Needs a Hero."

323 **On that same day:** Rich Johnston, "Stan Lee's Super Subs—JC Lee's Plans for Her Father's Legacy," Bleeding Cool blog (April 10, 2018), https://www.bleedingcool.com/2018/04/10/stan-lee-super-subs-jc-lee-legacy/.

323 **Stan appeared to beat back:** "Stan Lee Denies Reports," *TMZ.*

323 **sued Olivarez for theft and fraud:** Rich Johnston, "Stan Lee Sues Hands of Respect's Jerry Olivarez, Claiming Elder Abuse," Bleeding Cool blog (April 14, 2018), https://www.bleedingcool.com/2018/04/14/stan-lee-jerry-olivarez-elder-abuse/.

323 **The "diabolical and ghoulish scheme,":** First Amended Complaint, *Stan Lee v. Jerardo Olivarez et al.,* no. SC-129127, April 13, 2018 (County of Los Angeles, Superior Court of the State of California): 30–37.

324 **Hands of Respect's own website:** Gene Maddaus, "Stan Lee's Ex-Publicist Drained Accounts and Sold His Blood, Suit Claims," *Variety,* April 13, 2018, https://variety.com/2018/biz/news/stan-lee-elder-abuse-sold-blood-1202753267/.

324 **Just a few days later:** Abigail Gillibrand, "Stan Lee's Final Public Appearance at Infinity War Premiere Saw Him Thank Fans for Years of Support," *Metro* (November 12, 2018), https://metro.co.uk/2018/11/12/stan-lees-final-public-appearance-at-infinity-war-premiere-saw-him-thank-fans-for-years-of-support-8132819/.

324 **"As some other pros have already said":** Peter David, "Max Anderson and Stan Lee," PeterDavid.net blog (March 15, 2018), https://www.peterdavid.net/2018/03/05/max-anderson-and-stan-lee/.

324 **Superstar comics artist and toy entrepreneur:** Todd McFarlane, "My Recent Visit . . . 'Stan Lee. I Wonder How He's Doing?' " Facebook photo (April 5, 2018), https://www.facebook.com/liketoddmcfarlane/photos/my-recent-visitstan-lee-i-wonder-how-hes-doingits-a-question-i-think-many-of-us-/1871196022924471/.

324 **That said, McFarlane reported:** *Celebrating Marvel's Stan Lee* (Marvel Entertainment, December 20, 2019), unaired portion.

325 **Larry feared for his brother:** Larry Lieber, interview with Abraham Riesman (December 27, 2018).

325 **Its name is POW Entertainment:** The company's representatives refused to grant me

information or interviews, and someone with reason to know informed me that it's because they're still smarting from what I wrote in my 2016 Stan Lee profile for *Vulture*.

325 **The company released a statement:** Gary Baum, "Stan Lee's Company Worried over 'Upheaval' in His 'Personal Management and Life,'" *The Hollywood Reporter* (April 12, 2018), https://www.hollywoodreporter.com/heat-vision/stan-lees-company -worried-upheaval-his-personal-management-life-1102222.

325 **Instead, POW plowed ahead:** Gary Collinson, "Stan Lee's The Virtue of Vera Valiant Heading to the Big Screen," Flickering Myth blog (May 14, 2018), https://www .flickeringmyth.com/2018/05/stan-lees-the-virtue-of-vera-valiant-heading-to-the -big-screen/.

325 **Two days later, it became clear:** Yohana Desta, "Stan Lee Files $1 Billion Lawsuit Against the Company He Co-Founded," *Vanity Fair* (May 16, 2018), https://www .vanityfair.com/hollywood/2018/05/stan-lee-billion-dollar-lawsuit.

325 **Morgan sent me candid:** "2018 05 14 New Recording 153," audio recording (May 14, 2018).

325 **POW was certainly suspicious:** David Reid, "Marvel Comics Legend Stan Lee's $1 Billion Lawsuit Is 'Preposterous,' Chinese Firm Says," *CNBC* (May 18, 2018), https://www.cnbc.com/2018/05/18/marvel-comics-stan-lee-1-billion-lawsuit -preposterous-says-chinese-firm.html.

326 **his Facebook and Instagram:** Stan Lee (@TheRealStanLee), "Help! Someone has hijacked my Facebook and Instagram. I want everyone to know whoever is writing them is a fraud and is impersonating me. How do I get them back? Can you guys help?" (May 15, 2018), https://twitter.com/TheRealStanLee/status /996429458197307392.

326 **that praised industrialist Elon Musk:** Stan Lee (@TheRealStanLee), "I agree with @ elonmusk that the media should be held accountable to tell the truth. Many reporters are honost but Fake news outlets like Hollywood Reporter should not be spreading lies. Go Elon!" (May 26, 2018), https://twitter.com/therealstanlee/status/10005525893 0847744l?lang=en.

326 **circumstances that remain murky:** Rich Johnston, "Stan Lee's Restraining Orders Allege Keya Morgan Swatted the Police, Committed Elder Abuse," Bleeding Cool blog (June 14, 2018), https://www.bleedingcool.com/2018/06/14/stan-lee-restraining -orders-keya-morgan-swatted-police-elder-abuse/.

327 **Morgan was arrested and charged:** Rich Johnston, "Stan Lee Associate Keya Morgan Arrested Today in Hollywood," Bleeding Cool blog (June 11, 2018), https:// www.bleedingcool.com/2018/06/11/keya-morgan-arrested/.

327 **A temporary restraining order:** Steve Gorman, "Stan Lee's Caregiver Keya Morgan Hit with Temporary Restraining Order," *Huffington Post* (June 14, 2018), https:// www.huffpost.com/entry/stan-lee-caregiver-restrainingorder_n_5b2209fce4 bobbb7a0e4a280.

328 **JC released a video:** Rich Johnston, "Video Message from Stan Lee at Home with His Daughter JC for Father's Day," Bleeding Cool blog (June 18, 2018), https://www .bleedingcool.com/2018/06/18/stan-lee-fathers-day/.

328 **A further image of peace was projected:** *Guardian* staff, "Stan Lee Drops 'Confusing' $1bn Lawsuit Against His Former Company," *The Guardian* (July 9, 2018), https://www.theguardian.com/books/2018/jul/09/stan-lee-lawsuit-dropped-pow -entertainment-marvel.

328 **Stan dropped the lawsuit:** Keya Morgan claims that act was done after Stan was pressured by an LAPD officer, who he thinks was being paid by POW, but he wouldn't allow me to talk about the only evidence he offered me—which was already dubious—until after his criminal trial for elder abuse was over.

328 **continued to announce Stan-related projects:** Rich Johnston, "Stan Lee's New

Webcomic Backchannel Publishes in a Month's Time," Bleeding Cool blog (August 31, 2018), https://www.bleedingcool.com/2018/08/31/stan-lee-webcomic-back channel/.

328 **Stan Lee Shanghai Comic Universe:** Samantha Kennedy, "Stan Lee-Themed Comic Convention Set to Premiere in Shanghai this Fall," *That's* magazine (July 18, 2018), https://www.thatsmags.com/shanghai/post/24233/pow-entertainment-announces -a-shanghai-comic-con.

328 **Bolerjack told Bleeding Cool:** Rich Johnston, "Stan Lee Will No Longer Do Public Signings," Bleeding Cool blog (August 5, 2018), https://www.bleedingcool.com /2018/08/05/stan-lee-no-longer-public-signings/.

328 **Stan and POW released a statement:** POW, "Stan Lee and POW! Entertainment Pledge," The Real Stan Lee blog (July 11, 2018), https://web.archive.org/web /20180711233049/http://therealstanlee.com/stan-lee-pow-entertainment-pledge/.

328 **A statement was released to Bleeding Cool:** Rich Johnston, "Stan Lee Issues Statement about Keya Morgan's 'Hostage Videos' to Bleeding Cool," Bleeding Cool blog (October 7, 2018), https://www.bleedingcool.com/2018/10/07/stan-lee-statement -hostage-videos-keya-morgan/.

329 **Morgan had been attempting:** I spoke with the reporter who was trying to do the story, and he confirmed that this was occurring.

329 **Ebner arrived at Stan's home:** Mark Ebner, "Stan Lee Breaks His Silence: Those I Trusted Betrayed Me," *Daily Beast* (October 8, 2018), https://www.thedailybeast .com/stan-lee-would-like-to-set-the-record-straight-will-anyone-let-him.

330 **Stan had one more visitor:** Roy Thomas and Aaron Couch, "Marvel Veteran Recalls His Final Saturday with Stan Lee," *The Hollywood Reporter* (November 13, 2018), https://www.hollywoodreporter.com/heat-vision/stan-lee-my-final-final-saturday -comic-book-icon-1160986.

330 **taken to Cedars-Sinai Medical Center:** Karen Mizoguchi, "Stan Lee's Cause of Death Revealed: Cardiac Arrest, Respiratory and Congestive Heart Failure," *People* (November 27, 2018), https://people.com/movies/stan-lee-cause-of-death-revealed/.

330 **Less than a day after news of his death:** "Stan Lee's Daughter J.C. Lee Reveals They Created a New Superhero," *TMZ* (November 13, 2018), https://www.tmz.com /2018/11/13/stan-lee-daughter-jc-lee-new-dirt-man-superhero-father-death/.

330 **brought an announcement from Camsing:** Andreas Wiseman, "Chinese Firm Camsing Vows to Push On With POW! Entertainment Projects Following Stan Lee's Death," *Deadline* (November 13, 2018), https://deadline.com/2018/11/stan-lee-china -camsing-pow-entertainment-death-1202500899/.

331 **In addition, in the immediate wake:** Alan Duke, "Episode 2: Stan Lee's World: Murder? Nancy Grace Analyzes Mysterious Clues Concerning Stan's Death," podcast audio (November 21, 2018), http://stanleesworlds.com/index.php/episode/episode-2 -stan-lees-world-murder-nancy-grace-analyzes-mysterious-clues-concerning-stans -death/.

331 **Though POW released a statement:** @TheRealStanLee, "A Statement from Stan Lee's POW! Entertainment" (November 16, 2018), https://twitter.com/TheRealStan-Lee/status/1063568652820111360.

332 **the mouth of his business partner:** Zhang Ruinan, "Legacy of Comics Giant Stan Lee Heads to China," *China Daily* (November 29, 2018), https://web.archive.org /web/20181202040215/chinadaily.com.cn/a/201811/29/WS5bfecaf4a310eff30328ba38 .html.

332 **helped JC craft a lawsuit:** Though Peter Paul is not mentioned in the suit, I can confirm that he showed me an early draft of a press release about it and seemed to be orchestrating it. See *Joan Lee v POW! Entertainment,* case no.: 2:19-cv-0835 (United States District Court, Central District of California, September 26, 2019).

332 **The Chinese government seems to have a vendetta:** Evelyn Cheng, "Major Chinese

Wealth Manager Tied Up in Criminal Detention Case," *CNBC* (July 9, 2019), https://www.cnbc.com/2019/07/09/major-chinese-wealth-manager-tied-up-in-criminal-detention-case.html.

334 **He had finished his decades-long run:** D. D. Degg, "Larry Lieber Retires from the Amazing Spider-Man," *The Daily Cartoonist* (September 9, 2018), http://www.dailycartoonist.com/index.php/2018/09/09/larry-lieber-retires-from-the-amazing-spider-man/.

335 **"What's the famous line from":** *The Man Who Shot Liberty Valance,* directed by John Ford (United States: Paramount Pictures, 1962).

INDEX

TRUE
BELIEVER

–

ABRAHAM
RIESMAN

Random
House
Book Club

Because
Stories Are TM
Better Shared

RANDOM HOUSE BOOK CLUB

BIOGRAPHY IN THE AGE OF FANDOM:
A Q&A WITH TEGAN O'NEIL

———

Comics criticism is, as of now, a wounded art form. Too few media outlets even bother to cover comic books in and of themselves, as opposed to merely looking at them as the source material for big-budget movies and shows. But among the remaining people who devote themselves to analysis of the comics medium, few are as sharp as Tegan O'Neil. She is the winner of an Eisner Award (comics' top honor) for her writing at The AV Club *and publishes fascinating essays on her blog,* The Hurting. *She's a longtime watcher of all things Stan Lee, and was kind enough to interview me about the making and meaning of this book. The following chat was edited and abridged—the full version is available at* abrahamriesman.com.

It's worth saying these disputes about Stan Lee's authorship were known and discussed in fandom for a very long time. Stan's reputation took a hit eons ago, before either of us was born. This is an inherited argument three generations deep. How did you first become aware of the controversy?

To be honest, I'm not one hundred percent sure I remember when I learned that Stan Lee might not have been on the level. I sometimes have a vague memory of an embittered employee at my childhood local comic shop, One Stop Comics in Oak Park, Illinois, telling me that Stan was full of shit, but, unlike Stan, I'm prepared to admit that it may be an inaccurate remembrance. When I met him as an early adolescent, circa 1998, at the Wizard World comic-con in Rosemont, Illinois, I don't recall thinking Stan was a bad guy.

I also don't recall thinking he was a particularly *good* guy, at that point, either, insofar as I never worshipped Stan at any point in my life. I don't say that to condescend to people who *did* worship him—people have found the Stan Lee myth to be extremely potent and attractive. I can see why people would get seduced. I was more or less neutral on him throughout my life. I loved the characters he was credited with creating, and I found him amusing when he popped up in fourth-wall-breaking comics or in those live-action intros for the early nineties cartoon *The Marvel Action Hour*, the latter of which was my first exposure to him. But he was never an inspirational or aspirational figure for me.

I didn't come up reading old issues of *The Comics Journal*, I'm sad to say, so lots of the industry details were lost on me. That said, I got more details about Stan's deceptions when I was reading the great comics message boards and blogs of the aughts: Barbelith and Comics Alliance, mainly, may they rest in peace. Then came Sean Howe's book. I didn't pick up *Marvel Comics: The Untold Story* until late 2013, when it had been out a year or so, since I had largely given up on superhero comics from 2006 to 2012 or so. I got back into them as a casual reader, then started pitching stories about them to *New York Magazine* a few months after I started working there in 2013. Around then, I read a column on the now-defunct comics blog *Comics Alliance* by the writer Chris Sims about Stan that quoted heavily from Sean's book, and I realized I had to read the whole thing.

I snatched it up and devoured it. I'm being quite earnest when I say it changed my life. The information gave me a foothold for my reporting on the industry, but more importantly, it taught me that comics was an industry worth reporting on. There's so much meat in there. I do have to take issue with the fact that Sean presented as fact a lot of things that have turned out to be dubious—perhaps most notably Stan's account of his last encounter with Kirby—but no book is perfect and you can't travel back in time. You do your best, and he really crushed it. That was the beginning of me having concrete info about Stan's misdeeds and misdirections.

So in 2015, when *New York* editor David Wallace-Wells plopped a copy of Stan's graphic memoir on my desk and said I should "do something with it," I was all too eager to investigate Stan's life further in a big profile. I immediately started reading *Stan Lee and the Rise and Fall of the American Comic Book* by Jordan Raphael and the late Tom Spurgeon, which presented me with even more startling information. I didn't realize until a week later that David had just meant doing a capsule review of the book. But to his credit, he encouraged me to continue with my harebrained scheme, which culminated in a February 2016 profile, which in turn planted the seed for the book. I tried to present all the relevant existing data points about Stan's creative-credit problems, though I definitely can't take full credit for unearthing all of it. Sean, Tom, Jordan, and many others did the initial digging.

So, I know it can seem hard at times to see a positive to a lot of this material, steeped as it is in controversy and heartache. But the actual process of sifting through the reams of paper necessary for the book seems like it must have been an interesting experience. Could you describe that process in a little more detail? I'm always curious about effective research methods (partly because I'm terrible at it!), and based on both our conversations and your social media feed, I'd guess that research is something you enjoy quite a bit.

I do and I don't. My gripes are the inverse of those of the typical writer: I get enormously frustrated during the research stage and have trouble forcing myself to get working, then I have a total ball during the writing stage. I blame my ADHD, which makes staring at books or documents all day a big challenge. On top of that, there was so much material to get through that figuring out where to start on a given day was daunting. As such, I never really developed a system, to be honest. I sort of let my instincts tell me what to do each day during the research phase. It might be making cold calls to old friends of Stan, it might be reading a biography of one of his collaborators, it might be going through the endless scans of documentation from the University of Wyoming Stan Lee archive . . . it might just be reading some old comics! I'd spin the wheel and see where I landed.

That said, the research stage is where I had some of the most thrilling moments of the whole process. A few stick out in my mind. One was my first long interview with Larry Lieber. I'd called him, then had an initial lunch with him, and he'd told me his life story, but—to my great frustration—he wouldn't let me record it or take notes. He wants to write it all down for his memoir. The eventual interview was monumental, and I'll always be grateful to Larry for his time. Another was meeting with Keya Morgan after nearly a year of negotiation and getting to hear all the private tapes of Stan with his inner circle. I can't say it was a *happy* experience, as the tapes are extremely difficult to listen to. But, as a journalist, you have to be slightly sociopathic, so all that mattered was that I was getting insights into Stan's life and mind that no journalist had ever obtained before. I hope it was worth it for the reader. But perhaps my favorite part of the research was getting information about Stan's Jewish background. I'm Jewish, myself, and do a lot of reporting on the Jewish world, so that was a particular delight to indulge in. I hope I didn't bore anyone.

Now, I would like you to correct me if I am mistaken but, as an interested bystander observing the process from the out-

side in, it really seemed to me as if you and your book were situated in this instance to be the poster children for "killing the messenger." The message in this instance wasn't a particularly new or novel one in the context of the comics industry, but you had the misfortune of being one of the first books over the ridge after Lee died. Is my perception correct that you received a bit of backlash for being, if not the first person to tell this story, certainly the first person to do so on such a big platform? In other words, how'd the whole "telling people Santa Claus isn't real" thing go? People *love* that one.

Yeah, there were some negative responses, mainly in my Amazon reviews. There are a ton of one-star reviews there, many by people who proudly state that they haven't read the book. I don't get too worked up about those, although the cutthroat world of algorithmic rankings makes it such that I wish they'd been nicer. There was one YouTuber who—again, without having read the book, in his case because it wasn't out yet—said I was trying to "cancel" Stan. I get why you might think that, since the advance marketing copy was largely about debunking and disenchanting. But what's been gratifying is hearing from Stan fans who were skeptical about or outright hostile toward the book in advance, but then read it and realized it wasn't a hatchet job. Even if they don't end up being superfans, I appreciate their willingness to alter their opinions, which is something all too rare in the contemporary moment.

The one piece of "how could you do this to Stan?" criticism that seems to have risen above the din was the essay in *The Hollywood Reporter* that Stan's protégé, Roy Thomas, wrote just after the book was out. I hope I'm not mischaracterizing Roy when I say he had no real factual disputes, just ones about tone and omissions. He felt I didn't sufficiently highlight the positives of Stan's time at Marvel, and that this wasn't the Stan *he* knew. Fair enough, I suppose: I'm sure I wrote about a Stan—or series of Stans!—that was unfamiliar to him. But that doesn't mean he didn't exist. I went out of my way to point out Stan's unambiguous talents and accomplishments, so I don't think I made him out to be a monster. He wasn't a saint, but he wasn't Satan, and I was trying to flesh him out more than tear him down.

When I was doing research, I had a conversation with the great Peter Guralnick, who, among many other accomplishments, wrote a definitive two-volume biography of Elvis Presley. As it turns out, the Jewish world is small: He went to summer camp with my dad. We connected and chatted, and he said my challenge was going to be to do something bigger than a mere exposé. I had to think bigger than just saying, "Here are things this guy lied about." No one cares about that on its own. It's the 2020s—shame over hypocrisy or dishonesty isn't really a thing anymore. He said the *real* question is, "What was the story he was telling with his lies?" In other words, the lie, itself, is boring without the context of motivations and impact.

In an early press interview for the book, someone asked me what I thought the core theme of the book was. I used to think it was something about the American Dream, but by the time he asked me, I felt like maybe that wasn't the case anymore. I surprised myself when I blurted out that the book is about the agony of ambiguity. You can try to glean life lessons from Stan's arc, but I feel like they're all relatively obvious: thou shalt not lie, thou shalt not steal, thou shalt not covet, and so on. The harder thing to process is the twofold ambiguity of his life.

There's the factual ambiguity of who created the Marvel pantheon, which is a dilemma that will probably never be resolved. And then there's the moral ambiguity of asking whether he was a "good" man or not, which is a similarly unanswerable question, albeit for different reasons. The human mind wants to reject ambiguity; we want to say some things are incontrovertible facts and that the people we like or hate are objectively good or bad. But the reality of existence is uncertainty: constant, chaotic, and infuriating. You can either lie to yourself for certainty—and, to be sure, we all have to do that for certain aspects of life—or you can be honest and confront the answerlessness of the world. It sucks, but without that confrontation, you'll accept the wildest lies from people who can provide the illusion of certainty.

I'd like to ask you to take off your journalist hat for a minute and reflect on the project as a fan. How has the experience changed the way you look at Marvel? Has your relationship with comics and/or superhero fiction changed? Have you been back to revisit any of the sixties material since you finished the book?

Oh, man. It's become really, *really* hard for me to consume superhero media these days. My spouse and I just watched the new DC Comics movie adaptation, *The Suicide Squad*—not to be confused with *Suicide Squad*, the 2016 film for which *The Suicide Squad* is a sequel. Comics, everybody! Oh, wait, I mean movies. Wait, is there a difference anymore? Anyway, I really enjoyed it, but afterward, as I was discussing it with my spouse, I found myself getting increasingly defensive whenever she said I seemed to have liked it. Like, I'd say, "Y'know, the more I think about it, the less I like it," which wasn't even true. I couldn't quite understand why I was having this reaction, and then I realized that it's because the movie's writer/director, James Gunn, had dissed my book on Twitter when it came out. It's truly strange to know that someone of that stature specifically took time out of his day to prevent people from buying my work.

Plus, I know how comparatively little the people who created the Suicide Squad in comics are being remunerated for their efforts, especially compared to Gunn. And honestly, it's even worse with Marvel movies. At least DC used to have these little equity agreements that allowed creators of characters to get compensated as a matter of course when their creations were used, but Marvel has historically just dicked over anyone and everyone they can, and the Disney era has only made that worse. Ed Brubaker and Steve Epting came up with the idea and design for the Winter Soldier, the subtitular co-star of *Captain America: The Winter Soldier*. The movie comes out, they toss the two of them a few thousand bucks—which, they remind you, they're not legally obligated to give—and invite them to the premiere. That's it. Not even the premiere *party*—just the premiere, then it's, "Begone, so the grown-ups can talk." It's sadistic—but what do you expect? It's Marvel and Disney. Entertainment through exploitation has been the name of the game for both of them for nearly a century.

The comics are even harder for me to read, because at least there are a few people involved in the creative process of a movie who get big paydays and union jobs. There are no good comics jobs at Marvel and DC. Hell, if you're a writer or artist, there are no *jobs* at Marvel or DC, period, because you're an independent contractor. America is already an awful enough place to be a freelancer of any kind, what with our lack of universal health care and general disregard for the human spirit, but comics is one of those industries that's especially bad, insofar as they try to make it seem like *they're* doing *you* a favor by letting you come up with intellectual property for them. The big bosses rely on the fact that there are lots of people in their applicant pool who have been obsessed with Marvel for so long that they're willing to let their love of these characters and this universe override their instinct for self-preservation. No one sticks around at Marvel if they can afford not to. Seriously, look at the roster! Are there any Marvel "lifers"? No. Even Brian Michael Bendis left! It's a horrible place to work. Staffers, too! I know so many folks who have worked as editors at Marvel. All of them were miserable.

You can't lay *all* of that at Stan's feet, but he was instrumental in establishing this awful, rapacious state of affairs. He was genial and friendly with lots of his creators, and he would do individual good deeds for them, but there is zero evidence that he tried to fix anything at a systemic level. He was largely fine with none of the other creators having stable jobs, health benefits, or ownership. The only time he got on a soapbox about creator rights was when he was getting jilted over the movie and TV profits and sued Marvel in 2002, and that ended up with him getting screwed out of billions. Chickens, meet roost. So, along those lines: No, I haven't been revisiting the sixties comics since I finished the book. It's too painful to think of all the injustice that surrounds them and the industry they created.

Stan was nowhere near the son of a bitch Walt Disney was, but they shared a similar attitude toward self-promotion at the expense of everyone around them. It makes perfect sense that their companies ended up marrying one another. Do you think we'll ever get to someplace like that with Stan, where we can actually talk about the man without having to fight a reflexive desire on the part of many to defend someone they did not even know?

To the extent that anything is foreseeable these days, I don't think the Stan Myth is going anywhere, because the Mythic Stan isn't going anywhere. People love the fictional story of Stan as much as they love the man himself. When the book was first being advertised, more than a year before it came out, I had random Stan fans getting furious with me online because the subtitle was "The Rise and *Fall* of Stan Lee." The comments were always along the lines of, "Fall? He never fell! He died while Marvel was at the top of its game and he was more famous than he'd ever been!" What's interesting about such statements is that Stan had a publicly awful final few years. The tales of grift and elder abuse were all over the place, from legitimate sources to tabloids and beyond. He pretty conclusively fell! Even without reading my book, you could know that! But they chose not to. These are people who profess to be Stan diehards, but they were willfully blind to the arc of his story. I think it's because the Stan myth—the tale of a cheerful and loving man who struggled, then succeeded through hard work and being true to himself, and eventually rode off into the sunset as a champion—has been a huge inspiration and comfort to them. The fact that it's barely rooted in reality and that easily available information contradicts it is unimportant. We construct our lives and minds around stories, and when someone tries to take our stories away, we get defensive. Disney, Marvel, POW!, the Peter Paul group—they're all going to keep posthumously milking the Stan myth for as long as they can. Once those companies are gone, maybe the myth will die out and be replaced by the facts, but I don't think I'll live to see that day.

THIS IS NOT A SECRET
JEWISH HISTORY OF STAN LEE

———

This essay was initially published in slightly different form on Jewish Currents.org.

IN HIS RECENT BOOK *STAN LEE: A LIFE IN COMICS*, THE CON-servative columnist Liel Leibovitz proposes a skeleton key for understanding the life and work of Stan Lee, the legendary Marvel Comics creator, who died in 2018. In Leibovitz's telling, the superheroes of the Marvel pantheon that emerged in the early 1960s must be read "as characters formed by the anxieties of first-generation American Jews who had fought in World War II, witnessed the Holocaust, and reflected—consciously or otherwise—on the moral obligations and complications of life after Auschwitz." At length, he compares Spider-Man to Cain, the Thing to a golem, Mr. Fantastic to a dybbuk; he even goes so far as to argue that the Incredible Hulk and his alter ego are akin to the two versions of the biblical Adam theorized by the rabbinic scholar Joseph Soloveitchik. Leibovitz is not alone in his pursuit of Marvel's Jewish undertones. In Lee's twilight years and after his death, Jewish writers have repeatedly attempted to situate his work in the context of his Jewish background. In books and articles, speeches and seminars, Lee and the characters he is credited with creating are held up as icons of Yiddishkeit and extensions of the long Jewish textual tradition.

Given the existence of this mini-genre of Marvel exegesis, one might expect it would be possible to excavate a textured portrait of Lee's Jewish identity. I know I did: When I began research for this book, one of my primary concerns was investigating Lee's relationship to Jewishness. My motivations were perhaps not so different from those of the aforementioned scribes: Like many of my people, I have a perhaps unhealthy fixation on any famous Jew's Jewishness. And so—through genealogical research, an investigation of the cultural milieus in which Lee and his family lived, close readings of the rare comments he made about Jewishness, and a long and revealing set of conversations with his brother, Larry Lieber—I attempted to suss out the true story of Stan Lee the Jew. What I found instead was an artist who spent much of his life trying—with apparent success—to distance himself from Jewish practice, Jewish communal life, even from the designation "Jewish."

Stan Lee, I've come to realize, is an exemplary subject of a genre of writing, common in contemporary Jewish letters, that we might call the Secret Jewish History. Secret Jewish Histories take on a wide array of mainstream cultural objects—*Easy Rider* or James Bond or the music of Dolly Parton—fixating on the roles that Jewish people or institutions had on their creation or popularization. Criticism in this vein posits that the presence of Jews in the creation of a non-explicitly Jewish event or work is a crucial vector for understanding it. There's an element of rabbinic interpolation involved, not unlike the process of explaining that some heroic character in the Torah who seemed to act immorally—Jacob stealing his brother's birthright, King David committing adultery with Bathsheba—was, in reality, secretly enacting the will of God. The approach suggests that, if a Jewish artist says they didn't put Jewish themes and motifs into a work, they are merely lying to themself.

Such revelations of crypto-Judaism induce a thrill in no small part because they allow Jews to claim someone or something as distinctively *ours*. There is some truth to be found in this approach—who you are really does have an impact on what you do—but all too often it betrays a deep cultural chauvinism and parochialism. This is especially the case when it comes to Jews who, like Lee, almost or entirely walked away from Jewishness. And yet, for related reasons, Lee is irresistible Secret Jewish History fodder for many of his Jewish admirers. Millions of fans have found succor and meaning in the Marvel legendarium since the 1960s; Lee both helped to create the company's American myths and lived out his own as an avatar of upward mobility and moral uprightness. But myths work precisely because you can read into them nearly anything you want. And who wouldn't want Stan Lee on their team?

Some claims about Lee's Jewishness are indisputable. Stanley Martin Lieber, as he was originally known, was born to Romanian Jewish immigrants in Manhattan in 1922. He was raised and bar mitzvahed in Jewish communities in uptown Manhattan and the Bronx; some of the Yiddishisms he presumably learned in childhood would later make their way into his comic book dialogue and narration. Crucially, too, he entered the comic book industry around 1940, when it was dominated by Jewish businessmen and creatives, including his most significant collaborator—the comics writer and artist Jack Kirby, né Jacob Kurtzberg—a fellow New York Jew, and one whose Jewish identification ran deep.

Yet over the course of my research, I found virtually no instances of Lee publicly invoking his Jewishness. Late in life he told an interviewer, "Jewish people—and I include myself—I think we think a certain way." In private correspondence, he sometimes jokingly invoked bar mitzvahs or peace in the Middle East, and there's an anecdote about him once yelling at a bird that was bothering him, "For the Gentiles, you sing!" But those examples are the exception to the rule. In his co-written 2002 memoir *Excelsior!: The Amazing Life of Stan Lee*, Lee fleetingly identifies his forebears as Jewish—but never himself. Describing his and his wife's struggle to adopt a child in the 1950s, he wrote, "My parents were Jewish and Joan is Episcopalian, and in those days it was more difficult to adopt in a mixed marriage." The problem, in his telling, wasn't his Jewish identity—it was others' perception that he had one at all.

Those aforementioned Jewish parents, unsurprisingly, are central to any understanding of Lee's Jewish identity, or lack thereof. His parents, Jack (born Iancu Urn) Lieber and Celia Solomon, each escaped horrific antisemitism in Romania as young people. In New York City, neither was Orthodox in their practice, but they were openly and distinctively Jewish: Celia lit candles and prayed every Shabbat; Jack attended synagogue and became an ardent Zionist who often ranted about the struggles of the Jewish people. Jack was a difficult man: removed, judgmental, and possessed of a dourness that only grew more intense as he struggled to find work during the Great Depression. As Lee himself admits in *Excelsior*, much of his own career was built on an effort to distinguish himself from his unhappy, unsuccessful father. He became the opposite of Jack, at least in public: a cheerful, relentlessly optimistic raconteur who deracinated himself to the point where anyone could think of him as a beloved relative. After Lee had found steady work and some modicum of fame within the comics industry—and had adopted the distinctly non-Jewish pen name "Stan Lee"—Jack would chastise him for abandoning the community. "He'd send him letters all the time, drive him nuts," Lee's brother Larry recalled to me in an interview. "'Be more Jewish,' 'Observe the holidays,' that kind of thing." The letters became more plentiful after Lee married a Gentile and, a few years after Celia's death, had their newborn daughter baptized. As Larry put it, the act of telling Jack that his grandchild was a Christian amounted to "cruelty." By the time Jack died in 1968, there was little love lost between him and Lee, in large part thanks to these divisions over Jewish identity.

How should we read the comics Lee was credited on, in light of this ambivalent inheritance? (I say "credited on" rather than "wrote" because there is another complicating factor here: The Marvel stories to which Lee signed his name were in fact written collaboratively, and it seems likely that Lee's underlings were in fact their primary writers.) It is reasonable to speculate, as the writer Michael Chabon did in his popular 2000 novel *The Amazing Adventures of Kavalier & Clay*, that mid-century Jewish comics artists poured their own anxieties about assimilation into superheroes who, paradigmatically, had to hide their identities to make it in a world hostile to their true natures.

But some critics and fans have made wild leaps of logic, employing a sort of Talmudic exegesis of the comics attributed to Lee—a variation on the critical mode of philosopher Leo Strauss, long influential in conservative circles, in which great works harbor secret teachings, with exoteric meanings available to anyone and esoteric meanings available only to a chosen few. Spider-Man is an alienated neurotic who lives in Forest Hills, Queens, so these fans hold him up as a crypto-Jew—in fact, one recent Spider-Man movie features an alternate-universe version of Spidey who is implied to be Jewish. But there were a lot of alienated neurotics in twentieth-century Queens, plenty of them non-Jews. It's likewise true, as Leibovitz points out, that the intellectual Silver Surfer grapples with the godlike Galactus in a manner not wholly unlike Abraham arguing with the God of the Hebrew Bible. But attempting to negotiate with divinity is in no way a solely Jewish endeavor. The closest hit in this search for Lee-era Marvel's Jewishness is the rocky-carapaced Thing, who spoke in a Lower East Side brogue and, many decades later, was canonically identified as Jewish. But in the days when Lee was working on the character's stories, none of that was explicit, and any streetwise social reject could conceivably find themself in him. Yes, Lee's Jewishness may have informed these tales; no, we should not fall into the trap of an overly literalist reading of these comics.

All of this suggests we should be careful about any attempt to map out the Secret Jewish History of Lee's work—or, for that matter, anyone's. I have already confessed that I understand the temptation to indulge in Jewish mythmaking. Indeed, when first mapping out this essay, I had planned to identify Lee's distance from Jewish identity with the figure of the *echad rasha,* the Wicked Son of the Passover seder, who frustrates his elders by remaining aloof from his heritage. But would that not have been just another attempt to embellish the Jewish bona fides of someone who didn't want them? I maintain that Lee's Jewish saga is crucial for understanding how he developed, but I have had to resist the temptation to read the influence of that Jewishness on his work as though I were among a chosen few who could decipher it. There were, to be sure, secrets of Lee's Jewish history, but not, in fact, a Secret Jewish History.

To posthumously conscript Lee into a Jewishness he did not want is to play an intellectually dangerous and narcissistic parlor game. Let him dwell in the liminal spaces of Jewishness in death, as he did in life, joining all the other fascinating Jews of assimilation who have come before and since. Even if Lee was, in some ways, one of us, he does not really belong to us.

PHOTO: KRIS KRAIG—USA TODAY NETWORK

ABRAHAM RIESMAN is a Providence-based reporter. He has written primarily about arts and culture for *New York* magazine, but his work has also appeared in *The Wall Street Journal, The Boston Globe, The New Republic,* and *Vice,* among others. This is his first book.

ABOUT THE TYPE

This book was set in Bembo, a typeface based on an old-style Roman face that was used for Cardinal Pietro Bembo's tract De Aetna in 1495. Bembo was cut by Francesco Griffo (1450–1518) in the early sixteenth century for Italian Renaissance printer and publisher Aldus Manutius (1449–1515). The Lanston Monotype Company of Philadelphia brought the well-proportioned letterforms of Bembo to the United States in the 1930s.